A Touchstone Book

The Greek Passion

by

Nikos Kazantzakis

TRANSLATED BY JONATHAN GRIFFIN

A Touchstone Book Published by
Simon and Schuster · New York

17   18   19   20

For catalogues or information on other Touchstone titles
available, write to Educational & Library Services, Simon &
Schuster, Inc., 630 Fifth Ave., New York, N.Y. 10020

ISBN 0-671-21216-8 PBK.
LIBRARY OF CONGRESS CATALOG
CARD NUMBER: 53-10810

MANUFACTURED IN THE UNITED STATES OF AMERICA

Table of Contents

The Characters in This Book

THE ELDERS OF LYCOVRISSI

PRIEST GRIGORIS: A powerful, well-fleshed, domineering man, given to rages and gluttony, unable to brook interference of any kind, seeking to bend God to his will, for good or evil.

ARCHON PATRIARCHEAS: Hereditary leader of Lycovrissi; a "noble pig" living only for pleasures of table and bed, turning in his own small world of soft ease, spoiled, child-like, fat and imposing.

OLD LADAS: Arch-miser, mean and cowardly, starving as he gloats over his full coffers like a scrofulous cricket, planning to take ever more from the poor.

CAPTAIN FORTOUNAS: An old sailor, hardy and rough, retired from long years of adventure; a full life, joyously spent the world over, living in past dreams and present pleasures.

HADJI NIKOLIS: A dry individual, steeped in ancient glories of Greece and moaning her downfall; the ineffectual schoolmaster, living in a world of books, never resolving his fears and asserting himself.

THE VILLAGERS CHOSEN FOR THE PASSION

MANOLIOS, THE CHRIST: The strong and humble shepherd lad, turning away from worldly things to seek the true spirit of his Lord, becoming a saint in the hearts of his friends.

YANNAKOS, APOSTLE PETER: The sturdy merchant-pedlar, traveling the countryside; warm-hearted, naïve and impetuous, sunny-tempered, finding simple joy in his beautiful donkey.

MICHELIS, APOSTLE JOHN: The archon's son, born to wealth and position, handsome, deeply sensitive, bewildered by treachery, neither of the village nor apart from it.

KOSTANDIS, APOSTLE JAMES: Owner of the café, thin, crabbed, willing to give, but always tied to his possessions and his family, willing to share, but confused in spirit.

PANAYOTAROS, APOSTLE JUDAS: The Plaster-eater, the saddler of the village and its buffoon, a wild, undisciplined man crazed by lust, hating all, waiting only for revenge.

WIDOW KATERINA, THE MARY MAGDALEN: The prostitute of Lycovrissi, ripely beautiful, husky-voiced, good-hearted, generous with her possessions, willing to sacrifice her life for that which she believes.

THE TURKISH HOUSEHOLD

THE AGHA: Lord of Lycovrissi, fattening in Oriental splendor on gifts from his Greek subjects, cruel, demanding, sensuous and fuddled, living for the pleasures of raki and pretty boys.

HUSSEIN, THE GUARD: Standing always ready with trumpet and whip; a giant Oriental, wicked as a monkey, ill-favored, a lackey succumbing to his master's habits.

YOUSSOUFAKI: A dimpled, pretty boy, softly sweet and gentle.

BRAHIMAKI: The second pretty boy, wild and demanding.

OLD MARTHA: A hunchback slave, spider-like and bright-eyed, hating her master and finding her pleasure in the meager drama of other's lives.

THE OTHER VILLAGERS

MARIORI: Grigoris' only child, divinely fair, winsome and soft-spoken, betrothed to Michelis, hearing always the wings of the Archangel Michael hovering over her.

LENIO: Handsome, rosy love-child of old Patriarcheas, bursting with desire for passionate love, happy as a lark and bright as the morning.

MOTHER MANDALENIA: The village coffiner, laden with little bags of herbs and charms, ministering to the ill and dying, gossiping, enjoying the attention bestowed on tragedy.

ANDONIS, THE BARBER: Kindly, thick-witted, willing to do his share.

DIMITRI, THE BUTCHER: Honest and generous, cursing his age and his lameness, giving his portion to help.

CHRISTOFIS, THE MULETEER: Foul-mouthed, loud, earthy, relishing his reputation for humor.

NIKOLIO: The dark, wild, mountain boy, half goat, wrestling with the ram and sheep, flinging the notes of his pipes to the sun.

CHARAIAMBOS, THE BEADLE: Sly, fearful, scuttling to do the priest's bidding, sure he should have been bishop.

MADAM KOSTANDIS: A hard worker, an honest woman, inspiring fear with her vicious temper.

GAROUFILIA: Wife of Panayotaros, old and haggard, stunned by her shame and misfortune.

PELAGHIA, CHRYSSOULA: Her daughters, dark and vivacious, restless with sensual longings, giggling, heartless.

OLD PENELOPE: Wife of Ladas, squalid, in rags, an old molted stork withdrawn forever into a world of silence.

THE WANDERERS

PRIEST FOTIS: Leader of the starving ones, unconquerable, great-souled, praying for guidance, acting with magnificent strength and wisdom, the firm rock to which all turn, the fountain from which both common sense and abiding faith flow without stint.

LOUKAS: A colossus, firm, slow, the banner bearer.

CHARILAOS, PAULES: Old men, weary of privation.

PETRES: A rebellious younger man, despairing of finding haven.

PANAGOS: An ancient, bearing on his back the bones of his ancestors.

THE TOWN DWELLERS

YERASSIMOS: The jolly innkeeper, loud, affectionate.

KRONSTALLENIA: His buxom, hearty wife.

THE BISHOP: A fat, mean-hearted, waspish, grasping man of the cloth, jealously guarding the "rights" of the church.

ANGHELIKA: His niece, a sad girl, mistreated and sullen.

FROM A NEARBY VILLAGE

KOUNELOS: The garrulous innkeeper, honest and solemn.

ALI AGHA SOULATZADES: The ignorant lord of the village.

FATHER MANASSE, SUPERIOR OF SAINT PANTELEIMON MONASTERY: A holy, saintly man.

The Greek Passion

Wanted: a Judas

Sitting on his balcony above the village square, the Agha of Lycovrissi smoked his pipe and sipped raki. A thin, warm rain fell softly; on his fat mustaches, which were freshly dyed black, tiny drops hung and twinkled; warmed by the raki, the Agha licked his lips and enjoyed the cool. At his right hand, holding a trumpet, stood Hussein, his squire and bodyguard, a giant Oriental, wicked as a monkey, and with a squint. At his left, seated on a velvet cushion with his legs tucked under him, a dimpled boy ceaselessly relit his pipe for him and refilled his cup with raki.

The Agha half shut his heavy eyelids and savored this world below. All that the good God has made is perfect, he thought: this world's a real success. Are you hungry? here's bread and minced meat or pilaff with cinnamon. Are you thirsty? here's that water of youthfulness, raki. Are you sleepy? God has made sleep; nothing like it when you're sleepy. If you're angry, He's made the whip and the *raia's** buttocks. If you're depressed, He's made the *amanés*.† If, lastly, you want to forget all the sorrows and worries of this world, He's made Youssoufaki.

A wonderful artist, Allah! he murmured sentimentally, yes, indeed, a wonderful artist Who knows His business and is ingenious, too. How the devil did He get the idea of making raki and Youssoufaki?

The Agha's eyes moistened with tears; he had drunk so much raki that his soul was filled with tenderness. Leaning over his balcony, he watched the *raias* strolling in the square, just shaved, in their best clothes, with their broad red sashes, freshly washed

* Non-Moslem subject under Turkish domination
† Turkish air or melody

1

breeches, long blue leggings. Some wore the fez, others the turban, others the sheepskin cap. The smartest had a sprig of basil or a cigarette behind the ear.

It was Easter Tuesday; Mass was just over. Exquisite weather, tender: spring sun and rain; the lemon blossoms were fragrant, the trees budding, the grass reviving, Christ rising from every clod. The Christians were coming and going across the square and embracing one another with the Paschal greeting: "Christ is risen!" "Risen indeed!"—after which they would go and sit at Kostandis's café or in the middle of the square under the old plane tree. They ordered narghiles, with their long tubes and bubbling water, and coffee, and at once there began an endless chatter, like the light rain.

"This is what it'll be like in Paradise," hazarded Charaiambos the beadle, "soft sunshine, a gentle rain falling without a sound, lemon trees in blossom, narghiles, and agreeable conversation, forever and ever."

At the other end of the square, behind the plane tree, freshly whitewashed and with its graceful bell tower beside it, rose the village church: "the Crucifixion." Today its doorway was decked with palm and laurel branches. All around were small shops and stalls:

There was Panayotaros the saddler's (a clown with the nickname "Plaster-eater": once, when a plaster statuette of Napoleon was brought to the village, he had bolted it. After that, they had brought another, of Kemal Pasha; bolted again. Finally, one of Venizelos; bolted like the others).

Next door, Andonis the barber's with its signboard saying "Andonis." Above the door an inscription in thick, dark-red letters announced: "Teeth also extracted."

Farther on, the butcher's shop kept by old lame Dimitri: "Fresh calves' heads, HERODIADE." Every Saturday he killed a calf; before doing so he gilded its horns, painted its forehead, hung red ribbons round its neck and, limping, led it through the village, singing its virtues.

Lastly the famous Café Kostandis, a long narrow room where it was cool and there was always a balmy smell of coffee and tobacco and, in winter, sage. On its walls hung—the pride of the village— three impressive portraits on glossy paper: on one side Saint Genevieve, half naked in a tropical forest; on the other, Queen

Victoria, with blue eyes and an enormous nurse's bosom; right in the middle, hard-faced, gray-eyed, glowering and wearing a tall Astrakhan cap, Kemal Pasha.

Fine men, all these villagers, hard workers, good fathers; and the Agha, too, was a fine man with his love for raki, for the heavy scents—musk and patchouli—and for the pretty boy seated at his left on the velvet cushion. Amused, the Agha gazed upon the Christians, like a shepherd upon his flock, and was well pleased.

Excellent fellows, he thought, this year again they've filled my cellar with their Easter presents—cheeses, coronets of sesame bread, brioches, scarlet eggs. . . . One of them, may Heaven preserve him, has brought me a box of Chian mastic for my Youssoufaki to munch and make his little mouth smell nice. The Agha felt happy: My cellar, he thought, is bursting with good things, the rain is falling gently, the cocks are crowing, and, close beside me, crouched at my feet, my Youssoufaki munches his mastic and smacks his tongue. The Agha suddenly felt his heart overflowing. He bent his neck and was about to begin singing the *amanés*; but the effort was too great; turning toward Hussein he signed to him to put his trumpet to his lips to silence the *raia*s. After which, he turned to his left:

"Sing, Youssoufaki (my blessing be upon you), sing me *'Dounia tabir, rouya tabir, aman, aman!'* Sing it to me or I shall burst!"

The pretty boy, without hurrying, took the mastic from his mouth, stuck it on his bare knee, leaned his right palm against his cheek and began to sing his Agha's favorite *amanés:* "World and dream are but one, *aman, aman!*"

His fluting voice went up and down with dove-like cooings. The Agha, enchanted, shut his eyes and, as long as the boy sang, forgot to drink.

"One of his good days," whispered Kostandis as he served coffee, "blessed be raki!"

"Blessed be Youssoufaki," said Yannakos, smiling maliciously. He was the village carrier and courier: a thick pepper-and-salt beard, eyes of a bird of prey.

"A curse on destiny, the blind hag, for having made him an Agha and us *raia*s," growled the priest's brother, Hadji Nikolis, the village schoolmaster; a dry individual with glasses and a jutting Adam's apple that bobbed up and down when he talked.

He kindled, thought of his ancestors, sighed:

"There was a time when our people, the Hellenes, were the masters of these lands. The wheel turned and the Byzantines came—Hellenes too, and Christians. The wheel turned again, and the children of Hagar came. . . . But Christ rose again, my friends, our country will rise again, too! Here, Kostandis, another round!"

The *amanés* finished, the exquisite boy put back the mastic into his mouth and resumed his sleepy rumination. The trumpet sounded again: the *raia*s could now laugh and shout freely.

Captain Fortounas, one of the five village Elders, appeared at the door of the café: a tall, corpulent character, formerly a boat owner who for many years had ploughed the Black Sea, transporting Russian corn and not above smuggling. He had not a hair on his chin: complexion olive, a parchment skin, deep wrinkles, tiny, sparkling, jet-black eyes. He had grown old, and his boat with him. One night it had smashed on a reef off Trebizond: shipwrecked and disillusioned, Captain Fortounas had come back to his native village, intending to put away as much raki as possible and, when the time came, to turn his face to the wall and die. His eyes had seen too many things; he had had enough; no, he hadn't had enough; he was tired, but ashamed to admit it.

Today he was wearing his captain's boots, his yellow belt and his notable's cap—real Astrakhan; in his hand the long staff of an Elder. Two or three villagers stood up respectfully and invited him to a glass of raki.

"No time, my children, even for raki," said he; "Christ is risen! I'm going to the priest's house, we've a notables' meeting. In less than an hour's time, all those who've been invited should be there. Quick, cross yourselves and come; you know what the business is today, surely. Ah, one of you should go and fetch saddler Panayotaros with his devil's beard; we need him badly."

He was silent for a moment, blinking, then said maliciously:

"If he isn't at home, he'll be at the widow's." They all burst out laughing.

Christofis, the old muleteer, who had learned love in his young days—and a heavy price he had paid for it—came out with this violent retort:

"What are you sniggering at, you chicken heads? He's quite right. Do as you damn well like, Panayotaros, and pay no attention to what they say! Life's short, death's long. Go ahead, my lad!"

Fat Dimitri, the butcher, shook his close-shaved skull:

"God preserve the widow, our Katerina! The devil knows how many horns she saves us from!"

Captain Fortounas laughed.

"There, children, don't argue. Every village should have its odd woman, so that the honest ones mayn't be upset. It's like the fountain by the roadside, that's it: those who're thirsty stop there and have a drink. Otherwise they come knocking at all our doors, one after the other; and the women, when they're asked for water . . ."

He turned, and noticed the schoolmaster.

"What, you here still, old one? Aren't you on the council, too? Turn even the café into a school? Class is over, come along!"

"Don't you want me to come, too?" said old Christofis, with a wink to the company. "I'd do for Judas."

But Captain Fortounas had already started up the slope, leaning heavily on his stick. He was not in good shape today; his rheumatism was at him with its pincers; he had not closed an eye all night. Of course he had gulped down two or three big glasses of raki that morning by way of remedy, but, devil take it, the pain hadn't given him a moment's peace. Even the raki hadn't done the trick.

If I weren't ashamed, I'd start screaming: that might quiet the pain a bit. But there's this damned self-respect and look jovial. And if I let slip my stick, I shan't let any young imp help me, I shall stoop and pick it up by myself. . . . Come on, Captain Fortounas, bite your lips, hoist your sails, steer into the waves, my lad! Don't go covering yourself with shame! By God, sir, life, too, is a squall; it'll pass!

He growled and blasphemed to himself. As he climbed the hill a lurch hurled him from one wall to the other. He stopped a moment and looked around him: nobody was looking; he sighed noisily and this relieved him a little. Raising his eyes toward the upper end of the village, he caught sight of a white patch among the trees, the indigo-shuttered house of the priest.

What the devil was he thinking of, the old sod, going and building his house at the top of the hill, he grumbled. His curse upon me! And he resumed his climb.

Two notables had already arrived; seated cross-legged on the divan they were waiting in silence for the dish to be brought in. The priest had gone to give his orders in the kitchen, where his only daughter, Mariori, was preparing the coffee, the cool water, and the preserves.

Close to the windows the first Elder of Lycovrissi sat throned: corpulent, lordly in manner, wearing breeches of fine linen, a gold-braided bolero and a stout gold ring on his forefinger—his seal with his initials interlaced: G.P., George Patriarcheas. His hands were fat and soft, like a bishop's. He had never done anything in his life, having a whole tribe of servants and serfs working for his service. He had swollen intestines, spreading buttocks, a pendulous paunch and three tiers of chin which, one on top of another, rested on a well-fleshed, hairy chest. He had two or three teeth missing in front—it was his only defect and made him lisp and stammer. But even this defect added to his distinction, for it forced whoever was speaking with him to lean toward him in order to hear what he said.

At his right in a corner, thin, grubby, with a cadaverous head, bleary eyes and huge calloused hands, sat in a heap, humble and self-effacing, the second notable: the richest man of the village, old Ladas. Bent over the land, for seventy years he had ploughed it, sowed it, reaped it, planted it with olives and vines, pressed it, drunk its blood. Not once since he was a lad had he cleaned it off him. Insatiable, he had hurled himself on it, demanding that it yield him a thousand to one. Yet he never once said, "God be praised!" but grumbled, eternally discontented. Now, in his old age, the land was not enough for him. As his death approached and he felt himself getting near the end of his scroll, he was impatient to devour the whole village. He had taken to lending money at high rates; men down on their luck pledged their vineyards and their houses and, when payment was due and they hadn't a penny, saw their property sold at auction and old Ladas gobbling up the lot.

And yet he moaned without stopping, and never had enough to eat; Penelope, his wife, went barefoot, and when the one and only daughter he had managed to produce fell ill, he had let her die through not sending for the doctor.

"It costs a lot of money," he had said; "the big towns are a long way off; how can I get a doctor out? And then, what do they know, more than others? Plague on them! We've got our priest; he knows the old medicines, and I shall only pay him for the extreme unction. She'll get well just the same, and it'll be cheaper."

But the priest's electuaries were no use, the holy oils had no effect, and the young girl died at seventeen and shook free of her father. He, too, was freed from the expense of a wedding: one day, not long after his daughter's death, he had done the accounts: dowry about so much; linen, tables, chairs so much. And then wouldn't he have been obliged to invite to the wedding all those relatives, who put away victuals like the gluttons they are? So then meat, bread, wine so much . . . He had added it all up, a pretty figure: his daughter would have reduced him to beggary. So what did it matter? We shall all die. . . . Besides, she had escaped from the worries of this world—husband, children, illness, housework. . . . In fact, she'd been lucky, God rest her soul!

Mariori came in with the dish, greeted the notables and, with eyes cast down, stopped first in front of the archon. She was pale and had big eyes, fine-drawn eyebrows, and two great tresses of chestnut hair made her a crown. The old archon helped himself to a full spoonful of wild bitter cherry conserve, looked at the young girl and raised his glass.

"To your loves, Mariori; my son's getting impatient."

The priest's daughter was engaged to his only son, Michelis, and the priest boasted that such a match would soon bring him grandchildren.

"I begin to see why he's so impatient, the young dog. He can't stand it any more, he says," the old man added with a laugh and winked at the young girl.

She blushed to the roots of her hair and became tongue-tied.

"Joy to us all!" said Grigoris, the priest, as he brought in a bottle of muscatel wine. "With the blessing of Christ and the Virgin!"

Green still, getting stout, with a perfectly white forked beard, he smelled of incense and fat. He saw his daughter's confusion and, to change the subject:

"And when, God willing," he asked, "do you think of marrying off that adopted daughter of yours as well—Lenio?"

Lenio was one of the bastards the archon had begotten on his servants. He had betrothed her to his shepherd, the faithful

Manolios, and given her a generous dowry in the shape of a flock of sheep, which Manolios minded on the Mount of the Virgin, close to the village.

"God willing, quite soon," he replied; "Lenio's in a hurry. She's in a hurry, the lucky girl! I do believe her breasts are swelling and she needs to nurse a son. 'Here's the month of May,' she said to me the other day, 'here's the month of May, master, it's high time.'"

He laughed again, wholeheartedly, and his triple chin shook.

"Only donkeys wed in May," he said; "she's right, Lenio is, it's high time. They're human, too, after all, even if they are servants."

"Manolios is a good lad," said the priest; "they will be happy."

"I agree, I love him like my own son," said the archon. "It was when I went to Saint Penteleimon Monastery that I saw him. He must have been fifteen. He brought me the dish of welcome in the parlor. A real little angel, only the wings missing. My soul had pity on him and I said to myself: 'Pity so handsome a lad should fade away in a convent, like a eunuch. I went to the cell of his Superior, Father Manasse; he'd been there for years, paralyzed. 'Father,' I said to him, 'I've a favor to ask you; if you grant it, I'll present the monastery with a silver lamp.' 'Anything you like, archon, except Manolios.' 'That's just it, it's him I want, Father; I want to take him into my service.' The old monk sighed. 'I look on him as my son, and so he is, and I've no fault to find with him. I'm feeble and all alone; I've no other company. Every evening I talk to him about the ascetics and the saints: that way he learns and I pass the time.' 'Let him go into the world, Father, and have children and live; when he's had enough of life, he'll become a monk.' In the end, by sheer talking, I managed to get the boy. Now I'm giving him Lenio. Good luck to them!"

"And he'll bring you grandchildren," said old Ladas, with a mischievous sneer. He took a cherry on the tip of his spoon, munched it, drank a mouthful of muscatel and with a bow said:

"May our labor be rewarded; God grant we may not die of hunger. The vineyards and the crops aren't doing well this year. We're in a bad way."

"God provides for all things," replied the priest in his crusty voice. "Courage, friend Ladas. Tighten your belt; no excuses; eating too much is harmful. Renounce extravagance; don't throw your money away, as you do, on the poor."

The archon burst out laughing so loudly that the house shook.

"Charity, Christians! Father Ladas is dying of hunger," he whined, holding out his huge hand.

A heavy tread sounded; the stairs creaked.

"Here's Captain Fortounas, our old sea wolf," said the priest. He got up to open the door. "Wait, Mariori, don't go, we must offer him something to drink. . . . I'll go and get a big glass and the raki; he turns up his nose at wine."

The captain paused a moment on the threshold to get his breath again. He came in with a smile on his lips, but the sweat was dripping from his forehead. Close on his heels and out of breath, the schoolmaster appeared; he was fanning himself with his cap. At the same moment the priest came in with the raki.

"Christ is risen, my hearties," said the captain to the three old men. Then, gritting his teeth, he sat down as lightly as he could on the divan and said to the young girl:

"No preserves and no coffee for me, little Mariori. They're all right for ladies and old men. That little glass, which the rest of you call a tumbler, will do for me. To your wedding!" he said, emptying his glass at one go.

"Today is a great day," said the schoolmaster, tasting his tiny cup of coffee; "our people won't be long in coming; we must hurry up and take a decision."

Mariori went out with the dish, and the priest bolted the door. His broad, sun-bronzed face suddenly took on a prophetic grandeur. Below his bushy eyebrows his eyes sparkled. He was a priest who ate his fill, drank deep, swore when he had got going and used his fists when he was angry. Even nowadays, old as he was, his blood stirred when he looked at women. His head, chest and stomach were full of human passions. But when he said Mass, or when he raised his head to bless or to pronounce the anathema, the wild wind of the desert blew over him and priest Grigoris, the glutton, the drunkard, the lecher, turned into a prophet.

"Brother councilors," he began in grave tones, "this day is a solemn one, God sees us and hears us. Take heed; all that we are about to say in this room, He will note down upon His tables! Christ is risen, but He is still crucified in our flesh. Let us see to it that He rise in us also, Elders, notables, my brothers. Archon, my friend, forget for an instant earthly things, you and yours are fortunate upon this earth. You have eaten, drunk, embraced more

than your share; raise your spirit above all these good things and
help us to make a decision. And you, old Ladas, forget on this
solemn day your oil, your wine, and your Turkish gold, which you
keep piled in your coffers. To you, brother schoolmaster, I have
nothing to say; your spirit remains always above the pleasures of
the table, of gold, and of women, turning itself toward God and toward grace. As for you, captain, old sinner, you have filled the
Black Sea with your iniquities; think at the last of God and give us
what help you can to make a just decision."

The captain bridled.

"Let the past alone, priest," he cried; "God is there to judge
it! If we, too, were free to speak, I think we should have something to say about your holiness."

"Speak, priest, but pay attention to what you say; you are addressing notables," said the archon, frowning.

"I'm speaking to a lot of worms," bellowed the priest furiously;
"and I, too, am a worm. Don't interrupt. Our guests will be here
any minute, and we must have our decision ready. So listen: it is
an old custom, transmitted from father to son in our village, to
name, every seven years, five or six of our fellow citizens to revive
in their persons, when Holy Week comes around, the Passion of
Christ. Six years have passed; we are entering upon the seventh.
We must today—we, the heads of the village—choose those who
are worthiest to incarnate the three great Apostles, Peter, James,
John, and Judas Iscariot and Mary Magdalen, the prostitute. And
above all, Lord forgive me, the man who, by keeping his heart pure
throughout the year, may represent Christ Crucified."

The priest paused a moment to draw breath. The schoolmaster
seized this chance, and his Adam's apple began working up and
down.

"The ancients," he said, "called this a Mystery. It began on
Palm Sunday under the church porch, and ended in the gardens on
Holy Saturday, at midnight, with the insurrection of Christ. The
idolaters had their theaters and circuses, the Christians had the
Mysteries . . ."

But Grigoris the priest cut short his flow.

"All right, all right, everyone knows that, schoolmaster. Let me
finish. The words become flesh, we see with our eyes, we touch the
Passion of Christ. From all the villages around, the pilgrims come
flocking; they pitch their tents around the church, groan and

smite their breasts all through Holy Week, then begin the festivities and dancing to the cry of 'Christ is risen.' . . . Many miracles
take place during those days, as you will remember, brother councilors; many sinners shed tears and repent. There are rich proprietors who display the sins they have committed to enrich themselves and give the church a vineyard or a field for the salvation of
their souls. Did you hear me, father Ladas?"

"Continue, continue, priest, and cease throwing stones into the
garden," burst out old Ladas, exasperated. "With me those tricks
don't work, just get that into your head."

"We are therefore met together today," the priest continued,
"to choose—and may God enlighten us—those to whom we shall
entrust this sacred Mystery. Speak freely; let each put forward
his opinion. Archon, you are the first notable, therefore speak first;
we are listening."

"Judas! We've got him," the captain interjected. "You'll never
find a better one than Panayotaros, the Plaster-eater; sturdy, spotted
with the smallpox, a real gorilla, like the one I saw at Odessa; and
what's even more important, he's got the beard and hair for the part:
red as the Devil's in person."

"It's not your turn to speak, captain," said the priest severely;
"don't be in such a hurry, there are those whose turn comes before yours. Well, archon?"

"What shall I say, priest?" replied the archon. "I desire only
one thing: that you should choose my son Michelis to act Christ."

"Impossible," the priest cut in. "Your son is a young archon,
big and fat, eating and drinking and enjoying life, while Christ was
poor and thin. It isn't suitable, forgive me. And besides, is
Michelis capable of going through with so difficult a part? He will
be scourged, he will have to wear a crown of thorns, he will be
hoisted up on the cross: Michelis won't have the strength; do you
want him to fall ill?"

"And the most important of all," the captain cut in, "is that
Christ was fair, while Michelis's hair and mustache are as black as
boot blacking."

"For Mary Magdalen we've just the thing," said Ladas, clucking: "widow Katerina. The bitch has everything required; she's
a fine whore with golden hair; I saw her one day in her yard,
combing her hair, and it came down to her knees; devil take her,
she'd damn an archbishop."

The captain already had his mouth half open to utter some jest, but the priest gave him a look which made him hold his tongue.

"The bad ones are easy to find," said the priest; "Judas, Mary Magdalen. But the good ones? That's where I'm waiting for your advice! Where shall we find, where shall we find—Lord forgive me!—a man resembling Christ? Let him but resemble Him physically more or less, that will be good enough. I—for days and weeks I've been hatching this idea in my head and many nights it's kept me awake. But I believe God has had pity on me; I've found the man."

"Who?" said the old archon, stung; "out with it."

"With your permission, archon, someone in your service, whom your lordship also loves well—your shepherd, Manolios. He is mild as a lamb, he can read, has been in a monastery, too; has blue eyes and a short beard as yellow as honey, a real Christ like an icon. And pious into the bargain. He comes down from the mountain every Sunday to hear Mass, and every time I've confessed him and given him Communion I've found not the least peccadillo to reproach him for."

"He's a wee bit crazy," squeaked old Ladas; "he sees phantoms."

"No harm in that," the priest assured him; "it's enough that the soul be pure."

"He can stand the scourges, the crown of thorns and the weight of the cross. What's more, he's a shepherd, another advantage; Christ is also shepherd of the human flock," said the schoolmaster sententiously.

"I approve," concluded the archon, after having reflected for a good while. "And in that case, my son?"

"He'll do very well for John," said the priest enthusiastically. "He has everything required: well-fleshed, black hair, almond eyes, and of good family, just as the well-beloved disciple was."

"For James," said the schoolmaster, watching his brother the priest timidly; "it seems to me we couldn't do better than Kostandis who keeps the café. He's thin, fierce-looking, crabbed, and that's how they represent the Apostle James."

"And he has a wife who worries the life out of him," said the captain. "Was the Apostle married, too? Well? What's your opinion, most learned of all the learned?"

"Stop joking about sacred things, blasphemer!" cried the priest angrily. "You're not on your boat here, telling dirty stories to your scum. We are considering a Mystery."

The schoolmaster plucked up courage.

"A passable Peter," he said, "would, I think, be Yannakos the carrier: narrow forehead, gray curly hair, a short chin. He loses his temper and calms down, flares up and goes out as easily as a tinder; but he's a good heart. I can't see a better Peter than him in all the village."

"A bit of a cheat," said the archon, shaking his big head. "But what can you expect of a tradesman? It doesn't matter."

"They say he killed his wife," wheezed father Ladas; "he gave her something to eat and she died of it."

"Lies, lies!" cried the priest; "don't come telling that story to me! One day, out of sheer greed, his late wife ate a whole spoonful of raw chickpeas; it made her so thirsty she couldn't bear it. The poor woman, she drank a whole jugful of water. She swelled up and died. Don't damn your soul, father Ladas!"

"Served her right!" said the captain; "that's where drinking water leads to; she need only have drunk raki."

"We still need a Pilate and a Caiaphas," said the schoolmaster; "I think we shall have trouble in finding them."

"A better Pilate than your lordship we shall never find, my dear archon," the priest hazarded, in a honeyed voice. "Don't frown; Pilate, too, was a great nobleman; proud in manner, well stuffed, double-chinned, well groomed, with just your bearing. A good man, too; did what he could to save Christ, and at the end even said: 'I wash my hands of this.' By that he escaped sin. Accept, archon, and you'll enable us to give grandeur to the Mystery. Imagine what a glory it will be for our village and what a crowd it will draw when people hear that the worthy archon Patriarcheas is to act Pontius Pilate!"

The archon gave a self-satisfied smile, lit his chibouk, with the amber mouthpiece and long stem, and was silent.

"Father Ladas would make a first-rate Caiaphas!" said the captain, breaking in again; "we couldn't find a better. In your opinion, priest, since you paint icons, tell me, what do they make Caiaphas look like?"

"Well," said the priest, swallowing, "rather like father Ladas: skin and bones, grimy, cheeks hollow, nose yellow and narrow . . ."

"And was his mustache, too, scurfy?" asked the captain, who liked giving pinpricks. "Didn't he, too, grudge giving a drop of water even to his guardian angel? Didn't he, too, walk about with his boots under his arm so as not to wear out the soles?"

"I'm going!" shouted Ladas, jumping up. "And you, captain, why don't you take a part? What are you waiting for? There's not a smooth skin needed, by any chance, is there?"

"I? I form the reserve," said the captain, with a laugh and the gesture of twirling mustaches. "Perhaps in the course of the year —after all we're men, and not young!—one of you will go west: you for instance, Ladas of the mustaches, or even his lordship Pilate . . . If so, I shall take his place, to save the Mystery."

"Find another Caiaphas, that's all I've got to say!" bawled the old skinflint. "Anyhow, I must do some watering. I'm off!" And he made for the door.

But at one bound the priest was there and, with outstretched arms:

"Where are you going? Our people are coming; you shan't leave. You don't want to make us all ridiculous?"

Then, wheedling:

"You must make a sacrifice, like the others, father Ladas. And think of hellfire; many of your sins will be forgiven you if you aid us in this work, which is pleasing to God. A better Caiaphas than you we shall never find. Don't hold out against us. God will note it on His tablets."

"I don't want to be Caiaphas!" shouted old Ladas in terror. "Find another! And as for those tablets—"

But he had no time to finish his speech: the villagers were already coming up the stairs and the priest unbolted the door.

"Christ is risen, notables!" About ten villagers came in, their hands on their chests, lips or foreheads. They formed a line along the wall.

"Risen indeed!" replied the notables, placing themselves more squarely on the divan. The old archon passed round his tobacco pouch.

"My children, the decision has been taken," the priest announced; "you have come at the right time, welcome to you!"

He clapped his hands and Mariori entered.

"Mariori, give these young people something to drink and offer each of them a red egg for the resurrection of Christ!"

They drank, each one took a red egg, and waited.

"My children," began the priest, stroking his forked beard, "I explained to you yesterday after Mass what we expect of you. A great Mystery will be represented next Easter in our village, and all, great and small, must lend a hand. Remember, all of you, six years ago, what a Holy Week we had! What tears flowed beneath the porch, what piercing groans: then, on the Sunday of the Resurrection, what joy, what a lighting of candles, what an opening of arms; how ardently we threw ourselves into the dance; we sang 'Christ is risen again, trampling death by death'; we were all become brothers! Next year the Passion of Christ must be as fine, finer still; do you agree, my brothers?"

"We agree, Father!" they answered, as one man. "With your blessing!"

"With the blessing of God!" declared the priest, rising to his feet. "We, the Elders, have chosen those who will this year incarnate the Passion of Christ—those who will be the Apostles, also Pilate, Caiaphas, and Christ. In the name of the Father, approach, Kostandis."

The proprietor of the café took the corner of his apron, tucked it into his wide red sash, and advanced.

"You, Kostandis, are the man we have chosen to be James, the austere disciple of Christ. A heavy burden, a divine burden; bear it with dignity, do you hear? Do not dishonor the Apostle. From today you must become a new man, Kostandis. You are good, but you must become better. More honest, more affable. Come to church more often. Put less barley in the coffee. Stop cutting the slabs of Turkish delight in two and selling the halves as wholes. Above all, take care not to beat your wife, because from today you are not only Kostandis, but also, and above all, James the Apostle. You understand? Do you?"

"I understand," replied Kostandis, withdrawing to the wall and blushing. He was on the point of saying: "It isn't me who beat my wife, it's she beats me," but he was ashamed.

"Where is Michelis?" asked the priest, "we have need of him."

"He stopped in the kitchen and is talking with your daughter," replied Yannakos.

"Let someone go and fetch him. Now it's your turn to come forward, Yannakos."

The carrier took one step forward and kissed the priest's hand.

"You, Yannakos, have drawn a difficult number; you will be the Apostle Peter. Attention! Forget the old man, this is a baptism. Yannakos, I baptize thee in the name of the Father; thou art the Apostle Peter! You can read a little, take the Gospels; there you will see what Peter was like, what he said, what he did; you, too, are mule-headed, Yannakos, but good-hearted. Forget the past, take a new road, enter into the way of God: don't give short weight, stop selling a cuckoo as a nightingale, stop opening letters to find out people's secrets. Do you hear? Say: 'I hear and I obey'!"

"I hear and I obey, Father," replied Yannakos, withdrawing to the wall as quickly as he could. He was trembling lest this devil of a priest should start unpacking all his little tricks in public.

But the priest had pity on him; he was silent. Then Yannakos grew bold:

"Father, I ask a favor. I believe that in the Gospel there's also an ass. When he entered Jerusalem, I think, on Palm Sunday, Christ was riding on a donkey. So we shall need one: I should like it to be mine."

"Your will be done, Peter; your ass is accepted," the priest answered. All burst out laughing.

At this moment Michelis came in. Stout, fresh and pink, with a flower behind his ear and a gold ring on his finger, he had on fine linen and satin. His cheeks were burning; he had just touched Mariori's hand; he was still all flame.

"Welcome, Michelis, dear child," said the priest, his eyes brooding over his son-in-law to be. "Unanimously we have chosen you to incarnate John, the well-beloved disciple of Christ. It is a great honor, it is a great joy, Michelis. It will be you who will lean upon the bosom of Christ to comfort Him. It will be you who will follow Him up to the last minute upon the cross, when the other disciples have dispersed. It will be to you that Christ will entrust His mother."

"With your blessing, Father," said Michelis, blushing with pleasure. "From childhood I've admired this Apostle in the icons; he was always young, handsome, full of sweetness; I liked him. Thank you, Father. Have you any advice to give me?"

"None, Michelis. Your soul is innocent as a dove, your heart overflowing with affection. No, you won't dishonor the Apostle; receive my blessing!"

"Now we must find a Judas Iscariot," he went on, looking at the villagers one after another with the eye of a bird of prey. They shivered as they felt his hard gaze fall upon them. "Come to my help, O Lord," murmured each one. "I don't want, no, I don't want to be Judas!"

His gaze came to rest on the red beard of Plaster-eater; his voice rose:

"Panayotaros, come a little nearer, I want to ask you for a service!"

Panayotaros, like an ox trying to get rid of its yoke, shook his heavy shoulders and his thick neck; for a second he felt like shouting out: "No, I don't want to!" but he had not the courage in front of the notables.

"At your orders, priest," he said, approaching heavily with a bear's gait.

"It's a very painful service we are asking of you, Panayotaros, but you won't wish to disoblige us; for all those churlish manners of yours, you've a tender heart. You're like the almond—a shell as hard as stone, but, well hidden inside it, a sweet almond. . . . You heard what I said, Panayotaros?"

"I heard, I'm not deaf," he answered, and his face with its hail of small pox went purple. He guessed what was wanted of him, but the honeyed words and flattery disgusted him.

"Without Judas, no Crucifixion," the priest went on; "and without Crucifixion, no Resurrection. It's therefore absolutely necessary that one of us should sacrifice himself and take the part of Judas."

"Judas? Me? Never!" declared Plaster-eater, bluntly. He clenched his fist, his red egg broke, its yellow daubed his hand.

The archon jumped up; he raised his chibouk in a meaning gesture.

"So! It's the end of the world!" he shouted; "so all of you now are going to be in command! This is the Council of Elders, not Kostandis's café! The Elders have decided, and that's that; the people must obey. Do you hear, Plaster-eater?"

"I respect the Council of the Elders," Panayotaros retorted, "but don't ask me to betray Christ. I'll never do it!"

The archon puffed and foamed. He would have liked to speak; he was choking. The captain took advantage of the confusion to fill his glass again.

"You're a bent stick, you see everything askew, Panayotaros," the priest broke in, studiously keeping his voice mild. "It isn't you, you idiot, who will be betraying Christ, you'll be *pretending* to be Judas and to betray Christ, that we may crucify Him and raise Him up again afterward. Your brain is sluggish, certainly, but pay attention and you'll understand; for the world to be saved, Christ has to be crucified. For Christ to be crucified, someone has to betray Him. For the world to be saved, as you see, Judas is indispensable, more indispensable than any other Apostle. If an Apostle's missing, it doesn't matter; but if Judas is missing, nothing can be done. . . . He's the one that's most necessary, after Christ. . . . Have you grasped that?"

"Me, Judas? Never!" Panayotaros repeated, kneading the broken egg in his hand. "You want me to be Judas; I don't want to be; that's all!"

"Come, my good Panayotaros, to please us," said the schoolmaster; "be Judas, your name will become immortal."

"Old Ladas, too, begs you to do it," said the captain, wiping his lips; "and as for the money you owe him, he won't press you, so he says. He'll even, so he says, make you a present of the interest."

"Don't meddle in other people's affairs, captain," yelped the old miser, beside himself. "I never said anything of the kind. Do what the good God bids you, Panayotaros; I never make a present of interest to anyone!"

Everyone was silent. Panayotaros' quick breathing became audible; he was gasping as though he were climbing a mountain.

"Let's not keep hanging about," said the captain; "let the poor devil digest the thing; it's no joke becoming Judas. It's not a thing you do just like that, without a moment's notice. Reflection and raki are what's needed. Where's Manolios? Let's get on with it."

"He was seen telling sweet nothings to his Lenio; it's hard to pry him away from that!" said Yannakos.

"Here I am," said Manolios, blushing. He had slipped into the room unnoticed and was in the farthest corner. "At your service, archon and notables."

"Approach, Manolios," said the priest in a voice all sugar and honey, "approach and receive my blessing."

Manolios stepped forward and kissed the priest's hand. He was a fair-haired, timid young man, poorly dressed. He smelt of thyme and milk. From his blue eyes one could tell his candor.

"You have drawn the winning number, Manolios," said the priest in solemn tones. "You are the one whom God has chosen to revive by your gestures, your voice, your tears, the Holy Passion. . . . It is you who will put on the crown of thorns, it is you who will be scourged, it is you who will carry the holy cross, you who will be crucified. From today till Holy Week next year you must think only of one thing, Manolios, one thing only: how can I become worthy to bear the terrible weight of the cross."

"I am not worthy," said Manolios, trembling.

"No one is. Yet it is you God has chosen."

"I am not worthy," Manolios murmured again. "I am betrothed, I have touched a woman, sin is in my soul; in a few days' time I shall be married. . . . How then could I bear the terrible weight of Christ?"

"Do not resist the will of God," said the priest severely. "No, you are not worthy, but Divine Grace forgives, absolves, chooses. You are the one It has chosen; be silent!"

Manolios was silent, but his heart beat to bursting with joy and terror. He looked out of the window: the plain in the distance was green again, wet, serene; the drizzle had ceased. As he raised his eyes, Manolios suddenly trembled. An immense rainbow, all emerald, ruby and gold, was binding heaven and earth together.

"His will be done," said Manolios, laying his hand wide open upon his chest.

"Let the Apostles now approach," said the priest. "You too, Panayotaros, come; don't scowl; no one's going to eat you. Approach and receive the blessing."

All four approached and ranged themselves to right and left of Manolios. The priest stretched out his arms above their heads.

"With the blessing of God," he said; "may the Spirit of the Lord breathe upon you. As in the springtime the trees swell with sap and burst into buds, so may your hearts, though but dead trunks, flower in their turn! May they accomplish the miracle which shall make the faithful who will see you during Holy Week say: 'Is that Yannakos, Kostandis, Michelis? No! No! It's Peter, James, John.' May they, when they see you, Manolios, in the crown of thorns climbing Golgotha, be possessed with terror. May the earth tremble once more, the sun be darkened, the temple be rent in twain, from top to bottom, within their souls! May their eyes be filled with tears, may they be purified and suddenly discover that we are all brothers! May Christ rise again, no longer only on the steps of the church, but in our hearts. Amen!"

The three Apostles and Manolios were bathed in a cold sweat; their knees gave; dread hovered over their heads; their hands fumbled for one another and joined; they formed a chain, united in danger. Panayotaros alone clenched his fist and would not join the others; he gazed at the door, impatient to get out.

"Go your ways," said the priest, "with the blessing of God. A new road is opening before you. It's a very rough one. Tighten your belts, cleanse your hearts, and may God aid you!"

They withdrew, bowing one by one before the priest and saluting the elders, then passing through the door in silence. Then the notables stood up and stretched their arms and legs.

"Thanks to God's power," said the archon, "all's properly fixed up. You managed things very nicely, priest. Your blessing!"

Just as the notables were about to cross the threshold, Captain Fortounas burst out laughing and slapped his thighs.

"Oh, I say, we forgot to choose the Magdalen!"

"Don't worry, captain," said the old archon, swallowing his saliva, "I'll have her come up to me and I'll talk to her. . . . I feel sure I'll succeed," he added, smiling.

"If you must sin with her, archon," said the priest, frowning, "do it before speaking to her; for as soon as she's the Magdalen it will be a great sin, you know."

"You did well to tell me, priest," said the archon. He drew in his breath as though he had just escaped from a great danger.

Once he was alone, The devil take us, thought Captain Fortounas as he descended the slope, leaning heavily on his stick. For that sort of business, old man, you need a pure heart; we are Sodom and Gomorrha. This gobble-all priest of ours? He's opened a drugstore and calls it "church" and there dispenses God by weight. He cures all sicknesses, so he says, the charlatan. "What's wrong with you?" "I've lied." "Good! Take three grams of Christ, so many piastres." "I've stolen." "Four grams of Christ, so much. And you?" "I've done a murder." "Oh, you poor man, you're very ill. This evening, before you go to bed, you will take fifteen grams of Christ; it costs a lot, that." "Isn't there a little rebate, Father?" "No, that's the price; pay it, or you'll go right to the bottom of Hell." He shows him the images he has in his shop,

representing Hell, with flames, pitchforks and devils; then the customer has gooseflesh and empties his pocket. . . .

Old Patriarcheas? A pig on two legs; nothing but belly from
head to foot; even his skulls full of guts. If you placed beside
him, on one side, all he's eaten during his life and, on the other, all
that's come out of him, above and below, it'd make two enormous
stinking mountains. That's how he'll appear when the Day comes,
with two mountains, one on his right, the other on his left, in front
of the good God.

Hadji Nikolis, the schoolmaster? A half-helping, the poor fellow! Chicken-livered, moth-eaten; an ugly mug with a pair of dirty
glasses—and takes himself for Alexander the Great! Puts on a paper
helmet and crowns the brains of all the brats with ancient paper
helmets. A schoolmaster! What good can come of that?

Old father Ladas? Lousy, stingy. Not an ounce of self-respect.
Sits on his barrels of wine, on his jars of oil, on his sacks of flour,
and starves. He's the one who said to his wife, one evening when
he had guests: "Woman, go and cook an egg, there'll be four of
us to supper." Always hungry, always thirsty, goes about barefoot
and bare-arse—and why? To die in a rich man's skin! Ugh! The
devil take him!

And me? Well, must I say it? String and sacking! You need
tongs to touch me without getting dirty. The eating and drinking,
stealing, killing and cuckolding I've got through in my life! O
Lord! How did I have the time for so much dirty work? A health
to my hands, my feet, my mouth, my thighs! Friends, you've done
a good job: my blessing!

As he soliloquized, Captain Fortounas struck the stones of the
road with his stick; he had taken off his cap and was fanning himself with it; he was hot. He looked at the sun: it was past noon. He
hastened his step: that very morning the Agha had invited him to
lunch; they would once more fill their bellies and get drunk. Let's
get a move on, he growled, life is good, let's take what we can!
Reaching the threshold of the Agha's house, he paused before the
red-painted door and spat upon it. This relieved him: it was as if
he had spat on the whole of Turkey, as if he had raised a small, a
very small standard of liberty, and had for a moment become free.

He spat again, then knocked at the door, relieved. He was going
to eat and drink well; the Agha was a fine fellow, not close-fisted;
they would once more knot their napkins around their skulls to

stop them from bursting, and they would drink neat raki in tumblers.

In the courtyard a dry sound of clogs, of short steps, was heard. The door opened. The Agha's aged slave, hunch-backed Martha, greeted the captain peevishly:

"If you believe in Christ, captain, don't go getting drunk again; I've had enough, yes, really, I've had enough!"

The captain laughed. He stroked the old woman's hump:

"Don't worry, Kyra Martha, we won't get drunk. And if we do get drunk, we won't be sick. And if we are sick, well, you'll bring the basin to stop us dirtying the floor. Upon my word!"

That said, with great dignity he crossed the threshold.

Men Hunted by Men

T OWARD EVENING the three Apostles and Manolios started along the road by the small lake of Voidomata, which was not far from the village, to lighten their hearts by having a chat. All four were filled with a mystic thrill, as though they had taken Communion.

The drizzle had stopped, the trees and stones were shining, the earth was balmy, a joyous, mocking cuckoo whistled. The sun, like a great nobleman appeased, was caressing the earth with affection. All was pure tenderness and serenity. Raindrops were still at play on the tips of the leaves. The world was smiling and weeping in the damp air of evening.

For a long time the four companions walked in silence. They were now on one of the soaking paths which divided the gardens; the blossoms of the lemon trees gleamed among the dark foliage. As though Christ were not yet risen, the whole flower-laden earth was in tears. A warm wind, one of those that make the sap rise, was on its way by, and all plants, even the lowliest, were reviving.

Kostandis was the first to speak:

"What a heavy burden the priest has put on our backs!" he said in a low voice. "God help us to carry it through. Last time, if you remember, Christ was acted by Master Charalambis, a man of property, a good family man. But he tried so hard to follow in the footsteps of Christ, he struggled so, during the whole year, to be worthy to bear the cross, that in the end it turned his head. On Easter Day he put the crown of thorns on his head, heaved the cross upon his shoulder and, abandoning everything, went off to the monastery of Saint George of Soumela, over there, Trebizond way, and became a monk. It was the ruin of the family; his wife died of it, his children became beggars in the village. Manolios, do you remember Master Charalambis?"

Manolios said nothing. He listened to Kostandis's words without hearing them; his spirit was plunged in a profound meditation; his throat was tight, he could not speak. The thing to which he had aspired from his tenderest childhood, the thing he had desired during so many nights as he sat at the feet of his Superior, Father Manasse, listening to the golden legend—behold, now God was granting it to him. To follow in the footsteps of the martyrs and the saints, to pare away his flesh, to go to his death for his faith in Jesus Christ, and to enter Paradise bearing the instruments of martyrdom: the crown of thorns, the cross and the five nails. . . .

"Don't you think we shall go crazy, too?" said Michelis with a bantering smile; but deep down inside him he felt a vague disquiet. "Can't you see us imagining we're the Apostles? God preserve us!"

"Who knows?" said Yannakos, shaking his huge sun-baked head. "Man, it seems, is a delicate machine, which gets out of order easily. It's enough for a life to come unscrewed, and . . ."

They had reached Voidomata, and they halted. Dark green waters, thick reeds, wild duck. Two storks rose and passed over their heads with slow, indifferent flight. The sun was about to set.

Far from the world, they gazed at the lake lost in shadow, but none of them saw it: their spirits were absent, pursued by strange anxieties. They were silent. At last Yannakos spoke:

"It's true, Kostandis, the task is difficult, very hard. I—God forgive me!—have got into bad habits; how shall I set about losing them? 'Don't give short weight,' he said; 'don't open other people's letters.' The priest imagines it's easy. If you don't give short weight, how do you expect to make money and be somebody some day? If you don't read other people's letters, just to see, what'll you do to amuse yourself? I got into that habit when my late wife left me. Not to do any harm—God preserve me!—but I was bored. . . . It's the only pleasure I've got left, except my ass—blessings on him! It's the only pleasure I've got left: coming back from my round, bolting my hut door, boiling some water and steaming the letters open. . . . I read them, I find out what this or that one's up to, I stick them up again, and I take them around next morning. And now here's the priest, telling you . . . You know, friend, it's not easy for crow to become dove—God forgive me!"

Smoothing his thin black mustache, Michelis smiled. He was

pleased with himself. He didn't cheat; he didn't read other people's letters; Grigoris the priest hadn't found anything to reproach him with; he was proud of it. He pulled out his tobacco pouch and handed it to his companions; they began, all four of them, rolling fat, close-packed cigarettes. They lit these, inhaled the smoke, and felt more calm.

Michelis could not keep his pride to himself:

"The priest told me I needn't change any of my habits: as I am, I shan't dishonor the Apostle."

Hardly had he uttered the words than he went red with shame, but he could not take them back.

Manolios turned toward him and looked at him severely. At first he thought he would say nothing: Michelis was his master's son, was he not? But he remembered that from now on he was not merely Manolios, he was something deeper, greater; and this emboldened him.

"All the same," he said, "who knows, master, if your lordship, too, won't have to change quite a few of his habits? To eat less—think of all the people in the village who are hungry—and not display so much luxury: fine linen breeches, embroidered waistcoat, brand-new leggings—think of all the people who shiver in the winter because they've nothing to wear. . . . To open your cellars and larders from time to time and give a little to the poor . . . you've more than you need, God be praised."

"And if the old man got to suspect that I was giving alms?" said Michelis in terror.

"You're not a child now, you're twenty-five, you're a grown man," Manolios answered. "Besides, above your father there is Christ, He is the real Father, He alone commands."

Michelis turned dumbfounded toward his servant. It was the first time he had been spoken to so boldly. I believe he's getting a swelled head because they've made him Christ, he thought. I'll tell my father to call him to order. He threw his cigarette away nervously, but said nothing.

"Must buy a Gospel," said Kostandis; "that's what I think. That's where we'll find the road we have to follow."

"In our house there's a great big Gospel, my grandfather's," said Michelis. "It's bound in wood and pigskin. The boards of its binding are like fortress gates. It has a lock, too, with a huge key. When you open it you think you're entering a great city. It's quite simple—we can meet every Sunday at my house and read it."

"I must have one too, up on the mountain," said Manolios. "Up to now I've been bored all alone; I've been taking bits of wood and carving spoons, sticks, snuffboxes, saints, goats, anything that came into my head. I've been wasting my time. But now . . ."

He fell silent and meditative.

"And I—when I've done my round with my donkey and sat down under a plane tree for a bit of a breather—it'd be no bad thing if I had a little Gospel to read. . . . You'll be telling me I won't make much sense of it, but what's that matter, there'll always be something to the good!"

"I'm the one who has most need of it," Kostandis burst in. "When my wife starts shouting and my temper gets up, I'll open it to calm me down. And I'll say to myself: 'All I put up with, all this martyrdom of mine, what is it to the Passion of Christ?' Otherwise . . . You mustn't blame me, Yannakos; she's your sister, but she's beyond bearing. Once she threw herself upon me and tried to tear my eyes out with a fork. Even the day before yesterday she picked up the pot in which the mashed beans were cooking and chased me round and tried to hit me on the head with it. I said to myself: 'Either she'll kill me, or I shall kill her.' Now I shall read the Gospel and she can shout as much as she likes!"

Yannakos laughed. "Poor Kostandis," he said sympathetically, "God knows how I feel for you. But patience: every man has a woman in his fate; make the best of yours and say nothing."

"The trouble is," Kostandis went on, "that I can't read very well. I get the letters mixed and end up all in a muddle."

"That doesn't matter," Manolios assured him; "it's better so. You read one syllable and you understand the whole word. Besides, the Apostles were simple people, like us, not educated, fishermen most of them."

"Could the Apostle Peter read?" asked Yannakos, anxiously.

"I don't know," replied Manolios, "I don't know, Yannakos. We'll ask the priest."

"Better ask, too, whether he sold the fish he caught or gave them to the poor," murmured Yannakos. "Because surely he didn't give short weight, but did he sell them? That's the question. Did he sell or give away?"

"We ought to read the lives of the saints as well," Michelis suggested.

"No, no," protested Manolios, "we're simple men, we'll get everything mixed up. When I was with the monks I used to read them, and I nearly went off my head. Deserts, lions, dreadful diseases, leprosy; their bodies were covered with boils, eaten by worms, or became like the shells of tortoises. . . . At other times temptations came like a beautiful woman. No, no! Only the Gospel."

They walked slowly round the lake in the invading shadow. It was the first time in their lives that they had had such a singular conversation. They turned over and over in their minds the strange words of Grigoris the priest: "May the Spirit of the Lord breathe upon you. . . ." To breathe, was it then a wind, this Spirit? A wind that makes the sap rise, like the damp, warm wind of evening whose breath brings buds out on the branches? The Spirit—could it be a wind like that one? Could it breathe upon our souls?

And the four companions reflected, wondered, tried to understand. But none of them were willing to question his neighbor, yet it was secretly and strangely delightful to him to be gripped by an anxiety like this.

So they remained for a long while without speaking, silently watching night fall. The evening star sparkled on the far horizon. By the lakeside the frogs began to croak, for all they were worth. On the left, already drowned in shadow, rose the green, well-tilled Mount of the Virgin, where Manolios had his shepherd's hut and guarded his master's sheep. On the right, the wild mountain called Sarakina was changing from violet to midnight blue, and the many caves which pitted its flanks yawned black. But on its summit, freshly whitewashed and shored up by enormous rocks, shone the chapel of the Prophet Elijah, all white, and tiny as an egg. . . .

Down below, on the soft earth, between the rushes, here and there a glowworm had kindled its belly and was gleaming serenely, patiently, loaded with love, and waiting.

"Night is coming," said Michelis, "let's go home."

But Yannakos, who was walking in front, stopped suddenly, he put his hand to his ear and listened: a sound of footsteps could be heard, like a crowd on the march, a far-off but full murmur like the humming of a swarm; from time to time a deep and powerful voice seemed to be giving orders.

"Look, you others, look!" cried Yannakos. "What's that ant heap coming out from the plain? Seems like a procession."

They strained their eyes to distinguish something in the half-darkness, and listened hard.

A long troop of men and women was coming into view among the corn, between the vines. They looked as if they were running; no doubt they had seen the village and were hastening their steps.

"Listen!" said Michelis, "aren't they singing a psalm?"

"More like weeping," said Manolios, "I can hear sobs."

"No, no, it's a psalm; hold your breath, so we can hear better."

Motionless, they listened. Then clear, triumphal in the calm of the evening, the old Byzantine canticle rang out: "Lord, Lord, save Thy people. . . ."

"Those are our brothers, Christians!" Manolios shouted. "Let's go and welcome them!"

All four began running. The head of the procession had already reached the first houses of the village. The dogs were jumping about in the road, barking as if mad; doors were opening, the women were coming out on to the thresholds, the men were running up with their mouths full; it was the moment when the people of Lycovrissi took their meal, seated cross-legged about low tables. Hearing the psalm-singing, the weeping, the noise of footsteps, they had leaped up. The three Apostles and Manolios arrived in their turn.

The last rays of sunset still lit the houses and the lanes of the village. The procession was now near, and they could clearly make out, at its head, a thin priest with sun-tanned face and flaring black eyes under bushy eyebrows, and with a sparse, pointed beard, quite gray. He clasped in his arms a great Gospel with a heavy binding in chased silver. He wore his stole. At his right hand, a giant with black, drooping mustaches bore the old church banner on which was embroidered a tall Saint George in gold. Behind them, five or six gaunt old men carried huge icons, holding them dead straight. Then followed the flock of women and men accompanied by children crying and weeping. The men were laden with bundles and tools: shovels, spades, picks, scythes; the women with cradles, stools and tubs.

"Who are you, Christians? Where've you come from? Where

are you going?" shouted Yannakos, bowing before the priest just as the troop began to spread over the village square.

"Where is priest Grigoris?" replied the old man hoarsely; "where are the notables?"

He turned to the villagers, who had run up, surprised and anxious.

"We are Christians, my brethren, have no fear: Christians, persecuted Greeks! Call the heads of the village, I must speak with them. Have the bells rung!"

Exhausted, the women sank to the ground; the men laid down their burdens, wiped the sweat from their faces, and looked at their priest without a word.

"Where have you come from, by the grace of God, granddad?" Manolios asked an old man, bent with years and laden with a very heavy sack which he still kept on his back.

"Don't be impatient, son," the old man answered, "don't be impatient; priest Fotis will speak."

"What have you got in that sack, granddad?"

"Nothing, son, nothing. Things of mine . . ." he said, laying the sack down carefully on the ground.

The priest remained standing, holding the Gospel closely to him. A young man ran to the belfry, seized the rope and set the bell ringing wildly. Two owls, terrified, flew out from the plane tree and were lost in the darkness.

The Agha came out on his balcony, completely drunk; the square appeared to him to be filled with a strange flock which did not belong to him. His ears had begun to hum. Somewhere somebody must be shouting, weeping or singing—he could not manage to understand. And that thing making Hell's own din was perhaps —was it?—the bell.

"Hey you, Captain Greenhorn," he said, going in again, "come and explain me this mystery. What's this herd in the square? This din? These bells? Am I dreaming?"

Captain Fortounas ran to the balcony. He had tied a white napkin around his head for fear it might explode. This was his habit every time he spent an evening drinking with the Agha, because, so he pretended, the raki might make it burst into a thousand pieces. From time to time he would untie the napkin, plunge it into a basin of cold water and roll it again about his burning head.

The captain leaned out, straining his eyes. He thought he could make out, down below around the plane tree, men, women, a banner. . . .

"Well, what is it, Captain Greenhorn?" the Agha asked again. "Can you understand something of what's going on down there?"

"It's people!" answered the captain. "It seems to me to be people. And you, Agha, what do you think?"

"To me, too, it seems to be people. . . . Where've they come out from? What do they want? What ought I to do? Let them alone? Kick them out? Go down with my whip? What do you think?"

"Don't worry, Agha! What's the good of shouting, going down with a whip, fretting and fuming? Let them alone and let's have some fun. Shall we have another?"

"Youssoufaki," the Agha called, "bring the cushions here, my treasure, and the glasses and the demijohn. And come and have a squint yourself, my dear. Those are *romnoi*,* d'you see—Greeks: it won't be long before they come to blows."

"Where is priest Grigoris?" asked priest Fotis once more. "Where are the notables? Isn't there a Christian who'll go and fetch them?"

"I'll go!" replied Manolios. "A little patience, Father."

Then, turning to Michelis:

"Michelis, go and tell your father, will you? Tell him there are Christians arrived, Christians who are pursued and are falling at his feet, asking for his protection. He's archon, it's his duty. I'm going over to priest Grigoris's. You, Kostandis, run to old Ladas's. Tell him there are people from another village, and that they're selling their stuff for a crust of bread because they're starving. That's what you must tell him, or he won't come. And you, Yannakos, cut across to the captain's cottage, and tell him there're shipwrecked men arrived from the Black Sea, and they've come here because they've heard tell of him. On your way turn off and call the schoolmaster; tell him they are Greeks and in need!"

An urchin piped up:

"The captain's on the spree with the Agha. Here, there he is, up there on the balcony. . . . I say! he's got his head tied up in a napkin. That means he's quite drunk."

"The archon's snoring!" said an amused voice behind them; "a cannon-shot wouldn't wake him."

* Greeks

They wheeled round. It was Katerina, the opulent and seductive widow, with her fleshy lips, arriving breathless. She was wearing a brand-new shawl, with big red roses on a green ground. Her cheeks were on fire. Her teeth, polished with walnut leaves, glittered.

"He's asleep, he's in bliss, and he's snoring!" Katerina repeated, casting a roguish glance at Manolios. She added with a laugh: "You're wasting your time sending messengers to him, Manolios!"

Manolios looked at her and lowered his eyes in fear. What a tigress! he thought, a man-eating tigress. . . . Get thee behind me, Satan!

The widow approached him, simpering; she smelled of musk, like a real wild beast in heat. She heard a dull bellow behind her, and turned. Frowning, glowering darkly, Panayotaros was there and was gazing at her. He, too, must have been running, for he was panting and his pitted face was crimson.

"Let's go! let's go!" said Manolios impatiently.

All three started up the hill, running, and disappeared into the dark lanes.

Furious, gritting his teeth, Panayotaros took one step, then another, and was beside Katerina.

He leaned over her shoulder: "What are you after, slut, in the archon's house, the old tomcat? What were you up to, there, eh? You whore, I'll eat you up raw!"

"I'm not made of plaster!" mocked the widow. She slid through the crowd and took refuge near the colossus carrying the banner.

"Courage, my children," the priest was crying, as he came and went among his flock. "Courage, the notables will soon be here, the Reverend Father Grigoris will come, our torments will have an end. We have escaped, with the aid of God, from the jaws of death; we shall put forth new roots into the earth, our race will not vanish! No, it will not vanish, my sons, it is immortal!"

A rumor arose, like the humming of a hive, then all was silent. Several women opened their bodices, let out their breasts, gave suck to their children to silence them. The colossus leaned the banner on the ground, and the hundred-year-old Elder rested his callused hand upon his sack with a smile.

"God be praised," he murmured; "we shall take root again!" and he made the sign of the cross.

All this time the people of the village were arriving breathless;

the dogs, tired of barking, were sniffing at those people from elsewhere; the young man clinging to the rope was still ringing the bell and rousing the village.

Velvety, pricked with two or three big stars, the sky stretched infinite above them; the refugees raised their eyes and stared into it. They waited confidently for the arrival of the notables who would decide their fate. All were silent. For a moment the singing of the stream between the pebbles could be heard.

"Come, devil's captain, pour out the drinks," said the Agha, hearing the water flowing; "it's a dream, it's our stream, a sweet stream; pour out the drinks to stop us waking. And keep your eyes skinned. Soon as the *romnoi* get going, let me know and down I go with the whip."

"Don't worry, Agha, I'm all eyes; I'll let you know; I'm coming on watch!"

"Call Hussein and let him come with his trumpet. I may need him. Youssoufaki, light me my chibouk."

The handsome boy lit the long chibouk with its amber bowl. The Agha shut his eyes and began to smoke. Seated on his cushion between the demijohn and his Youssoufaki, he softly entered Paradise.

Manolios returned, out of breath; he stretched out his arms and shouted:

"Make way, make way, brothers, here comes the priest!"

The men jumped up, the women raised their heads and sighed. The banner staggered and took up its position by the side of priest Fotis; the old men carrying the icons lined up in front. Their priest crossed himself:

"God succor us!" he murmured, and waited without moving.

Michelis in turn arrived. He approached Manolios and whispered in his ear:

"He's asleep; he's snoring. Impossible to wake him; he's drunk too much and eaten too much. I shook him, he didn't stir. I called him, he didn't hear. So I left."

Then came Kostandis:

"That damned old man's a real fox," he said, beside himself; "he smelt a trap, so he pretends he's too busy and can't come; if it's a collection that's being made for the beggars who've invaded the village, *he* hasn't a single penny to give, he says. Don't let them come knocking at his door, he won't open."

At this moment Yannakos arrived:

"I found the schoolmaster reading his books; he'll finish reading and then come. And anything priest Grigoris decides to do, he says, will be right. There you are!"

"Talk of heads of the village!" muttered Manolios with a sigh. "There's one who's snoring, another getting tipsy, another reading, and the old skinflint brooding over his shekels. But I rely on priest Grigoris who's coming. He—he's the voice of God. He's the one who'll speak!"

A pale young woman gave a piercing cry and let her head sink on her breast. She had not eaten for three days. Used to an easy life, she was at the end of her strength; she was dying.

"Courage, little Despinio, courage," the women around her said to her, fanning her; "here we are, come to such a rich place, and they've already gone to get us food to give us back our strength. Just a little courage!"

But she wagged her head; her eyes rolled back and then closed.

All of a sudden joyful cries rang out; the crowd stirred.

"He's coming! He's coming!"

"Hey, Smooth-skin, what's happening?" asked the Agha, raising heavy eyelids.

"I keep telling you not to fuss, Agha. . . . You're in Paradise, don't come out. I'm at the gate, on the alert, I'll keep you posted. I think it's Grigoris, the priest, turning up."

The Agha burst out laughing.

"Has the horde of strangers got its priest, too?"

"Yes," said the captain, refilling his goblet.

"Good, then we shall have some fun, you'll see. The two priests will come to blows. They're like women, those blessed priests. They've long hair, and when there are two of them who meet, they tear each other's tresses out. Where's Hussein? Let him go down and tell 'em to speak up so that I can hear."

Meanwhile, in his pursuit of the widow, Panayotaros had arrived close to the banner.

"I'll gobble you up now, creature!" he growled again, leaning toward her ear. "What are you after here, among all these men? Off with you, home, quick. Get out of here! I'm at your heels."

"Haven't you any heart, then, you?" said the widow, turning on him fiercely. "Can't you see the torments of Christendom? Haven't you any pity for all these starving people?"

She was silent a moment and turned her back on him. And suddenly she could no longer contain herself, a heavy word was choking her; she turned again and screamed at him:

"Judas!"

Immediately, she twisted among the refugees and escaped.

Panayotaros felt the earth turning under his feet. He was giddy; there was a dagger planted in his heart. To prevent himself from falling he held on to the staff of the banner and remained there doubled up, with his mouth open, waiting for the earth to come to rest.

"There he is! There he is! Grigoris the priest!" cried voices on all sides.

The throng raised its eyes and saw him. Tall in stature, lordly, in a cassock of aubergine satin streaked by his broad black belt and by his heavy silver cross which lay flat upon his vast paunch, priest Grigoris, God's representative in Lycovrissi, stood up before the starving crowd.

Men and women knelt; their gaunt priest opened his arms and stepped forward for the accolade on the shoulder, in the monastic manner, toward the fat minister of God. But he raised his fleshy hand, frowned and stopped him. With a fierce glance around, he saw these people in rags, these starving people, these dying people; he did not like them at all, and his voice arose:

"Who are you? Why have you left your hearths? What are you seeking here?"

At his voice the women shrivelled up, the children ran to their mothers and clung to their skirts; the dogs began barking again. The captain, on the balcony, cocked his large ear and listened.

"Father," replied the priest of the refugees, calmly and with decision, "Father, I am priest Fotis, of a distant village, Saint George, and here are the souls God has entrusted to me. The Turks have burned our village, they have chased us from our lands, they have killed as many of ours as they could; we have escaped and departed with heavy hearts; Christ marches at our head and we follow. We are seeking new lands on which to find a hold. There."

He was silent a moment, his mouth had gone dry, the words would no longer come out.

"We, too, are Christians," he resumed after a while; "we are Hellenes, a great race; we must not vanish!"

Leaning on the balcony with his head buzzing, the captain listened to the dry, proud voice of the angry priest. Little by little, as the fumes of the raki dispersed, his brain became more clear.

Devil of a race, all the same, he said to himself; what tenacity! Where do they manage to find this courage! Octopus, we are! One tentacle cut off, then other—and at once we grow new ones!

He untied the napkin from about his head; it was so hot that it steamed. He plunged it in the basin of water, which was within reach, and encircled his head with it once more and felt refreshed.

Priest Fotis shouted:

"We shall not vanish! For thousands of years we have kept alive; we shall keep alive for thousands more. . . . Blessed be the hour of our meeting with you, priest Grigoris!"

That's a real captain of a priest! thought Captain Fortounas. What fire, what vigor, what courage the animal has! By the sea, I think he's right. We Greeks are an immortal race. In vain they uproot us, burn us, cut our throats: they can't make us lower our flag! We take the icons, the tubs, the cradles, the Gospel, and, quick march! off we go to pitch our tent farther on!

The tears came into his eyes, and suddenly he leaned out from the balcony and yelled:

"Bravo, captain priest, bravo, old friend!"

Heads were raised in the direction of the balcony, but the shout was lost in the clamor which had been aroused by the priest's words. The women uttered strident cries, remembering their homes; the children, remembering bread, began to weep.

Then, all at once, the clamor died down. Priest Grigoris had raised his dimpled hand; he was speaking:

"All that happens in this world happens because God has willed it," he said in a powerful voice. "He sees the earth from on high, He holds a balance and weighs. He allows Lycovrissi to enjoy what it has, and plunges your village into mourning. God knows what sins you have committed!"

He fell silent a moment for the crowd to take in the grave words he had just pronounced. Raising his hand again, he cried in tones of reproach:

"Priest, tell the truth! Confess what you have done to fall into this disfavor with God."

"Priest Grigoris," replied priest Fotis, curbing the fury which was beginning to neigh within his breast, "priest Grigoris, I, too, am a minister of the Most High; I, too, study the Scriptures; I, too, hold in my hands the Chalice with the Body and Blood of Christ. Whether you like it or not, we are equals. It may be that you are rich and I am poor. It may be that you have fat fields in which to lead your flock to pasture, while I, as you see, have not where to lay my head. Nevertheless, before God, we are equal. Perhaps, even, I am nearer to God because I am hungry. Lower your tone of voice then, a little, if you wish me to answer you."

Priest Grigoris choked. He too felt anger swelling within his breast, but held himself in. He saw that he was in the wrong, he realized that all the villagers were there as witnesses and that no doubt they approved this fierce and tattered priest.

"Speak, speak, priest," he said, softening his voice; "God is listening to us, the people are listening, we, too, are Christians, and Greeks. We shall do all we can, and more, to save the souls that are hanging around your neck."

"Priest Grigoris, your name was known over there, in our villages; now we see you in the flesh before us and we listen to your words. You have asked me how misfortune fell upon our village, and I will answer you. Listen, priest Grigoris; listen, notables, even if you have disdained to come and see us; listen, all of you, Christians of Lycovrissi."

Manolios's heart was beating violently. He turned toward his three companions:

"Let's get near him," he whispered, "let's get near so as to hear and see better."

"Manolios, that's how I imagine the Apostle James," said Kostandis.

"And I the Apostle Peter," said Yannakos.

The priest began rapidly, nervously, as though reluctant to remember and to reopen wounds. His words leaped from memory to memory, shuddering.

"One day voices were heard on the roofs of our village, crying: 'The Greek Army! The Greek Army! We can see the kilts upon the hilltops!' I at once gave the order: 'Ring the Easter peal! Let the people assemble, I wish to speak to them!' But all the inhabitants had rushed to the cemetery; they were scrabbling at the graves and each crying to his father: 'Father, they've come! Father, they've come!' They lit the oil lamps on the crosses and poured out wine to bring the dead to life. Having done with their dead, the people piled themselves into the church. I went up into the pulpit: 'My brethren, my children, all the faithful! The Greeks are coming, earth and heaven are uniting; men and women, take up arms, and chase the Turks to the gates of Hell!' "

"Not so loud, priest, not so loud—your blessing be upon me," Yannakos breathed into the priest's ear. "Not so loud: the Agha's on his balcony; he's listening."

Just at this moment the Agha gave a jump. Sleep had gained him, but his ear had caught a few words of rebellion.

"Hey, you, Captain Greenhorn! There are things happening which I don't like at all. My ear caught . . ."

"Take things easy, I tell you, Agha. Go to sleep. Go to sleep. I've got my ear cocked!"

"I want to sleep, that's right, captain . . . But if you see the priests bandying strong language and tearing each other's hair, shake me awake and I'll go down with the whip and restore order."

He turned toward Youssoufaki:

"Come here, Youssoufaki, stroke the soles of my feet and let sleep take me," he said, letting fall his heavy eyelids.

Priest Fotis had lowered his voice:

"We bring out the arms from among the beams, I gird on my cartridge pouches, I take my cross, and I muster the inhabitants in the square: 'My children, before we set forth, let us all sing together the national hymn!' What voices! What a resurrection of Christ that was! The earth shook with it: all together we sang the hymn. . . ."

And priest Fotis, forgetting once more, began to sing aloud: "From the sacred bones of the Hellenes, Liberty has arisen. . . ."

"Not so loud, not so loud, Father," whispered Yannakos again in his ear.

At the same moment, like an echo, there rang out upon the balcony, continuing the national hymn of the Greeks, the huge, hoarse voice of the captain: "Valiant as ever, greetings, greetings, O Liberty!"

The Agha stirred for a moment as if a flea had bitten him, then fell back into slumber.

Down below in the square, all jumped. They raised their eyes to the balcony, but the captain had sat down again on his cushion and was refilling his goblet with raki.

"Come, a health to you, holy Greece," he murmured with a sob, "you shall rule the world!"

"Captain Fortounas is drunk," said Kostandis. "He's all lit up, just like a minaret on a night of Bairan. God grant he doesn't take the pistol the Agha has in his belt and blow out his brains! That'd be the end of us!"

"Let it be the end of us!" said Michelis, all on fire; "this priest makes me want to bellow like a calf."

"Quiet, brothers, quiet, let's hear what he's saying," said Manolios, who was hanging on priest Fotis's lips.

Priest Grigoris in his anger was puffing for all he was worth. "This ragamuffin priest's turning all their hearts upside down," he told himself; "it's a bad business. I must find some way of making him move off my ground."

"Speak, speak, priest," he said, protectively. "Why have you stopped? We're listening."

"Don't force me to tell what happened then, Father," sighed priest Fotis, and groaned. "I've a heart here, and it's not a stone, Father. It will break."

He began to weep and his voice cracked.

The captain leaned on the balcony again and wiped his eyes with his wet napkin.

"The devil take me," he muttered; "I've gone all to seed."

"It is the will of God," said priest Grigoris; "to complain would be a great sin."

"I do not complain," priest Fotis burst out, having recovered his voice; "I am not afraid; we are immortal. My heart, look, has found calm again; I will speak. The Hellene battalions were decimated and beat a retreat; we remained. We remained and the Turks returned. The Turks returned: that word says all. They burned, stabbed, raped; they're Turks, after all. I mustered all my people I found still alive; there, those are they, whom you see on their knees before you, Christians; some men, a few more women, a great many children. . . . We have saved the icons, the Gospel, the banner of Saint George; we have brought all we could. I took the lead and the exodus began. . . . Pursuit, famine, sickness; it's three months we've been on the road; several of us have remained by the wayside, we buried them and moved on, we survivors! Every evening we lay down exhausted. I took my heart in both hands, I rose up and read them the Gospel and spoke to them of God and of Greece; we gained new strength, and in the morning the march began again. . . . We learned that beyond, near the Mount of the Virgin, there were good people, a rich village: Lycovrissi. We said to ourselves: 'They are Christians, Greeks; their cellars are full, they have land in plenty, they will not let us die. We have come, here we are; God be praised!'"

Priest Fotis wiped away the sweat which stood in beads on his brow, made the sign of the cross, leaned over the Gospel and kissed it.

"We have no other hope, no other consolation than this," he said, brandishing high his heavy Gospel.

All eyes filled with tears; the people shuddered with terror. Manolios leaned on Yannakos's arm in order not to fall, and Michelis, nervously twisting his mustaches, held back his tears. Even the eyes of Panayotaros were wet; just now they looked on all things with kindness and tenderness. The widow, too, wept over Christendom and Greece, over the men and women around her, over herself, her guilt and shame. Up above, on the balcony, Captain Fortounas pressed his large hand over his mouth and swallowed back his sobs so as not to wake the snoring Agha.

Only the two priests were not weeping, the one because he had lived all these misfortunes and was past tears, the other because he did not cease to ruminate anxiously what way he could find to get rid of this famished band and of its fierce guide who upset men's souls.

"Some of us," priest Fotis went on, in a less violent tone, "had the time to go as far as the cemetery. They took the bones of their fathers and are transporting them with them, that they may become the foundation of our new village. Look, that old man, who's a hundred years old, has been carrying them on his back for three months."

But priest Grigoris was beginning to lose control:

"All this is very fine, priest," he said; "but what do you expect of us?"

"Land," replied priest Fotis; "land in which to put forth roots! We have heard tell that you have waste land, for which you have no use: give it us, we will share it out, we will sow it, we will harvest it, we will make bread for all these starving people to eat. That's what we ask, Father!"

Priest Grigoris growled like a sheepdog. What? would these

beggars force his fold? He stroked his beard slowly and reflected.
Men and women hung on his lips. A heavy silence fell.

The Agha started up, annoyed:

"Why are they silent? Didn't I order them to shout?"

"Go to sleep, go to sleep, Agha," said the captain, "the fray
hasn't started yet."

"Well, what's the matter? Your voice is quavering—why? Are
you drunk?"

"Ay, raki's raki, it isn't water." He's caught me out, the dirty
dog, muttered the captain, wiping his eyes.

Manolios could contain himself no longer. Where did he, a
servant, find the courage to hurl himself forward and speak before
the whole village?

"Priest Grigoris, Father," he cried, "listen to their voice. Christ
is hungry, He is asking alms."

Priest Grigoris turned toward him, mad with rage:

"You, shut up!"

Silence fell again, heavier still. Kostandis and Yannakos came
and stood close to Manolios as if to protect him; Michelis, troubled, drew nearer.

"Go and wake your father," Manolios said to him, "go quickly.
He has a heart; he may have pity on them. Don't you pity them,
master?"

"I pity them. . . . I pity them. . . . But I'm afraid of waking
him. . . ."

"It's God you should be afraid of, Michelis, God," said Manolios; "not men."

Michelis blushed. How did his servant dare speak to him like
this? To whom was he speaking? Whose business was it to give
orders? He frowned, but made no move to go to wake his father.

Meanwhile priest Grigoris still remained silent, racking his
brains for what he would say and how he would manage to get
these starving wolves out of his fold. He could feel, all around him,
his whole flock stirring, on the point of escaping him. . . . What
was he to do? Call the Agha? What would the villagers say if he
gave over to the Turk for judgment these people who had been
uprooted from their homes for having fought the Turk? Call the
notables? The only one he trusted was old Ladas. The archon,
the old dotard, was easily moved to tears: he would say yes. And

the other, that lousy captain, would certainly say yes—what had he to lose? Likewise the schoolmaster, that wordy dreamer in spectacles with his grand ideas, who couldn't even divide the oats between two donkeys. . . .

"God is taking a long time, He's taking a long time to enlighten you, Father," said priest Fotis, beginning to lose patience.

"He's taking a long time," retorted priest Grigoris furiously, "because I, too, have souls hung around my neck; I shall have to render account to God."

"All the souls in the world," priest Fotis took him up, "are hung round the neck of each man. So don't make distinction between 'yours' and 'mine,' Father."

Had they been alone, priest Grigoris would have thrown himself upon him and seized his Adam's apple to strangle him. But as it was, what could he do? He controlled himself. In any case, he could no longer remain silent. All eyes were fixed on him. He opened his mouth:

"Listen, priest. . . ."

"I am listening," replied priest Fotis, gripping the heavy Testament in his hands as though he would have liked to throw it at his head.

Priest Grigoris had not yet thought of what he would say, but at the moment when he needed it, the miracle he desired happened. A wild yell rang out and poor Despinio fell down in a swoon. Her companions of the road rushed to pick her up, but recoiled in horror: she was green, her feet were swollen, her belly bulging and tight as a drum, her lips purple.

Priest Grigoris raised his arms to heaven:

"My sons," he cried, mastering his joy with difficulty, "at this terrible moment God Himself has given the answer. Look at that woman, go near, take a good look: distended belly, swollen feet, face gone green—cholera!"

All recoiled, seized with dread.

"Cholera!" cried priest Grigoris once more. "These strangers are bringing the appalling scourge into our village; we are lost! Harden your hearts, think of your children, of your wives, of the village! It is not I who am taking the decision, it is God. The priest wanted an answer, there it is!" and he pointed at the dead woman in the middle of the square.

Priest Fotis clasped the Gospel against his chest, and his hands trembled. He gave a bound toward priest Grigoris and tried to speak, but could not: he was choking.

Up above, on the balcony, the captain rose, tottering. He plunged his napkin again into the basin; the blood was going to his head; he tied the napkin again and was himself once more. The water was trickling over his faded cheeks, his beardless chin, his hairless chest tanned by the sea's salt.

The goat-beard, the fat soup-belly! he growled, and drunkenness made him stutter. He's beaten the poor priest of the refugees! Cholera, he says! Ugh! old swine! But it shan't end there, no! I'll go downstairs, I'll shout: "Liar! Liar!" I'm a notable, too, I too hold the rudder of this village, I, too, have a say, I shall speak.

He rose, tottering, reached the door by a zigzag course, kicked it open. For a minute he paused on the first stair; the lit lamp, the guns on the walls, the sleeping doubled-up Hussein, the yataghans, the red fezes were swirling; the whole house was crumbling. He held onto the banister, his leg stretched out; he seemed to have wings. The stairs rose and fell like waves. He placed his foot in the void and tumbled down the stairs, head first. At the din of his fall, the Agha woke up with a start.

"Hi, captain," he yelled, "who's broken his nose?"

He stretched out his hands in the dark and groped around the balcony: nobody. He made an effort to stand up, but fell back on the cushion, near Youssoufaki, who had gone to sleep with his mastic in his mouth. The Agha felt the warm, scented body with his foot, and smiled.

"My Youssoufaki," he said tenderly, "you're asleep, my treasure. . . ."

He leaned his head against the fresh chest, forgot everything and closed his eyes again.

The voice of priest Grigoris could be heard, calm now and full of mildness:

"My brother, you have told us of your sufferings, our heart is torn; you saw, we shed tears. We had opened our arms to receive you, but at that very moment God had pity on us and sent us a terrible warning. You are carrying foul death with you, my brethren; go with God's grace, don't cause the ruin of our village."

At these words, groans arose from the flock of refugees. The women began to beat their breasts and howl. The men looked haggardly at their priest. Dread took hold of the inhabitants of Lycovrissi; they looked in terror at the stiffened corpse and stopped their nostrils.

On all sides, voices cried out:

"Let them go! Let them go!"

"Bring chalk, throw it on the woman with the cholera, keep the air from being infected," brayed an old man.

"Have no fear, brethren!" shouted priest Fotis, "it's not true; don't listen to him! We are carrying no plague; we're hungry, that's all! And this woman has died of hunger, I swear it!"

He turned toward priest Grigoris.

"Priest with the full belly," he roared, "priest with the double chin, may God Who is above and hears us pardon you; I cannot! May your crime fall on your own head!"

"Leave, by the grace of God!" cried an old Lycovrissi; "I have children and grandchildren; don't cause our ruin!"

Panic took hold of the villagers; their hearts became as stone; they waved their hands, exclaiming:

"Go! Go!"

"Voice of the people, voice of God!" shouted priest Grigoris, folding his arms. "Go! God be with you!"

"May your crime fall on your own head!" cried priest Fotis again; "we are leaving! Courage! Arise, my children, they don't want us, and we don't want them either. The earth is wide, let's go on farther!"

The women stood up, swaying; they again took up their burdens. The men hoisted up their bundles and their tools off the ground; the banner bearer went and took his place once more in front. Manolios was weeping; he leaned forward to help the centenarian get up and set the sack of bones on his back once more.

"Trust in God, granddad," he said, "don't despair. Trust in God."

The old man turned on him sternly:

"In whom else, do you think? In men? Haven't you seen what they've just done? Ugh!"

Just as they were about to set off, priest Fotis suddenly stopped. He looked at his people—skeleton-like, at the end of their strength. His heart contracted.

"Brethren of Lycovrissi," he cried, "if I were alone, if I had to

account to God for my own soul only, I should never have deigned
to stretch out my hand to you as a beggar; I'd have preferred to
starve. But I pity the women and children, they can't stand any
more, they'll collapse from hunger on the road. For them I forget
dignity and self-respect, and I stretch out my hand: give alms,
Christians. We'll unfold our blankets, throw into them what your
heart tells you to—a piece of bread, a pail of milk for the children,
a handful of olives. . . . We're hungry!"

Two men undid a blanket and, holding it spread out, took the
head of the procession.

"In the name of Jesus Christ," said the priest, making the sign
of the cross, "we are taking to the road again. Forward, my lads;
courage; this cup also we shall empty. God be praised! We shall
go through the village, we shall knock at the doors; alas, to this
have we come! We will cry: 'Charity! Charity! Give us what you
have too much of, what you would have thrown to the dogs!' Grit
your teeth upon your grief, my sons. Courage. Christ will
conquer!"

Then, addressing priest Grigoris:

"To our next meeting, priest Grigoris! To our next meeting on
the Day of Judgment. We shall appear before God, both of us,
and it is He will pronounce the sentence!"

Widow Katerina was the first to rush forward. She untied her
new shawl, the green one with the huge red roses, and slipped it
into the open blanket. She searched again on her bosom, found a
small mirror and a bottle of scent, and threw them, too, into the
blanket.

"I've nothing else, my sisters," she said, weeping, "I've nothing
else; forgive me. . . ."

Kostandis hesitated a moment, then remembered that he was
taking up the heavy burden of Apostle. He leaped forward, opened
his shop, took a packet of sugar, a tin of coffee, a bottle of brandy,
some cups, a piece of soap and placed them all in the blanket.

"Not much," he said, "but plenty of friendship; God be with
you!"

They knocked at all the doors, one after the other. One furtive
hand hastily threw some victuals and clothes into the blanket, and
the door shut again sharply, not to let in the cholera.

They reached the house of old Ladas, and knocked. The door
remained closed. The light which could be seen shining through

the window went out. Yannakos, who was following with the three Apostles, knocked louder and shouted:

"Father Ladas, they're Christians; they're hungry, everyone's giving a bit of bread; give them one, too!"

But the angry voice of old Ladas was heard inside:

"When your garden is thirsty, don't throw the water out!"

"I'll settle with you one day, Antichrist!" shouted Yannakos, clenching his fists.

"Let's go on to the house of the archon Patriarcheas, my friends," cried Michelis; then, turning toward his three companions: "Quick," he said, "let's take advantage of the old man being asleep; we'll go to the cellar and lay hands on all we can."

"And if the old man gets annoyed?" Manolios mocked.

"He can just drink some vinegar and get unannoyed," Michelis answered; "let's be quick!"

They set off running, merrily, as though they were going to pillage an enemy town.

During this time the widow was on her way home. Her shoulders kept shivering, she was cold; but she smiled happily.

"That's nothing," she thought; "another woman will wrap herself in the shawl, and won't be cold. . . ."

At that moment a big voice sounded behind her. A warm breath passed over her neck and two huge hands imprisoned her neck.

"Bitch, I bought you that shawl with my heart's blood and you —give it away? I'll strangle you!"

The road was deserted, the widow was frightened. The man's vinous breath made her feel sick; two imploring eyes were fixed on her.

"Panayotaros," she whispered, "you're a wild beast, but you're good; have mercy on me, I won't do it again."

"Why did you call me Judas, eh? You stabbed me to the heart. You want me to have mercy on you, but haven't you any mercy on me? Won't you let me come with you this evening?"

A silence. Then, humbly:

"Let me come. I've no other consolation but you, Katerina."

The widow felt the man's warm, pressing desire envelop her, soaked in sweat and tears; she shuddered.

"Come," she said in a low voice. She led the way, swaying her hips.

His breath taken away, Panayotaros followed in the darkness, hugging the wall.

The troop of refugees reached the archon's house. Four men, each loaded with a great full basket, were waiting for them in front of the door.

"Brothers," cried Yannakos, "all this will never go into the blanket: let four stout lads lend their backs!"

"God keep you company!" said Michelis, "and may you forgive us. Forgive the archon Patriarcheas as well!"

"You are forgiven!" replied joyful voices of men and women. They had already sacked one of the baskets and their jaws were greedily at work.

"What do we need, children, to conquer death?" said the colossus carrying the banner; "what do we need? A bit of bread, that's it!" he said, seizing a big loaf.

"The old man's still snoring," said Michelis emerging from the courtyard.

"He's snoring and dreaming he's entering Paradise," said Yannakos. "In front of him, four angels are marching to show him the way: four baskets!"

They burst out laughing; their hearts were lightened.

They reached the end of the village. Night had fallen, feathery, blue, balmy. The dogs behind them stood still, barking a little, then went home satisfied with having done their duty. Mount Sarakina suddenly rose before the persecuted people, wild, abrupt, full of precipices.

"Let's go and say good-bye to the priest," said Manolios to his companions. "He's no priest, he's Moses leading his people in the desert."

They hastened.

Manolios seized the priest's hand and kissed it.

"Father," he said, "I believe our village has sinned. Intercede with God that the curse which weighs upon us be lifted."

With gentleness the dried-up hand of the priest was laid on the fair hair:

"What's your name, my child?"

"Manolios."

"I have nothing against the villagers, Manolios; they are simple, credulous people. They have leaders and obey them. That is right. But God forgive me, their principal leader, in the priest's cassock, is evil."

He reflected for a moment.

"What I have just said is grave," he went on. "He is not evil, he is inhuman; misfortune will soften him. And you, young man —who are you?" he asked, looking at Michelis who was taking his hand.

"He's Michelis, the son of the archon of the village," replied Manolios.

"Tell your father, young man, that God will note down these four baskets in the record He keeps for each living being; one day, in the other life, He will pay him for them, with interest over and above; that is how God pays, tell him. The four baskets will be multiplied, up there, as the five loaves were multiplied."

Yannakos and Kostandis approached in their turn.

"I'm Yannakos, a pedlar and a great sinner. He's Kostandis, who keeps the café. Your blessing, Father."

Priest Fotis blessed them too, laying his bony hand on their heads.

"Now, my sons," he said, "go home; God bless you!"

He turned and looked around him. The night was deep, serene. Not a leaf stirred. In the sky, a sparkling army of stars. Mount Sarakina rose immense above their heads.

"There are many caves, Father," said Yannakos. "I've heard it said that once upon a time the first Christians lived in those caves. There's one where you can still make out the Virgin and the Crucifixion painted on the rock. It must have been their church."

"There's water, too," added Kostandis. "Winter and summer, it drips from the rock; when you've climbed a bit you'll hear the murmur of it. And then there're partridges. And right up at the top, the Prophet Elijah."

"Tonight you can rest in the grottoes," said Manolios. "The mountain's full of brushwood and burnets. You'll light fires and you'll prepare the meal. If you find it suits you, you can settle there for a time, and rest. The Prophet Elijah, the patron of the mountain, loves the persecuted."

Priest Fotis raised his eyes toward the mountain. For a long time he remained in meditation. The four companions watched him, moved; the thoughts passed in waves over his ascetic face; his eyes plunged into the abyss.

Suddenly, as though he had just taken a decision, he made the sign of the cross.

"It is God Who speaks through your mouth, Manolios," he said.

"Men chase us from every place. Let us then share these caves with the wild beasts. God aid us!"

He raised the Gospel and blessed the mountain:

"Daughter of the Almighty," he murmured, "great stone; and thou, water, who knowest no sleep and wellest from the rocks to quench the thirst of the martlets and falcons; and thou, fire, who sleepest in the wood and waitest for Man to awaken thee to enter into his service; blessed be the hour of our meeting! We are men hunted by men, wild and sorrowful souls; martlets and falcons give us good welcome! We bring the bones of our fathers, the tools of our labor and the seed of Man. In the name of God! May the race take root among these uninhabited stones!"

Groping in the darkness, he found a path, turned back toward the throng which was waiting for him in silence, and cried:

"Follow me!"

Then, addressing the four companions:

"Christ is risen! My sons, health and joy!"

"Risen indeed!" they answered and, leaning against one another, they watched the refugees climbing up the mountain. In front went the priest, the banner bearer, the old men with the icons and the centenarian carrying the sack of bones; then, one behind the other, the women holding their babes in their arms. The men closed in the rear.

Soon they were lost to view in the darkness.

Saints and Robbers

For a whole week, the Passion of Christ and His glorious Resurrection had illumined the villagers' dwellings, by filling them with Easter cakes and red eggs; their gardens, by crowning them with flowers; their big peasant heads, by chasing out of them for a time the morose and interested reasoning of every day. For a week, their poor life felt delivered from its harness. Now it shook its heavy head and foamy nostrils and went under the yoke again for the daily task.

So, the festival over, Yannakos had gone in the early morning into the dark stable where the ass, his best friend, slept and dreamed. The stable smelled of the dung and fetid damp of the earliest ages; no doubt the world smelled like that in the first time of the creation.

The faithful companion placidly opened his great eyes with their long lashes, turned and recognized Yannakos, his master; by way of welcome he also wagged his tail and started braying full-throatedly.

Yannakos went to him and stroked his black and shining rump, his white and downy belly and his warm neck. Then he dug one hand into one of the great trumpet ears and, seizing hold of the beloved beast's muzzle with his other hand, began to talk to him:

"My Youssoufaki" (that was the fond name he gave him in secret, unknown to the Agha), "my Youssoufaki, the holiday's over. Christ is risen! We've had a good time, you can't complain. I've brought you double rations, I've scythed fresh grass to give you appetite, I've given you an Easter present in the shape of a collar of blue stones against spells and put it around that graceful neck of yours; I've even hung a clove of garlic on it as an amulet, to make doubly sure, for you're such a beauty, my Youssoufaki, and people are so wicked, they might cast the evil eye on you from jealousy! What would become of me without you? Don't forget we're alone, the two of us; I've nobody in the world but you. I wasn't worthy to have children; my wife died from eating too many chickpeas; you're all that's left me, Youssoufaki.

"And today I'm bringing you a piece of news that'll please you. Next Easter the Passion of Christ will be acted in the village; you must have heard talk of it. They need a donkey. Well, I asked the notables, as a favor, that you, Youssoufaki, should be that donkey of the holy Passion. It's on your back that Christ will enter Jerusalem. What an honor for you! With the Apostles and you, my son. You'll march at the head, carrying Christ; they'll make you a carpet of myrtles and palms, and the grace of God will descend upon your back, upon your belly; all your hide will shine like silk.

"And when I die, if God is willing to let me, poor sinner that I am, into Paradise, I shall stop at the gate, I shall kiss the porter's hand and I shall say to him: 'I've a favor to ask you, Apostle Peter; it's that he may enter Paradise, that we may go in together: otherwise I'm not going in!' And the Apostle will burst out laughing, and stroke your rump, and say: 'All right, I'll do that for you, Yannakos; get on Youssoufaki and ride in; God loves asses.'

"And then what joy, my Youssoufaki! Eternal joy! You will walk about with none of these heavy baskets, no load, no pack saddle, in fields where there'll be immortal clover, this high, coming right up to your mouth so you won't have the bother of stooping. In Heaven you'll bray every morning to wake the angels. They'll laugh. As light as down, they'll get on your back, and you'll gambol through the meadows with a load of blue, red and purple cherubs. Like a donkey I once saw at Smyrna, in the bazaar, with a load of roses, lilies and lilac, smelling wonderful . . .

"That day will come, it'll come, Youssoufaki, have no fear. Meanwhile, my son, we must work to earn our crust. So come and let me saddle you, come and let me tie on your back your baskets of wares. We're to start again on our round of the villages, selling reels of cotton, needles, hooks, combs, incense, trinkets and lives of saints. Help me, Youssoufaki, to make our business do well. We're companions, aren't we? associates, and you know whatever we earn is shared out honestly—the corn for me, the straw for you. And as I was saying, if our business does well, I'll order you from Panayotaros a pack saddle that won't make you sore and a new harness with red tassels.

"Come on, now. I'd say to you: 'Cross yourself.' But you aren't a Christian, you're a donkey. So stretch yourself, straddle your hooves, ease yourself and come and let me load you. Day's begun and we must be off, Youssoufaki, with the grace of God!"

Yannakos loaded his ass, took his staff and a small trumpet which he used to call customers, opened the door, made the sign of the cross, and they set out, the one after the other, both fresh and joyful, upon their first round after Easter.

The light was resplendent: it came leaping down from the sky and spread over the plain and the whole village; the stones, the doors, the windows, the cobbles took on a smiling air. Yannakos had an appetite: he pulled out from his bag a big piece of bread, a handful of olives and an onion, and began to eat happily.

What a thing the world is, in spite of everything! he thought, God, how good it is; like good bread!

The widow's door, his neighbor's, was open. Katerina, with her skirt hitched up and her bodice undone, was throwing bucketfuls of water over her doorstep to wash it. Her well-shaped, firm, smooth legs shone bare to the knees, and within her bodice two small, lively animals—her breasts—were jumping about, ready to escape.

A bad meeting so early in the morning, thought Yannakos, striking the donkey on the rump to make him pass by more quickly. But the widow saw him, stood up and, with her face all animated, leaned against the door jamb.

"Good business, Yannakos!" she shouted to him with a laugh. "You know, neighbor, I admire you; even if you do live alone like a cuckoo, you're always munching something and always in a good temper; how do you do it? I can't! I can't, my poor neighbor; I have bad dreams . . ."

"Any orders for me, Katerina?" Yannakos asked, to change the subject. "A pocket mirror? a bottle of lavender water? What do you need?"

The widow's ewe appeared on the threshold, bleating anxiously. It had a red ribbon around its neck and its udders were heavy with milk.

"She wants me to milk her," the widow sighed; "her udders are too full, they're bothering her. Ah well, she too is a woman, poor thing. . . ."

She bent down and stroked it tenderly.

"I'm coming in a moment, my treasure; patience. First I must wash the entrance and get rid of the marks of dirty feet."

She pushed the ewe gently in and turned again to Yannakos:

"Yes, I've bad dreams, neighbor," she repeated with a sigh. "Think, last night, at dawn, I saw Manolios: he was cutting up the moon into small slices and offering me them to eat as if it were an apple. You, Yannakos, you've seen other countries, you've been as far as Smyrna, so they say; you must know about dreams."

"That's enough, Katerina; be kind, don't torment people," answered Yannakos. "D'you think I didn't see you yesterday evening making eyes at Manolios? Would you make a set at that decent lad now, hussy? Have you got no pity for him? He's engaged, poor boy; don't go putting spokes in his wheels. And if Panayotaros gets wind of it, don't you see that he'll kill you? Change your ways, Katerina, take on a little ballast. Didn't old Patriarcheas tell you anything? Don't you know the notables have decided it's you who'll be the Magdalen in the Mystery that's to be acted at Easter next year?"

"I am, old Yannakos; I am the Magdalen already," said the widow, doing up her bodice to make sure he saw it was open. "No need for the archon to give me the message. The old sinner, ugh! the devil take him! Because I've fair hair, he says . . ."

"It's not that, Katerina," said Yannakos. "It's not that. . . . How am I to explain to you, when I don't understand very well myself. Look here, you'll not keep company with Panayotaros now, but with Christ. It's Him you'll run after. You'll wash His feet with perfumes and wipe them with your hair. Understand?"

"But it's the same thing, idiot! All men, even Panayotaros, are God for a minute. A real God, not just in words! Afterwards, they fall back again and become Yannakos or Panayotaros again, or an old dotard of a Patriarcheas. Understand?"

"Devil take me if I understand, Katerina . . . It's the end of the world, as old Patriarcheas says."

The widow, annoyed, seized her bucket and threw all its contents over the doorstep, splashing Yannakos's feet; Youssoufaki shook his ears—they too were splashed.

"Ugh! you're only a man," said Katerina mockingly, "you're only a man, you poor thing; how could you understand? There, good-bye—and good luck in your business. You understand that at least."

Yannakos lightly touched his donkey, who quivered and set off at a trot. His owner ran behind him, whistling, glad to have escaped from the widow.

"I'll call at the priest's first and see if he has any orders for me. He's furious when I don't start with him. 'My house first,' he says, 'then the notables'. I am the representative of God at Lycovrissi!' So let's call first at the head wolf's so as not to have trouble."

He turned and saw Katerina still busy washing her doorstep, with her skirt hitched up, half naked.

The trollop! he thought, what legs the good God has made for her, what calves, what a bosom for tempting men. . . .

While Yannakos was soliloquizing on his way, priest Grigoris in his purple cassock barred with a belt of black velvet, was coming and going bare-headed and barefoot in his yard, playing with his long rosary of black amber, a present from the bishop, and panting like a blacksmith.

Mariori came timidly forward and laid in the shadow of the trellis the tray with the breakfast biscuits and a piece of cheese— which the priest took every morning to give him an appetite. An hour later, he would eat his daily couple of soft-boiled eggs and drink a big glass of the old wine which he kept for his "favorite"— this was how he referred to his huge paunch—then render thanks to God for His infinite goodness and justice.

Having served him, Mariori started to water the flowers: basil, geraniums, African marigolds. Today she was still pale and thin; she had slept badly. There were two blue rings around her black almond eyes, and her lips were smarting. Her mother had died of consumption when still young; Mariori was like her mother. From time to time her father looked at her and sighed: Let her get married, he thought, let her get married very quickly and give me a grandson. Afterward, come what God wills. Michelis is a fine lad, solid, well set up, of good family, with property. He will perpetuate my seed.

Having finished her watering, Mariori was about to withdraw. The priest swallowed his last mouthful rapidly.

"Stay here," he said to her sharply, "where are you off to? I want to speak to you."

He could not control his anger, it must burst out. Mariori leaned against the door, folded her arms and waited. She knew what he was going to say to her, what he was going to talk about, and she trembled. Panayotaros had just left; she had caught a few disquieting words; she had heard her father say to Plaster-eater as he showed him to the door: "You did well to tell me. It was your duty! I'll give him the shaking-up he needs!"

"At your orders, Father," said Mariori, lowering her eyes.

"Did you hear what Panayotaros told me?"

"No, I was in the kitchen, getting the coffee ready," replied Mariori.

"It was about your fine fellow of a fiancé, Michelis!"

The priest sighed deeply, the veins on his temples stood out, he was preparing to speak. At that moment there was a knock at the door. Mariori started with relief: God had pity on her, all danger of trouble was averted. She ran to open.

"Who's there?" asked the priest, furiously, swallowing the rest of his coffee at a gulp.

"It's me, Yannakos, Father; Christ is risen! I'm starting on a round and I've come for your blessing. And if you have any orders, or a letter . . ."

"Be so good as to enter," the priest broke in, "and close the door."

"He's still in a bad humor today," thought Yannakos, "it's the Devil brought me along here."

He bowed to kiss the priest's hand.

"Let the hand-kissing wait, you rascal; let's talk first. I shall ask questions, and you will answer. What is all this I hear, eh? It seems your lordship was in it. The first and best of them. Why stand there open-mouthed? You're not going to pretend you know nothing; someone's just been and told me the whole thing from A to Z. Sacrilegious wretches, robbers!"

"Father . . ."

" 'Father' won't help you! You rob me of my property, you pillage my house and, when you've done, you turn up and try to kiss my hand as if nothing had happened! Hypocritical Jesuit! It's a pity I chose you for the Apostle Peter! Robber! Is that how you start your life as apostle?"

"Me? . . . Me? . . ." murmured Yannakos, dumbfounded.

"You, you, and those fine birds, your friends, Kostandis and Manolios! You tricked the innocent Michelis, that lamb of God. You know his heart's in the right place; you watched your chance, and you emptied his house by basketfuls. Robbers! O God, I have sinned in making you apostles. . . ."

"But it wasn't your cellars, Father," Yannakos dared to interrupt him.

"Whose? Yours, perhaps? Louse-heap! Mine, because Michelis is marrying Mariori and our two houses will be one. It's from my cellars you've taken cheeses, bread, oil, wine, olives, and sugar in basketfuls! And to distribute them to whom? To the cholera carriers! With hare-brained friends like you, he'll soon have given away all he has to the poor and to rebels; he'll leave my daughter destitute!"

He turned to his daughter who, motionless and terrified, dared not raise her eyes.

"Do you hear, Mariori?" he shouted, "do you hear the disgrace that's come on our house? If that's all the brains your fine fellow has got, what's to be done? We shall have to think very carefully before we decide."

Burning tears brimmed her eyelids and rolled over her wilted cheeks; but her mouth remained closed.

"Mariori, do you hear?" the priest asked again.

The young girl's head bent still more humbly, as if to say: "I hear and I submit."

The ass, tied to the ring of the door, began to bray; Yannakos started.

"Excuse me, Father, I must go. If it was wrong to take from the rich to give to the poor, may God forgive us!"

"God speaks by my mouth, mine!" shouted the priest, throwing back his head. "You cannot talk with Him direct! It is through me that His word passes. You are robbers, I tell you, you, Kostandis and Manolios, and I shall call a meeting of the notables to examine what we should do. Hardly have the cholera carriers got here, and already our village is contaminated!"

"With your blessing, priest," said Yannakos, darting to the door.

Red with wrath, the priest made no reply; he turned to his daughter.

"Bring me my shoes, my calotte and my stick; I'm going to find the archon and the notables."

He went back into the house and quickly swallowed his eggs, while Mariori ran to catch Yannakos, who was just untying his donkey. Hastily she whispered to him:

"Yannakos, help me; buy me what the women in the towns put on their cheeks to make them red. Get it to me secretly, and as for the price . . ."

"Don't worry, Mariori," replied Yannakos, "I know what you mean; I'll bring you some."

The priest could be heard shouting, with his mouth full:

"We'll speak more of this, you rascal!"

"The Devil's own priest!" muttered Yannakos, slamming the door; "God's representative, he says! All right! If the good God were made in his image, it'd be a bad lookout for poor people, he'd gobble up the lot of us alive."

He scratched his head and grinned:

"Up to now he only gobbles us up when we're dead. Things might be worse!"

He pricked his donkey lightly and said to him:

"Come, Youssoufaki, get those shanks of yours weaving, my son. That buffalo-head has made us late starting. There, don't be upset, my boy; it's a fact. Main thing is, you're all right! We'll call at the café for orders and then be off. Robbers, he said . . . Go to the devil, old gobble-all!"

The inn was packed; it was humming like an angry hive. All the villagers were collected there, commenting on the sad things they had seen with their own eyes the night before—the herd of refugees, the fierce priest with his Gospel, the woman falling stone dead, the chalk thrown over her to keep the cholera from spreading, also the old grandfather with his sack of bones. Some praised priest Grigoris for having saved them from the plague, others confessed their pity for the starving women and children, others again claimed to have seen fires on Sarakina toward midnight.

Panayotaros came in, venturing lowered glances round about him like a bull, then sat down in a corner. He called the café proprietor and surlily ordered:

"A coffee, without sugar."

"You look washed out, neighbor," said Kostandis. "You didn't have another bad night, did you?"

The saddler gathered his bushy eyebrows in a frown:

"A coffee, without sugar," he repeated, turning his back.

Old Patriarcheas, with his lordly fur *kalpak* on his head and his tall stick in his hand, came in at this moment and waved a protective salute to the villagers, who rose to wish him good day. He was not properly awake; his voice was hoarse and his eyes swollen. His thick tongue took away from him all desire to speak.

Kostandis brought him a cup of very strong, highly sweetened coffee, a slab of Turkish delight, and a glass of cold water.

"A good awakening to you, archon," he wished him.

The archon did not reply. Moistening his Turkish delight in the water, he swallowed it whole, drank the water, pulled out a big handkerchief, buried his nose in it and blew so loudly that the room rang. Feeling better, he began to drink his coffee, breathing loudly. His eyelids unswelled, his brain cleared a little, and he recovered his voice. A narghile was brought to him. The archon was gradually waking up.

Turning round, he saw Hadji Nikolis the schoolmaster. He made a sign to him. The schoolmaster, narghile in hand, came over to the archon's table and wished him good day.

"What news?" asked old Patriarcheas. "I slept heavily last night. I thought, in my sleep, I heard a great din; but I didn't wake up. Just now, as I was coming here, I overheard talk about some extraordinary people who'd arrived, a woman who'd given up the ghost, and a quarrel between two priests. . . . What's it all about? The end of the world! can you help me get all this straight, my friend?"

The schoolmaster cleared his throat, with satisfaction. He leaned forward and began talking in a low voice with a great many gestures, delighted at having to tell a terrible story, which made him, for a few moments, terrible. He forced the old archon to listen open-mouthed.

Panayotaros watched them, biting his mustache nervously. With eyes wide open he gazed at the heavy-jowled face of old Patriarcheas. He was waiting to see him lose his temper and, with the blood flooding up into his head, seize his stick and rush home.

But devil take it, no conflagration kindled in the lordly countenance. "That coward of a schoolmaster," growled the Plaster-eater, twisting on his chair as though he were sitting on pins, "that

coward of a schoolmaster daren't tell him everything for fear of
setting him in a rage. I'll tell him everything, I will."

He got up with decision and approached the two notables.

"With your permission, archon," he said; "I think this learned
personage hasn't told you everything; he hasn't dared. I'm not
afraid; I'll tell you the whole story when we're alone, the two of
us."

"Hadji Nikolis," said the archon, "leave us a moment, please.
Let's see what the saddler wants with me."

Addressing Panayotaros:

"Now speak. But not a lot of words; the schoolmaster's talked
me stupid."

"I don't go in for a lot of words," retorted Panayotaros, wounded.
"You know me. Here's the story in a nutshell: Manolios has bewitched your son; they took with them Kostandis here, the café
proprietor, and Yannakos the carrier. They went down into your
cellar, stuffed four great baskets full and slipped them to the cholera
bearers. All that time you were snoring. That's all I had to say and
I'm going."

This time the blood did storm the archon's heavy head. Once
more his eyelids thickened, his voice grew hoarse.

"Go to the devil," he yelled, "you've set my bile boiling of a
morning!"

He hurled down the stem of his narghile and looked around;
he could distinguish no one; the café room was whirling. He stood
up, took a step, then another, found the door, went out and,
weighed down with distress, took the steep lane up to his house.

"What the devil have you been and sung in his ear to make him
so mad, eh, Panayotaros?" cried some of the villagers, half amused
and half annoyed. "Haven't you any fear of God? He's old
and so fat already; he'll be having a stroke."

But Panayotaros had already gone out of the door and disappeared.

Yannakos's trumpet sounded, mocking, good humored.

"Hey, villagers!" cried Yannakos, standing in the middle of the
square like a cock with his hackles up; "I'm starting on my
rounds through towns and villages. Those of you who have orders
for me, come here. Those of you who have letters to send, bring
them. Those of you who have relatives, children, friends or business in the villages around, approach. I'll take the orders, I'll set

out and, if God wills, I'll be back on Sunday with the answers!"

Several villagers got up, went over to Yannakos, lowered their voices and gave their orders. Leaning on his ass, Yannakos wrote them down in order in his head.

The last of all, Kostandis, came and whispered in his ear:

"Take care you don't call on old Patriarcheas, if you don't want trouble. That swine of a Judas has told him something which has put him beside himself, and he's gone off home whirling his stick. He's surely going to thrash his son."

"For the baskets?" Yannakos asked in a low voice.

"Of course it's the baskets. I think it's going to be a bad business. We're going to have trouble."

"I know all about that; had some already. The priest too is beside himself. He certainly hauled me over the coals! . . . But I don't care a rap; don't you worry, let them storm away. We've done our duty."

"I, too," said Kostandis with a sigh, "I've had trouble already, no fear. It was scarcely day when your sister threw herself on me, ready to tear my eyes out. 'Dolt, waster, bandit,' she shouted, 'I know all about it; you've ruined the shop for the sake of those church robbers who've turned up among us, the plague carriers. We are hungry, your children are going short and wasting away, and you, you rogue, go and give away the coffee, the sugar and the soap!' "

"Who the devil went and told them?" said Yannakos in astonishment.

"The red devil; who else? You remember, he kept on our heels the whole evening. He took the first chance to go and tell everyone—the priest, my wife and now old Patriarcheas. He's mad with rage at being chosen as Judas when we're apostles!"

"Patience, Kostandis, old man," said Yannakos, who was sorry for the café proprietor because of all he suffered from his sister. "Patience, just pretend to be stupid, and on Sunday, when I'm back, we'll talk it over again."

Yannakos pricked his donkey with the tip of his staff, and disappeared up the steep track.

"You're the lucky one," muttered Kostandis, watching Yannakos depart. "You're the lucky one; everything's turned out nicely for you: no children, your wife dead; you've got peace . . ."

Yannakos stroked his companion's shining rump.

"Ah, Youssoufaki, we've a good life, we have," he murmured.
"We get on like brothers. Have we ever had a row? Never, God be
praised! Because we're both of us good fellows—or good asses, it
comes to the same thing—and don't harm anyone. Come, step out,
and right turn: we're changing route, didn't you hear what Kostandis told us? No archon today. Straight ahead to old Ladas, who
admires you so much his mouth waters. Come, get a move on, let's
get it over. Then we'll be out of the village; we'll be rid of the
notables and the priests, a curse on them! We'll be alone at last!"

Turning right, he made for the old miser's house.

There's just that poor Manolios I'd like to see, he ruminated,
to speak to him about Katerina before leaving. I'd like to tell him
to be on his guard and not get messed up. It's he who's to act
Christ, isn't it? So beware women!

Old Ladas was sitting in his yard on a stone bench, in rags,
with bare feet, in a good temper. His old woman, mother Penelope, had brought him, in a cracked bowl, his morning coffee made
with chickpeas and barley. She had also placed on the bench a
slice of barley bread and a plate of olives. While he ate and
drank, old Ladas spoke to his wife, who sat silent and indifferent
in front of him on a stool, knitting socks. She was a squalid woman,
in rags like her husband, barefoot likewise, with an interminable,
diving nose which made her look like an old, molted stork.

In the very first years, when she was young, she had answered
her husband back and had some stand-up fights with him. She had
been handsome, loved luxury, came of a rich family of notables.
But little by little the edge had blunted, the spirit tired and the
body withered; she had let herself slide, without realizing, without complaining, into decay. Mother Ladas had begun by saying
nothing; she had listened, scolding back from time to time and
kicking back inside herself, but had said nothing. After her only
daughter had died, she had ceased even to listen to father Ladas's
floods of words, ceased to get angry, ceased to oppose anything.
She was a dead woman; she still walked, ate, slept and woke up,
but did not live. She had the disinterestedness, beatitude and
dignity of the dead.

So father Ladas sat sipping his barley juice. He watched his
wife knitting her sock there, mute and resigned, and informed her
of a great scheme which, unable to sleep, he had set on foot during

the night. He was filling his coffer with gold earrings, rings, necklaces and gold pieces.

"I've worked it all out properly in my head, the whole thing's quite ready, Penelope; but I don't see whom I can let into the secret. For it's no small affair and it needs two. At this present time, my dear, the world's gone to the dogs; people are greedy, they're all scum who try to do you in. So whom can I trust? Hadji Nikolis is an idiot aping his betters: a schoolmaster—there's nothing more to be said. What can you expect from him? One's even thankful if he doesn't go throwing stones at people, like a madman! If it's his brother, priest Grigoris, you're thinking of, he's a guzzle-all: shrewd and knowing as the Devil, but thinks of nothing but his pocket. He's no good to me because, you see, I too want the lot for myself. You shake your head, mother Penelope; I suppose you mean old Patriarcheas: hoo! he can go hang! He's a paunch, not a man. In his house they're rich from father to son; he's never done a thing in his life. Sweat? He doesn't know what it means! I've heard tell that there are big ants, royal ants they're called, which stay lying full length, night and day: they have an army of slaves to feed them, and if they're not fed they starve. . . . He's like that: if only he'd have a stroke, the fat termite! He's no good to me, either. As for the other notable, Captain Fortounas, that one, well! That's not a man, it's a cauldron of raki always on the boil. So I've got to find some other partner for this job. But who? Haven't you got someone in mind, mother Penelope?"

But she to whom he spoke knitted away, lost in a super-terrestrial beatitude and torpor; she heard nothing. For a moment she raised her eyes; they were neither sad nor joyful, but dull. Her gaze seemed to go through old Ladas's skin and bones and, behind him, the wall of the house and, behind the wall, the road, the village, the plain and, farther still, Mount Sarakina and, behind Mount Sarakina, far, very far, the sea; and beyond the sea something infinite, still and menacingly black—the Void. She lowered her eyes once more to her sock and began again knitting quickly, and still more quickly, to finish it in time.

All of a sudden Yannakos's trumpet sounded. With a bound, old Ladas was on his feet; his little crafty eyes were gleaming.

"It's the good God has sent him!" he exclaimed. "Here's the man I was looking for; *he's* what I want! Eh, Penelope? He's got everything that's required: as carrier and pedlar, he goes from village to village; half-liar, half-robber, very good at small thieveries, no idea of the big frauds; a cheap-jack. That's my man. He'll keep some aside and at the end, bang! I'll bag the lot!"

He rubbed his knotted hands, no longer able to contain his joy. The ass stopped in front of the door. Old Ladas ran to open.

"Greetings, Yannakos!" he cried; "welcome! My friend, it's the good God has sent you. Come, quick, tie up your ass to the ring and come in. I want a word with you."

What the devil has the old fox got up his sleeve? Yannakos wondered; Keep on your guard.

He tied up his ass to the ring and came in.

"Shut the door properly, bolt it, so no one can hear us. I've a great secret to confide to you. Sit down. You've the devil's own luck, Yannakos. You, too, are going to get rich. You won't need anyone any more. No more need to drag yourself about the roads like a beggar, trying to sell your reels of cotton. I'll cover you with gold, do you hear, my friend? gold, I'm telling you."

Dumbfounded, Yannakos exclaimed:

"Don't burst my poor head, father Ladas. Explain. What gold?"

"Open those flaps of yours and listen. Those people—the plague carriers who came through—had property before the Turks have seized it, and now they haven't even enough to eat. Well, listen: They're sure to have hidden about them all they had in the way of jewels when they left—their earrings, their bracelets, their wedding rings, their gold pieces. . . . There you are, have you got it, Yannakos?"

"Not yet . . . not yet . . . I'm slow to catch on. Explain it a bit more."

"It's a work of merit, a divine inspiration, I'm putting before you, Yannakos. Last night I saw fires on the Sarakina. That's where they've gone to nest, up among the caves. Well, you take your donkey and go straight toward the mountain. You blow your trumpet, you call upon them all, men, women and children; they assemble around you. You speak to them and you say: 'Brothers, you're starving; have you no pity on your children? I've been thinking of you so much that I haven't closed an eye all night; I've been wondering what to do to save you, brothers. God has enlightened me, I've found the way: bring out the jewels you've managed to carry away; I'll give you in exchange all a man needs in order to live—corn, barley, oil, wine. You, give me what a man doesn't need, a little of that knick-knackery you surely have. If I lose by it, I don't care. You're Greeks, Christians, so it doesn't matter.' . . . This time, it's clear; do you understand, blockhead?"

"I'm beginning . . . I'm beginning . . ." Yannakos answered, hesitantly. He could not yet make out whether it was God or the Devil who had whispered this plan into the ear of old Ladas.

"A divine inspiration, I tell you! But mum's the word! No one must get wind of it. Come, my friend, think, you'll get rich and happy; even you, you poor devil. A man like you—it hurts me to see you set off along the roads, winter and summer, wearing out your youth. How old are you?"

"Fifty," replied Yannakos, concealing only two years.

"Well, you see? The flower of a man's age! Don't waste your life, Yannakos! You, too, might set up a fine house, like a fellow of standing, marry anyone you liked in the village and have children—I think the priest's daughter wouldn't suit you badly. And then you'd be able to help your friends, you'd become the benefactor of the village, and when you passed, people would stand up and bow. A new life, Yannakos, and a lordly one, not a beggar's life! How many years have we got on this earth? At least let's live them in comfort, don't you agree? Come, make up your mind. I'm speaking to you for your good. We mustn't let someone else cut the grass under our feet. I fear the worst from the priest!"

"I'm afraid of God," said Yannakos, in indecision. "I'm afraid of God, father Ladas. Is it right to fleece our persecuted brothers?"

"We're not fleecing them, you hen-wit; we're refleecing them, you idiot, we're saving them from death. . . . They've got to eat, the poor things, they've got to live; they're our brothers; I, too, have a heart and I'm sorry for them. It's an exchange we're making, we're not robbing them. Of course, look to our interest also, as much as possible. We're doing business, we're not fools; a small profit isn't disagreeable. Here, come closer, take a bit of bread; here's some olives, eat! We shall be associates, friends, now. So we must share and share alike. I've left some coffee, too; drink it!"

"I'm not hungry," said Yannakos; "my head's going round. I'll just sit down for a moment on the bench and digest what you've said to me. You're opening a new road before me, father

Ladas; let me get my wits together and think the business over before deciding."

"The trouble is, there isn't time, my friend. The thing's urgent. Why do you want to stop and think it over? Go to the Sarakina, don't let's dawdle. I'm alarmed of the priest, I tell you—the priest, that hook-fist!"

Yannakos sat down on the bench, put his head in his hands and remained for a long time without speaking, with his elbows on his knees. His brain was boiling like a pot, his temples throbbing. In his head, all was mixed up, entangled: the earrings were coming away from thousands of ears, the necklaces from thousands of necks, the wedding rings off fingers, the gold coins rolling . . . and all this was coming and piling up in a great chest which stood in his hut and was full of his dead wife's old clothes. Gradually an immense house rose into the air: not a house—a palace, with gardens, courtyards, balconies, soft beds and a beautiful young woman smoothing her hair. . . . The great door opened, it was a Sunday morning. The sun was shining, the church bell announced Mass, and Yannakos, in fine linen breeches, wearing a notable's *kalpak* and leaning on a tall ivory-handled stick, advanced toward the church with lordly step, while all the villagers rose as he passed and saluted him with many bows. . . . Then he saw a Yannakos seated in his courtyard, and Kostandis standing in front of him in an attitude full of respect. He took from his fob a small bag bulging with gold pieces: "Here, my good Kostandis, take this money and let's see a smile on your face. You've been through some hard times with my cat of a sister, you deserve better!" Then he called Manolios: "Approach, Manolios, you too; I've bought you a flock of sheep; take it, and you won't any longer be a servant to that old crock Patriarcheas." Yannakos's thoughts went one way, then another, and he saw on the belfry of the village church of Lycovrissi an enormous clock, like one he had seen at Smyrna. Around its face these words were written in golden capitals: "Gift of the notable Yannakos Papadopoulos, our great benefactor!" They went another way, and the clock disappeared: in Yannakos's brain there now shone a well-padded pack saddle covered with velvet and spangled with gold; he took it in his arms and entered the stable, crying: "Youssoufaki, I've bought you the saddle I promised you; look, no king has the like. Your miseries are over! Now all you have to do is eat and drink, my little Youssoufaki. Every Sunday, after Mass, you shall parade in the square with a new saddle, you too, the archon of asses. Everyone will draw back with respect, and they'll salute you as if you were a man."

Yannakos burst out laughing and, as though waking up, shook a head swollen like a pumpkin. He looked at the old woman, knitting without ceasing and still engulfed in her beatitude. He saw father Ladas waiting, with eyes fixed upon him.

"Half and half," he said; "agreed, father Ladas?"

Old Ladas put out his big paw:

"Give me your hand, Yannakos. Agreed. Half and half. It's the normal thing. In the evening you'll bring me your harvest of jewels and I'll give you the corn, oil and wine according to what you've arranged with them, and when we've scraped up all there is to be scraped we'll do our accounts. All you have to do is to mark in your book what's given you and what's taken from you, so that you'll know, and won't go thinking I'd stoop so low as to do you. And to let you see I trust you, here! I'm giving you three Turkish pounds in gold on account."

He pulled out of his pocket a bag firmly attached by a stout string, plunged his hand into it and slowly took out the three pounds, which he counted, one by one, trembling. Yannakos seized them greedily, his dazzled eyes filled with gold.

"I'll prepare the receipt," said old Ladas, "and you can sign it when you come back. That all right like that? D'you trust me now? What I've said to you isn't just words, it's gold. Go, let's not lose time, with the peace of God!"

He pushed Yannakos and opened the door.

"The good God keep you company! Go and try out the ground!" he cried after him, hastily shutting the door for fear his accomplice should repent.

"Penelope," he said, laying a finger on his lips, "mum's the word! Did you see the way I handled the thing? Did you see how cunning I was? My brain's like a razor, I tell you! Did you see, Penelope, how I caught him with the hook of gold? For three lost, a thousand gained. Come, now, do something for me: get the coffee ready. Quick, my dear!"

But she remained motionless on her stool. She knitted, went on knitting, watching, without seeing, the needles as they crossed, parted, crossed again, while the sock she was making for old Ladas grew longer. And what she saw in the sock was not the old man's lanky leg, but the bone itself, long, dry, half gnawed by worms.

Meanwhile the ass was pursuing his path, and behind him Yannakos all in a dream. He could feel, in his left side, a sad weight lying on his heart; but on his right another weight, a very agreeable one, in his waistcoat pocket. He staggered as though drunk; sometimes he bounded from stone to stone, sometimes he stopped all of a sudden and began to reflect. The little donkey turned, looked at him in astonishment and stopped dead and waited for him.

"If only I see no one and no one sees me," Yannakos muttered. "Get on, Youssoufaki, hurry up, why've you stopped? Turn this way. We've changed route: a thunderclap, my dear!"

The ass shook his head, perplexed; he could not understand. Where were they going to, this way? What had come over his master? What fanciful creatures men are—they never know what they want!

"If only I see no one, not even Manolios. I've other fish to fry now. He can go to blazes with Katerina, for all I care! Come, Youssoufaki, get a move on!"

But as he rounded the last houses of the village, after which there was nothing but fields, he found himself face to face with Manolios and two other lads, carrying Captain Fortounas. They were walking with short steps, their heads lowered, and before them went Hussein with his yataghan and red fez.

Yannakos made his ass draw in to let them pass. He went close and saw the unlucky captain unconscious, with his split head tied up in a white napkin stained with blood. . . .

"Well, what's happened to our captain? Tell me, Manolios."

"He tumbled down the stairs at the Agha's, poor fellow," Manolios answered, "and he's smashed his skull. If you see my Aunt Mandalenia, tell her to come and change his bandage. She knows how, she was a midwife before she became a coffiner."

"Poor fellow," muttered Yannakos, "he must have been very drunk."

Hussein turned and guffawed:

"Don't you worry, dirty Greek; he's bust his head, it'll mend again Greeks are tough, especially the hairless ones."

"Manolios," said Yannakos, "I must have a word with you."

"So must I with you," replied Manolios. "But let's first put the captain to bed. Follow us and wait for me in front of the door; I'll come."

They moved on slowly, for at every jerk the captain groaned. Reaching the house, they took the captain in. Yannakos tied up his donkey in the shade of an olive tree and waited.

"It's true, fate she was full as a cow, that night. What'll she give birth to, now? Heaven protect us!"

He took his tobacco-pouch, rolled a cigarette, leaned against the olive tree trunk and began smoking to pass the time. He was sorry he had spoken to Manolios; it was a waste of time and, he thought, speed was necessary for the important business he had undertaken. He felt in his pocket, fingered the coins and smiled.

God be praised, he thought, I wasn't dreaming. How often in my sleep I've seen myself with gold pieces in my hands. And in the morning I felt for them, like a fool, under my pillow. But this time, God be praised, they're there!

He fingered the coins again, and his mind was set at rest.

Manolios appeared on the doorstep. He wiped his forehead, saw Yannakos under the olive, and approached.

"Our friend's heavy, that he is; we're tired."

"I'm in a hurry," said Yannakos, "I've two things to say to you, and then I'm off. I've a lot to do today. . . . Listen, Manolios, to begin with, don't set foot at your master's all today. He knows about the baskets. He went up in the air, and took his stick and went off to thrash his son. So look out and wait till the storm's passed."

"If that's how it is, I must go and take my share. It's my fault, too."

"It's mine, too, but I'm not going. You'll tell me that's shameful, but I don't mind. . . . Don't go, wait, there's something else. Katerina, the widow, is setting her nets and she'd like to get you wound up in them. She sees you in her dreams, she told me; yesterday evening in the square she was making eyes at you, but you, of course, didn't even notice! Be on your guard, Manolios, a she-devil, that's what Katerina is; she'd even lead bishops astray. Think a bit about next Easter and when you'll act Christ. Don't get soiled."

Manolios bent his head, blushing. The night before, he, too, had seen the widow in a dream, he couldn't remember how, but when he woke he had rings round his eyes.

"Christ will come to my aid," he muttered.

"He can't do everything, the poor thing, by Himself, Manolios; you too must stir yourself! Well, I'm in a hurry. Your turn; I think you had something to tell me."

Manolios hesitated. He did not know how to put it so as not to hurt his friend.

"You must forgive me for what I'm going to say," he began at last, "but the four of us now have the same aim, a great and sacred one. From now on we're one. If one of us is taking a false step, the others must hold him back. If one is lost, we're all lost. That's why I'm bold enough . . ."

"Speak out, Manolios, don't beat about the bush," said Yannakos, beginning to untie his donkey. "I'm in a hurry, I tell you."

"Today you're going back to work," Manolios went on, softly, taking Yannakos by the arm. "You're starting out on your rounds again. Don't forget, I beg you in the name of Christ, don't forget the advice the priest gave us yesterday. . . ."

"What advice did the priest give me?" cried Yannakos, in a voice suddenly rough.

"Yannakos, please, don't take it in bad part. Not to give short weight, for instance; not to . . ."

Yannakos felt his temper going. He loosed his ass sharply and twisted the rein nervously round his arm:

"All right, all right . . . He thinks it's easy, his holiness does . . . What would the priest say if I had advised him to tighten his belt, not to stuff his stomach so full, and to give what's over to the poor? And then not to make a mixture of paste, flour and spices and dish it out to you as a remedy for all diseases, the charlatan! And didn't he, only last year, leave old Mantoudis unburied for three days, till he was stinking, and all because he insisted on the heirs paying him in advance? And another time, didn't he put up to auction the vineyard of poor Yeronimos the cobbler because he owed him something? And this very year—yes, not long before Holy Week—didn't he give out his prices: so much for a baptism, so much for a burial, without which, he said, I'll perform no baptism, no marriage, no burial? And he has the face, the fat paunch, to give me advice, me who haven't a penny. . . ."

"Don't swear at him like that," Manolios interrupted; "everyone will have to give account for his soul; you attend to yours, Yannakos! This year we must be pure and without spot; you will be the Apostle Peter, don't forget. What does one do before Communion? One fasts, one eats no meat or oil, one doesn't swear, one doesn't lose one's temper. For us, now, it's like that, Yannakos."

But Yannakos was warmed up. He felt Manolios was right, and this irritated him all the more. Leaving the priest, he turned on his companion and burst out shrilly:

"Well, and you too, Manolios, don't forget it's not an apostle you'll be acting, it's Christ Himself. Well then, ought you to touch a woman? No! And yet you're nearly to marry! Yes or no? Why do you make that noise? Is it yes, or is it no? Then let's all go to the devil, that's what I say. Holiness is no small affair . . ."

Manolios hung his head and said nothing.

"Yes or no?" Yannakos resumed, more and more roused; "when you see Lenio your mouth waters. And the Devil brings her to you in your sleep as you'd like her to be, stark naked. I, too, was a sucker like you, and I know all about the tricks of Satan . . . He brings her to you while you're asleep, you commit the sin and in the morning you get up with rings round your eyes . . . When you come before us to act Christ Crucified, you'll be newly married. They'll put you on the cross, but a lot that will mean to you! You'll know that it's all a game, that it's Another who was crucified, and at the moment when you cry out on the cross: 'Eli, Eli, lama subachthani!' you'll say to yourself that soon you'll be home, after the crucifying, and that there'll be Lenio waiting for you with hot water to wash in, clean linen to change into, and the two of you, after the crucifying, will go to bed. So keep quiet, Manolios, and don't come giving me lessons! It won't do, no! it won't do!"

Manolios listened, hanging his head, overcome.

He's right . . . he's right, he told himself. I'm an impostor, yes; an impostor!

"Why don't you say anything? Isn't it true, what I say?" shouted Yannakos, enchanted at seeing Manolios tremble.

"But yesterday, Yannakos, you still . . ." Manolios began.

Yannakos did not let him go on:

"Yesterday, Manolios," he said, giving his donkey a pull preparatory to going, "yesterday, Manolios, things were different. It was a holiday, don't you see? We had food inside us, the donkey was in the stable, interest was asleep. Today, look, the donkey's loaded, our bellies are empty, Easter's over, trade's starting again . . . and trade, young man, means: if you want to eat something, take it; if you want to have something, steal it. Otherwise, instead of becoming a tradesman, I'd have done better to go to Mount Athos and become a monk. See?"

He was silent a moment, now somewhat relieved. Pulling at his donkey, he looked at Manolios, satisfied at having said what was on his mind.

"Good luck, Manolios, and think over what I've said, and God aid you."

But down inside him anger was still rumbling. He turned toward his friend once more:

"A tradesman's duty is to rob people, Manolios. A saint's duty is not to rob them. There! Mustn't get mixed up. Good luck for your wedding, Manolios! The road for us, Youssoufaki!"

Manolios remained alone. The sun was already high. Men, oxen, dogs and asses were harnessed to their daily tasks. Old Ladas had put on his glasses and was drafting unhurriedly, attentively, all smiles, the receipt for the three Turkish pounds. At the moment when the priest, beside himself with fury, was setting forth in search of old Patriarcheas, someone came to ask him to bring the Sacrament to a dying man, and he changed direction. As for Captain Fortounas, he was groaning on his bed, cursing mother Mandalenia, who was changing his bandage and tying up his broken head.

Lenio was sitting before her frame and humming as she wove the final sheets for her dowry. Her heart was dancing. It rose to her throat, went down to her stomach, and jumped from one breast to the other. . . .

Up above, in the master's room, Lenio heard the noise of a dispute—father was shouting, the son answering back, and they came and went as if they were fighting, and the ceiling trembled. But Lenio, leaning over her frame, did not worry about their quarrel. She did not even worry at hearing the yells of her master. She was casting loose from the bonds of his authority; the chain was on the point of breaking and she of departing with her Manolios to live on the mountain among the sheep. She had had enough of old Patriarcheas, even though he did love her as his own daughter and had found her a husband and given a generous dowry. He disgusted her, and she did not want to see him any more.

At this moment the dispute upstairs redoubled. The old man's clamor rang out more distinctly, and Lenio lent an ear.

"As long as I'm alive," he was shouting, "I'll be the one who gives orders here, not you! It's the end of the world!"

He choked, stuttered; his words got mixed up, and Lenio could not catch any more. But a moment later she clearly heard this phrase:

"No! I don't want you to have more to do with Manolios than you can help. Don't forget he's a servant and you're an archon. Keep your station!"

The dirty old man! murmured Lenio, the old swine! He doesn't even respect his white hairs, but brings here that bitch of a Katerina and slobbers over her! And then he won't have Manolios, in case he should spoil his precious . . . Ugh! I want to get away, and not see any more of him, not hear any more of him, the old horror!

She suddenly stood up, unable to stay in the room any longer, and went out into the yard to take the air.

The old beast! she was still muttering, if only he'd have a stroke!

She went to the middle of the yard, drew some water from the well, plunged her face into it and felt cooler. She was small, well-fleshed, with full lips, alert and smiling eyes, and an aquiline nose just like the old archon's. She was very dark and seductive, and of an evening she would stand on the threshold and, when a man passed by, poke out her neck curiously and examine him with mingled desire and compassion, like a cat which, drawing in its paws and about to spring but suddenly seized with pity for its prey, lets this one go and watches greedily for another. . . . This implacable and motionless hunt took place on the threshold every evening. After a while, giving up the struggle, Lenio would go in again, exhausted, as night fell.

Just as her bucket came up and she was about to plunge her burning face into it, the yard door opened and in came Manolios.

"Welcome, Manolios!" the girl burst out, with a first impulsive movement toward him, which she suddenly checked, contenting herself with a glance burning with desire. Then, with an eye rapid as lightning, she inspected his arms, his neck, his chest, his thighs and his knees. As though she had to wrestle with him she sized up his robustness and his staying power.

Manolios said no word; he crossed the yard with great strides, leaned his stick in a corner and made to climb the stone stairs leading to the master's room. From the road he had heard shouting; he was impatient to share the archon's wrath with Michelis.

Manolios looked tired and worried. As soon as he saw Lenio he was struck all of a heap: she was just the person he did not want to see at this moment. He hurried to get across the yard and reach the staircase. But Lenio did not see things in this light.

"Oh," she cried, "didn't you notice me, my lord?"

"Good morning, Lenio," said Manolios faintly; "excuse me, I'm in a hurry. I've got to see the master."

"Let him alone, what do you want with that dirty old thing?" said Lenio under her breath. "He's just having a row with his son and heir, so leave them to scratch each other's eyes out! Here, come and see . . ."

She took his hand to lead him into the house. She sniffed him, turned around him, brushed against him and suddenly drew back blushing.

"When are we going to get married, Manolios? The old man's impatient."

"When God wills!" said Manolios, trying to break away.

"I bow before His greatness," said Lenio, suddenly grave, "I bow before His greatness, but tell Him to be quick. It'll soon be May and people don't marry in May. Must we wait till June? Or July? It's time wasted."

"Time gained, Lenio. Don't be impatient. We don't have to hurry because we're getting old. And I've got business to finish first. After that, if God wills . . ."

"What business?" said Lenio, surprised. "What business? Have you other business, besides a shepherd's?"

"Yes, I have. . . ." said Manolios, edging gradually toward the stone staircase.

"What business? Who with? Why won't you tell me? I shall soon be your wife, I ought to know."

"I'm going to see the master first, then I'll tell you. . . . I must speak with him first, Lenio. . . . Let me go."

"Manolios, look me in the face, don't lower your eyes. What's the matter with you? In a single day and you've changed. What have they done to you?"

She looked at him, worried, then annoyed and breathing quickly:

"Someone's cast the evil eye on you!" she cried. "We must find your Aunt Mandalenia. She'll burn Good Friday branches and recite the magic formula to charm away the evil eye, Manolios . . . Come here, I've something to tell you, my treasure . . ."

Manolios felt the girl's breath on his neck. A bitter smell rose from his sweating body. Now and then her full, firm bosom brushed against his hand. His blood coursed through his well-nigh bursting veins.

"I'll go and find mother Mandalenia, I can't bear to see you all scowling like that. Don't go!" said Lenio firmly. She went in, slipped on her best dress, bound up her hair in a kerchief, and filled a basket with some red eggs, a little coffee, some sugar and a bottle of wine to pay old Mandalenia for her trouble. Returning, she saw that Manolios had already climbed the staircase and was hesitating in front of the master's door.

"Don't go, don't go!" she shouted to him. "I'm coming!"

The dispute had died down. Michelis must have left the room. All Manolios could hear, through the door, was the heavy steps of the old man, who strode up and down muttering.

He pushed the door and entered. As soon as the old man saw him he rushed at him.

"It's your fault," he roared, raising his hand to strike, "it's you who've turned my son's head, it's you who've egged him on to give away my substance, my heart's blood, you vagabond!"

The veins of his temples, neck and hands were black. He had opened his shirt, and his old man's chest was swelling and collapsing, ready to burst. He tumbled onto a sofa in the corner, took his head in both hands, coughed, and his throat rattled.

Leaning against the wall, Manolios watched the speechless old archon remorsefully. What a wild beast the heart of man is! he thought. What a wild beast! Even you, my Christ, could not tame it.

Suddenly the old man got up, he had regained his strength. He seized Manolios by the collar.

"It's your fault," he shouted again, spattering Manolios's cheeks and neck with saliva. "It's your fault! I brought you down from the mountain to marry my Lenio, whom I love like my own daughter; I kept you here all through the holiday; I forgot you were my servant and on Easter Sunday I had you sit at my table! And now, look at the thanks I get, traitor! You've turned my son's head, you've gone into my cellar while I was asleep, and you've robbed me! Robber! Robber! And as if that weren't enough, here's Michelis resisting me for the first time. 'I'm a man, now,' says he, 'I shall do whatever comes into my head!' Do you hear that? The insolence! He'll do whatever comes into his head, says he. And when I shouted at him: 'Have you no fear of your father?' he dared to answer me—the effrontery!—'I fear God, and nobody else!' No, d'you hear that? Nobody else! It's all your tricks, Manolios. Why didn't you break a leg, the day you came down from the mountain to celebrate Easter with me? . . . Why don't you say anything? Why do you keep looking at me with those round eyes? Say something, I'm bursting!"

"Master," said Manolios calmly, "I've come to ask permission to go back to the mountain."

The old man opened his eyes to their full width; his lips quivered and he stuttered:

"What's that you say? Go back to the mountain? Say it again if you've the face!"

"I came, master, to ask your permission to go back to the mountain."

"And the wedding?" cried the old man, his neck swelling afresh; "when'll we have that, you fool? In May? May's when the donkeys marry. So it will be in April. That's why I had you come. I'm the one who gives orders!"

"Give me a little more time, master . . ."

"What for? What do you want? What's happening to you?"

"Well, I'm not ready yet, master."

"Not ready yet? What's the meaning of that?"

"I don't know myself, master. . . . Look here, how'm I to say it? I feel I'm not ready yet. My soul . . ."

"What soul? I think you've gone crazy. Just listen to him! His soul, he says! Have you a soul?"

"How'm I to tell you, master? There's a voice inside me. . . ."

"Shut up!"

Manolios put out his arm to open the door. The old man seized it.

"Where are you going? Stay here!"

He started striding up and down the length and breadth of the room again, banged the table with his fist, hurt himself and bit his lips.

"You'll kill me today, between the two of you. It's the end of all things! My son isn't afraid of me, he says, he's only afraid of God. . . . And this—this dirty servant talks to me of his soul. . . ."

He turned furiously on the shepherd:

"Get out, go to the devil! Get out, out of my sight! If the wedding doesn't take place this month, I'll have no more of you in my service; you get out of my house! I'll find another husband, a better one, for my Lenio. Off you go, make yourself scarce!"

Manolios opened the door, tumbled down the stairs two at a time, gave a glance at the yard. Lenio was not yet back. He scooped up his stick and took the road to the mountain, running.

Near Saint Basil's Well, outside the village, he stopped to breathe. It was an old and famous well, surrounded by tall bamboos, with a rim of polished marble deeply cut into by the ropes which for centuries had raised and lowered the buckets. In the evening the young girls came there to draw the cool water: it was said to be miraculous, able to cure many illnesses—the stomach, the liver, the kidneys. Every year, on Twelfth Night, the priest came to bless it. Saint Basil of Cesarea, loaded with toys for the little children of the whole earth, passes by this well, they say, and drinks its water before doing his round, on New Year's Eve. That is why it is called Saint Basil's Well, and also why the water is miraculous.

The sun, hanging at the highest point of the heaven, fell plumb upon the earth, a still cataract. In the fields, ears of yellowing green raised their delicate heads and drank the nourishing sun. The olive trees dripped light from every leaf. In the distance, the Sarakina was smoky within a fire-colored, diaphanous veil. The black holes of its caves could be made out and, right at the top, the Chapel of Saint Elijah, molten in the dazzling light.

Manolios seized the rope, drew water, plunged his face into the bucket and drank. Opening his shirt, he wiped the sweat from his chest. His gaze came to rest on the Sarakina, and priest Fotis, ascetic, fierce, all fire and flame like the sun itself, rose up in his mind. Manolios gazed at it without thinking of anything, without asking himself anything, molten himself, like the Chapel of Saint Elijah, in the burning light.

For a long moment he remained like that, in ecstasy; all of a sudden he felt his hands, his feet, his heart pierced by fearful pains, as though he were crucified upon the light. Months later, at a fatal hour, this moment of ecstasy in front of the rim of the well came back to his mind, and he suddenly realized that this moment had been the greatest joy of his life. No, not a joy: something deeper, more cruel, passing all human joy and pain.

When he rose to climb the Mount of the Virgin and return to his sheepcote, the sun was setting.

"I must have gone to sleep," he muttered, "evening's fallen. . . ."

He stretched, tightened his belt and picked up his stick. He was impatient to rejoin the friendly companions of his solitude—sheep, rams, dogs. Also his shepherd lad, that young, wild, sun-baked boy, the curly-haired youth Nikolio.

He was just going to start when all of a sudden he heard the reeds rustle. Behind him a fresh, seductive, imploring voice said:

"Eh, Manolios, are you so frightened that you're leaving us? Wait, I want a word with you."

He turned. Katerina the widow emerged from the rushes with her jug on her shoulder. His eyes ran quickly over the dazzling throat, the bare, well-molded arms and those red and smiling lips.

"What do you want with me?" he asked, casting down his eyes.

"Why do you run after me, Manolios?" said the widow, in a voice now full of passion and pain. She leaned her jug on the rim of the well and sighed. "Every night I see you in my dreams; you won't let me sleep. Why, at dawn today I dreamed you were holding the moon and cutting it into slices like an apple, and giving me the pieces to eat. What's between you and me, Manolios? Why do you run after me? My seeing you in my sleep means that you're thinking of me."

Manolios kept his eyes lowered. He could feel the widow's breath flow round him, burning. His temples were throbbing hard. He said nothing.

"You're blushing, you're blushing, Manolios," said the widow, and her voice was warm, slightly husky; "I was right, you do think of me, Manolios. And I, too, think of you. . . . And when I've got you there, in my thoughts, I'm ashamed, as if I were naked in front of you. As if I were naked, and you were my brother and you saw me."

"I do think of you," replied Manolios without yet raising his eyes. "I do think of you and I'm sorry for you. All through Holy Week you were in my mind. Forgive me!"

The widow sat down on the rim of the well. She suddenly felt a sweet but unconquerable lassitude; her legs could no longer carry her. She, too, was silent, now. Leaning over the well she saw, at the bottom, her face in the green and black water. Her whole life passed in a flash through her head: an orphan girl, daughter of the priest of a faraway market town, she had met her husband at the festival of the Virgin of the Myrtles. He had been much older than she, going gray already; but he had had some property. She was poor. He had taken her to wife, or rather bought her. After the wedding he had brought her to Lycovrissi. He had wanted children but never been able to have any. Then he had died. The young lads of the village were then unable to sleep. They roamed at midnight before her door, under her windows, in her yard, and sang her serenades and sighed like calves. Inside her house, she, too, sighed. This martyrdom went on for a year, two years. One night, a Saturday, she could bear it no longer. That day she washed her hair and scented it with oil of laurel. She looked at her body and was sorry for it. She opened her door and a young lad, the first who happened to be there, entered. In the morning twilight, before the village awoke, he went away. The widow knew then a great comfort. She also felt that life has hardly any length and that it is a great sin to let it be lost. The following evenings, at midnight, she again opened her door.

She stood up; her face disappeared from the green and black water.

"Why are you sorry for me, Manolios?" she asked.

"I don't know, Katerina; don't ask. But it's true, I'm sorry for you, as if you were my sister."

"Are you ashamed for me?"

"I don't know, don't ask me that. I'm sorry for you."

"What do you want of me?"

"Nothing! I want nothing!" cried Manolios, frightened, moving to escape.

"Don't go, don't go, Manolios!" she said, in a voice full of witchery.

Without turning, Manolios stopped. They were silent once more. After a moment the widow spoke again:

"You look to me like an archangel, Manolios, an archangel who wants to take my soul."

"Let me go," said Manolios. "I've nothing to take from you. I want to go!"

"You *are* in a hurry," said the widow, offended, and her voice once more sounded mocking. "You're impatient to get to the mountain, drink milk, eat meat and set yourself up again. You're going to be married, Manolios, you're going to be married, and Lenio stands no nonsense!"

"I'm not going to marry!" cried Manolios. What he had just said frightened him. It was the first time he had thought of such a thing. "I'm never going to marry; I want to die!"

Having said it, he felt relieved. Turning, he looked the widow in the face this time, as though he no longer feared her. As though he found himself freed from a great weight.

"Good-bye," he said, calmly, "I'm going!"

The widow followed him with her eyes as he departed, and her heart contracted.

"Don't think of me, Manolios," she cried despairingly. "Don't trouble my sleep any more. I've taken the bad road, leave me alone!"

I'm sorry for you, my sister, I'm sorry for you, and I don't want you to be damned, Manolios thought, but without turning and without replying. He was already on the path to the mountain.

The Fight with the Ram

THE SUN ROSE and struck the peak of Sarakina, touching with pink the Chapel of Saint Elijah. On the slopes, partridges began to cackle. The whole mountain grew light and there appeared, scattered among the abrupt rocks, a few stunted carob trees, wild pears with their prickly trunks, and wind-torn holm oaks.

Men must have lived there in the past—you can still make out a crumbled wall, some fragments of pottery, some fruit trees which, when their tamer departed, turned wild once more. The paths are obliterated under a raving of grass and rubble; the houses have returned to their original elements; the domesticated trees have grown thorns; the wolves, foxes, and hares, which had fled before Man, have come back in triumph. Earth, trees, and beasts breathed again, recovering their liberty; no longer now would they know the menace of the ephemeral two-legged monster, which had appeared for a moment, altered the law of eternal things, then disappeared.

And lo and behold, that perpetually agitated animal was back again. The wild beasts hid behind the high rocks to watch him. The sun had hardly risen when men, women, and children emerged from the caves, found the water where it dripped from the rocks, leaned over it, arranged stones and lit fires. They stood on tiptoe and looked out into the distance: below in the plain spread the prosperous village of Lycovrissi; all around, a sea of hills with their olives, figs, and vines; farther off, the peaceful Mount of the Virgin, golden green, with its rich flocks of sheep and goats. Still farther beyond, rose-pink and blue mountains stood out against the sky.

Priest Fotis made the sign of the cross:

"My children," he said, "here is the dawn. We have a great deal of work to do today. Come here, around me, and let us call on God together, that He may hear our voice."

The old men and the old women dragged themselves to form a circle around priest Fotis where he stood on his rock; the women ran up with their children; behind them, heavily, came the men, with downcast heads full of cares. A ragged barefoot lot they were, with cheeks scored by fatigue and hunger, defenceless in the middle of these inhospitable stones and these sparse trees without fruit. One might have expected supplications and tears, begging hands raised toward Heaven; on the contrary, from these breasts there arose, joyous and full, the triumphal hymn of the Byzantine church—the whole mountain rang with it:

> *Save Thy people, O Lord, bless Thine inheritors,*
> *Grant us victories over the barbarians! . . .*

Swinging his arms rhythmically, the priest conducted the singing; his own voice dominated and led, deep and martial.

The bowed heads were raised, the women unhooked their bodices and gave suck to their babies, while others crouched down, threw branches on the fires and placed pots upon them.

"My children," cried priest Fotis, "it is here, on this sheer mountain, that with God's aid we shall take root. For three months we have been on our way; the women and the children are exhausted, the men have grown ashamed of begging. Man is like a tree: he needs earth. This is where we shall put forth roots! I saw in a dream last night Saint George, our patron, exactly as he is painted on our banner—a young man with fair hair, beautiful as the spring, riding on a white horse, and behind him on its back the beautiful princess whom Saint George had saved from the horrible monsters of the fountain; she was holding out toward him a ewer of gold and pouring out for him to drink. . . . Who is this beautiful princess, my children? It is the soul of Greece, our soul! Saint George has taken us up on his horse and has brought us here, onto this deserted mountain where we are. Last night I saw him in my dream; he stretched out his arm and placed in my hand the seed of a village—a little, little village in my palm, with its church, its school, its houses, its gardens—and he said to me: 'Plant it!' "

From the crowd rose a murmur, a rustle like that of the wind in the reeds. And when priest Fotis opened his hand, several women saw in it a little, little village, like an egg placed to hatch in the sun.

"It is here," priest Fotis pursued, embracing the mountain with a gesture of his open arms, "among these stones and caves, this rare water, and under these thin wild trees, that we shall plant the seed which Saint George the Knight has entrusted to me. Courage, my children, arise and follow me. This day is a great day, we are planting our new village! Arise, father Panagos, hoist your sack of bones on your back again, and march!"

The centenarian raised his dried-up head, and his little steely eyes kindled:

"My children," he said, "three times I've seen villages planted and uprooted. The first time it was the plague that ravaged them, the second time an earthquake and the third time, this time, the Turk. But three times also I've seen the seed of man put forth, now in the same place, now farther on. A priest gave his blessing, the masons began to build, everyone threw himself on the earth and dug, the men took wives and, within the year, what joy it was, my lad! Ears of corn were poking from the earth, smoke was rising from the houses, new-born children were wailing—the village was a-growing! Courage, my children, it will put forth again!"

"Bravo, father Panagos!" cried the men, smiling; "you grand-dad, have got the better of Charon himself! You're the dragon who conquered death, aren't you?"

"That's me, for sure!" replied the old one; "that's me, the dragon!"

Priest Fotis, having meanwhile put on his stole and fashioned a sprinkler of savory and thyme, now filled a gourd with water and called and grouped around him five or six urchins whom he had taught to sing psalms and chant the responses.

The whole throng stood up and ranged itself behind its leader, the men on the right, the women on the left. Above them the sun, the indefatigable, obstinate athlete, was climbing the sky to perform yet again his ever-renewed exploit.

"In the name of Christ, my sons!" cried priest Fotis, "in the name of Christ and of our country! Our village has been razed to the ground, our village is building again. The root of our race is immortal! What am I to say, my brethren? I rejoice, being a man, when some happy thing comes to me, but I rejoice still more when the difficult hour comes! Then I say to myself: 'It's now, priest

Fotis, that you will show whether you're a real man or a rabbit.' "

Men and women burst out laughing. At this solemn moment these virile words, full of good humor, made their hearts less heavy. A hard fighter from far-back times arose in each breast, looked at the stones, the sterile trees, the hungry mouths, and rolled up his sleeves.

"Follow me, all of you, my children; I'm going to mark out the boundaries of the village!" cried the priest, plunging his sprinkler into the water he had blessed. "In the name of Christ! In the name of Greece!"

The colossus raised the banner of Saint George; the men took their tools, spades, picks, shovels; the old men lifted the icons in their arms; and the old grandfather took the lead with the sack of bones on his back. Two or three dogs which had accompanied them followed also, barking joyfully. There was a great noise. At this moment a trumpet sounded at the foot of the mountain, but nobody heard it.

The priest dipped the sprinkler in the holy water and with a wide gesture sprinkled the stones, the bushes, the carob trees, as though tracing in the air the boundaries of the village. It was the first time he had founded a village, and he improvised the prayers out of an overflowing heart.

"Lord, Lord, I trace with holy water the boundaries of our village! May the Turk never come inside it, may the plague never enter it, may no earthquake overthrow it! We shall make for it four fortified gates: place at them four angels to guard them, O Lord!"

He paused, sprinkled a huge stone with the sign of the cross and, turning toward his companions:

"Here, toward the east," he said, "we will build one of the gates of the village, Christ's Gate!"

He raised his arms to heaven:

"This is Thy gate, O Lord! Here is where Thou wilt enter when Thou deignest to hear our voice and to descend on earth at the hour of danger. For we are men, Thou knowest, we have a soul, we have a voice, we shall cry to Thee! If it happens that we say too much, be not angry; we are men, tormented creatures, we have many cares, there are moments when the heart cannot bear any more, it bursts, utters an insolent word and is relieved. Life is a heavy burden, Lord; and if Thou wert not there, we should take one another by the hand, men and women, and go and throw ourselves over the precipice to have done with it. But Thou hast being, Thou, joy, consolation, protector of the oppressed, our God! Here is Thy gate, enter!"

They moved to the south. Again the boundaries were marked in the air. The priest intoned a psalm, and all around his deep voice the slender voices of the children twittered like swallows.

The priest paused before a hollow of rock filled with limpid water:

"Here," he said, "we will build the Gate of the Virgin, protectress of the human race! Make a mark!"

He stretched out his arms:

"Virgin Mother," he cried, "Rose that cannot wither, blossoming Hawthorn enlacing the wild Oak, our God! We are good people persecuted, hear our voice! Thou art seated here on earth, close by us; Thy lap is a soft nest in which human beings hide. Thou art Mother, Thou knowest the meaning of sighs, hunger and death. Thou art a woman, Thou knowest the meaning of patience and love. Our Lady, look down on our village, give its women patience and love, that they may endure in this strife of every day and may without complaining bear with their fathers, brothers and husbands, their children and the torments of the house! Give to the men the strength to work and never despair, that dying they may leave behind them a yard filled with children and grandchildren! Give, Our Lady, a peaceful and Christian end to the old men and women! Here is Thy gate, Our Lady of the Gate; enter!"

At this moment a loaded ass appeared at the back of the procession, but nobody noticed it. It stopped suddenly, astonished, and turned its great velvet eyes to its companion to ask him what to do. Out of breath, soaked with sweat, cursing the sun and stones, Yannakos appeared in turn behind the donkey.

He stopped, amazed like his Youssoufaki. He had heard the chanting and the words of the priest; he looked around, bewildered. "Here is the gate," he says . . . Where do you see a gate? What village is this they're going to build? What with? Out of air? In the air? Hang it all, they're starving and yet they talk of building villages? They can't even stand up on their legs and they sing you warrior psalms: "Grant us victory over the barbarians . . ." Mercy of God, they're mad!

He tied up his ass to a stunted oak and took his place, silently and unseen, in the procession. With wide eyes and ears cocked, he had not yet decided whether he ought to laugh or cry. He followed the others and watched the priest lunging with the sprinkler and tracing the boundaries with an astounding assurance, as though he already saw in the air the streets of the future, the houses, the church, the dwelling of the notables.

The old man paused for the third time, at the side opposite Christ's gate, looking westward, and climbed onto a great rock which had been split by a wild pear tree now covered with blossom.

"Here we will build," he said, "the gate of Saint George the Laborer! He who, like us men, bends and tills the land; who leads the goats and sheep to pasture, guides the oxen, prunes and grafts the trees. For Saint George is not only a noble warrior but also a great laborer. We put our trust in your grace, patron of our village! Make our goats and our lambs to prosper, let them give us milk for our children; let them give us meat for our body and help it to carry our soul; let them give us wool, that the snows may not overcome us! Bless, Saint George, all the creatures that love and serve Man—the oxen, the asses, the dogs, the chickens, the rabbits. . . . Bend over the land and bless that, too. We shall throw the seed into your bosom, and you will make the rain fall when it is needed, that the seed may grow. . . . Land, men, saints, all together, one army, with God at our head showing us the way! Saint George, here is your village, and here is your gate. We have designed it high, that you may enter on horseback. Enter!"

Yannakos listened with his mouth wide open. He rubbed his eyes and looked around him. Nothing but rocks and brambles, broom and thyme . . . Two crows on a carob tree took fright and flew away, flapping their wings and croaking lugubriously.

What are these creatures? he asked himself with dread, men? wild animals? or saints? He looked at the men with their drooping mustaches, the women with their heavy tresses and broad hips. They're stark, staring mad, Lord help me!

To the north, opposite the Gate of the Virgin, the priest paused once more, in front of a ruined wall invaded by grass. He brandished his sprinkler, blessed the stones three times and turned toward his companions:

"Here," he said in a voice that trembled, "here, my brethren, we will build the gate of our last Byzantine king, Constantine Palaeologos! It is here, my friends, that one day, surely, the messenger soaked with sweat will enter to announce to us: 'Brothers, once more Constantinople is ours!' "

Those present were overcome; wild cries arose; they turned to the north in ecstasy, gazing afar toward the holy city, Constantinople: they could already see the messenger coming, carried by the wind.

"Father Panagos," the priest called out, "approach, lay down your sack, at the gate of King Palaeologos!"

Then, addressing the men who had tools:

"Dig!"

They did so, with great strokes of the spade, opening a wide grave, deep enough for a man to stand in. The grandfather went down into it. One by one he took from the sack skulls, shinbones and ribs, and piled them in the trench reverently, in silence. Priest Fotis sprinkled the bones with what was left of the holy water, then threw his sprinkler into the trench and cried:

"Fathers, patience a little longer; do not crumble into dust: behold, the messenger is coming!"

Yannakos wiped his eyes. There was a tightening in his throat.

"Come out now, father Panagos," the priest ordered; "come out; we're going to fill the trench." Two young men ran up to hoist him out.

"Leave me, lads," the old man implored them, "I'm all right here. Why do you want me to eat bread I have no right to? I can't work any more, I can't have children, I'm good for nothing, leave me!"

"Father Panagos," said the priest severely, "your hour has not yet come; don't be in a hurry."

"Father," replied the grandfather, beseechingly, "leave me here, I'm where I should be. I've heard say that if a human being is not sealed up in the foundations of a village, that village soon crumbles! Where could I find a better death? Bury me!"

"That cannot be," the priest protested. "God gave you life, and only God can take it away. We haven't the right, father Panagos. . . . Pull him out, my sons!"

The two young men bent down and stretched out their hands to pull him up. But the old man had already lain down upon the bones and was crying:

"Leave me, lads; leave me, I'm where I should be!"

Yannakos could no longer hold himself in. He leaned over the trench and saw the old man. He had turned over on his back and was lying still, with his face to the light. He was smiling happily.

"I'm all right here . . . I'm all right here," he kept murmuring, with his arms crossed on his chest.

Yannakos's tight throat loosened, and a sob was heard.

The priest turned, saw Yannakos and recognized him.

"Make room, my sons," he cried, "here's Yannakos, a good man from Lycovrissi; he's come to see us and give us courage in our misfortune. Greet him, my brethren! He's one of our four benefactors with the baskets."

"Welcome, Yannakos!" he said, shaking him by the hand with emotion. "For the love of you and your friends, God will not consume Lycovrissi with His flames."

Yannakos could control himself no longer: he burst into sobs.

"Why are you weeping, brother?" said the priest, clasping him in his arms.

"I've sinned, Father, I've sinned!"

"Come with me!"

He took him by the arm and they went apart a little.

"Why are you weeping? What is wrong? Tell me what's hurting you, my son. You are one of the founders of our village," he said, showing with outstretched arms the future village.

Yannakos's legs failed him and he sank down upon a stone; the priest, standing over him, gazed at him, worried.

"Is there something you want?" he asked; "is there something you've done? Don't weep!"

"I've sinned, Father! I want to confess it all!"

And he began to tell him—his words tumbling over each other, his breath short—why he had climbed up the Sarakina, and of the agreement he had made with father Ladas and of the three gold pieces he had accepted on account.

The priest listened attentively without a word. Yannakos looked at him in dread.

"What are you thinking, Father?" he said at last, in a quavering voice.

"I'm thinking that Man is a beast, a savage beast. . . . Don't weep; I'm thinking also that God is great."

"Worse than a beast," Yannakos muttered, and spat as though he suddenly felt sick; "a slimy worm, that's what a man is, a dirty worthless worm, foul. . . . Don't touch me, Father: don't I disgust you?"

The priest said nothing; he withdrew his hand, lowered his eyes and sighed.

Yannakos leaped up from the stone on which he had sunk down, dug his fingers into his waistcoat pocket and brought out the three gold pieces.

"Father, I've a favor to ask you: take these three gold pieces and buy some sheep for the village, for the children, they need milk. And if you can, lay your hand on my head and forgive me."

The priest did not move.

"If you don't take them, my soul will never rest again."

And, after a moment:

"You said Man was a savage beast: tame him, Father. One good word is enough. For me, at this moment, redemption hangs on your lips."

The priest threw himself into Yannakos's arms and in his turn wept.

"Is it for me," cried Yannakos, "is it for me you are weeping?"

"For you and for myself and for the whole world, my son," murmured priest Fotis, wiping away his tears.

He kissed Yannakos on the eyes and stroked his gray, woolly hair.

"Be forgiven, Yannakos! Peter also denied Christ, three times, and three times was saved by tears. Tears are a great font of baptism, my son. . . . I take this gold of sin which you are giving me; your crime will be changed into milk for our starving children. My blessing on you, Yannakos!"

Yannakos threw himself on his knees before the priest and tried to kiss his feet; but the priest hastily stooped and raised him.

"No, no, they can see us," he said; "they're coming!"

"Father, Father," cried fear-stricken voices.

"What's happening, my sons?" said priest Fotis, alarmed.

"Old Panagos has given up the ghost, Father; we tried to pull him out of the grave—he was dead."

Priest Fotis crossed himself.

"May God forgive him," he said. "He died happy, and there he is, he has entered into the foundations of our village. God grant

us also, my sons, an end like his; I'll come and give him the blessing." Then, addressing Yannakos:

"Come, my son, fear nothing; Christ is with you!"

Yannakos bowed, kissed the priest's hand and went off to find
his donkey.

Joy had given him wings, he jumped from stone to stone like a
young lad of twenty. He could feel his back thrilling as though
wings had sprung there.

Devil take old Ladas, he muttered, devil take his gold; I feel
as light as a bird.

He stroked his donkey, who was waiting patiently in the shade
of the oak, and untied him, humming a tune.

"Off we go, Youssoufaki," he said, "our business has gone well,
God be praised!"

Turning, he saw the wild rocks, the gloomy caves and the lean
men grouped round the grandfather's grave beneath the future
Gate of King Palaeologos, listening to the burial service and making the sign of the cross.

God give body to your village! he murmured; I—I've put three
gold pounds into its foundations.

He began to go down, singing.

You said the truth: Man is a wild beast, he told himself. Yes, he
does what he chooses. If he chooses to take a road, he takes it.
The gate of Hell and the gate of Paradise are close together, and
he goes in at whichever he chooses. . . . The Devil can only go
into Hell, and the angel only into Paradise, but Man into whichever he chooses!

He laughed. Then he intoned an old song which he had forgotten since God knows how long; and now here it was on his lips
once more:

> I am son of the lightning, and grandson of the thunder:
> I make the lightning flash at my will,
> The thunder rumble, and the snow fall.

At the foot of the mountain he stopped:

I'm hungry, I'm going to have something to eat. Youssoufaki's
hungry, too. I'll go and get him some fresh grass, so he mayn't be
jealous at seeing me eat. We'll have a bite together, side by side,
like brothers.

He went a few steps, gathered some thistles, jumped over a

hedge and cut a few cabbage leaves, bunched the lot together and brought it to his companion.

"There, eat, my Youssoufaki. I'm going to do the same. Enjoy your dinner!"

He opened his bag, pulled out bread, olives and an onion and began munching slowly and placidly, like a rabbit.

It's mighty good, this bread is! he murmured. It's as if I were eating bread for the first time. But it isn't bread, it's crust; goes straight into the bones and gives them strength.

He took out of the bag his wine bottle, on which he had carved a two-headed eagle. He tilted it above his mouth and a joyous gurgle could be heard.

You'd think it was the first time I'd drunk wine, he thought. The way it goes down, the rogue, straight to the heart and makes it rejoice. God had a famous idea when He made vines and grapes, and blessed was the man who thought of treading the grapes to get wine out of them. Here's one more drop!

He put the gourd to his mouth again and shut his eyes.

"Enjoy yourself, Yannakos!" said a fresh voice.

Yannakos opened his eyes and saw Katerina before him, carrying a heavy bundle on her back; behind her came her ewe, with a red ribbon round her neck.

"Hey, Katerina," he cried, "what are you after, out here? Where are you taking that ewe of yours? Are you selling her?"

"Yes," said the widow with a smile.

"Come, sit down a moment and have a bite and a drink. Priest Fotis was just wanting to buy a ewe, to give the little ones milk. . . . It's God who's sent you!"

The widow sat down on the ground. With her black kerchief she wiped the sweat from her face and neck. Her eyes sparkled with pleasure.

"How hot it is," she said. "Summer's come, Yannakos."

"Eat something," said Yannakos, cutting her a slice of bread, and handing her the olives. "Like an onion?"

"No, I never eat onions," answered the widow, taking the bread and olives.

"To keep your mouth from smelling bad, hussy?" laughed Yannakos.

"Yes," she said, and her voice had suddenly changed. "You see, neighbor, we ought always to smell of scented soap and lavender."

She pushed away the bread and olives.

"I'm not hungry," she said. "I'm sorry."

Yannakos was ashamed, and swallowed.

"It's me should be sorry, Katerina," he muttered, "I'm an ass."

The widow picked a piece of grass and sucked it without saying anything.

They remained silent a moment; Yannakos no longer felt like eating; he shut up the bag.

"What have you got in your bundle, Katerina?" he asked, by way of ending a silence which weighed on him.

"Some odds and ends of clothes for the children."

"You're going to give them to them?"

"Yes."

"And the ewe?"

"The ewe as well, for the milk."

Yannakos lowered his head, abashed. As if to excuse herself, the widow added, after a moment:

"You see, neighbor, I've had no children, and it's as if all the children in the world were mine."

Yannakos felt a tightening of his throat.

"Katerina," he said in a strangled voice, "I'd like to throw myself on the ground and kiss your feet."

"Patriarcheas, the old lecher, made me come and see him the day before yesterday, and told me the Council of Elders had decided I should be Mary Magdalen, next year. I've heard tell of what Mary Magdalen was. That's what I've come to—the village Mary Magdalen! When he told me that, I was ashamed; but now, Yannakos, I'm not ashamed any longer. If I met Christ, and if I had a bottle of lavender water, I'd empty it out to wash His feet and then I'd wipe them with my hair . . . I think that's what I'd do, and I'd stay by the side of the Virgin Mary without feeling ashamed. And she wouldn't be ashamed, either, seeing me beside her. Do you understand a bit what I've just been telling you, Yannakos?"

"I understand, Katerina, I understand," Yannakos answered, with tears in his eyes. "Since this morning I've begun to understand, Katerina."

He added:

"I'm a much greater sinner than you, Katerina. That's why I understand. Before, I was a bit of a robber, a bit of a liar, not much, just trifles. This morning I was a criminal. But now . . ."

He fell silent. His heart had wings. He took his gourd:

"To your health, Katerina," he said. "I hurt you just now; forgive me. An ass can only do what asses do."

Having drunk, he carefully wiped the neck of his gourd.

"You have a drink too, Katerina, so I can be sure you've forgiven me."

"Your health," said the widow, putting her head back. Wiping her mouth, she stood up.

"I'm off," she said; "the ewe's getting impatient, she's bleating, as if she were unhappy. I haven't milked her, poor thing. I want them to have it up there."

"Won't you miss her, Katerina? I know how you love her."

"If you gave them your donkey, would you miss him?"

Yannakos shuddered:

"Don't say that, neighbor, it tears my heart."

"It tears mine too, Yannakos. Good-bye. Good luck!"

She hesitated for a second:

"Will you be seeing Manolios?" she ventured at last.

"I'll be doing a round of the villages. On my way back I expect I'll turn aside and go to see him. . . . Want me to tell him anything?"

The widow had put the bundle on her back again and was pulling hard at the reluctant ewe.

"No," she answered, "nothing."

And she began to go up.

In the meantime Manolios had reached the mountain. The dogs scented him a long way off and ran up, wagging their tails, followed by Nikolio, the sunburned shepherd boy with the pointed ears, who bounded from rock to rock like a kid as he came to meet him. He had grown up in the mountains with the goats and sheep. He was a very dark, wild creature, who seldom spoke, but bleated with the sheep and rams. His curly hair, sticky with resin and muck, twisted and gave him two small pointed horns. He was now fifteen, and looked at the sheep with a ram's scowl.

When they reached the sheepfold, Nikolio set bread, cheese and roasted meat on the bench.

"Eat," he said.

"I'm not hungry, old Nikolio. You eat."

"Why aren't you hungry?"

"I'm not."

"They been doing things to you, down there?"

"Yes."

"Why did you go?"

Manolios did not answer. He lay down on his bed of straw and shut his eyes. It was true: why had he gone? Till then, he had gone down to the village on Sunday mornings; he had heard Mass, taken the holy bread and come back quickly to his mountain. Down there in the plain he stifled. When he looked at the women he became wild; when he passed in front of the café where the men were drinking and playing cards, the smell of tobacco and narghiles seized him by the throat, and so he passed as quickly as he could to get back to the pure air. And now . . .

He remembered Lenio, her mischievous eyes, her smile, her bewitching voice and, above all, her breasts stretching her pink bodice to bursting. He sat up on the straw. He was too hot: he pulled off his shirt; it was soaked with sweat.

I must be patient, he told himself, and keep pure, and not touch a woman. I shall have to give account. This body isn't mine any longer now; it belongs to Christ.

The image of Christ rose up in his mind, as he had seen it when he arrived at the Monastery, on the iconostasis in the chapel: a long blue tunic, bare feet which touched the ground so lightly that the blades of grass were not even bent. Thin, transparent, weightless like a mist. From His hands, from His feet and from His uncovered chest there flowed a thin thread of rose-pink blood . . . A young woman with golden hair floating on her shoulders was darting forward to touch Him; but He, austerely, raised His hand to stop her. From His mouth issued a garland of words, unrolling; Manolios read them but could not catch their meaning. He had asked his Superior: "What is Christ saying there, Father?" And he had answered: "Woman, touch me not!" "Who is the woman, Father?" "Mary Magdalen."

"Woman, touch me not!" Manolios closed his eyes. Suddenly he saw the widow Katerina shaking her head and throwing aside her black kerchief; her fair hair came undone and reached to her knees, covering her nakedness. Then a gust of wind stirred her hair, and two breasts appeared, round and firm.

"Help!" cried Manolios, bolt upright on his bed.

The shepherd boy was eating and could not quench his hunger. He turned impassively, with his mouth full:

"Been dreaming, master? Was someone after you? I, too, have people after me in my dreams. There! Dreams are lies; don't be a fool, go to sleep!"

"Light the fire, Nikolio, I'm cold . . ."

"But it's stifling hot!" protested the shepherd boy, unable to tear himself away from the bread and meat.

"I'm cold. . . ." repeated Manolios, and his teeth were chattering.

The little shepherd boy got up, without stopping munching; grumbling, he went and took wood from a corner, laid it with twigs on the hearth and set light to it. Approaching Manolios, he looked at him attentively and shook his head.

"They've cast the evil eye on you, master," he said and went back to eating greedily.

Manolios dragged himself to a corner of the hut, wrapped himself in a rug and huddled himself together. He watched the fire consuming the wood: Lenio, Mary Magdalen, Christ came by, dancing in the flames, drawing together, apart, together again. . . . The flame danced a little and Christ came to life; emerged from the ash; grew smaller, bent double, arose, then disappeared in the smoke.

Exhausted, Manolios let his head fall on his knees; sleep took hold of him.

A heavy, sticky sleep; all through the night, Manolios fought to get free of it. He was caught in the midst of clinging seaweed and water serpents, and at dawn a cascade of fair tresses came leaping and crumbling, and wrapped him round. "Help!" he cried, stifling. Still asleep, unable to tear himself out of slumber, he was now floating on his back at the mercy of a river, and groaning.

Two or three times Manolios's piercing cries woke the young shepherd.

"He's still dreaming they're after him, poor fellow," he muttered, and turned over and went to sleep again.

At dawn, Manolios opened his eyes and saw through the hole of a window a milky sky; he crossed himself. "God be praised," he said, half-aloud; "the night's over, and I'm saved!"

His joints were aching, his red eyes were burning, and he was shivering. The fire had gone out. He was thirsty. He longed for

some hot milk; but Nikolio had already gone off to pasture the
sheep, and he did not feel like getting up. He gazed around, as if
he saw the tools of his trade for the first time: pots, milk pails,
wooden spoons hanging on the wall, fashioned and carved by his
hands with delicate craft. Even as a small boy, whenever he had
come on a piece of wood he had taken his knife and tried his hand
at engraving on it cypresses and birds; later he had begun to en-
grave women; then it had been men on horseback; finally, after
he had gone to the Monastery, saints and men on crosses.

"You, my son," a monk who passed by the sheepfold had said
to him one day, "you ought never to have become a shepherd.
You should have become a monk. We'd have given you wood, and
you'd have made us icons."

The sun came through the window. Manolios went and sat in
its rays to unstiffen himself. As he got warm again, he again saw
his dreams of that night—the river of golden hair; and he shuddered.

"Lord Jesus," he murmured, "don't let me yield to temptation!"

Somewhat calmed, he rose, lit a fire, took some milk from a
bucket, warmed it and drank it. It gave him back some strength.
He went out and sat on the stone bench in the enclosure. The sun
was an arm's length high in the sky; the world was awakening;
the whole mountain was glittering. In the distance he heard Nikolio leading the sheep.

I'm all right now, he thought. It's in the night that temptation
comes; the sun has appeared, God be praised!

Looking around, he saw by the doorstep a log cut from a box-
tree trunk. His heart gave a bound of joy. He bent down, picked
it up, put it on his knees and stroked it. It was stout and round
like a head. Its grain showed sinuous and ramified, like the veins
on a head.

Manolios felt an itch tickling his fingertips. He stood up suddenly, went into the hut and fetched a small saw, a chisel and a
file. With a hasty sign of the cross, he kissed the wood and began
working at it.

The sun was reaching the zenith, and still Manolios was at work,
bent over the piece of wood, which he held clasped against his
chest. He had completely forgotten his exhaustion; the open air
had swept the earth clean like the sky; all temptation had fled to
the four winds.

Rapt by the wood he was carving, Manolios turned his eyes in upon himself. His whole soul became an eye, contemplating, at the bottom of his heart, a calm face, all kindness, silence and sorrow. Manolios strove to reproduce faithfully, just as he saw them, the hollow cheeks, the suffering eyes, the broad brow beaded with big drops of blood . . . and a wound between the eyebrows, not to be found in the icons, seen by Manolios alone.

The sweat was dripping from his temples; he had cut his fingers with the chisel, and blood stained the wood red. But Manolios did not stop. He was in haste to copy the holy face and fix it in the wood, before it should vanish.

While he was feverishly carving, two women appeared on the path, a young one followed by an old one whose face was ringed with a kerchief. When the young one saw Manolios, she turned and laid her finger on her lips; both approached stealthily, curious to see what Manolios could be doing. At one moment, the old woman stumbled and sent a stone rolling; but Manolios was so absorbed that he heard nothing.

The young woman, unable to hold back, hastened her steps and touched Manolios on the shoulder.

"Hello, Manolios!" she cried.

He jumped; the holy form vanished within him; overcome, he leaned against the wall, with his head thrown back.

"What's the matter, Manolios? Why do you look at me haggardly, as if you'd seen a ghost? It's me, Lenio, your betrothed; and here's your aunt, mother Mandalenia. She's come to exorcise you."

"You've been hurt by some demon or other, that's certain, my child," said the old woman, approaching breathless.

Manolios looked at her with dread.

"What do you want?" he asked at last, turning the piece of wood face downward.

The old woman was about to answer, but Lenio pushed her aside.

"Leave us, mother Mandalenia," she said; "go and gather the herbs you need, and leave us alone; I want a word with him."

The old woman went off grumbling to look for her plants. Lenio slid onto the stone bench, close against her betrothed.

"Manolios," she said softly, taking him by the hand, "turn

and look at me. Don't you like me any more? Don't you love me any more?"

"I love you," answered Manolios quietly.

"When are we going to get married?"

Manolios said nothing. How far his marriage was from his thoughts at this moment, Almighty God!

"Why don't you say anything? The master's told me everything."

"I'd rather you hadn't come," said Manolios, standing up.

"Perhaps I should have asked your leave first?" cried Lenio, her cheeks on fire. "You're not my husband yet; I'm free."

She got up and stood in front of him. Stretching out her arms she ordered him:

"Don't go!"

Manolios leaned against the wall and waited. Lenio watched him. In her breast hate and love were contending.

"My mother was only a servant," she said at last in a strangled voice; "my mother was only a servant, but my father's a noble: I'm not going to force myself on anyone. I've my dowry, I've my youth, I shall find another better than you."

Manolios pressed the carved wood against his chest so hard that he hurt himself.

"As you will, Lenio," he said, calmly, but his heart beat as if it would burst. Hardly had he uttered these hard words than he regretted them; his courage weakened.

"Lenio," he began again, lowering his eyes, "leave me alone here for a few days to decide. If you love me, do that for me."

"You love someone else, eh? Which? Out with it and I'll go."

"No, no, Lenio, I swear I don't!"

"Very well; when you've decided, let me know. I'll wait . . . But you'd better know—perhaps I'll love you all my life, perhaps I'll hate you all my life, it depends on one word from you; on a yes or a no; choose!"

And, turning toward the old woman:

"Hey, mother Mandalenia, we're going!"

They set off; Lenio walked in front, furious; not once did she look back. Her father's proud blood was boiling in her.

Manolios sank down on the bench. He looked at the log he held in his hand; he had not the slightest desire to carve. The flame had gone out, the holy form which had been in him had disappeared.

He went back into the hut, wrapped the piece of wood in a rag, slowly, as one covers up an ember with ashes so that it may not go out. He could not bear now to remain alone, he was stifling. He grabbed up his crook and went to join Nikolio and the sheep.

The sun was pouring vertically down upon the mountain. Not a breath. The shadows were gathered fearfully at the feet of the trees. The birds, crouching voiceless in their nests, waited for the panic to pass.

Nikolio suddenly felt his strength brim over. He looked round in search of someone or something to expend this overflow of vigor upon. Nothing. Nobody. Neither a man to fight, nor a woman to hurl on her back in the grass. The sheep, stunned by the heat, lay in the shade under the holm oaks; it would have been shameful to set on them. But here came their chief, the great ram Dassos, with his long spiral horns, thick greasy fleece, and at his neck the leader's big bell. With a dull eye he glanced over his drowsed sheep lying in the shade, gave a bleat of contentment, then made off, heavily, for his walk, with measured steps and all the arrogance of a monarch: a reek of male haunted the air. Nikolio threw himself upon him, as though he had suddenly lost his head, and struck him furiously with his stick on the horns, back and belly.

Haughtily the impassive male turned. His adversary appeared to him a puppy—no horns, no thick fleece, only a couple of feet to walk with; a slight butt would have been enough to knock him sprawling. So he pursued his saunter among the sheep.

Nikolio followed him, seized him by the horns and leaped onto his back. Then Dassos became annoyed; shaking his head, he threw the shepherd boy.

"Swine! I'll show you!" shouted Nikolio, picking himself up, bleeding at the elbows.

He hunched his neck between his shoulders, lowered his head and took a run to butt. Dassos also took a run. The shock stunned Nikolio. He spun round and the mountain, too, began spinning. But he managed to keep his balance, picked up his stick, rushed at the animal in a rage and hit it as if he would break its horns.

Just at this moment Manolios came up. He put two fingers into his mouth and whistled. Nikolio turned and saw him, but he was too far gone, he could not stop, and he hurled himself once more upon the ram. Manolios picked up a stone and threw it at him.

"Hey, Nikolio," he shouted, "having a fight with the ram? Come here!"

Grumbling, swearing and sweating, Nikolio came. The two of them leaned their backs against a rock; the young shepherd, fuming with anger, gave out a smell of ram. From time to time he whistled and threw a stone, trying to hide his fury. But deep down in him rage was boiling: Dassos had won, had humiliated him.

The eyes of Manolios were lost in the void. He was trying hard to recover his spirits and to find once more in his heart the holy form he had been carving in the wood. The enchantment of this morning! Forgotten his torments; the world wiped away; they had remained alone between heaven and earth—he and a bit of wood! Then suddenly a woman's voice, two full lips . . .

"Hey, Nikolio, take your pipe out of your belt and play us something . . . I'm not well, my lad. My soul's all vague. Play a bit, that'll make me better!"

The little shepherd laughed.

"I'm just the same, Manolios," he said. "My soul's all vague, too. There are moments when I feel I'm going to burst. I play my pipe, but it doesn't make me better at all. That's why I fought the ram."

"What can make your soul all vague? you've not yet any hair on your chin."

"Devil take me if I know. Here, when I'm all alone, Manolios —well, I feel sad!" the boy answered, kindling.

He took out his pipe and placed his bronzed fingers on the holes.

"Got a tune in your head, Nikolio?"

"Me? Never. I play as it comes."

He began to play.

The slopes became covered with goats and sheep, and rang with bells: the mountain was going out to pasture. The countryside was in motion, streams leaped from stone to stone, warbling. Little by little, streams, sheep bells and mountain fell silent; no, they were not silent, they stirred with fresh, joyous, provocative laughter. . . . A melodious sea stretched there, a shore scattered with shells; there were smiling women bathing. . . . Arms and legs apart, they threw themselves into the water, teased the waves which bowled them over, uttered little cries; and the whole shore was tickled and laughed with them.

Crouched in on himself and panting, Manolios listened. The women's laughter echoed madly all along the seashore, it welled up, calmed down, then came back again mingled with the waves. In the end, all was silent, and Katerina rose from the sea, naked.

"Stop, that's enough!" cried Manolios, jumping up.

Nikolio turned his head to look at him, but went on playing, for he, too, was carried away by the music. He held the pipe pressed hard against his lips.

"Stop, I tell you!" repeated Manolios.

"You've broken my thread, just at its best," said Nikolio, put out, resting the pipe on his knees.

Tears stood in Manolios's eyes.

"What's the matter, Manolios? Are you crying?" exclaimed the little shepherd, taken aback. "Come, don't be sad, it was only a pipe; all that isn't real, it's only wind!"

Manolios wanted to walk a few steps, but his knees failed him.

"I don't feel well," he muttered, "I don't feel well."

"Did you hear the water?" the little shepherd asked, smiling.

"What water?"

"I was thinking of water as I played—a lot of water, because I was thirsty. . . ." he said, and with a bound was under the holm oak where he had hung up his gourd. Manolios had given it to him and had carved a goat on it.

"I'll go and lie down," thought Manolios, "I'm shivering . . ."

"Keep an eye on the sheep," he called to Nikolio, "I'm going back to make the cheese."

"I've got the fire ready," Nikolio answered, wiping his lips and his chest where the water had dripped. "Boil the milk, I'm coming."

He watched him go, staggering over the stones, and felt sorry for him.

"If you don't feel well," he shouted again, "leave the cheese; I'll make it, you lie down!"

"Why did you say that?"

"Because your feet are all mixed up, master, and you look yellow."

"Poor lad!" he muttered sympathetically, as he watched Manolios disappear, tottering, behind the holm oaks. "I saw Lenio coming in the distance—curse her! She'll suck your marrows dry, old one!"

He picked up a stone and threw it a long way, angrily.

"Damned females!" he shouted at the top of his voice.

He saw Dassos advancing before him, provocatively. He seized him by the horns, bent the long head away from him and hurled himself on top of him.

When he reached the enclosure, Manolios revived the fire to make the cheese, but he had not the strength. He sat down on the bench in the sun, to get warm again. He was shivering. The sun was dipping toward the horizon. A few minutes later, he heard bells approaching and the cries and whistling of Nikolio as he edged the animals toward the enclosure, throwing stones at them.

Manolios's thoughts flew off and slipped down to the village, slid past the houses, the café and the square, took the steep path, entered the priest's house, saw the notables distributing the parts —who shall act Peter, who Judas, who Christ . . . He again saw priest Fotis and the Christians uprooted from their houses, the painful duel with the other priest, the woman who had cried out and given up the ghost. The hard, mocking words of Yannakos rang in him afresh: "You're going to be Christ, and at the same time you're getting ready to marry and soil yourself . . . fraud!" He climbed up to the room and saw the archon and, down in the yard, Lenio clinging to him, with her breasts leaning against his chest as she asked, in cajoling, pressing tones: "Manolios, when are we getting married? when? when?" And then . . . then, when he had left for the mountain and had stopped for a moment to get his breath by the well . . .

His heart melted.

I'm sorry for her, he murmured, sorry for her; she's taken the evil road, she'll be lost. . . .

She rose up in his memory—black kerchief, white neck, teeth scraped by the walnut leaves . . . He heard once more her despairing appeal:

"Don't go, don't go, Manolios!"—as if she expected her salvation of him alone.

In a flash her dream came back to him, and its meaning seemed to him clear. Yes, yes, she was right, the poor woman; he alone could save her. God Himself had warned her of it in her sleep. In his hands Manolios held the moon, cut it into slices and gave it her to eat, like an apple. Suddenly he understood the dream's hidden meaning, and trembled: the moon is the pure light, the word of God which lights up the night. It is the will of God, the command of God, that Manolios should share it with her. It is he who should save Mary Magdalen, the sinner.

I must see her, he muttered; yes, I must, and quickly. Every minute that passes may make her sink farther into sin . . . I must, I must. . . . It is my duty.

He could see the narrow lane where she lodged, the arched doorway with its green paint and its iron ring. He could see the stone doorstep shining clean. He had never crossed that doorstep, but he remembered how, one Sunday, the door had been open and he had cast a furtive glance inside—he had caught a glimpse of a small yard paved with big, freshly washed cobbles, some pots of flowers—and sweet basil—on the low wall which went round it, and two fat groups of red carnations near a well.

Manolios's thought slipped down the mountain path, reached the village, went along the narrow lane, crossed the threshold, entered. . . .

Must see her, must see her . . . he kept repeating; it's my duty.

He felt a strange joy. Now that he understood that it was necessary for him to see her, that it was not himself but God that was ordering it, he was relieved. He knew now why he was obsessed night and day by the desire to go and see her. While he had believed that it was Satan who was impelling him, he had been ashamed and had resisted; but now . . .

He jumped up. He was not cold any more, and his knees no longer shook. He lit the fire, put the pot on it and boiled the milk.

What ways God takes, he said to himself, to enlighten a man's soul! Think—this time His will turned into a dream and descended upon the widow's pillow. . . .

Nikolio was arriving, the air was all bleats, the sheep were reentering the fold. The sun was setting, tranquil and sated; day done, he was going home to his mother for dinner.

"Hullo, Nikolio!" Manolios shouted from the door in a serene voice; "go and milk the ewes and then lay the meal; I'm hungry!"

He had not eaten all day; nothing had managed to get by his contracted throat. Now that it was loosening, his appetite was coming back.

Nikolio looked at him and burst into a laugh.

"So you've come back to life, master! Good news?"

"I'm hungry; get going. I'll lend you a hand."

They brought the copper buckets, knelt down side by side and began to milk the ewes one after the other. The ewes kept quiet, glad to be relieved of their good burden. The skilled fingers seemed to them like beloved lips sucking.

Having done, they washed. Nikolio laid the meal outside on the bench. They crossed themselves, then, famished, fell upon the bread, meat and white cheese. Nikolio still kept thinking with annoyance of the strong ram and of Lenio. The two were indissolubly bound together in his resentment: the flock's leader and the plump young woman. They were now one, and sometimes he saw Lenio on top, astride, sometimes underneath, smiling . . .

"Curse her . . . curse her . . ." he grumbled. He picked up a stone and threw it into the air.

"Well, Nikolio, what are you mumbling about?" Manolios asked with a smile. "Who are you throwing stones at?"

"The Devil's roaming round me," replied the little shepherd, also smiling, "and I'm throwing stones at him."

"Have you seen him, Nikolio?"

"Yes, I've seen him, just fancy."

"What's he like?"

"That's his secret," the shepherd boy jerked out, plunging his red face into a bucket of water.

When he had finished his meal, Manolios crossed himself and rose.

"Nikolio," he said, "I'm going down to the village this evening. Good luck!"

"The village again?" cried Nikolio angrily. "What'll you do down there now? I believe you too, master, have got the Devil roaming round you."

"It's not the Devil, my good Nikolio, heaven preserve us, it's God."

He pulled out a small mirror from his pocket, wetted his hair and combed it. Then he put on his best clothes, his Sunday ones. He slipped his little mirror, his comb and a handkerchief into his belt. Why? What need had he of them? Did he know? He simply took them and, for no reason, hid them away in his belt.

"The Devil, I tell you," the lad repeated, angrily, as he watched Manolios.

"God, God," repeated Manolios, and left, crossing himself once more.

"He's surely gone to look for Lenio. The devil take the two of them!" muttered Nikolio, and spat with disgust.

The Demon and the Mask of Christ

NIGHT WAS FALLING. Amorous or famished, the night birds were uttering their cries. In the sky the first stars, the biggest, were kindling.

Must wait till it's darker still: mustn't be seen in the village, Manolios said to himself, as he went slowly down the twisting path. As he walked he rehearsed in his head what he would say in order that the word of God might reach the widow's heart. I'll knock, he reckoned; she'll come and open. She'll be surprised to see me, we shall go in and she'll bolt the door. . . . He had already seen the courtyard with its carnations, sweet basil and well head— he was not afraid of that. . . . But inside? Manolios took fright. He paused to draw breath. There, inside, there'll be the bed . . . he told himself, and shivered.

All became mixed up in his mind. He no longer knew what he ought to say, or even why he was going down from the mountain at such an hour, in the middle of the night, to knock at her door. She would see him blush and lose countenance, and she would laugh. So, Manolios, she'd say to him, there you are, and you don't even know, yourself, why you've come? Can it be, you, too, have had a dream? Has the fiend come looking for you in a dream, Manolios? or perhaps the Virgin Mary? or even both—that too happens, Manolios. And so you've come, and you'll start by talking to me of God and Paradise, then afterward, gradually, without either you or me noticing it, Manolios, we'll find ourselves clasped tight together in bed. You're a man, aren't you? I'm a woman. That's the way God has made us. Is it our fault if, when we're close to each other, we get giddy and lose our heads and open our arms and legs and become one. . . .

Manolios felt the blood rising to his head. These shameless words rang in his brain, with complete clearness he heard the widow uttering them as she smiled and drew close to him. Already he was breathing her breath with its scent of mastic and cloves. From her open bodice rose the warm smell of her body, with its reek of sweat and nutmeg.

Suddenly he was tired, his knees gave way and he sank down on a stone.

Who was it, spoke inside me? he asked himself in terror. Who laughed? Whose was that knee which touched me and made my knees double up? He had really heard those words and the widow's laughter, and his nostrils were still soaked with her smell.

"O God, help me," he cried, raising his eyes to Heaven.

But this evening, Heaven seemed to him very high, a very long way from man, silent, indifferent, neither a friend nor an enemy. Terror took hold of him. The stars were watching him; Manolios's heart froze. Sometimes on winter nights he had seen, around the fold, between the snow-laden branches, the still, yellow, jealous eyes of wolves; this evening the stars appeared to him like wolves' eyes.

The memory of the widow began again to flow in his blood, like honey. In the presence of the chill and hostility of the world, it was a great consolation. She did not speak or laugh now. She lay on her big bed cheerfully and cooed like a grateful turtledove.

Manolios stopped his ears; his head was buzzing; the veins of his neck swelled. He could feel flaming blood mounting to his head. His temples were throbbing violently, his eyelids grew heavy, there was a prickling all over his face, as though thousands of ants were biting his cheeks, his chin, his forehead, and were devouring his flesh.

A cold sweat flowed over his whole body; he passed his hand over his face and stood up.

"O God," he tried to cry out, but could not. Again he passed his hand over his cheeks, his lips, his chin: they felt swollen. His lips were so distended that he could not open his mouth.

What is the matter with me? Why am I swollen? he asked himself, desperately feeling his face all over, down to the neck. His whole face was like a drum, but he felt no pain. Only his eyes were burning, and tears began to flow.

Must see, see, I want to know! he gasped. He pulled out the

mirror from his belt, stooped, lit a sprig and looked at himself. In the dancing glow he caught sight of his face, and gave a cry: it was all bloated, his eyes were no more than two tiny balls, his nose was lost between his ballooning cheeks, his mouth was a mere hole.

This was no human face, but a mask of bestial flesh, repulsive. No, it was no longer his face; a foreign face had fixed itself over his own.

A sudden thought crossed his mind: My God, could it be leprosy? He collapsed on the ground.

Seizing the little mirror again, he at once turned his head away in horror. That, a man? No, a demon. He got up. I can't go now . . . How could she look at me? How could I talk to her? I'm horrible. I'll go home!

He turned back and climbed the path at a run, as though he were pursued.

When he reached the fold he stopped and entered it furtively, trembling at the thought that Nikolio, if he woke up, would strike a light and see him. Tomorrow morning, with God's help, perhaps I'll be all right. This thought calmed him a little.

He sat down on the straw mattress, crossed himself and implored God to pity him. O God, kill me if Thou wilt, he prayed, but do not humiliate me before men . . . Why has Thou stuck this meat over my face? Take it away, my God, hurl it far from me. Tomorrow morning make my face be clean and human, as before!

Having placed his trust in God, he felt some consolation. He shut his eyes and dreamed that a woman in black—it must be the Holy Virgin—was leaning over him and slowly, softly stroking his face. Immediately it felt cooler, lighter, and Manolios, stretching out his arms, took the miraculous hand to kiss it. But a fresh, mocking laugh burst out, the black veil fell away, and Manolios woke with a cry. It was not the Virgin, it was the widow . . .

In the opposite corner Nikolio heard the cry and awoke: he sat up and saw his master, with his face turned to the wall. He began laughing, peevishly.

"Why, you're back, are you, Manolios? Done your business already?"

But Manolios, turned to the wall, kept on feeling his face: he was desperate. The swelling had not gone down at all, and wounds must have opened in it, for his finger tips were now moist with a thick and sticky liquid.

I'm done for . . . done for . . . he thought. It must be leprosy!

Day was breaking. Nikolio got up quickly to take the sheep out to pasture. The little shepherd was just going out of the door when he turned. The first rays were coming through the window, and the hut was all illumined.

"Manolios," he said, "see you this evening."

Completely forgetting the state he was in, Manolios turned to answer. Nikolio saw him and leaped out into the yard.

"Holy Virgin!" he cried, coming back.

Manolios's face was flowing with muck; it was all over furrows of pus. He tried to speak, to calm the little shepherd, but he could not get a syllable out. He merely waved his hand to reassure him.

Nikolio leaned his cheek against the door jamb, with his body still outside, ready to escape. Unable to take his staring eyes off that face, he gradually grew bolder and recovered his spirits.

"In Heaven's name, it is you, isn't it, Manolios?" he said; "cross yourself, so as I can be sure!"

Manolios made the sign of the cross. Nikolio plucked up courage again and recrossed the threshold, but still did not go near.

"What's happened to you, poor lad?" he asked him, compassionately. "The Devil must have set upon you and left you with that mask, God protect us! The Devil, I tell you, that's sure! The same thing happened to my grandfather."

Manolios shook his head and turned to the wall so as not to frighten his young companion. He sighed to him to go.

"See you this evening," said Nikolio again, timidly, rushing out as though he had someone on his heels.

Left alone, Manolios sighed and got up. He felt strong and had no pain anywhere. He was not shivering any more and, strangely enough, was filled with an inexplicable joy . . . He picked up his little looking glass again, and went over to the window and looked at himself: the swollen skin had cracked, a yellowish, thick matter was oozing out and coagulating in his mustache and beard. His whole face was blood red, like meat.

He crossed himself:

If that comes from Satan, he said, inwardly, exorcise me, Jesus.

And if it comes from God, welcome to it. He, I know, cannot wish me evil. My misfortune must have a hidden meaning. I will be patient until He lays His hand upon my face.

As soon as he had given this meaning to his adversity he felt at peace. He lit a fire, put the pot on it, poured in the milk they had drawn the evening before. Feeling hungry, he filled a spoon with it: he could not manage to open his mouth. So he took a straw, dipped it in the milk and began sucking this up and drinking it greedily.

Then he went out and sat on the stone bench.

The sun had waked the birds and filled their little throats with tunes. Having climbed over the peak of the mountain, he spread over its slopes and the plain, opened the doors in the village, and went in. He found the widow still in bed after a sleepless night; she was pale; he slid furtively in among her hair. He found Mariori in her yard, busy watering her flowers, and hung himself around her neck. He went to look for all the women of the village in the same way, and caressed them like a master.

He sat down finally on the stone bench in front of the fold; Manolios stretched out his hands to him in welcome.

Where does this joy I feel come from? he wondered; what is this relief? I don't understand.

With his handkerchief he wiped his bloated face, which was oozing in the sun.

I don't understand, I don't understand, he kept repeating, spreading out his handkerchief again and again in the sun to dry it.

One day at the monastery his Superior had spoken to him of an ascetic whose skin had gone into crevasses from which there had come worms. When a worm fell to the ground, he bent down, carefully picked it up and put it back into the wound. "Eat," he said to it, "eat the flesh, my brother, that my soul may be lightened." For years Manolios had not thought of that little worm; what a consolation it was today and what a lesson in endurance and hope!

He rose, went back into the hut, picked up in his arms the rag with the piece of wood wrapped in it, got the file and chisel, came out again and sat down in the sun. He had all of a sudden felt the holy image arising within him and filling his heart. He could make it out clearly, contemplate all its features. His gaze bent upon it, he began again, with emotion, passionately, to fix it in the wood.

The hours passed swiftly; the sun for a moment held the zenith, then began little by little to descend . . . Chips littered the soil, lightening the wood. Serene, suffering, full of resignation and kindness, the face of Christ could be seen appearing. For a long time Manolios tried to render Christ's quivering mouth, but he could not: sometimes the mouth smiled, sometimes furrows dug themselves about it and it was weeping, sometimes again the lips contracted as though in an effort not to cry out with pain.

Toward evening, Nikolio brought in his flock; he found Manolios still sitting on the bench, holding on his knees the entire face of Christ carved in the boxwood. It remained for him to scoop out the inside of the head, so that he might place it over his face. This would be the mask he would wear on the day of the Passion.

Nikolio stopped, gave a rapid glance at his master and at once turned away. He could not recognize him. The pus furrowing his cheeks had now coagulated on his face and beard, forming a crust. It was as if there was sitting on the bench a demon with the face of Christ on its knees.

"You needn't come and help, I'll milk them myself," he exclaimed, fearfully.

Manolios turned away and shut his eyes. He was exhausted but relieved. He pressed the carved wood between his palms and felt happy at having managed to render faithfully the face which had arisen in his heart. It would not vanish now, a trembling form in the air; he had confirmed his soul in the wood. Slowly Manolios balanced the holy face between his hands and admired the Lord's mouth. Full face, it smiled; turned to the right in profile, it was weeping; turned a little to the left, it tightened, resigned and proud . . . His eyes shut, Manolios now slowly and tenderly caressed the face of Christ with his finger tips, as Mary would have caressed the divine Child.

With infinite care he wrapped and enfolded the carved wood in the rag, like a new-born babe in swaddling clothes, and took it in his arms.

Nikolio, meanwhile, had finished milking. He returned to the hut without glancing toward Manolios and began to prepare the dinner. "Poor old lad," he thought with secret pleasure, "a newly-married man with a mug like that? Why, if Lenio sees him, she'll be scared and take to her heels!"

He came out onto the doorstep.

"Coming to have dinner, Manolios? Can you open your mouth to eat?"

Manolios got up. He was hungry; he had forgotten to eat at noon. He filled a large bowl with milk, took the straw, knelt down and drank his milk, sniffing it. He filled the bowl a second time.

When it got dark, they did not light the oil lamp. In the blackness Nikolio could no longer see the swollen face, and fear left him. He was in an excellent temper, without very well knowing why; as soon as he had done eating, he sat down near the fireplace and poked the fire with his staff.

"I was telling you how my grandfather," he began, happily, "became a monk, after he'd killed, robbed and done a lot of dirty work. Haven't you, too, heard say that when the Devil grows old he turns hermit? Well, my grandfather—God forgive him!—had gone apart near Saint Penteleimon Monastery, where you, too, were monk, for the space of a moon . . . But, lo and behold, there was a village over by the convent, and in the village, women . . . For that matter there's no lack of them anywhere, the bitches!" he added, spitting into the ash.

"Are you listening?" he asked, turning to try and make out Manolios's face by the glow from the flame. Manolios nodded his head, as much as to say: "I'm listening."

"Well, look: one day, as I was saying, the Devil gets up on his back. 'I got to have a woman,' says he, 'got to have a woman; I'm going to the village and there I'll find one. I've had enough! Married, unmarried, old, young, lame, hunchbacked—I don't care, so long as it's a woman!' So one evening when the monks are asleep, there goes our lad jumping over the monastery wall and making off, hell for leather. He meant to do his business, see? and be back in less than it takes to count two, so nobody'd know a thing. He ran and he ran, with his skirt hitched up, bleating like a ram in the summertime when he catches sight of the ewes . . . But the good God had seen him, He took pity on him, and just at the moment he was coming into the village, lo and behold, He sends him a foul disease, the leprosy—you've heard tell of that. His body was covered with boils as big as hazelnuts—what was I saying?—walnuts, or rotten apricots . . . And then they burst and the stuff trickled down, and didn't it stink? Poor old chap, he did get a fright, God forgive him! 'Where am I to go now?' he says to himself, 'would any woman touch me? Better go back . . .' "

Manolios was listening hard. He stretched out his hand and tapped Nikolio on the knee, with a gesture which meant: "Go on!"

"Old wives' tales!" said Nikolio with a laugh. "It was my poor mother used to tell them to me, may she prosper! Even she laughed at them. You can imagine our scamp—monks indeed! He goes back to the monastery, does the wall all over again and hides in his cell . . . Next morning, the monks found him with his face like a water skin."

Manolios again urged on the little shepherd by signs.

"How it all ended, you mean? How should I know? I was a child, I didn't pay any attention . . . It's a long time now since he packed off, poor old fellow; no more trouble with women for him!" he said, and burst out laughing. Then he began brooding again.

"I'm sleepy," he said, "I'll go and lie down in the yard. I'm dying of heat."

He was not in the least hot, but was afraid to remain in the hut with Manolios. He got up.

"I've straightened your bed. Go to sleep, you'll be better tomorrow."

He took his rug, spread it in the yard, put a stone on it as a pillow and shut his eyes. He remembered Lenio and his senses kindled; but he was tired: he turned over and went to sleep.

Manolios threw another bundle of firewood on the fire: he was afraid to remain alone in the dark. He watched the flames dance, and whistled. With his ear cocked toward the open door, he listened to the voices of the night: owls were moaning, minute animals were burrowing in the earth, the mice above his head were scampering over the roof beams with sharp squeaks. And within him, insistent, the small voice, only heard at night when complete silence reigned and he was alone.

He got up, went out on the doorstep and looked at the stars. The Milky Way was flowing peacefully; Jupiter was blazing; the spangled sky was glittering insensitive and afar. All at once the words of the shepherd boy came back to Manolios's mind, and his heart began beating hard.

"Lord Jesus," he thought, "is this a miracle? Is it not Thou, Who has stretched forth Thy hand at the moment when, like the old monk, I was rushing to throw myself over the precipice?"

He put his hand up to his face, this time without repulsion and

without fear. He felt his swollen cheeks and his chapped flesh
with gratitude.

Who knows? Who knows? he thought, caressing his sickness;
perhaps it is to you that I owe salvation. . . .

Soothed, he went in again. A goodly heat was coming from the
fireplace. He felt a wish to go to sleep. Sometimes, when his soul
was struggling in the dark, a dream showed him the way.

Perhaps, he thought, God in His mercy will come to me again
in a dream tonight to enlighten me.

He closed his eyes and plunged at once into sleep.

The fire went out, the night passed. The cocks were beginning
to crow when, benumbed by the cold of morning, Manolios opened
his eyes. He did not remember having had any dream. But his
heart was at peace. He crossed himself, his lips moved, and this
hurt him as though a wound were reopening; but he managed to
say distinctly: "Glory to God!"

He rose and went to sit outside on his bench.

The sun appeared flush with the horizon, red-faced, round, jovial. He was coming back to his rich domains; everything was as
he had left it yesterday evening: the fat plain, the green Mount
of the Virgin, the escarpments of the Sarakina, the round and
brilliant mirror of Lake Voidomata and the especially beloved village, Lycovrissi, with its narrow lanes busy with those ants called
men. With the warmth Manolios's face began to ooze again.

"Glory to God," Manolios murmured once more, wiping his
cleft face with his handkerchief.

Up there on the mountain Manolios was striving, sometimes
with the wood to give it form, sometimes with God or the demon,
sometimes again with Lenio and the widow. At the same time, on
the Sarakina, priest Fotis was putting things in order. He outlined
a task for everyone: there were those who would dig and sow
what little earth remained between the stones, those who would
build, those who would go hunting to bring back hares, wild
rabbits and partridges to feed them all. In addition to the widow's
ewe, he bought three more with Yannakos's three gold pieces;
the children were now provided with milk. He planned also to take
the old icon of Saint George and make a round of the villages and
monasteries, asking for help. "We are Greeks," he repeated,
"Christians, an immortal race: we shall not vanish!"

Down below, in Lycovrissi, Captain Fortounas was still groaning on his bed: his split head was taking time to heal. The Agha, seized with pity, sent his guard constantly with fresh ointment, and with messages telling him to hurry up and get well enough for a good carousal. Old Patriarcheas was not at all well either. He coughed, breathed with difficulty, and kept shivering. After which he would sit up in bed, stuff like a pig, be sick, and start guzzling again. He kept sending to Katerina to ask her to come and massage him. But the widow snapped her fingers at him and sent word in reply that she herself was ill, she, too, needed massage.

Priest Grigoris had serious worries of his own, concerning his only daughter, Mariori. Day by day he saw her melting like a candle; he was impatient to throw her into the arms of Michelis, that she might give him a grandson as soon as possible. It had become his life's most ardent wish. Old priest Grigoris saw in it the one way of conquering Death.

Panayotaros, the Plaster-eater, was also the victim of a dark depression. For three nights now the widow had not opened her door to him; she would have none of him any more; she must certainly be casting her eyes elsewhere. At every moment she would run off to the church—this saintly Mary Magdalen—and light candles. Panayotaros had taken to drink by way of forgetting. Every evening he went home completely drunk, beat his wife and his two daughters and then lay down full length in the yard, which at once rang with his snores. The village urchins fell upon him when they saw him drunk, treading on his heels and goading him with: "Judas! Judas!" He would rush at them to catch them, but stagger, stumble and fall flat.

Every morning old Ladas lectured his wife as she sat in front of him, knitting socks. She never answered, did not even hear what he said.

"He's taking his time, Penelope; that Yannakos is taking his time, the rotten plank! And the receipt for the three pounds still isn't signed. He hasn't yet showed up with a single lot of earrings. What do you think, Penelope? Is there a woman, however poor, who hasn't at least one jewel? No, no, there isn't! God in His mercy wouldn't allow it. You'll see; Yannakos will turn up with the jewels: don't worry, my dear."

Old Ladas's ears kept ringing; he had the impression, every

moment, that there had been a knock at the door; he kept thinking he heard an ass braying. He ran barefoot to open and scanned the road from end to end: not a sign of Yannakos!

Yannakos was finishing his round of the villages, trading combs, reels of cotton, pocket looking glasses and lives of saints against corn, wool and chickens. He went on with his business, but now he had quite different things on his mind. So much so that he actually gave true weight and honest measure. "When is a man saved?" a Moslem saint was once asked. "When," the saint answered, "at the moment of buying and selling, his spirit is in the garden." Yannakos's spirit was in the garden at the moment when he was buying and selling.

From time to time he thought of father Ladas and imagined his cries and lamentations on his return. He remembered also his sister, the shrew who tortured poor Kostandis. Or Manolios, who must have gone back up his mountain, and was probably having great trouble in reconciling Christ and Lenio—the hare and the hounds. But all this only passed through his head: Yannakos's thoughts were centered on priest Fotis, on the arid and inhospitable mountain, on those souls clinging to the stones, from which even Charon could no longer detach them.

In the café of the last village he found his friend the proprietor, Chirogiorgis, also known as Kounelos. He had welcomed Yannakos with delight, helped him unload, led his ass to the stable, and hurried back to entertain his friend and gossip with him. Meanwhile the whole of the little village had collected around Yannakos, that traveled merchant, who went from village to village and brought fresh news. To every question he knew the answer. "Question him, friends, question him," cried the innkeeper, "for tomorrow morning he's off again; and don't forget to order coffee."

Gathered thick about him, they had already begun eagerly asking him what was happening in the world—the great powers, the Bolsheviks, the war, earthquakes . . . They lowered their voices and shuddered. "Yannakos, do you know anything about the Greek troops that came and then vanished again like a flash of lightning? What's happening over there in Greek territory, where our Evzones came from? What massacres, what burnings and what disasters? We here—Lycovrissi and the villages round about—are out of the way, we seldom hear anything. The sound of their lamentation has not pierced through to us, but you,

Yannakos, you get about, you do pick up something; tell us, we do want to know, we're bursting with curiosity."

Yannakos, too, shrank. He could not help thinking of priest Fotis and his village, which the Turks had burned down in revenge, scattering its inhabitants to the four winds . . . From Smyrna as far as Afiuru-hara-Nisar and beyond, whole rows of Greek villages were smoking ruins, the Greeks were a hunted people, Greece was in danger . . .

But Yannakos was sorry for them, and did not want to disturb them.

"Have no fear, friends," he answered; "think of the thousands of years Greece has lived already! She is deathless. Some villages must be burned to the ground, so they say, some men will be killed, but the Evzones will return, they'll build the villages up again, they'll bring fresh children into the world, to people Anatolia once more. Let's have a drink; it's on me."

"Blessings on you, Yannakos," shouted an old man, who was sitting in a corner with his chin resting on his stick, listening open mouthed and taking in the traveled merchant's every word. "Blessings on you, Yannakos! It'd be a sad thing if you stopped visiting our village; you're always welcome because you come with news from the great world."

The hubbub had already subsided, when Ali Agha Soulatzades came into the café. He was the village Elder and carried, slung from his belt, a ring with the keys of all the houses he had rented out. Kounelos's café was his. He had heard about the well-known traveler, put on his red slippers, grabbed up his longest chibouk, and now made his appearance, to talk with the famous merchant. A grave worry was tormenting him. Perhaps that damned Greek could clear the matter up for him.

Yannakos rose, laid his hand on his heart, lips and forehead, to give him the full formal greeting. He was his best customer: he had a large harem, and his wives, daughters and grandchildren loved spices, rouge, scent and sweets. So he rose, greeted him and ordered coffee for him.

"I've a great worry on my mind, my dear merchant."

"Tell me what it is, Agha, and anything I can do . . ."

"What exactly is what they call Switzerland, little Greek?"

Yannakos scratched his head. He too had heard of it, but only very vaguely.

"Why do you ask?" he said, to gain time for reflection.

"Because my son Chouseinis has gone off to Switzerland to study there and become a doctor. I'd like to send him a jar of rice and spinach, and another of charcoal to light his narghile with, but I don't know where Switzerland is, or how to send them."

While the Agha was speaking, there came a twilight in Yannakos, and he remembered.

"Switzerland is a country at the end of the world, which makes milk and watches."

"Does it also make doctors?" asked the Agha uneasily.

"Yes, doctors too, the best in the world. When Charon catches sight of them—how am I to put it, Agha, without shocking the whole café?—yes, then he pisses in his pants."

"Good, little Greek, you've your heart in the right place. But the two jars?"

"Yes, I'll tell you. Switzerland doesn't let charcoal into the country, but you can give me the rice and spinach, I know a way. . . ."

Yannakos had already made his plan. He would take the rice and spinach to the Sarakina, to give the starving people something to eat for Chouseinis's sake.

"I'll go at once and fetch it," said the old man, and got up. He stopped at the café door and hesitated, then turned again to Yannakos.

"And what does it cost to send it to Switzerland?"

"Leave that to me," said Yannakos, and raised his hand. "To do Ali Agha a service."

"It won't do to hang on to it and eat it," the innkeeper burst out, as soon as the Agha had gone.

"God forbid," protested Yannakos. "An honest deal, friend."

Then he turned to the peasants:

"Excuse me, friends," he said, "I'm tired after the journey and I'd like to have a sleep. You can ask me more questions tomorrow and give me your orders and letters. Call your wives and daughters too, when you hear the trumpet, so they can come and make their purchases. Good night."

He leaned against the wall, stretched out his legs and went to sleep.

It might be noon. Having done his business in the villages, Yannakos was approaching Lycovrissi. The ass was trotting gaily; he was already sniffing again his warm stable, his well-stocked rack, his trough full of clear water. His heart was beating like a human heart; already he was lifting his tail, to bray the better.

But his master seized it and pulled it down.

"Don't be in too much of a hurry, Youssoufaki; turn off toward the mountain. We're going to see Manolios first."

Yannakos had treated him roughly the other day, given him hard words, behaved badly to him; and he was sorry. He desired ardently to beg his pardon.

I was right, he thought, but still . . . He's such a sensitive lad, Manolios, the sort you can wound with a feather. Ass that I am, I went at him with a cudgel!

In turn priest Grigoris, old Ladas, Michelis and the widow crossed his mind; he did the round of the whole village but came back to Manolios.

I've not behaved well, not well at all . . . he muttered again. I forgot that the four of us are in this together, all this year. You might say, associates: not for making money, but for making Paradise!

He laughed at his own joke, then became pensive.

Devil take it, he thought, goods and goodness aren't exactly the same, then? No fear. In that case God and the Devil would be the same. God forgive me!

He heard behind him the bray of an ass and turned. It was Christofis, who had ridden up here from the village on his ass. He was old, tough and full of humor. He had been married three times, had brought many children into the world, he couldn't remember how many; some had died, others disappeared, and now he was free and went about laughing and cracking his jokes.

Yannakos stopped and waited for him.

"Good day, old Christofis," he said; "like to do me a favor? Want to do a good deed?"

"Say what it is, and we'll see. I'm tired of doing good deeds, Yannakos."

"Stop a moment on the Sarakina—your way takes you close by —and give this jar to priest Fotis. And if he asks you who gave it to you, tell him: 'A sinner,' that's all."

"What's in it, Yannakos? It's heavy," said old Christofis, and got down off his ass.

"Rice and spinach," he said, and told him the whole story.

Old Christofis burst out laughing.

"Bless you, Yannakos!" he said. "If only God had your talents! Then there'd be no more hungry children and no more hopeless widows in the world. I'll be getting along at once."

"Not so fast, not so fast. I've been away for several days. Is there anything fresh in the village? Is old Ladas still alive?"

"The skinflint avoids death. Much too expensive, see? He gets nothing out of the funeral. But that damned Captain Fortounas is in a bad way."

"Raki will be cheaper," said Yannakos, and laughed.

"Ah, but the barbers will go bankrupt," answered old Christofis.

"Hm. And sleek priest Grigoris?"

"Devil take him, he's alive and doing fine. He's found a new cure for sterile women, they say: long like a sausage, and he sells it by the ell. Take an ell of it, and the worst skinny cow will calve."

Both burst out laughing.

"May you live to be a hundred, old Christofis. If you die, laughter will die out, too. Fare you well, then; I'm going to buy a hundred ells of that sausage and fill the village with young men and maidens."

"Fare you well, Yannakos, And good luck to your business!"

They parted. Shortly afterward old Christofis's voice could be heard, like the clang of a bell:

"The swindler! God came across that sausage a thousand years ago and lent it to Adam!"

So he spoke, and the slope echoed with his laughter.

Standing up, Manolios saw Yannakos climbing toward him and pulling his ass by the bridle. Gathering his courage: "Manolios," he said: "now begins your martyrdom. Stick it out!"

For a moment he thought of going into the hut and sitting down in the darkest corner, for he was ashamed to show himself in the light of day. Again, that morning, he had examined his face in the mirror. "Only a demon," he muttered, "only a demon could be so ugly!" The mouth alone was becoming less swollen: he could at last talk.

Yannakos clambered up the slope, humming a tune; he was looking forward to seeing Manolios and making his peace with him. It was a load to be tipped out; he would be relieved.

Manolios waited for him standing, with his heart fluttering, in the golden light of the ending afternoon. He remembered the lips of the Christ, pressed tight so as not to show His pain; he pressed his own together as tight as he could. I shall get used to it, he told himself; it's difficult at the start, but gradually . . . Christ! Come to my aid!

Yannakos's tune became more and more distinct. Suddenly—joyous, triumphant—the trumpet rang out: Yannakos had paused on a rock and was blowing into his instrument to announce his arrival to his friend.

He's going to come in sight, thought Manolios; he's going to see me. Stick it out, my heart!

"Hey, Manolios, Manolios," cried a joyous voice, "where are you?"

"Here I am," replied Manolios as firmly as he could, and stepped forward.

Yannakos raised his head, opened his arms; but hardly had he seen him than he stopped, confounded, open-mouthed. Unable to believe his eyes, he rubbed them, drew nearer, looked hard and gave a cry:

"Manolios, Manolios, what has happened to you?"

He made as though to embrace him, but was afraid and recoiled, shuddering.

"Yannakos," said Manolios, "if you can't bear it, go back."

He went toward the fold so that Yannakos might no longer see his face.

Yannakos tied his donkey to a bush of holm oak and followed him. Manolios heard his friend approaching.

"Yannakos," he repeated; "if you can't bear it, go back."

"I can, I can . . . " Yannakos answered; "I can. Don't go."

Manolios crossed the threshold, went into the hut, shut the shutter and doubled up in a dark corner. I did stick it, he thought; God be praised! Yannakos came in and squatted on the doorstep. He took off his cap and wiped his forehead. There was a long silence.

"What has happened to you, Manolios?" said Yannakos at last, with his eyes fixed on the ground.

"Nothing," replied Manolios.

"How do you mean, nothing?" cried Yannakos. "A demon's come and settled on your face, Manolios. A demon: it's not you!"

"Yes, it is me," replied Manolios calmly. "In my life I've never been so true."

He was silent a moment.

"In my life! In my life!" he repeated, wiping with his handkerchief his oozing face.

"A demon, I tell you, has settled on you!" cried Yannakos again, struggling against his terror. "When I look at you, I'm frightened of you. Get up and get on the donkey and let's go down to the village."

"Why to the village? I'm all right here."

"You'll go and see priest Grigoris and he'll say a Mass to exorcise the demon."

"No, no; I've one service to ask you, Yannakos. Not a word to anyone."

"I'll only tell the priest, Manolios. If you're ashamed to go down to the village, he'll come up and read his Mass here."

"No, no!" cried Manolios, jumping up in irritation. "I've got to have this sickness on my face, Yannakos; got to have it."

"I don't understand that," cried Yannakos, jumping up in his turn. "Why got to?"

"For my salvation, Yannakos. Otherwise I can't be saved. Don't look at me like that, I can't explain."

"Is it a secret?"

"One that only God knows," replied Manolios, sitting down again in his corner, rather more calmly. "Only God and me. We are agreed."

"And suppose it's the Devil?" Yannakos ventured.

"It is the devil, Yannakos, you guessed right; it's the Devil who set upon me, God be praised; without that, I was lost . . ."

"I don't understand, I don't understand!" repeated Yannakos desperately.

"I didn't, at first. I didn't understand, Yannakos. Later I understood. I was desperate; now I'm calm. And not only calm, but I raise my hand and glorify God."

"You're a saint," murmured Yannakos, suddenly seized with respect.

"I'm a sinner, a great sinner," protested Manolios; "but God is full of mercy."

They fell silent. In the distance the bells of the flock could be heard; the dogs were barking. The sun was sinking in the west, the hut was invaded by great blue shadows. The ass, vexed at not seeing his master, began braying plaintively.

"Can you eat?" asked Yannakos.

"Only milk, through a straw."

"Have you any pain, anywhere?"

"No, nowhere . . . Heaven protect you; go, Yannakos; that's enough; but give me your word you'll say nothing to anyone. It's necessary—understand?—for me to stay here and fight alone."

"Against the demon?"

"Against the demon."

"And if he wins?"

"He won't win; have no fear. God is with me."

"You're a saint," Yannakos murmured again; "you don't need anyone. Good health! I shall come back and see you, I'd best tell you."

"Can you bear it, Yannakos?"

"I can, I can . . . See you soon!"

For a moment he had an odd impulse to clutch Manolios's hand and kiss it, but he controlled himself. He went out, untied his donkey, whose tail wagged with pleasure, and without a glance back started on his way down, pensively.

"What a mystery the world is," he muttered as he scrambled down the slope, "what a great mystery. You can't tell the good God from the Devil. There's many times, God forgive me, they look just the same!"

Next day, before dawn, Manolios kicked awake Nikolio, who was sleeping in the fold, lying blissfully on his back.

"Nikolio, get up! I want you to do something for me!"

The young shepherd's fine-featured head was raised, still dazed. The eyelids opened and the white of his eyes gleamed, timid, in the twilight.

"What you want?" he growled, yawning.

"Get up, get up! I'll tell you when you're awake. . . . Hop to it!"

The boy got up, grumbling. As he stretched he laid bare a

bronze belly. His arms, thighs and calves were covered with black, shining hair. He smelled of thyme and goat.

"Make your sign of the cross," said Manolios. "Even if you don't ever do that, you must do it today."

"Never mind that, master," said Nikolio, still stretching, and making his joints crack; "what good does it do?"

On the mountain where he had grown up among the rams, he had never had the slightest wish to make the sign of the cross. Any more than to go to church. What need had he, Nikolio, of all that? What he wanted was to be well, to marry when the moment came, have children, have some sheep of his own and grow old solidly and leafily like a holm oak. Signs of the cross and Holy Virgins were for the people down below.

Manolios sat on the doorstep waiting for Nikolio to wash and wake up completely. In the dark he had taken a terrible decision. He had not closed an eye all night; God and the demon had been fighting in him. At dawn, God having won, Manolios had got up and gone to kick his shepherd boy awake.

"Here I am," said Nikolio, smoothing his hair into place with both hands. "I'm awake. Now tell me what you want me to do."

"Nikolio," said Manolios in a low voice, "listen carefully; if you're afraid, don't look at me, look into the distance; but listen carefully to what I'm going to say."

"I'm listening," said Nikolio, turning to one side.

"You'll go down to the village, you'll go to the big master's house. It's day, the door will be open, you'll go in. You'll cross the courtyard and turn right, on the ground floor, where the loom is. There you'll find my betrothed, Lenio."

"Lenio?" said Nikolio, turning sharply, his eye lighting up.

"You'll find Lenio and you'll say to her . . . listen to my words carefully, Nikolio, carve them in your head: 'Manolios sends you his greetings and asks you to be so good as to come up to the mountain. He has something to say to you.' That's all. You'll say that, and you'll leave at once. Understand?"

"I understand, it's easy. I'm going."

He was moving already, impatient to go down to the village.

"Wait, you wild goat!" said Manolios, seizing him by the arm. "If she asks you how I am, say I'm well. Above all don't reveal that I'm ill, or it'll be the worse for you!"

"Don't worry, master, don't worry. I'll say: 'He's all right,' and I'll take to my heels."

"Run along!'

Nikolio darted off and disappeared.

Lenio was up already; she had made a tisane laced with rum and was mounting the staircase to take it to her master, old Patriarcheas. Blooming and with her hair fluffed out, she climbed the stone steps, warbling like a titmouse.

The old archon, seated on a soft mattress, was looking out of the window at the roofs of the village below him. His mind reviewed all the villagers, knocked at their doors, went in, said a kind word of condescension and pushed on. He walked up the mountain, passed quickly over the sheep, came to Manolios and lost his temper. "Ever hear the like? that dirty lackey, holding out against me! His soul, he says . . . his soul's not ready. Well, my poor fellow, if you don't marry Lenio by the end of April, out you go, I'll pack you off back to the monastery like a eunuch. You trample on the bread I've given you, you little swine! It's you who've turned my son's head, it's you, you beggar, who take pity on the poor—they're men too, you say, they're our brothers! All that's very fine when it's said in church, when the priest pronounces it on Sunday from the pulpit. But you blessed sucker, you must be completely cracked to put it in practice!"

The door opened and in came Lenio with the tisane. The thoughts of old Patriarcheas immediately left his son and his shepherd to settle on the sprightly seductive girl, bringing him his sage tea with such a swing of the hips. He narrowed his eyelids and watched her approach, admiring the impertinent breasts, the slim waist, the firm joints. What am I to do with you, you blessed bitch, he thought, since I believe you are my daughter? Your mother, too, was frisky like you, when she was young, God keep her soul! and one night . . . The archon stroked his mustache and sighed.

"How are you feeling today, master?" said Lenio cajolingly. "What makes you sigh?"

"Isn't there cause for sighing, my good Lenio? My fine fellow of a son and Manolios have skinned me between them. They tell me you went to the mountain the day before yesterday to look for him; what did the noodle tell you?"

"What do you suppose he told me, master?" said Lenio, sighing in her turn and sitting down on the edge of the bed at the old man's feet. "It's as if he'd been bewitched. He said things I couldn't make head or tail of; he couldn't find the words. Instead of looking at me like a man, he kept his eyes cast down or else raised them to Heaven and rolled them. What am I to say, master? Perhaps if you took him to priest Grigoris to have the exorcism read over him? Don't laugh: Manolios isn't at all himself, master!"

The old bogy watched Lenio fidgeting and blushing. He heaved a deep sigh.

"You love him, eh?" he asked, and began noisily drinking his tea.

"What do you expect, master? You gave him to me, he's my man. If you'd given me another, he'd have been my man. For me, you know, one man's like another."

"The old ones as well, Lenio?" asked her master, winking.

"No, indeed!" the girl answered flatly, bridling; "only the young ones."

"Up to what age?" the old man insinuated.

"As long as they can have children," Lenio answered without hesitation. She seemed to have already thought out these problems and passed a final judgment on them.

"Good, you've a brain as sharp as a razor, Lenio. Remember what I'm telling you: you know what you want; you'll go far."

The girl laughed and rose. She took the empty cup and went back to the door; but the old man stopped her.

"What's the date today? April the—?" he asked.

Lenio counted on her fingers: Sunday, Monday, Tuesday . . .

"The twenty-seventh, master."

"Good. Must wait three more days for his Excellency Manolios to deign to give us his answer. If he's fool enough to refuse such a king's morsel, don't worry, Lenio, I'll find you a better husband, a real one who won't have souls and such-like nonsense —and who'll fill your yard with children. There, run along. I propose to get up today and go to church, then take a walk around the village . . . Bring me clean clothes."

The old horror, Lenio muttered as she went down the stairs,

chuckling as if she were being tickled, he devoured me with his eyes . . . By my faith, if he weren't my father, I'd have egged the old man on to marry me; never mind if he couldn't produce children. What's it matter, there's others can. But the Devil's turned everything upside down. But, never mind! Manolios isn't so bad as that!

At this moment Nikolio appeared on the doorstep; he was hot, his body was steaming, and a smell of thyme spread through the yard. He was like a he-goat on its hind legs, or perhaps a young archangel in a rage.

When she saw him, Lenio stopped, seized with fear.

"Who's that?" she muttered; "how good he smells! What do you want?" she cried. "Is it you, Nikolio?"

"Me, Nikolio," the shepherd boy echoed in a voice just breaking.

"I can't believe it, you're a real man now! Growing a mustache already! What's brought you here?"

"Manolios sent me, this morning early, to tell you something, so here I am!"

"Manolios?" said Lenio, approaching Nikolio with her heart throbbing. "Don't shout, you're not up on the mountain. Speak more softly here. What did he tell you to tell me?"

"Well, he said like this: Greetings from Manolios; be so good as to come up to the mountain; he's something to say to you."

"Is that all? Well, you can tell him I'll come. Wait, don't go. And how is he?"

"He's all right, quite all right!" cried Nikolio, taking to his heels and leaving a bitter fragrance behind him.

At this moment Michelis came out into the yard. In rich Sunday clothes and carefully shaved and combed, he was making ready to go and listen to the Gospel in church and see Mariori. Standing in the middle of the yard, he shone like an angel. Lenio remained motionless a moment, all admiration. "That's what my father must have been like in his youth," she thought, "a Saint George!"

"Good morning, Lenio," said Michelis, putting on the *kalpak* he had in his hand. "I'm going to church."

"May it do you good," replied Lenio, mockingly. "Go straight there, master, don't take a wrong turning."

"You'll take a wrong turning, that's sure. You'll go straight to Manolios, I'm thinking," said Michelis, who had caught sight of the messenger just as he was making himself scarce. "You needn't grumble."

"I'm not grumbling—who said I was?" the girl retorted, stung to the quick. "We're human too, we servants, eh! The good God keeps us from needing to grumble. And if Manolios put your clothes on, master, he, too, would make a handsome archon."

"You're right, Lenio," Michelis answered as he crossed the threshold. "Yes, you're right; the clothes are the only thing that separates us."

The bell began ringing for Mass.

"Well, I'm off, Lenio. Bring us back good news from the mountain."

The church was balmy with wax and incense. On the iconostasis the icons gleamed softly; the walls, from flagged floor to cupola, were illuminated with saints and with angels' wings of many colors. Going into this ancient Byzantine church was like losing oneself in a Paradise full of fantastic birds and of flowers the height of a man, with angels like gigantic bees flying from flower to flower to take their booty. At the high point of the vault, fierce and menacing, the Almighty sat throned over the heads of mankind.

Below, on the stones, the faithful—men in front, women at the back—hummed: they too were bees. They came and bowed down before the icons, sniffed at them, then stood rapt in ecstasy, listening to the chanting. Beyond the bench with its dishes and candles, the stalls of the notables. No one expected old Patriarcheas to come. As for Captain Fortounas, poor fellow, just now he was tacking in his bed, and groaning. The only ones present today were the schoolmaster, with his spectacles and white collar, and by his side father Ladas, bitter-lipped. Last evening Yannakos had brought him bad news: those people in rags, who had been wandering in the highways and byways for three months, had sold, so he said, the last of their jewels; they had nothing left but bare fingers. What was the use of fingers, father Ladas? No more than of ears without earrings. He cursed fate. I've no luck, he grumbled, as he stood there, beyond the bench. The destroyed village ought to have been near Lycovrissi, so that I could get there in time . . . What use is it to me that it was burned? Devil take it!

The faithful kept coming in, placing a coin in the dish, taking a candle, crossing themselves and moving toward the iconostasis. Old Ladas's spirit was far away. Lucky he signed the receipt for the three pounds, the idiot. If it had been I . . .

But he had no time to follow up his train of thought. A heavy bulk came in and sat down close to him, making the stall creak. He turned peevishly, and saw old Patriarcheas, with pale and flabby cheeks, eyes dead and lips yellow and dry. That greasy fat pig will never die, he thought. Turning round properly, he greeted him.

"Wishing you better health, archon," he whispered faintly, then plunged again into his cares.

When Michelis entered, he lit up the church. He was late, having stopped to see Mariori, who was waiting for him. She was alone in the house, except for the deaf and devoted old nurse.

"You've been a long time," said Mariori, posted behind the door.

She, too, was dressed in her best. A necklace of gold pieces, left her by her mother, gleamed on her neck; she had made up her cheeks slightly with the rouge brought back the day before by Yannakos. But her eyes were subdued as if she had been crying, and a dark blue ring went around them. She held a handkerchief, and put it to her mouth from time to time.

"Why did you send for me?" began Michelis, worried; "why are you upset, Mariori?"

"Father's in a hurry," replied Mariori, lowering her eyes. "He's in a hurry; he wants us to get married."

"Didn't we settle on Christmas, Mariori? It's not yet a year since my mother died; it wouldn't be suitable."

"He's in a hurry," the girl repeated in an undertone. "He makes a scene every day; he gets up in the middle of the night and strides up and down and can't sleep."

"Why? What's the matter that he's in such a hurry?"

"I don't know, Michelis, I don't know." Mariori murmured, with a tremor in her voice.

She knew quite well why the old man was so impatient, but did not dare confess it. Deep down in her undermined body she perceived that her father was right, that they must be quick.

"My father didn't love my mother," said Michelis. "She was older than he, she had aged, she scolded him . . . He was sick of it, and so he wasn't sorry when she died. All the same, he daren't quite go against custom, and it's not yet a year. And he is archon of the village, must set an example. You understand, Mariori?"

"I understand, I understand. But father's getting impatient, I tell you, and he blames me. I can't bear it any more!"

She felt her cough rising, held it back and put her handkerchief to her mouth. Her little hand trembled in Michelis's moist palm.

Michelis looked at her suddenly in alarm. She had grown terribly thin. Under her downy skin the bones were sharp. Her face forecast a death mask.

"Mariori . . ." he murmured, pressing her hand and holding her to his breast, "Mariori. . . ."

It was as if she were going away from him and he could not hold her back, as if she were now only a handful of earth and were bidding him farewell.

"My Michelis," said the young girl, trying not to cry, "my Michelis, you must go now. Go to church. I'll come myself in a moment. We're late. Go. May God lay His hand upon us!"

She took his hand and held it against her breast, for some time.

"May God lay His hand upon us!" she murmured once more, then went in hastily and threw herself, almost fainting, into the arms of her nurse.

Michelis opened the door softly and walked with great strides to the church, with a tightening of the heart and throat.

He remained standing near his father's stall. The old man turned and admired him. That's what I was like, he thought, that's what I was like once. You jade, life! gone like a fairy tale!

Meanwhile Lenio had done her hair. She had sprinkled orange water on it and within her bodice, arranged on her head the yellow kerchief with the red fringe which her master had given her at Easter, and then gone out through the lanes of the village to the path leading up to the Mount of the Virgin.

Mass was over, the villagers had scattered over the square in their Sunday clothes, with their Sunday souls: they were walking up and down. Some of them, in the Café Kostandis, were drinking and laughing.

The Agha was smoking his narghile on his balcony. On his right he had Hussein with his trumpet, on his left Youssoufaki, who poured out his drink and munched his mastic. Narrowing his rheumy eyes, the old Agha watched the villagers in the square below, as the shepherd looks down on his flock, with condescension and solicitude. He knew that he was a man and the others were sheep. The Agha allowed them to feed in peace that they might provide him with wool, milk and meat.

Lenio clambered up the mountain with a light heart. She suspected what Manolios wanted. This week they would have the wedding: all that waiting over and done with, real life was about to begin—in the daytime the work of house and kitchen, at night the embrace and, at the end of nine months—hush-a-bye baby . . . I shan't be a servant any longer, I shall be a wife and mother . . .

She liked Manolios: a peaceable lad, hard-working, handsome, with his fair beard, blue eyes and tender expression—a real Christ. Her heart had wings, went up the mountain quicker than she could, reached the sheepfold, fluttered all round it, perched on Manolios's shoulder like a plump, tame partridge with red claws, and lovingly pecked at his nape and throat.

At this moment he must be sitting on the jutting stone at the end of the path and waiting for me. I expect his heart's flown off, like mine, she thought.

And it was true—Manolios had sat down on the jutting stone, incessantly wiping his swollen face, whose sores had reopened and were running.

I'm sorry for her, poor thing, I'm sorry for her, he said to himself, but it's got to be done. I've got to redeem myself from all temptation; my soul's got to be purified, my body's got to be purified, I've got to become worthy . . .

He cocked his ear, heard her quick, light step and smelled a scent of orange blossom in the air, her scent; his nostrils twitched.

She's coming, she's coming, he thought. Here she is, here she is!

The yellow kerchief came in sight. Lenio paused for an instant and shaded her eyes. On the jutting stone she saw her betrothed waiting for her, with bent head; she came on more slowly.

Here she is! repeated Manolios. He raised his head, stood up, and remained still.

Lenio pretended not to see him, so that he might bound forward, as his custom was, and seize her by the waist to help her, so he said, to climb up . . . But today Manolios stayed and did not move at all.

"Manolios!" she cried, unable to contain herself any longer.

Manolios did not answer. He stood on his rock, silent, without stirring.

Lenio began to run, drew near, raised her head, saw him and gave a cry:

"Holy Virgin!" She collapsed.

Manolios came down and picked her up. She covered her eyes with her left arm, and with her right warded him off.

"Go away! Go away!" she cried, stridently, "go away!"

"Look at me once more, Lenio," said Manolios softly; "look at me: then you'll loathe me forever and be rid of me . . ."

"No, no!" cried the poor girl, "go away!"

Manolios drew back and went and sat down again on the rock. Both of them remained for quite a while without speaking. Lenio was the first to break the silence.

"What is it?" she cried. "In heaven's name, tell me, what is it?"

"Leprosy . . ." answered Manolios tranquilly.

Lenio shuddered and turned her head toward the village.

"I'm going," she said. "Is that why you sent for me?"

"Yes, that's why," answered Manolios, still calm. "Can you marry me now? You can't. Do you want leprous children? You don't. Leave me."

Again they remained without a word. And suddenly the young girl was shaken with violent sobbing.

"Fare thee well, Lenio," said Manolios, turning his back on her to return to the sheepfold; "good-bye!"

Lenio did not reply. She wiped her eyes with her fine yellow kerchief and looked about her, numbed, not knowing where to go. Manolios had disappeared, the earth was a desert, turning without aim.

The sun was at midcourse: nothing could be heard but the bells of the sheep coming in to lie in the holm oak shade. For a moment a flute sang in the solitude, but almost at once fell silent on a plaintive tone.

"Leprosy . . . leprosy . . ." Lenio kept repeating with horror. In the overwhelming heat of noon she was shivering.

How long she stayed there, doubled up among the stones, she

could not have told . . . It seemed centuries, but it must have been only a few moments; for when she rose to go, the sun was still motionless at the summit of the sky.

The flute played again, plaintive, joyous, insidious, like another soul unable to bear the solitude.

Fascinated, not knowing what she was doing, Lenio walked toward the calling flute. It was as if she heard her name, was being asked for it. She went tottering, breathing in gasps. After a few steps she listened. The flute was nearer, more caressing, more beseeching: it was calling her, drawing her . . . She could not resist any more.

All at once, under a majestic holm oak which had grown in a hollow of the mountain, she saw sheep lying, leaning their throats on the ground to get a little coolness. Only two were still standing, as if inclined to chase and butt one another. Near them, standing, the shepherd boy, half naked, was gamboling and dancing with them, with a long flute pressed between his lips. From time to time he took the flute from his mouth and gave wild cries, clapped his hands, made bleating noises and then started playing again, louder, ever louder.

Spellbound, Lenio advanced hesitantly. The shepherd boy had his back turned to her: he could not see her. Lenio could now make out the whole scene: a ram with a heavy black fleece and twisted horns was pursuing a white ewe, trying to mount her, and she to escape. The ram reared up in fury, seized her again with his front feet and fell forward onto her with a feeble moan, as though beseeching her. The young shepherd followed the love fight: he leaped, danced and, with tender cries, joined the ram in beseeching.

"Go it, Dassos! climb on her, Dassos!" he yelled, and started again to play the flute.

Lenio, with no breath left, had come up right behind the little shepherd. Like the ewes, her tongue was hanging out and she was panting. Her breasts were hurting.

Exhausted, as though she, too, could no longer master her desire, the ewe suddenly stopped still. Dassos was on her with a bound and covered her completely. His tongue was hanging out; he began to lick her neck and bite. All his wool was bathed in sweat; the air was stifling, filled with the smell of male.

Nikolio threw down his flute, tore off his remaining clothes and began, stark naked and covered with sweat, to dance and sway like the ram.

The veins on Lenio's throat stood out, and her eyes darkened. All of a sudden, in his dance, Nikolio turned; he saw her, darted on her, and threw her to the ground up against the ram and the ewe.

Death of the Captain

Poor Captain Fortounas isn't at all well, Agha. The bones of his skull won't stick together again. The things we've done to them! The ointments, the pomades—and even priest Grigoris come in person to read prayers. A gipsy, too, has been and dealt the cards. They've lit a candle up at Saint Penteleimon the Healer's. He's been given a cat's parts to eat—it's said they have nine lives. And all for nothing! Neither God nor Devil wants our dead captain to get well."

The word "dead" had somehow escaped mother Mandalenia. She bit her tongue.

"May the fiend's ear be deaf," she muttered, and her tongue set off again merrily. "Today he sent for Michelis, the archon's son, so he could dictate to him his will, says he. And now, Agha, I'm on my way to fetch priest Grigoris to give him the Holy Sacrament. He's weighed anchor, our captain has, he's getting ready to sail. A moment ago he called me and said: 'Aunt Mandalenia, do me the kindness of going to the Agha and saying to him: all greetings from Captain Fortounas-Greenhorn: he's setting sail'—says he— 'and he's off; good-bye!' So I've come, Agha. Mother Mandalenia, that's me."

Sleepy, with puffy eyes, sagging cheeks and bare feet, uncombed, unwashed, the Agha was sitting on his sofa drinking coffee to wake himself up. He listened to mother Mandalenia as one listens to rain. When she had stopped, the Agha lazily opened his mouth:

"And his brain?" he asked in the midst of a yawn.

"It's working all right, Agha. A regular clock."

He was silent again. He felt slack and gave another yawn.

"Is he frightened?" he asked, with his mouth still open.

"Not a bit of it, the dear man, not a bit of it, Agha. You talk to him of God, and he laughs; you talk to him of the Devil, and he laughs at that too. God forgive me, he doesn't care that much for one or t'other."

"Does he drink?"

"He drinks, but not much."

"Good. When I've waked up, tell him, I'll come and say good-bye to him. Tell him also that I'll bring with me my guard, Hussein, to sound the trumpet. I'll bring Youssoufaki, too, tell him, to sing him his favorite *amané*—he knows which one. I've got to the coffee, then I'll have my chibouk and raki, and Youssoufaki will come and massage my feet and I shall wake up. Then I'll come down . . . Wait, listen: don't let him go and die before I arrive—you tell him that! He's to wait for me. Off with you now!"

Yellow, thin as a lath, with his bones sticking through his tanned skin and his head tightly bound in a wide red sash, stiff with dried blood, the captain lay on his bed with his back to the wall, calm, fearless, unrepenting. His little eyes sparkled maliciously, agile like those of the monkey he had once seen at Odessa.

Near him on a small table stood the raki and a chibouk; also a plaster statuette of Queen Victoria, which he had bought once upon a time in a distant port. A virago, he had said to himself, nice and fat, an ample bosom—I like her . . . and he had bought it. Since then he had always kept it by him. "She's my wife," he would say, and burst out laughing; "she has more mustache than I have, but what does that matter? I like her."

He turned his eyes and surveyed his poor hovel: dirty walls, beams covered with cobwebs, empty shelves, a long chest full of old clothes, old slippers, flannel waistcoats and junk, a water jug in a niche, a demijohn of raki in one corner. He rested his gaze a good while on each object, to bid it good-bye. On an old photograph pinned to the wall facing his bed, his eyes rested a long time. It showed his defunct ship—all sails set, the Greek flag at the poop and a siren with bare breasts on the prow. He himself stood there, a thirty-year-old captain, holding the tiller. In imagination he went aboard; the ship weighed anchor in the photograph stained with fly-droppings and stood out to sea. But a heavy mist had come down—Captain Fortounas could make out, very vaguely, islands and coasts, Turks wearing the fez on the mole, bare-breasted women like figureheads and, in port, taverns where you stifled in the fumes of cigarettes, chibouks and fried fish.

Everything had darkened, the joys along with the pains he had lived through, the wounds he had received when in the war of '97 he had volunteered with his boat to smuggle munitions and victuals into Greece. Once he had fallen in love and nearly lost his head—a Turkish girl, he couldn't recall her name now, or where . . . was it Constantinople? Smyrna? Aïvali? Alexandria? Was she called Chioulsoum? Fatima? Ermine? He couldn't remember. A thick fog was falling on this world below; from all his life one event alone emerged, bathed in light, through this opaque mist: the day when, at Batoum, in April, on Saint George's day, he had gone with three friends into a garden full of huge, dark-red flowers. They had sat down on some pebbles and begun to eat and drink, and to sing. They'd had their heads swathed in fringed turbans. The sun was blazing, the sea was balmy; no woman was with them. There were just the three of them, all fine sparks, fair-haired or dark. One of them was called George and this was his day. And lo and behold, as they were eating and drinking and singing, a light rain began to fall, fine and mild, purifying the huge leaves and speckling the pebbles in the gardens. The earth in turn smelled good, like the sea. Three Armenians had presented themselves, with mandolin, hautboy and tambourine. They squatted on the ground under the dark flowers and started singing *amanés*.

How delightful it had been, how gentle! Life had chirruped in the palm of man like a little, warm bird . . . Captain Fortounas racked his brain, but could remember nothing else. Nothing else. Decidedly his whole life had dispersed in smoke. That pleasure party and the light rain of Batoum had survived alone.

Well! is that all it is? he muttered; only that, the whole of my life? A little fine rain, three friends, a few red flowers. It's enough to make you lose your bearings: nothing else has happened to me! And me who thought I'd swallowed the world!

He stretched out his hand to take his glass of raki from the small table, but at this moment the door opened and in came the Agha. He had on his grand uniform with the red breeches, the silver pistols, and fine new leggings; a silk handkerchief floated under his arm, as if he were going to a wedding. Behind him came Youssoufaki, white and fresh as good bread, half asleep, munching. After him, fierce and scowling, came Hussein with his trumpet.

"Wishing you a calm sea and a fair wind, Captain Fortounas!" cried the Agha, briskly. "So you've gone on board, they tell me, and you're off!"

"Sails set, Agha, a following wind, good-bye!"

"And where the devil are you bound for, you blessed old Greenhorn?" said the Agha laughing and flopping down onto the old chest. "What's your idea, leaving this world? Stay a little longer. A few days ago they brought me some more raki—exquisite, my friend, a spirit with black mulberries soaking in it. That's all I'm going to say. Stay and drink it with me, you can go afterward."

"Good-bye, I'm telling you, Agha, it's all over. I've weighed anchor, taken hold of the tiller, and I'm setting sail. Drink it by yourself."

"And where are you bound for, my poor friend? Do you know where you're bound for?"

"The devil only knows. I'm bound where the wind sends me, that's it!"

"And that *romnoi* religion of yours? What's it got to say?"

"Olalala!" answered the captain with a wave of his hand; "if I'm to believe my religion, I'm making straight for the Devil's."

The Agha laughed.

"If I'm to believe mine, I shall go straight to Paradise. It's stuffed with pilaff, women and Youssoufakis! But tell me, Captain; suppose both our religions were fooling us? This world's a dream, life is raki, one drinks and one gets drunk. Our brains veer with the wind: you play the *romnios,* I the Turkish agha. Let that alone. Greenhorn—to tell you the truth, it worries me!"

He turned to the pretty boy:

"Get up, Youssoufaki, my eye has spied a demijohn over there in the corner; get up and pour us out drinks."

Old Mandalenia came in, leaned over the captain and whispered in his ear:

"Captain, the priest will be here in a moment with the Holy Sacrament; don't go drinking raki."

"What priest, old witch? Shut up! Take the demijohn and serve us."

The old woman groaned. With a trembling hand she filled the glasses. The Agha stood up, approached the bed and clinked glasses with the captain:

"A fair journey, Greenhorn!"

"A fair journey to you, Agha!"

They laughed. Both of them felt good.

"Captain," said the Agha, wiping his mustache, "if our Mahomet and your Christ had drunk raki and clinked glasses like us two, they'd have become two friends, and they wouldn't be spoiling to scratch each others' eyes out. Through not drinking, they've rolled the world in blood. Think, how did you and I become friends, eh, Captain? Haven't we had a good time? Haven't we taken things easy?"

"Here's the priest coming to give me communion, Agha," said the captain, whose head was beginning to spin. "Good-bye!"

"Wait, friend, don't be in such a hurry. I've brought you Youssoufaki to sing you your favorite *amanés* you like as you cast off. Won't do to leave without a song. Dear old friend . . . Come, Youssoufaki, out with your *amanés*, my little one!"

Youssoufaki took the ball of mastic out of his mouth, stuck it on his knee and languorously leaned his right hand against his cheek. He was opening his mouth when the Agha stretched out his arm.

"Wait, my treasure," he said. "First the trumpet must sound."

He turned to his bodyguard.

"Open the door," he ordered. "Stand on the threshold and sound the charge."

Hussein opened the door, put his trumpet to his lips and began blowing fit to burst.

"That's enough!" cried the Agha. "Your turn, Youssoufaki; now give us our *amanés!*"

Once more the small, clear, passionate voice arose. The captain listened hard, and his breast filled with regret and sweetness. "*Dounia tabir, rouya tabir* . . . World and dream are but one, *aman, aman!*"

Never had the captain felt so deeply how world and dream are but one. He must surely have fallen asleep and dreamed that he was a captain and had plied between the ports of the White Sea and the Black Sea, that he had gone to war, that he was Greek and Christian and that now, so it appeared, he was passing away. But no, he wasn't dying, he was waking up, the dream was over, day was breaking.

He stretched out his hand soberly:

"Thank you, friend Agha, you alone have understood my torments. Good-bye, you too, Youssoufaki; may your little mouth never rot, may it change into rubies under the earth."

The Agha was moved. He wiped his eyes.

"Go, dear old captain. And if I've sometimes called you Greenhorn, you know it was from affection. Must forgive me. There, a fair voyage!"

He leaned over and kissed him. The eyes of both were filled with tears.

"Well, I never knew how fond I was of you, dear Agha," said the dying man in sorrowful tones. "Fare you well!"

They parted. Once aside, the Agha turned to his bodyguard:

"Play a charge once more to give the captain back his courage. I want the whole village to know that everyone's to be present for his burial. A pillar of the village is crumbling."

The sky was covered with light summer clouds. A few drops of rain fell.

"Let's hurry, my children," exclaimed the Agha. "I've my new clothes on."

All three began to run.

Michelis met them; he was carrying paper and an inkwell.

"Agha, how is he, our captain?"

"Well, young man. Better off, indeed, than us living. Look sharp!"

Old Mandalenia opened the door wide. She was expecting the priest with the Holy Sacrament; instead of the priest, Michelis appeared, breathless.

"Needn't hurry, my son," the old woman whispered to him. "He's still holding out; he's a grip on life, has the dead one."

Michelis entered; she closed the door behind him.

The captain was exhausted and had closed his eyes. The blood had begun again dripping onto his cheeks and onto the sheets. The old woman approached, wiped him and whispered in his ear:

"Captain, Michelis has come with the pen and ink; make an effort."

The captain raised his split head and opened his eyes. "Welcome to his young lordship," he said.

He closed his eyes again and went to sleep. Michelis sat down on the chest, put the papers down near him and waited.

"A good man he was, poor thing," said the old woman in a low voice, wiping her eyes and her running nose. "A good man for all his cross manner. My late husband, too . . . " and she began, in muted tones, the story of her misfortunes. It seemed to bring her relief. Michelis rolled a cigarette and began to smoke. He had misfortunes of his own, but he confided them to nobody. He listened to the old woman, but his spirit was far away.

A dog barked plaintively close by. The old woman got up angrily:

"Accursed animal! He must have seen Charon, to bark like that!"

She opened the door, picked up a stone, threw it, and came back. The captain opened his eyes.

"Michelis," he said, "where are you? Come nearer. I can't speak very loud now. Take a piece of paper and write!"

"Don't tire yourself, Captain," said Michelis. "There's no hurry."

"Write, I tell you, and keep your consolations. Out of nine lives, eight have gone. There's only one left, and here it is on my lips, ready to go, too. Look sharp, write while there's a little life left in me."

Michelis approached the pillow, unfolded his paper and dipped the pen into the ink.

"I'm listening, Captain."

"To begin with, write down that I'm in my right mind and that I'm an Orthodox Christian. My father was called Theodore Kapandais. I've no children, or nephews, or dogs; I'm not married, I had a lucky escape, God be praised! I had some money; I've eaten it. I had some fields; I sold them and ate them, too. No, I didn't eat them, I drank them. I had a boat, too, the one there in the photograph: it was wrecked off Trebizond and went to the bottom. There's what's left to me, all in all!" he said, pointing to the wreckage around him.

"I want to share them out between the poor and my friends, so they'll remember me. Aunt Mandalenia, sit yourself by my side and say them over to me as they come. Anything I forget will be for you. There; write, Michelis. Ready?"

"Ready, Captain."

"The demijohn of raki here, in the corner, I leave to the Agha: let him empty it to my health. Let my gold tooth be pulled out and given to the widow Katerina, to make a gold earring of. My chibouk with the amber end I give to the Café Kostandis: when a stranger of mark comes, he shall smoke it to make him forget his village. The ten kilos of barley I've got left I bequeath to Yannakos's ass: let him eat them on the evening when he enters Jerusalem with Christ on his back. The two or three coins remaining in my purse—let priest Grigoris take them, otherwise he won't bury me, the old goat's-beard, and I shall rot; that's all for that. In the chest there are some rugs, some oilskins, some old caps, whites, captain's boots, a dark lantern, a compass and some bits of junk. Give the lot to the poor people living in the caves on the Sarakina. Give them also my pots and pans, my stove, my crockery and the clothes I've got on. Yes, and also the coffee, the sugar, the onions, the bottle of oil, the cheese and the pot of olives. The lot, the lot: I'm sorry for those poor people!

"Have you written it all down, Michelis?"

"Wait a moment while I catch up. Don't be in such a hurry, Captain."

"I'm in a hurry, young man, for fear I mayn't finish in time. Write quickly. I also have a book, *The Arabian Nights*. Used to read a story from it on Sundays when the others went to church; it helped pass the time. Kostandis of the Café can come and take it, and on Sundays, after Gospel, when the village people come to the café, let one of them read it aloud—it'll open your eyes, you poor souls. I don't say the Gospel's not very fine, but *The Arabian Nights* is worth two of it. Have you written it down, Michelis?"

"I've written it, Captain. Go on, but don't tire yourself."

"Look around, mother Mandalenia. Look all around the house. Is there some precious jewel I've forgotten?"

"Your slippers, Captain."

"Pf! they're down-at-heel, fit for the rubbish heap. Wait, I'm going to leave them to old Ladas, poor wretch. Every time I used to go and see him I found him barefoot. Let him take them, the old close-fist; can't have him catching cold and dying, the gem of our village! Have another look, Mandalenia."

"The photograph."

"Ah, that I'm taking with me. You'll put it on my tomb, in its frame. I'm taking my raki glass too; it's served me so well, I can't leave it behind. Ah, there's also this plaster statuette. Plaster-eater shall have it, then after all the others he can eat the Queen of England."

"There's still the most important thing," said Michelis, "the house."

"The house I bequeath to the old woman here present, to Mandalenia, who's behaved to me like a real sister. I've put her through some scenes, poor woman, I've sworn at her more times than many. I think she's even had a good few blows with the stick. Mustn't blame me, mother Mandalenia. Don't cry—unless it's joy you're crying for?"

He tried to laugh but could not; he was in pain. He began bleeding once more.

"There's all my fortune," he said. "Finish writing and pass me the paper for me to put my name at the bottom."

Michelis brought the paper, the old woman held the captain up and Michelis guided his hand. He signed: "Captain Yakoumis Kapandais, son of Theodore."

Religious chanting came to their ears.

"Here's the priest with the Holy Sacrament," said the old woman, running to open both leaves of the door.

"Another sort of bother," the captain muttered; "come on, let's get it over."

The old beadle came in first with a lighted lantern; behind him came priest Grigoris, wearing his stole and lifting high the Holy Chalice under a cover of gold-embroidered red velvet.

"Here cometh the Lord!" he said solemnly as he crossed the threshold. "Leave us alone."

Michelis and mother Mandalenia crossed themselves, kissed the priest's hand and withdrew. The beadle waited outside with his lantern.

"Captain Fortounas," said the priest, approaching the dying man, "the terrible moment has come, when you will present yourself before the Lord. Confess your sins, purify your soul, speak!"

"How am I to tell you my sins, priest?" replied the captain angrily. "D'you suppose I can remember them? The good God has a book where He writes them down. All He's got to do is to rub out what's written there, if He has a mind to. There's something I'd have liked to bring Him as a present from the earth. I doubt if there's anything like it to be found in Heaven."

The priest listened with embarrassment. The captain's tone set him on edge.

"Just one thing," the captain insisted, "that I'd have liked to bring as a present to the good God."

"What?" asked the priest with a frown.

"A sponge."

"Aren't you ashamed? Aren't you even frightened at this terrible moment, impious man?"

"We're ants," the captain went on, imperturbably; "we've eaten a grain of corn too many, one dead fly more than our share—what's it matter? Rub it out! Aren't you ashamed to reproach us ants? You, the fat elephant?"

"Captain," said the priest gravely, "respect God. You are now before His door, poor wretch; it is soon going to open and you will see Him. Do you feel no terror?"

"Priest," said the captain, stopping his ears, "I'm tired. The Agha has been here, boring me, and Michelis has been to take down my will. While I think of it, I've bequeathed you what money I have left, so you may bury me and not let me rot like others. And now here you come with your bogy man. I can't now; I'm tired, I tell you; fare you well."

He turned to the wall and shut his eyes. He began to breathe painfully, then was siezed with a sudden, hoarse rattling.

"Good night!" he managed to say.

The priest covered the Holy Chalice once more with the red velvet.

"I cannot administer to you the Body and Blood of Christ," he said. "God forgive you!"

"Good night!" murmured the captain again, at the last gasp.

He made two or three convulsive movements, groaned softly, as if he were choking, and opened his mouth: blood flowed over the pillow and sheets.

The priest made the sign of the cross over him.

"God forgive you," he muttered; "I have not the right."

He opened the door and called old Mandalenia for the laying out.

Next day, when they buried him, a fine rain was falling, just as on that Saint George's day at Batoum when he had enjoyed himself with his friends on the pebbles in the garden. Transparent clouds were sailing the sky; the church bell rang the knell; a sweet odor of camomile rose from the little cemetery. All the villagers were present at the funeral. In front, lamenting and tearing her hair, went old Mandalenia. Yannakos wanted to bring his donkey to follow in the procession, for he had heard from Michelis that the captain had bequeathed him his barley. But priest Grigoris lost his temper.

"Isn't he, too, one of God's creatures?" protested Yannakos.

"He has not an immortal soul," replied priest Grigoris indignantly.

"If I were God," muttered Yannakos, "I should let all the asses, too, into Paradise."

"Paradise is not a stable, it is the dwelling of God," cried the priest, pushing Yannakos away.

"I should have let them into Paradise," grumbled Yannakos obstinately as he followed the procession; "I should have let my Youssoufaki in—but on one condition: that he didn't make droppings and dirty the heavens."

When all was done and everyone had thrown a handful of earth into the grave, Yannakos took Michelis and Kostandis aside, for he could not keep his secret to himself any longer.

"There's a thing I've got to tell you, brothers, but you must keep the secret; nobody knows yet . . . Manolios has caught a foul disease in his face: it's like an octopus, a mask covered with blood, as if a demon had settled on his face. I don't know what to say, lads. Or would Manolios be a saint, and us only now able to see it? For it's only saints and ascetics, so I've heard say, catch diseases like that."

"It must be because he's a saint," said Kostandis. "He is a saint, yes, he's a saint, and all these years we didn't know it."

"Don't get carried away so fast, Kostandis," said Michelis, disturbed by the news. "Wait. We must go into it first and get a doctor."

"What I say is," proposed Yannakos, "that Sunday afternoon we all three go up and visit Manolios. Besides, I have a present for him."

So saying he pulled out of his waistcoat pocket a little book with gilt edges.

"The Gospel. It's priest Fotis who sent it to me, yesterday eve-

ning. He said we were to read it, the four of us, the basket men—
it's his little token of friendship for us; and he sends us his blessing along with the Gospel."

They stepped over the tombs covered with camomile, where lay
their ancestors. Softened by the rain, the earth smelled good. They
stopped for a moment, sniffed the damp warm fragrance, and their
brains were lightly overlaid with soaked camomile.

Michelis sighed. He had suddenly thought of Mariori; his betrothed, with her pale, thin face, her great eyes ringed with blue
and her little white handkerchief which she kept pressing to her
mouth.

He remembered how, as a small child, he had come with his
father to this cemetery: they were disinterring a young girl whom
he had once seen at his home, beautiful, blooming, with blue eyes
and curly hair, all smiles. He had lingered beside his father at the
edge of the opened tomb. The gravedigger threw out the earth in
big spadefuls which piled up around the grave, and searched for
the remains of the young girl. His father stood there holding a
wooden box into which they gathered them. Suddenly the gravedigger plunged both hands into the earth and pulled out a skull.
Little Michelis burst out sobbing. Was that the pretty head of the
young girl with the curly hair? What had become of her eyes?
Where were her lips, her red cheeks?

From that day, for twenty years, he had never managed to
enter the cemetery without remembering the beautiful girl and
that skull.

"What are you sighing for, Michelis?" asked Yannakos.

Without replying, Michelis pushed the gate with its iron cross
on top.

"Let's go," he said gloomily.

They made for the village, in silence. Heavy steps sounded behind them. They turned.

"Panayotaros!" said Kostandis. "Even that bear has come to
the funeral."

"He must have heard," said Yannakos, "that the captain's left
him something, too. It's to the dead man's house he's hurrying so,
to the Queen of England, to eat her."

"Let's stop and take him along with us," proposed Michelis.
"We'll coax him a bit."

They stopped. Panayotaros did not greet them, but hastened

his steps to pass them. Ever since the Council of Elders had chosen him to act Judas, because of his red beard, so they said, he had been unable to bear the sight of the ones chosen to be the faithful and holy Apostles.

"The face they've got to act the Apostles!" he kept saying. "I'm better than they, savage though I am. Because I've suffered, I have, more than them, in my house and out of my house and in myself. It's when I'm alone I weep; they weep when everyone can see. I know what love is, the sort that makes the whole village laugh at me; when they lose anyone, they're happy and joke about it. They're disgusting; plague upon them! One's got his donkey, t'other his café, t'other his rich father and his Mariori. I've got nothing. There's times I'd like to set fire to my shop, chuck my wife and children out and kill the woman I love. Well, which of us is Judas? Them, that have all they want, them, the satisfied, or me?"

"Hey, Panayotaros," Yannakos shouted to him, "too grand to see us?"

"Greetings to the Apostles!" grunted the Plaster-eater; "what's become of our fake Christ?"

"Not got over that yet?" said Kostandis. "But it's only make believe, my friend, do you still not realize?"

"Make believe or not," replied the saddler, "you've stuck a dagger in my heart. My wife calls me Judas, the kids in the street make long noses at me; the women bolt their doors when they see me pass. Plague take you, you'll make me into a Judas forever!"

"Everybody likes you," said Michelis, "don't get in a huff for that. Why, the captain remembered you when he was dying and he's left you a legacy."

"Plaster to eat, so that I'll eat the Queen of England as well, eh? May his bones sweat pitch!"

"Don't damn your soul," Michelis protested; "his body's still warm. Take those words back."

"May his bones sweat pitch!" cried Panayotaros again, and his pock-marked face went purple. "And do you want me to tell you to go to hell?"

With which he strode off, mumbling.

"How do you pick up a sea urchin without getting pricked?" said Yannakos. "We'd have done better not to speak to him."

"He's been cut to the quick," said Michelis sadly.

"There's the widow as well," Kostandis explained. "And the bottle, too. He's off now to give his wife and daughters a thrashing. He's always threatening to throw them out of doors."

"Judas has got into his skin and is busy there," said Yannakos. "We're going to have trouble. I'm scared for Manolios, God grant I'm mistaken!"

"For Manolios?" said Michelis anxiously.

"The widow's got her eye on him, I think; on our Manolios," Yannakos answered. "Someone saw her the other day talking with him down by the well. Panayotaros got wind of it and he's furious. 'I'll kill him!' he cries, every time he's drunk, 'I'll kill him, the swine!' and he sharpens his knife on the stones."

"Suppose we went to see Manolios this evening?" Michelis proposed. "What you say is upsetting, Yannakos."

"Let's go straightaway!" said Yannakos. "I'm afraid Panayotaros may get there first. I've an idea he was making for the Mount of the Virgin."

"We've only to take that turning and go quick up the path," said Kostandis. "Quickest is best."

They turned off and started up the path. They did not speak, but hurried as if they had a presentiment of some disaster.

They caught sight of Panayotaros sitting on a stone at the bottom of the mountain, deep in thought, with his head in his hands. He did not see them, and they passed him without speaking to him.

The rain had stopped, the clouds were torn, and here and there the vault of the sky appeared, a limpid blue. The sun, still high, was blazing.

Bells tinkled; a flute rang out, gay, lively. They passed near some sheep. Nikolio took his flute from his mouth and stared at them.

"Hey, Nikolio," Michelis shouted, "is your master at the fold?"

"He's not there. I haven't seen him. Go and see for yourselves."

"How is he, Nikolio?"

"Like a crab in the embers!" replied the shepherd boy, with a burst of laughter; "sings as he cooks!"

"Nice temper he's in, the little goat!" said Yannakos. "Let's push on!"

Michelis started to laugh.

"I've got a secret for you, too," he said. "Yesterday evening Lenio went to see my father. She's got her ear to the ground, she must have heard of Manolios's illness. 'I don't want Manolios,' she lets fly at the old man. 'Why not? Do you love someone else?'—'Yes.'—'Who?'—'Nikolio, the shepherd lad.'—'Him? but he's a greenhorn, hasn't a mustache yet; what good would he be to you? Can he give you children?'—'He can, he can,' she said. 'He's what I want, he can, I tell you, he's what I want!' And she sets to work stroking and cajoling the old man.—'All right,' says the old man, 'take him and much good may it do you!' "

"That girl! She'd have accepted a goat, God forgive me!" said Yannakos.

"Manolios is well out of it, God be praised!" said Kostandis, remembering his own wife.

Reaching the sheepfold, they went in. Nobody. They went all around it; got up on the jutting rock; called. No answer.

"God preserve us," muttered Yannakos, "can he have killed himself?"

"What's that you're muttering?" said Michelis, worried.

"Nothing," he answered.

They returned to the path, with heads bent. The sun was sinking, the mountain was wrapping itself in shadows. They turned aside to pass close to the little chapel built on the rocks. It was abandoned, and was used only once a year, for Saint Michael's day. On that day a modest service for the Saint was celebrated there, and those who came lit candles, which revealed half-effaced frescoes. Then the wings of the Archangel Michael, black edged with red, stirred again. Toward evening the pilgrims went away, the candles went out, the angels' wings as well; they waited till next year to kindle again.

They entered. It smelled of damp earth. Like a tomb. A big candle was burning before the almost rubbed-out icon of Christ. They pushed through into the sanctuary and looked: nobody.

"He's surely been here," said Yannakos; "it must be he who lit the candle. But afterward, afterward . . . where can he have gone?"

"May God take this in hand," murmured Michelis, and crossed himself.

Manolios had indeed passed by the chapel. He had lit the candle and, kneeling in the half-light, contemplated Christ during the whole day, hesitating but not daring to speak to Him. He did not know how to express what he had to say to Him. Christ, on His side, watched him but kept silence for fear of frightening him.

Christ and he thus passed the whole day facing one another, without a word, like two great friends whose hearts are overflowing, but whose mouths are drawn tight by emotion.

As evening fell Manolios stood up and kissed the hand of Christ. They had confided everything to each other, had nothing more to say; Manolios opened the little door and made his way toward the village.

"I said all I had to say," he thought, comforted; "we are agreed, He has given me His blessing, I've now only to go."

He had muffled his face in his big handkerchief, leaving only his eyes uncovered. Night was falling as he entered the village. He chose the most deserted lanes, walking very fast. He stretched out his hand resolutely and knocked at Katerina's door.

Immediately the widow's clogs tapped in the yard.

"Who's there?"

"Open," replied Manolios with his heart panting.

"Who's there?" the voice repeated.

"Me, me, Manolios."

The door opened at once; the widow held out her arms to him.

"It's you, Manolios," she exclaimed joyfully. "What's brought me this honor? Come in."

He went in and she shut the door behind him. He was afraid.

He paused, looked at the two pots of carnations in the half-darkness and at the white cobbles of the yard. His heart was beating violently.

"Why've you got your face wrapped up?" asked the widow. "Are you afraid of being seen? Are you ashamed? Come in. Come in, Manolios, don't be afraid, I shan't eat you."

Manolios stood still, without a word, in the middle of the courtyard. He could vaguely see the widow's face, her white arms, her half-naked bosom.

"Day and night I think of you, Manolios," the widow was saying; "I can't sleep any more. And when I do sleep, I see you in my sleep. Day and night I cry out to you: 'Come! Come!' And here you are, you've come! Welcome, my Manolios!"

"I've come so that you may be rid of me forever, Katerina," said Manolios, calmly. "So that you may never think of me any more and never call me any more. I've come so that you may be disgusted with me, Katerina, my sister."

"Me, disgusted with you?" cried the widow. "But you're the only hope I have in the world. Without your knowing it, without your wanting it, without my wanting it, you've become my salvation. Don't be frightened, Manolios. It isn't my body that's speaking to you, it's my soul. Because I, too, have a soul, Manolios."

"You've lit the lamp. Let's go in, you must see me."

"Let's go in," said the widow, taking Manolios tenderly by the arm.

The widow's bed, wide and very clean, took up the whole room. Above it was the icon of the Holy Virgin, lit by a tiny lamp. On the right, in a corner, an oil lamp was burning.

"Courage, Katerina," said Manolios, going and placing himself under the flame of the lamp. "Come nearer, look at me."

So saying, he slowly untied the handkerchief.

His outrageously swollen lips appeared; then his chapped cheeks, from which a thick, yellow liquid was flowing; finally his distorted forehead, scarlet like a piece of meat.

With round eyes the widow watched him, bewildered. Suddenly she shut her eyes and rushed to Manolios, weeping.

"Manolios, Manolios, my love," she cried.

Manolios pushed her away gently.

"Open your eyes, look at me!" he implored her. "Don't cry, don't take me in your arms. Look me in the face, sister."

"My love! my love!" cried the widow, powerless to leave him.

"Aren't you disgusted at me?"

"How could I be disgusted at you, dear one?"

"You must; you must, Katerina, my sister. So as to be rid of me. So that I, too, may be delivered."

"Don't want to be rid of you. Separated from you, I'm lost."

In desperation Manolios sank on to a stool, near the bed.

"Help me, Katerina," he begged, "help me to find my salvation. I, too, think about you, and I don't want to. Help me, that my soul mayn't be soiled!"

Livid, the widow steadied herself against the wall. She looked at Manolios and her heart was breaking, as though her child in danger were calling her in the night.

"What can I do for you, my dear one?" she murmured at last. "What do you want me to do?"

Manolios was silent.

"Do you want me to kill myself?" said the widow. "Do you want me to kill myself so you may be delivered?"

"No, no!" cried Manolios, horrified. "That way, your soul would go to Hell, and I don't want that!"

They were silent again. Then, after a while:

"I want to save you," said Manolios. "It's by saving you that I shall be saved myself, my sister. I have charge of your soul, you know."

"You have charge of my soul, Manolios?" said the widow, trembling. "Take it, lead it where you will; it's yours. Think of Christ. That's how He, too, had charge of the soul of Mary Magdalen."

"It's He I'm thinking of," said Manolios, feeling suddenly more calm. "It's He I think of, night and day, my sister."

"Follow the same road as Christ, Manolios. How did He save Mary Magdalen, the prostitute? Do you know? I don't. Do what you like with me."

Manolios rose.

"I'm going. You have said the word which has set me free."

"You too, Manolios, you've said the word which has delivered me. You called me 'sister'."

Manolios bound up his face again. Only his eyes could be seen.

"Fare thee well, sister," he said. "I shall come again."

The widow took his arm again to guide him across the yard. In the darkness she stretched out her hand and picked a bunch of carnations.

"Take these," she said; "Christ be with you, Manolios!"

She put the carnations into his hands and, in the blackness, opened the door and looked out; nobody in the road.

"I shall open my door to no one now," said the widow. "I shall wait for you to come again."

Manolios crossed the threshold and vanished into the night.

God Is a Potter; He Works in Mud

THE FIRST OF MAY. Summer is coming. In the still green plain the corn is already turning gold, the olives are knotting and growing, the vines are adorning themselves with little acid clusters, a bitter milk flows in the green figs which will soon be all honey. The inhabitants of Lycovrissi are eating garlic to keep themselves well—the whole village reeks of it. Old Patriarcheas is beginning once more to keep good cheer; he has become pot bellied, his blood has thickened. The other morning Andonis the barber cupped him to save him from a stroke. Old Ladas, too, munches a sprig of garlic without thinking of it, while his spirit wanders between debit and credit: how much oil, wine, corn will he harvest this year? who owes him money, how much, and how is he to get it back? He thinks also of Yannakos's three pounds: he means to put his goods to auction and get hold of his donkey.

The betrothed languish. In May, no weddings; in June there is the work in the fields, no time for marriage feasts. Then, the month after, there is the threshing; the month after that, the wine harvest. They must wait till Holy Cross Day, in September, when there is less to do; when the harvest is being reckoned up. Then the priest will come and bless the new couples who, with many cares out of the way, will have plenty of bread and oil to eat, and wine to drink. That will give them the vigor to beget and bring forth children.

Priest Grigoris has many worries. Mariori is still not married and Michelis has got into bad ways. He was never very bright, but Manolios and his friends have managed to deprive him of the little brains he had: they found a ripe pear, and now he never stops distributing flour and oil to the poor without telling his father,

and from time to time Yannakos's accursed ass—may he die a violent death!—carries fresh baskets of provisions to the refugees on
the Sarakina . . . With a brain all askew like that, grumbled
priest Grigoris, he'll soon have got through his fortune, the idiot,
and then what'll become of my daughter?

But worst of all is this: the priest of the Sarakina, that goat-
beard, says Mass every Sunday in a grotto on the mountain and
indulges in sermons. Already some inhabitants of Lycovrissi are
deserting him, priest Grigoris, to go off and listen to this half-
crazed vagabond priest. Every village is a hive, priest Grigoris
kept telling himself, and in a hive there's not room for two queens:
let him go off and swarm somewhere else. The Sarakina is my
hive!

On the Sarakina, too, the month of May has made its entry,
but hollow-bellied and in rags. Here and there a few wild flowers
between the stones, some eglantine and hawthorn blossoms and a
myriad green and gray lizards which have crept out to warm themselves in the good sunshine. No olives here, or vines, or gardens.
Nothing but hostile, untamed rocks. At long intervals, a tree bent
by the wind, twisted, tormented, bearing bitter fruit that is all
pips—a wild olive, a carob tree or a wild pear—thorny, with nothing but hate for Man.

Sunday. The grotto with the half-effaced frescoes was all illumined. The ascetics had awakened, some with chins or beards
gnawed away by time and damp, others with head or feet missing,
mutilated. Of the big Crucifixion there remained only the face of
Christ, covered with verdigris and mildew, and a fragment of cross
with two livid feet from which blood dripped.

All the morning, men and women had crowded the grotto, chanting. They came out at length and sat in the sun, and priest Fotis
joined them. Every Sunday, after Mass, he was in the habit of
addressing his flock, to restore their courage. First he would greet
them, find a good word for each one, then he would begin to preach
to them the word of God and his own. At the start his voice was
always calm, but little by little he would warm up and his words
would seem to dive from somewhere very high, the better to fall
into men's souls.

"We are still alive, we have not given up; greetings, my children!" he said once more that day, gaily, to comfort them.

Sometimes he would quote them parables, sometimes speak to

them of his own life, of all he had seen and suffered; sometimes again he would take the Gospel, open it at random, read a few sentences to get him going. And before the subdued eyes of his flock there opened starry skies, and their rags changed into wings. Even their hollow bellies forgot their hunger.

"We call truth legend," began priest Fotis, that day. "I'm going to tell you a legend. Come closer, my children. Hey, you women who are crying, it's you I want to talk to; approach!"

The women bunched together with their children and crouched down in a circle round him. Behind them the men remained standing; leaning on their sticks, the old men were all ears.

"Once upon a time," priest Fotis began, "there were two fowlers. They went up a mountain and spread their nets. Next day they came back, and what did they see? The nets were full of ring doves. The poor creatures were fluttering about desperately to escape, but the meshes of nets were too fine—how could they have got through? Then in terror they bunched together and waited. 'Rotten birds, nothing but skin and bones,' said one of the hunters, 'how are we to sell them at the market?' 'We've only to feed them for a few days; they'll fatten up,' said the other. So they threw them mash in plenty and brought them water, and the ring doves began to eat and drink for all they were worth. Only one paid no attention and remained without eating. On the days that followed, more mash. The doves became fatter day by day. There was only one who got thinner, and struggled obstinately to get out of the net. This went on until one fine day the hunters took them to the market. The ring dove who had remained without eating had got so thin that by a last effort, he managed to squeeze through the meshes and flew away; he was free.

"That's the story, my children. Why have I told it to you? Who'll find the meaning? You, the old man, what do you think? Cudgel those brains a bit!"

All the old men were silent. Suddenly the giant banner bearer stood up.

"Seems to me, Father, you mean our hunger, and that it'll help us find our liberty. You mean that we are like the pigeon who didn't eat. But then, I don't see . . . my brain won't go any farther, sorry."

"You've got the essential, Loukas, I give you my blessing," said the priest. "I shall explain you the rest, my children. In our prosperous village we had begun to go too far, eating too much, overloading our souls with victuals. Peace, security, an easy life—the flesh had grown bold; it was enslaving our soul. We told ourselves: all's well, justice reigns in the world, no one's hungry, no one's cold, there is no better world than this.

"God had pity on us—he sent us the Turk who chased us away, threw us on the roads; we were persecuted and we learned that the world is full of injustices. We've been hungry and cold, there are others who feast, who've always a fire in their fireplace, and at the sight of people in rags and starving they laugh.

"Misfortune has opened our eyes, we have understood. Hunger has opened our wings, we have escaped from the net of injustice and of the too-easy life. We're free here! Now we can begin a new life, a nobler one, God be praised!"

No one breathed a word. The old men shook their heads, the women continued moaning softly; only the men looked the priest in the eyes, feeling deep down in themselves courage and obstinacy unshakeable.

The banner bearer alone raised his voice again.

"Father, well spoken; God has had pity on us and sent us misfortune. Same as the way a horseman whips his horse when it's broken-winded. Misfortune's whipped up our blood, it's opened our hearts, we've got free. But now, how are we to finish with misfortune? That's what you must tell us. If we don't finish with it, it'll finish us. It'll beat us, father!" he cried, and his eyes were swollen with tears. He remembered George, his little boy, who had died on the way.

"Fear nothing, Loukas; we'll yoke misfortune!" the priest answered. "It'll work for us, you'll see. Labor, patience, love—those are our weapons. Have confidence. When I shut my eyes, I see stone houses all round me, a church with its bell tower, a school with two stories and a huge yard full of children; round about the village, gardens, vineyards and cornfields. We've started already. We've found a little earth among the stones, we've sown it with seed. We've captured the rebel water in channels; we've grafted the wild trees. We've even begun to build. There are still a few men with hearts in that proud village of Lycovrissi, the Wolf's Fountain; they think of us. One day, one of them brings his whole fortune, three gold pounds; another day another sends us baskets of food, or a sinful woman offers us her ewe. Another sinner, who died the day before yesterday, thought of leaving us a full chest—God forgive his sinful soul! We're taking root, my children, we're once more getting hold of the earth, we're sprouting afresh, we're growing trunks and branches; have confidence!"

"Are we going to start the same all over again, Father?" cried a rough young man with a rag around his waist, and pale from privation. "Always the same thing, Father? Must the whole thing start again? You remember very well, there weren't only rich people at home, there were poor, too. My mother died of hunger, at a time when the village was swimming in oil and wine and when all the neighbors' ovens were baking batches of loaves; the very smell of it made my mother faint . . . So it's still the same old song, father? Once more rich and poor?"

Priest Fotis bowed his head. He remained in thought a long while.

"Petres," he said at last, "you're blunt, you don't beat about the bush, I like you. What you're asking me, I ask God day and night, and I pray Him to enlighten me. I cry to Him: 'New foundations, Lord, we want new foundations for our new village. No more injustices; let everyone be hungry and cold, or else let everyone have food and clothes and warmth. Can't we, Lord, bring justice on earth?'"

"And what was the good God's answer?" asked the young man harshly.

"Little by little, according to its strength, my poor brain receives the divine light. Misfortune, let's be just to it, has made us at last equals, we've all become poor, no one now has an oven to bake his bread in or can fall into the sin of refusing to give to the hungry. What was difficult then—now's the moment to put our shoulder to it, my children. The soul has been freed from full bellies; it can fly now."

He turned to an old man who, with his hands crossed on his stick, was listening and shading his head:

"Father Charilaos, if you'd been asked, three months ago, for your vines and olive trees, that they might be shared out among the poor, would you have given them?"

"Never! God forgive me," answered the old man. "Would you have cut off your arms, your legs, your lungs to give them to the neighbors? For me, my olives and my vines were the same."

"And your lordship, father Paules, would never have opened his chest to share out the gold pieces in it to those in want."

An old man facing the priest frowned and did not answer. He simply heaved a deep sigh at the remembrance of his coffers.

"The man who has land," cried priest Fotis in sudden irritation, "the man who has land and trees becomes himself land and trees, and his soul loses its divine countenance. The man who has coffers becomes coffers. You were nothing more than a coffer, poor Paules, you were nothing more than earth, even in advance of your death, miserable Charilaos! But God be praised, we are saved! You've at last seen for yourselves, you rich property owners, what it means to be naked and hungry; you've learned what a poor man's suffering is."

"Yes," sighed old Paules, "I've learned."

"Now we shall make a clean sweep of all that," went on priest Fotis; "there'll be no more thine and mine, no more fences, locks or coffers. Here we shall all work and we shall all eat. Each one will do the work he can do, and as much as he can. One will go fishing on the Voidomata, another hunting, another will work the land, another will take out to pasture the animals God will send us. We're brothers, are we not? We're a single family; we've one father, God.

"Let's lay new foundations in our village, new foundations in our soul," cried the priest, opening his arms toward them all; "new foundations; it's very difficult, help me, my brethren! Labor, patience and love—and faith in God!

"What did the first Christians do? They met in catacombs, underground, and gave new foundations to the world. These caves in the belly of the earth are our catacombs, we, too, have Christ with us; we have known injustice, we shall establish order! Have no fear, Petres my son, forget the past, let it be exorcised! All together, help in the establishing of a new world!"

They all rose; gripped, they surged round their priest.

"All together!" the priest cried once more. "All together! there's our new watchword, it will save us!"

"All together!" cried the men and women, raising their hands as if swearing an oath.

Old Charilaos crossed himself.

"Poverty has made my heart wider," he said, and his eyes were wet. "Don't give me riches, O God; I shall become bad again!"

"Have no fear, father Charilaos," cried Petres with a laugh, "have no fear, we shan't let you get rich!"

The priest took off his stole, folded it and handed it to a little old woman who had become sacristan.

"My children," he said, "today is Sunday; rest. Tomorrow work will start again. Let the young play bowls, let the men meet and hold council, let the women assemble, chat and console one another. I must go to the mountain opposite, where our friends of the baskets are waiting for me. Till this evening, my children, God be with us!"

So saying, he took his stick and walked away.

Surrounding Manolios, the three Apostles, Peter, James and John, had opened the little Gospel which Yannakos had brought that morning; they were about to begin the reading.

They had got used to Manolios's swollen face. Their first terror over, they dared look straight at him, without disgust and without fear. Unknown to Manolios, Yannakos had asked priest Fotis to come and examine their friend's affliction and give his opinion. The priest had seen much and suffered much, he knew all the afflictions of the flesh and of the soul, he might, who knows? find a remedy. Perhaps what Manolios needed was not ointments or drugs. Perhaps this sudden affliction had its roots elsewhere, perhaps it was the work of the Devil and the priest would exorcise the unclean spirit.

So, that day, the three of them had gone up the mountain, each with his present for his sick friend: Yannakos the little Gospel, Kostandis a box of Turkish delight, Michelis a small icon—the Crucifixion; it was very old, and he had it from his mother. It showed Christ on the cross and all around Him innumerable swallows painted—not angels, swallows perched on the arms and top of the cross, with beaks open as if they were singing. The whole cross had blossomed; from bottom to top it was entwined with tiny pink flowers which made it look like an almond tree in bloom. In the midst of the flowers and birds, the crucified Christ was smiling. At the foot of the cross Mary Magdalen the prostitute, all alone, had undone her hair and was wiping away the blood which flowed from the feet of Christ.

Manolios was waiting for them in front of the sheepfold, sit-

ting on his bench. He had washed his hair and put on his Sunday
clothes. He was holding the mask of Christ which he had carved,
and was looking at it, now full face, now turning it to the right,
now to the left, to contemplate the weeping eyes, the suffering
mouth, His melancholy smile.

Manolios took the presents, kissed the Gospel and spent a long
time examining the Crucifixion.

"It's not the Crucifixion, it's the spring," he murmured.

He looked at the woman at the foot of the cross, with her sparse
gold hair, and sighed.

He put his lips to the feet of the Christ, but at once recoiled
in horror. It seemed to him that he had kissed the fair hair and
naked neck of the prostitute.

Yannakos took the icon from Manolios's hands.

"Come, Manolios," he said, "open the Gospel and read."

"What shall we read, Yannakos?"

"Open it at random! And whatever we don't understand, we'll
discuss until we do."

Manolios took the Gospel, bent forward to kiss it and opened it.

"In the name of Christ," he said, and began to read, separating
the syllables:

"And seeing the multitudes, he went up into a mountain: and
when he was set, his disciples came unto him. And he opened his
mouth and taught them, saying, 'Blessed are the poor in spirit:
for theirs is the Kingdom of Heaven.' "

"That's easy," said Yannakos, pleased. "God be praised, I understand. And you, Kostandis?"

Kostandis was doubtful:

"What's it mean, 'poor in spirit'?" he asked.

"All those who aren't learned," explained Yannakos. "All those
who haven't been to the big schools to air their brains."

"No, not those who aren't learned," Manolios corrected him.
"You can be learned like priest Fotis and enter the Kingdom of
Heaven. You can be unlearned and not enter, like old Ladas.
It means something else, Yannakos. What do you think, Mich-
elis?"

"Those who are without malice," suggested Michelis. "All those
whose mind is simple, pure, who don't split hairs, but believe in
all innocence and all confidence. That's how I see it. We'll ask
priest Fotis."

"Next!" said Yannakos impatient; "that'll do for that; next!"
Manolios went on reading:

"Blessed are the meek, for they shall inherit the earth."

"That anyhow, that's perfectly clear!" cried Yannakos triumphantly. "Joy to the meek, that's to say kind, mild, peaceful. Those are the ones who'll win in the end, and the whole earth will be theirs. That's to say, it's not through war but through love that they'll conquer the world. Down with war! Down with war! We're all brothers!"

"And the Turks?" asked Kostandis, hesitating to accept this.

"The Turks as well," replied Yannakos enthusiastically, "and the Agha, and Youssoufaki, and Hussein, the whole lot!"

"And the ones who destroyed priest Fotis's village?" asked Kostandis obstinately.

Yannakos scratched his head again.

"I don't know about that," he said. "We'll ask priest Fotis. Next!"

"Blessed are they which do hunger and thirst after righteousness: for they shall be filled."

"Ah!" they all exclaimed, "may it be God's will, we shall be filled with righteousness."

Yannakos stood up, excited.

"Blessed," he cried, "are those who hunger and thirst after righteousness! That's us, it's to us Christ was talking, us lads, us four who hunger and thirst for righteousness. I feel as if my heart has wings, brothers. It's as if Christ had turned His face toward me and spoken to me. Courage, lads! Next, Manolios!"

"Blessed are the merciful: for they shall obtain mercy."

"Listen to that, father Patriarcheas," cried Yannakos, jumping up again. "Listen to that, you guzzler who won't greet us in the street any longer because we were merciful and gave four baskets of food to the poor! Listen to that, priest Grigoris, you low-down swallow-all who chase the starving away from the table loaded with meats! You stuff your paunch so full that if it bursts it'll stink out the whole village! Listen to that, father Ladas, old skin-flint who wouldn't give a glass of water even to your guardian angel! Barvo, Michelis, for not being like your father. You'll enter the Kingdom of Heaven, with the four baskets. Because the food was yours, it wasn't ours!"

"Where did you learn to unravel all that, Yannakos?" said Kostandis in amazement. "I say, you've the brain of Solomon!"

"I don't explain it with my brain, old man," replied Yannakos. "I explain it with my heart; that's the King Solomon! Go on, Manolios, next!"

"Blessed are ye when men shall revile you and persecute you, and shall say all manner of evil against you falsely for My sake. Rejoice, and be exceeding glad: for great is your reward in Heaven: for so persecuted they the prophets which were before you."

"Read it over once again, Manolios," said Yannakos. "And not so fast, please. That seems to me, God forgive me, a bit muddled."

Manolios read the passage again. "It seems to me perfectly clear," he said: "In the village, all the notables and the well-to-do and the liars and the dishonest will be after us one day, the four of us, and they'll chase us out because we'll have told the truth. They'll bring along all their hangers-on to bear witness against us. They may throw stones at us, they may even kill us. Didn't they do the same to the prophets? But we ought to be very glad, brothers, because we'll be giving our lives for the love of Christ. Didn't He give His life in the same way for love of us? That's what that means."

"You're right, Manolios," said Yannakos, his eyes darting flames. "I can see priest Grigoris marching in front like Caiaphas, and Ladas behind him shouting: 'Kill them! Kill them! They'd open our chests and share out our gold pieces between them!' And I can see old Patriarcheas—you mustn't mind me, Michelis—acting his Pilate and saying: 'I wash my hands of this; I've nothing to do with it, kill them!' But deep down in his heart he's very pleased, because we disturbed him. We didn't leave him in peace to guzzle his sucking pigs, paw his servants and have the widow Katerina up to massage him—that's what he said—because he'd caught a chill. Hey, you ungodly, you misers, you pleasure seekers, it will come, it's coming, it's already here—the justice of God!"

He was drunk with words. Leaning over the village, he threatened it with his outstretched arm; but turning around, he suddenly saw before him priest Fotis, and swallowed his tongue.

"Your pardon, Father," he said, in confusion; "but we were reading the Gospel and my heart caught fire."

Priest Fotis had approached on tiptoe, and the four friends, absorbed in the words of the Gospel, had not noticed. He had been there some time and was listening with a smile.

"Good luck to you, my sons," he said, drawing near, "God be with you!"

They all rose joyfully, and made room for him on the bench. But the priest, at the sight of Manolios, cried out:

"What is it, my child? What's happened to you?"

"God punished me, Father," replied Manolios, hanging his head. "Don't look at me. Turn your eyes upon the Gospel, and explain it to us. We were waiting for your holiness to enlighten us. We aren't instructed; how can we understand?"

"Our brain," Kostandis added, "is a badly squared plank. Come and square it, Father."

"Me, help you?" said priest Fotis. "But all the sages in the world ought to come here and stop and listen to you, so that they, poor things, might at last understand the words of Christ. You're right, Yannakos, the Gospel's not a thing you read with the brain; the poor brain doesn't understand much; you read it with the heart. It understands everything. One Sunday, Yannakos, you'll come to our church, in our catacombs, and explain to us the word of God. Don't laugh; I mean it."

And turning to Manolios:

"All afflictions, my child, come from the soul; it is what governs the body. Your soul is sick, Manolios; it is what needs healing! And the body, willy nilly, will follow. But let's talk first. Why did you send for me? How can I help you? Tell me. Then you and I, Manolios, will talk alone."

"Father," answered Michelis, "it was because of Manolios's illness that we sent for you. We said to ourselves: 'Perhaps there's a devil that's settled on his face and your holiness may know an exorcism to chase him away.'"

"Also, there's lots of things I don't understand, Father," added Yannakos. "Doesn't everything come from God? Why on Manolios and not on the Agha, let's say, or on priest Grigoris, or on old Ladas? What sort of justice is that? I don't understand."

He turned to Manolios:

"Why don't you protest, too? Why don't you raise your voice to God and ask Him questions? You're content to stay there with your arms folded and your head bent forward, saying: 'God is punishing me.' But what have you done? Why is He punishing you? Kick back, you're not a sheep, hang it, you're a man, question

Him! That's what a man is—a living creature that kicks back and asks questions!"

Priest Fotis stood up, stretched out his hand, and shut Yannakos's mouth.

"You're putting far too many questions," he said, "you're raising your voice too loudly, Yannakos, you're asking God to come down and render you accounts. Who are you, to wish to make God come down on earth?"

"I—I want to understand," muttered Yannakos, intimidated.

"Understand God, Yannakos?" said the priest, horrified. "But Man is a blind earthworm at God's feet; what could he understand of an incommensurable greatness? I, too, when I was young, used to protest and question like you. I didn't understand. One day my Superior, on Mount Athos, told me a parable. He often expressed himself in parables, God keep his soul!

" 'Once upon a time,' he said, 'there was a little village, lost in the desert. All its inhabitants were blind. A great king passed by, followed by his army. He was riding an enormous elephant. The blind people heard of it. They had heard a great deal about elephants and were moved by a great desire to touch this fabulous animal, to get an idea of what it was. About ten of them, let's say the notables, set out. They begged the king for permission to touch the elephant.—"I give you permission, touch it!" said the king. One of them touched its trunk, another its foot, another its flanks, one was raised up so that he might feel its ear, another was seated on its back and given a ride. The blind men went back enchanted to their village. All the other blind people crowded round them, asking them greedily what sort of thing this fantastic beast, the elephant, was. The first said: "It is a big pipe that raises itself mightily, curls, and woe to you if it catches you!" Another said: "It is a hairy pillar." Another: "It is a wall, like a fortress, and it, too, is hairy." Another, the one who had felt the ear: "It's not a wall at all; it's a carpet of thick wool coarsely worked, which moves when you touch it." And the last cried: "What's that nonsense you're telling? It's an enormous walking mountain." ' "

The four friends burst out laughing.

"We are the blind ones," said Yannakos, "you're right, Father. Forgive me. We explore His little toenail and we say: 'God is hard, like stone.' Why? Because we haven't gone farther."

"We've no right to ask questions," said Michelis. "God must have a reason for striking Manolios. Only we can't see it, because we're blind."

"Father," said Manolios raising his head, "the four of us are bound together this year, inseparably. I think, then, it's only right for me to confess in front of all, so we may try all together to find out why God is punishing me and how to cure it. I myself think that as long as I've still got this demon on my face it'll mean that I haven't repented and that God won't accept me."

"You are right, Manolios my son," said the priest; "that is what the first Christians did. They confessed their sins before their assembled brethren. All tried together to find the way of redemption. In the name of Christ, we are listening to you, Manolios. Don't forget that we are all sinners, and that at this moment God is above us and can hear us."

Manolios concentrated for a long time. His whole life passed before his eyes—poverty at home, then left an orphan, and his Aunt Mandalenia had brought him up, with much grumbling; later, sweetness and peace at the monastery; his Superior, Manasse, a grave and gentle voice, told him the lives of the ascetics in the Thebaid, spoke to him of the Apostles on the shore of the lake of Gennesareth and, finally, of Christ crucified. What joy it was, the Kingdom of Heaven on earth! Then, one morning, the archon Patriarcheas arrived with his retinue, filling the courtyard of the monastery with mules, red rugs and joyful cries.

Manolios raised his head:

"I don't know where to begin, Father," he said. "All my life is passing again through my head. Help me, Father, question me. Brothers, question me, you too."

"Don't look for a beginning, Manolios," priest Fotis answered. "There is no beginning, there is no end! Speak, say whatever comes into your mind. Shut your eyes, Manolios, what do you see? Don't think, answer: what do you see?"

"In priest Grigoris's house. All the notables, in full assembly, have taken a decision. They have allotted each one his task for Holy Week next year. For the terrible Mystery which is to be played under the church porch. Priest Grigoris comes toward me, he places his hand on my head and blesses me: 'It is you,

Manolios, whom God has chosen,' he says to me. 'It is you whom God has chosen to bear the burden of the Cross.' My heart flew into a thousand pieces."

Manolios opened his eyes, his eyelids fluttered, his thoughts returned to his companions.

"It's true, at that moment my heart burst into a thousand pieces," he began again. "Like the bottle of perfume Mary Magdalen the prostitute was holding, which she broke at the feet of Christ.

"When I was small, I had lots of imagination, I used to read the lives of the saints and my mind was in a fever. I wanted to be a saint. When I went into the monastery I had one thing in my head: the ascetics. I wanted to go myself to the Thebaid, and not to eat, not to drink, to do miracles. You see, brothers, right from childhood I was damning myself, Satan was poking the fire in my heart, and I was burning. I presumed to want to do miracles, I too! Forgive me, Lord!

"When I left priest Grigoris's house, my head was buzzing. It seemed to me that the village had become too small for me, that I wasn't any longer Manolios, the lowly shepherd of old Patriarcheas, the ignorant, the wretched, but as it were a man chosen of God and with a great mission: to follow the footsteps of Christ, to be like Him!"

"A terrible presumption!" muttered Kostandis. "You, Manolios, who are so gentle, so humble . . ."

"Kostandis, my son," said the priest, "Manolios's heart is overflowing. Let it brim over; afterward you will judge."

"Forgive me, brothers," Manolios murmured, "Lucifer, the spirit of pride, was in me. I'm ashamed to say all this, but I'm confessing; I've got to bring everything into daylight; God is listening."

"Speak, speak, Manolios," said the priest, "don't be ashamed. The heart of man is a gulf of serpents, toads and swine. Empty your heart, let it be lightened!"

Manolios plucked up courage again.

"I swelled like a turkey, I came and went saying over and over to myself full of pride: 'It's you God has chosen, Manolios, it's you!' Well, one day—thanks be to you, friend Yannakos . . ."

He took his friend's hand and would have kissed it; but Yannakos withdrew it in dismay:

"What's that, Manolios? You'd kiss my hand? mine?"

"Yours, Yannakos," said Manolios, "because it's you who opened my eyes. And I saw that I was a hypocrite and a liar. You remember, Yannakos, when you found me in front of the captain's house and you said to me, God bless you: 'Liar! liar! you want to be like Christ and you're preparing to get married. After you've been on the cross, Lenio will bring you warm water to wash in, she'll bring you clean linen to change into, and you'll go to bed with her after you've been on the cross!'"

"Forgive me, Manolios!" cried Yannakos, throwing himself into his friend's arms. "You've no idea what devil was driving me, that day! One day I'll confess, too, and you'll see how disgusting. . . . The priest knows."

"Let him bring it all into the daylight, brethren, that he may be relieved," said priest Fotis once more, making Yannakos sit down. "Speak, Manolios; you must already feel a bit lightened."

"As I talk, Father, as I talk, it does me good. It's a mystery, confession, a great mystery! Now I've got my courage, I'll unveil it all, all!"

"We're listening, my son," said the priest, laying his hand on Manolios's shoulder, as if he wished to pass on strength to him. "Speak, my child!"

"From the moment when Yannakos laid my heart bare in that way, I started back. I saw the precipice, I stopped. 'Aren't you ashamed, Manolios,' I said to myself, 'you think it's play, the Crucifixion? Do you imagine you're going to take in God and men like that? You love Lenio, you want to sleep with her, and you'd like me to believe that you're Christ? Shame on you, impostor! Make up your mind, hypocrite!' From that moment I resolved: 'I won't marry! I won't touch a woman! I'll remain chaste.'"

Once more Yannakos could not contain himself:

"I said so, Manolios, you're a saint!" he cried.

"Wait, wait," said Manolios, "you'll see and your hair will stand on end. I haven't yet got to the end of my sins. I'd taken my decision about Lenio, I had a row with the master, I set off for the mountain, for solitude, far from temptations. 'Up there,' I said to myself, 'where the air's pure, I will consecrate myself to Christ.' Well, at the moment when I was going to take the path and was about to be saved, lo and behold at Saint Basil's Well, just outside the village, Satan was waiting for me."

Manolios sighed. His face was beginning to ooze again and he wiped it with his handkerchief. He remained a long while silent, and his hands were feverish.

"Courage, Manolios," said the priest. "I am a greater sinner than you. One day I'll confess before you, and you'll shudder with horror. I, whom you see, have soaked my hands in the blood of a man. The Devil took hold of me one day: I was young and had hot blood. I was a shepherd and I'd gone down to the village to celebrate Easter with some friends. I'd taken on my back a lamb to put on the spit. It was noon, the trees were in blossom, the earth smelled good. With all the village people we'd settled down on the grass, lit fires and were roasting the Easter lambs on the spit. We'd set the giblets for the *mezes** cooking in the embers, we were drinking and our hearts were warming up. When the lamb was cooked we set it on its back in the grass. I took a big knife, sharpened it and was getting ready to carve the beast. At that precise moment Satan drove me to cry out, laughingly: 'Hey, if I had a priest within reach now, I'd slit his throat!' It was the Devil, I tell you, made me say that. For I was a priest's son and respected the priests. When I met one on my way I used to run to kiss his hand. But I said it, like that, by way of a joke. We'd been drinking and I'd got going. But a peasant beside me, as drunk as me, heard me and shouted to me with a laugh: 'There's a priest behind you. Keep your word, if you're a man!' I turned, I saw a priest, I threw myself on him and I slit his throat."

Priest Fotis made the sign of the cross and was silent. They all remained speechless, terrified. Each went down into the recesses of himself, saw his soul and shivered. What murders, what infamies, what acts of shame there are boiling in the depths of us! We stay good because we are afraid. Our desires remain all our life hidden, unslaked, furious; they poison our blood. But we contain ourselves, deceive our neighbors and die honored and virtuous. In the light of day we have done no evil all our life. But there is no deceiving God.

"I," said Michelis at length, in a stifled, unrecognizable voice, "I'm worse than you, Father. When my father falls ill, I feel a satanic joy. A demon arises in me and dances, because I'm sick of my father, he's like an obstacle in front of me, I'm impatient for him to die. Let him die—the man who brought me into the world, and

* Canapé

whom I love! I don't know what a criminal's soul is like, but the soul of the honest man, of the good man, is a hell! A hell that contains all the devils. And we call good people and honest Christians all who keep the demons hidden inside them and don't let them leap out to commit foul deeds, to rob, to kill. But all of us, at the bottom of our hearts, God forgive me, are criminals, assassins, robbers!"

Yannakos burst into sobs. He too had looked into the depths of himself, and he was appalled. The priest stretched out his hand:

"My children," he said, "our turn to confess will come. Now it's Manolios's turn. Shut your hearts, he has opened his. Let him finish. Speak, Manolios. Do you see now? Do you understand? We are worse than you. I, the priest, and Michelis, the good and charitable man, the pride of your village!"

Manolios wiped his eyes, which were filling with tears, pulled his courage together and went on:

"Satan was sitting, my brothers, on the rim of the well and smiling at me: Katerina the widow, the prostitute of our village. Her lips were made up and her bodice partly open. I saw as far as the tips of her breasts and the blood rose to my head and I turned giddy. She spoke to me beseechingly; I had only one desire, to hurl myself upon her. Only I was afraid of men, I was afraid of God and I fled. I left her, but I took her with me, in my thoughts, in my blood; day and night I now dreamed only of her. I pretended to be thinking of Christ; lies! lies! It was of her I was thinking.

"One evening I could hold out no longer; I washed, combed my hair, took the path—I was going to the widow. I told myself: 'I'm going to save her soul. I'm going to talk to her and lead her into the way of God.' Lies! Lies! I was rushing to sleep with her. Then . . .'"

Manolios stopped once more. He was breathing hard. They all turned toward him and looked at him with compassion. Manolios was changing under their eyes. From the swollen flesh of his face there ran a muddy liquid which collected and coagulated drop by drop on his mustache and beard.

"Then, salvation came," the priest finished, taking the hand of Manolios between his and stroking it. "I understand, Manolios. I've stumbled on the hidden path God took to save you. A great miracle, my brethren! Who could ever guess the strange unforeseen roads salvation takes to reach our souls?

"Then, suddenly—let me finish, Manolios, you are tired—then, suddenly, you felt your face swelling, putting on a covering of repulsive flesh, becoming a hideous wound. It's no demon, Manolios, that has settled on you. It is God who has clapped this mask upon you to save you. God has taken pity on you, Manolios."

"I don't understand," murmured Kostandis, "I don't understand."

"Neither do I. Neither do I. . . ." murmured the other two friends. Only Manolios was silent, sighing.

Priest Fotis stroked Manolios's hand, as though he would have liked to share his suffering.

"You were going toward the abyss, Manolios, you were on the edge of the gulf, and God fixed this flesh upon your face to make you stop. You were going to commit a sin, enter the widow's bed; but now, with a face like that, how would you look at her? How would she look at you? You were ashamed and you retraced your steps. You retraced your steps and at once you were saved."

With his face hidden in his large handkerchief, Manolios was silent. His breast was shaken with sobs. Once he murmured: "God be praised!" then fell silent again.

The three friends also bent their heads, transfixed with terror. Shuddering, they felt that God besieges each one of us, like a lion. Sometimes you feel his breath, hear his roaring, see his eyes piercing the darkness.

The priest seemed to guess their thoughts.

"My children," he said, "an eye is open in us day and night, and watches. An ear is open deep in our heart, and listens: God."

And Michelis cried:

"How can God let us live on the earth? Why doesn't He kill us to purify creation?"

"Because, Michelis," the priest answered, "God is a potter; he works in mud."

But Yannakos grew impatient:

"What you say is all very fine, Father, but here we have a sick man. Can't you lay your hand upon him and say a prayer? Couldn't we all pray together to the good God to have mercy on him?"

"Manolios doesn't need prayers," replied priest Fotis, "any more than exorcisms. The prayers of others won't make him better. In himself, day and night, slowly, ceaselessly, salvation is at work. Haven't you seen, my brethren, how the caterpillar in winter enters and hides within a tightly shut shroud? Its head is transformed, it becomes fierce, it waits motionless. Slowly, in its vitals, in the midst of the darkness, is laboring deliverance. Behind all that ugliness she is wearing a light down, a brilliant eye, wings. One fine spring morning she pierces the shroud and comes out, a butterfly. That is how in us, through the darkness, deliverance is busy. Courage, Manolios, pursue your way. Behind your visage, salvation is falling into place. Courage!"

"How long must I wait, Father?" asked Manolios, raising supplicating eyes toward the priest.

"Are you in a hurry, Manolios?"

"No, no," replied Manolios, ashamed; "when God wills."

"God is never in a hurry," said the priest. "He is still, He sees the future as though it were already past; He works in eternity. Only ephemeral creatures, not knowing what will happen, hasten out of fear. Let God work in silence, as He likes to do. Don't raise your head, don't ask questions. Every question is a sin."

The sun was midway. It fell drop by drop on the five heads gathered together. They had drawn near one another in silent affection.

On the opposite slope of the mountain Nikolio's flute sang, suddenly joyful, strident, passionate.

"Nikolio," said Michelis with a smile. "He, too, suffers and is relieving his heart."

They all cocked an ear and listened. The shepherd's tune discoursed, laughed, danced in the kindled air. A white orange-spotted butterfly fluttered for an instant above the five heads and went to settle on priest Fotis's hair. It beat it wings and plunged its snout into the gray hair, taking it for brambles in blossom. Then it flew off, climbed very high and was lost in the sun.

After a moment, the voice of Manolios rose:

"Father, brothers, forgive me and may God forgive you! I feel relieved as though a great weight had come away from my heart. I see; thanks to you, Father, I understand, I accept! Now my affliction seems to me like a cross; I carry it, I feel I am going up. Above the Crucifixion, I know, there is the Resurrection. I shall gather my strength together to bear my cross. Help me, comrades, that I may not fall!"

"All together!" cried the priest, rising. "This morning I was speaking to my people on the mountain. For we, too, are climbing, we, too, are carrying our heavy cross, we stumble, we complain, we are impatient. I spoke to them and cried to them: 'All together, and we shall be saved!' "

"But in that case," said Yannakos, "pain, sickness, sin . . ."

"So many caterpillars," said the priest, "which can change into butterflies."

He remembered what the four friends had been reading.

"Blessed," he said, "are they who suffer, because they will feel how great is the mercy of God. While those who do not suffer will never experience that celestial joy. See what a divine benefit suffering is. Do you understand, Manolios?"

But Manolios, exhausted, had let himself fall against Michelis's shoulder; he had shut his eyes and, relaxed, slid peacefully into sleep.

His companions gently raised him and laid him on his mattress, then tiptoed out.

"The grace of God, in the shape of sleep, has descended upon Manolios," said the priest. "Let's leave him alone, my sons, to God's guard."

They took the path in single file and went down it in silence. The priest led, bare-headed, his gray hair waving over his shoulders.

Toward the end of the afternoon, when Manolios opened his eyes, he saw, sitting at his bedside and watching him in the half-light, Panayotaros. His eyes were fierce, bloodshot and strangely fixed. His mouth exhaled a strong smell of wine.

"Welcome, brother Panayotaros," said Manolios, smiling at him.

Panayotaros did not answer. His heavy head with the red hair leaned over Manolios and stared at him fixedly. His upper lip protruded; big, sharp, yellow teeth were visible.

"Is there something you want from me?" asked Manolios with a shudder; he thought he was the plaything of some bad dream.

Panayotaros opened his mouth with difficulty, his words were coated.

"I've been here an hour, leaning over you, watching you," he stuttered.

"Is there something you want from me, brother?" Manolios asked again. "Why are you looking at me like that?"

"Can't look at you in any other way," grunted Panayotaros angrily. "I can't!"

Then, immediately:

"You'll be the death of me, Manolios!"

"Me?" said Manolios sitting up on the mattress. "Me? What have I done to you?"

"The worst any man could do to me, you've done it, curse you! All the joy I had in the world, poor me, you've killed it. I can't bear it any longer. I've come with a present for you. I was waiting for you to wake up so as to give it you—take it!"

He plunged his hand inside his shirt and pulled out a large knife, which he laid on Manolios's knees.

"Take it," he mumbled, "take it, curse you, and kill me. Finish off the work you've begun. You'll be doing a good deed. Kill me!"

"Panayotaros, brother," cried Manolios, "what have I done to you? What, do you speak to me like that? Me, kill you?"

He tried to take his hand, but Panayotaros pushed Manolios's arm away furiously.

"Don't touch me," he roared, "none of your soft words; that disgusts me. Kill me. Finish off, I tell you, the work you've begun. What should I do with life now? Kill me!"

Manolios burst out sobbing.

"What have I done, what have I done, Panayotaros, brother?" he muttered once more.

"I've men who are mine," answered Panayotaros, "and follow Katerina wherever she goes. There's an old woman next door and I pay her. Day and night she hides behind her door and watches. The other night she saw you go into her house, with your face hidden. You stayed an hour and a half with her. Ever since that night Katerina has refused to open her door to me, she refuses to see me, she stays shut up in her house, weeping, the woman next door told me. Who's she weeping for? For whose sake is it she won't eat any more and is wasting away? For whose sake is it she won't open her door to me? For yours, yours, so deformed it makes a man sick to look at you, yours! They told me the state you were in; I was glad to hear it. I said to myself: 'Now I'm rid of that thief who plays the saint to us. When Katerina sees him she'll be disgusted and she'll get rid of him. That way I'll be rid of him, too.'

"And yet you weren't ashamed to go to her in that state, and you stayed an hour and a half. What spell did you cast on her, eh? Instead of being disgusted with you, here she is can't forget you; she strikes herself and cries out your name, you dirty leper! It's no use my beating my wife every day, I can't get relief. I thrash my daughters, no relief! I've shut my workshop, I get drunk, I wander about the streets with the urchins on my tail loosing at me a word that strikes me to the heart, like a knife. You know what word, you know! Cursed be the hour when that goat's-beard of a priest called me into his dirty shop. Since that day I've been done for!

"I'm done for, I can't bear it any longer, and this evening I've brought you the knife. Get up, Manolios, if you're a man, and kill me! I kiss your hand; kill me, and I'll find rest."

Manolios leaned his head on his knees and could not keep back his sobs.

What can I do, he asked himself, how can I save this wild soul that's floundering in love?

"Leave the tears, you doll!" cried Panayotaros, mad with rage. "Take the knife, I tell you, don't be afraid, I've whetted it properly, here's my throat, cut it."

He stretched out his long neck toward Manolios.

"Why don't you kill me?" asked Manolios.

"What good would that do me?" replied Panayotaros despairingly. "My misfortune will only get worse; that way I'll lose Katerina forever. It's only if you kill me that I'll be saved. And I'll take you with me to Hell."

At these words he burst into sobs.

He wept abundantly, mooing like a calf, and with his neck still stretched out.

Manolios, in tears, took him in his arms and began talking to him.

"Forgive me, brother Panayotaros, forgive me, I won't see her again, I won't go in at her door again, it's I who'll die and you'll be rid of me. It's I, I, I, I swear to you. It's I who'll die. Can't you see the state I'm in? I'm rotten. It's I who'll die, brother, don't cry."

But the other kept on mooing. He tore his neck violently away from the arms of Manolios and stood straight up. He took two steps toward the door, tottering. He tried to get across the threshold, but stumbled and fell full length.

Manolios rushed to pick him up, but he was up already and, staggering, dead drunk, reached the path, mooing.

At this very moment Nikolio appeared with the flock. Panayotaros dashed at it and with stones pursued the sheep, which stampeded away in terror.

"Hey, hey!" cried Nikolio furiously, "leave my sheep in peace!"

But Panayotaros kept on tearing up stones from the ground and throwing them and swearing.

"Bite him, bite him!" cried the little shepherd then to his two dogs, which ran up with their tongues hanging out.

The dogs hurled themselves on Panayotaros, who, leaning against a rock, picked up big stones to throw at them. The dogs went for Panayotaros, barking, and he too began to bark and rushed at them, but his knees failed him. He picked himself up and fell again. The dogs, now furious, leaped on him; one of them seized him by the thigh and would not let go, the other jumped at his throat and bit him on the chin: Panayotaros's beard became red with blood.

"At him! At him!" cried Nikolio in excitement.

Manolios heard the cries and barks and ran to the rescue. The shepherd boy was looking on, laughing and shouting:

"Leave them, master, let them to eat him!"

Manolios called the dogs, seized a stick and beat them off, then turned to help Panayotaros. But he had already taken flight and was sliding down the slope, shouting.

Nikolio climbed on the raised stone, put his hands to his mouth and yelled:

"Judas! Judas!"

The whole mountain echoed.

"Shut up, you!" cried Manolios. "Aren't you sorry for him?"

"Judas," shouted Nikolio again, throwing a great stone as hard as he could.

Night was rising. It had already invaded the foot of the mountain and was gaining height. The world was darkening. The dogs, out of breath, had lain down at the feet of Nikolio and were licking their wounds. The big ram, Dassos, was jerking his bell paternally and waiting for the flock to regroup behind him for the journey back to the fold.

Manolios had gone back into the hut. He hid the sharpened knife under his pillow, then hung up the icon of the Crucifixion on the wall above his mattress.

"O God," he murmured, "place Thy hand upon his heart and grant him healing! He, too, is sick. Thou art Almighty, take his suffering from him, console him!"

Murder in the Village

SEVERAL DAYS had gone by since that Sunday of the Confession, as they called it later—the day on which Manolios opened and relieved his heart before his friends.

All this time the earth below and the sun above were working in concert without rest to ripen the grain. The ears, swollen with milk, became hard. The plain was red with poppies. The singing birds had gathered hair, straw, and mud and had built their nests; the female was already brooding with outstretched wings. In front of her, perched on a branch, the male sang to encourage her. From time to time longed-for and rare showers brought some coolness, but soon the sun reappeared and, chasing away the clouds, went on with his task, old as the world, of helping men and birds.

Old Patriarcheas ate, drank and quarreled, sometimes with Lenio, who neglected the housework, spent her time on the mountain and sizzled with impatience to get married, sometimes with his son, who had taken to reading, just like an old gentleman or a low-down monk.

"Reading," he scolded, "is for common people and schoolmasters; an archon's son is made for good living, old wine and other people's wives. You're the disgrace of our family, Michelis."

He saw him go off from time to time to see Mariori, his betrothed, but he came back more and more sad and taciturn. The old man shook his head contemptuously. "My father," he thought, "used to jump on a mare and do the rounds of the villages where he had mistresses. He'd tie up his mare to the ring on the door. On seeing him the husband would change direction and wait till my father had left before going home. I had mistresses, I used to go secretly at night, like a thief, I had my fun. This one has a fiancée and, God forgive me, he touches no more than her finger tips. How could she help drying up, the poor thing, and going sick in the chest? Woman's like sweet basil: if you don't water her she fades. The race of Patriarcheas is certainly in a bad way, it's gone flat, it's done with!"

Old Ladas kept stopping Yannakos and saying to him:

"Yannakos, bring me the three pounds, bring them with the interest; otherwise, you wretch, you'd better know, I'll force you to sell your donkey. I'm a poor man, I am, don't try to ruin me."

In the house of priest Grigoris, things were going badly. For months there had not been a marriage or a christening in the village, and none of the inhabitants would consent to die. The gravedigger kept shielding his eyes with his hand and looking toward the village. No one in sight. He listened: no knell.

"Won't the Devil make up his mind and take one or two?" he growled. "My children'll starve."

The widow, shut up in her house with lock and bolt, opened her door to nobody now. Panayotaros wandered, drunk as a lord, throwing out threats to right and left; and the young lads burned with exasperated desire and began to hang around the houses of honest folk.

"Curses on the widow!" grumbled all the ones with pretty wives. "Now she's playing the honest woman, there's no keeping people away from our houses; nothing but serenades under our windows; the honor of the village is in danger!"

Every day, at the end of the afternoon, the villagers met in Kostandis's café, tired out with fighting the land, with drawing water and watering vegetable gardens and orchards to keep them from drying up; they smoked their narghiles, exchanged two or three words exhaustedly and relapsed quickly into a heavy silence. Luck had not even willed that the village should have its madman: they would have tormented him a bit for fun. Not even a fire or a thrush that could whistle like a man to help them pass the time.

Sometimes Panayotaros would pass by, completely drunk; he brought them no relaxation, because he had a fierce temper and if you annoyed him he picked up stones and threw them at your face. Hadn't he, only yesterday, smashed the spectacles of the schoolmaster, who had chanced to be in the café and had received a stone full in his forehead?

From time to time the Agha made them dance under the plane tree, when his soul had vague yearnings and was melancholy. But that wasn't very lively. The villagers soon had enough of it, left dancing and went back to the narghiles, and the café fell to a morose chirping. If someone got drunk, broke a leg or found a thief in his vegetable garden, a great fuss was made about it for a moment, but it soon all died down and the village relapsed into a weighty silence.

But behold, one morning a terrible piece of news flew from mouth to mouth, from door to door: Youssoufaki had been found, at dawn, murdered in his bed!

Martha, the Agha's old slave, had slipped out of the Agha's house at break of day, and had gone, all trembling, to find her lifelong friend, mother Mandalenia.

"The village is lost!" she cried, as soon as they had locked the door, "lost, my dear Mandalenia! Youssoufaki's been found assassinated!"

"Who can have killed him, Martha? This news is fire, that you've brought; it'll burn us all. Who, my dear?"

"No one was at the house yesterday evening: the Agha, Youssoufaki, Hussein and me, nobody else! Run, warn the Christians to look out, let all those who can get away, get away! I've my suspicions, I have, but I'm not sure, so mum's the word!"

This said, she stole back, doubled up and hugging the walls, into the Agha's house and bolted the door.

Old Mandalenia seized her black kerchief and ran from door to door, sowing terror with secret, unavowed delight. The men abandoned their work and assembled at the café to see what would happen, venturing stealthy glances at the Agha's balcony. All was shut up, doors and windows. From time to time wild cries could be heard from inside, a pistol shot or the noise of something being smashed. Then, again, silence.

The notables and the Elders met in consternation at priest Grigoris's. The heart of father Patriarcheas nearly burst with terror.

"If the murderer isn't found," he kept saying, with more of a stutter than usual, "if the murderer isn't found, we're done for. He'll throw us all into prison. And if he's drunk, perhaps he'll send us to the gallows!"

"He'll have a ransom out of all of us to pay for the crime," sighed old Ladas.

"He'll close the school and the church and proclaim the persecution of our race," said the schoolmaster.

Priest Grigoris strode up and down his yard, nervously telling his beads. He felt the whole village hung about his neck.

"I am responsible," he thought, "God has entrusted me with the souls of the village. 'Take My lambs,' He commanded me, 'and guard them.' We absolutely must find the murderer."

He went over all the villagers one by one, to see who could have killed that accursed boy; but he found no one. Yet the murderer must certainly be a Christian: in the village there were only three Turks—the Agha, his bodyguard, and Youssoufaki. All the others were Christians. "Woe to us; if the criminal is a Christian, the whole village will be put to fire and slaughter!"

Kostandis arrived, breathless.

"The Agha is brandishing his pistol, he shoots at the first thing, he's breaking everything in the house—stools, demijohns, jars. Then he throws himself on Youssoufaki's body and starts to wail. It's Martha, the old twisted hag, told me."

The door opened again and in came Yannakos.

"Hussein's gone onto the balcony and is sounding the trumpet!"

Another appeared:

"The crier is on the square, and he's announcing something!"

"What's he saying?"

"I couldn't keep track of it, Father; there were some names I caught, but I can't remember which!"

"To blazes with you!" growled old Patriarcheas, and the veins stood on his neck as though they would burst.

"One of you go and get the news," priest Grigoris ordered. "Here, you go, Yannakos."

At that moment the voice of the village crier could be heard approaching. All ran to the door and opened it. The crier stopped at the crossroads. He coughed, cleared his throat, struck the ground with his staff and stretched out his neck. Wavily, psalmodically, monotonously, his voice rose, and all the neighboring doors opened a little.

"Oyez, villagers, oyez, *raias!* Open your ears, listen! Order from the Agha! Priest Grigoris, the notables: Patriarcheas and Ladas, Hadji Nikolis the schoolmaster, and with them Panayotaros the saddler, known as Plaster-eater, known also as Judas, will present themselves immediately at the dwelling of the Agha! Let the rest of the *raias* go home; no one in the café, no one in the streets, no one in the fields; all of you home; there, wait! Oyez, *raias*, oyez, villagers, I have spoken! Have a care!"

Kostandis supported old Patriarcheas, who was on the point of collapse; he made him sit down on the stone bench. Mariori ran up to fan him. Father Ladas leaned against the wall, yellow as a lemon, and with his mouth wide open. Yannakos was sorry for him and approached:

"Courage, Mr. Notable. Is there anything I can do for you?"

"Is it you, Yannakos? Who is it?" he asked, dribbling.

"Of course, Yannakos the carrier. I was asking if you had any order for me."

The eyes of old Ladas came alive again:

"Wretch," he said, "bring me the three pounds, or I'll be after you!"

Meanwhile the priest had gone in. He hung around his neck his silver cross, which had, chased upon it, the Crucifixion on one side and the Resurrection on the other. He took his tall silver-handled staff and crossed himself before the icon of Christ.

"Christ," he murmured, "this is a difficult moment, help me, help the Christians! Stretch out Thy hand over our village, let me not lower myself."

He prostrated himself before the icon, and gazed at the calm and gentle face of Christ.

"Christ," he repeated, "let me not fall below myself!"

He crossed himself again and came out into the courtyard.

"Let us go, brethren," he said in serene and solemn tones. "You go first, father Patriarcheas; don't forget that you are archon. The archon is not the one who eats and drinks more than the others, but the one who, at the hour of danger, has his place in the van of the people to protect them. This is the moment to show that you are archon; lead the way! You, father Ladas, don't dishonor our village, be courageous! Don't start blubbering in front of the Agha, keep up a brave front. We are innocent, but if we have to die to save the village, let's make a good end! I, too, like life in the world below, but more still the life of Heaven. We are on the threshold. Behind us, earth, before us Heaven, be it as the Almighty shall decide! For you, Hadji Nikolis, I've nothing to say.

What you have so long been teaching the children about the heroes of ancient Greece and the martyrs of Christianity, now is the moment to remember it and to put it into practice. Don't let your pupils see you blanch. Stand up before death as a hero and as a martyr! Are we ready, my brethren?"

"Ready!" answered old Patriarcheas, rising painfully. "Don't be impatient, Father. The body is afraid, but the soul—no. I shall not dishonor my name."

Priest Grigoris inspected his companions:

"Father Ladas has his belt undone and his breeches will come down. Here, Yannakos, fix his belt for him, pull it tight and fasten it, don't let him put us to shame."

Yannakos approached and tightened his belt for old Ladas, who lifted his arms and let himself be dressed, like a child.

"Now wipe his mouth, Yannakos, he's dribbling," the priest ordered again. "Health to you, Mariori!"

"Come," said Hadji Nikolis, "we are the heads of the village, everyone's eyes are on us. In the name of Christ and Alexander the Great!"

They made the sign of the cross and went out over the threshold. At their head, the priest, behind him the three notables, in the rear, Yannakos and Kostandis.

"Hey, Kostandis, why has the Agha sent for poor Panayotaros as well? What's he got to do with the notables?"

"They say he was seen last night, at midnight, wandering round the Agha's house, shouting threats."

"But what's he got to do with Youssoufaki? It's the widow he's running after."

"How should I know, Yannakos? The Agha is fit to be tied, he doesn't know what he's doing. His slave, Martha, tells me he's threatening to ride out on his mare and cut off the heads of all the giaours he meets. God protect us."

Doors opened stealthily, and people watched the Elders in their slow advance; all crossed themselves, as at the passing of a funeral.

"I forgive those notables all they've eaten and done in their lives," said an old man. "Just now they're paying for it all at one go; they're paying their debts."

They went without haste, solemnly, as though they were saying good-bye. Sometimes priest Grigoris turned toward the half-open doors and raised his head toward the windows:

"Fear nothing, Christians," he said, "great is our God."

Poor father Ladas had clung to the arm of old Patriarcheas: "Archon," he whined, "keep near me, hold me up."

"Are you frightened?" asked the old archon, sorry for him.

"Yes, I'm frightened," answered father Ladas in a washed-out voice.

"I'm frightened, too," said the archon, "but I'm pretending not to be; it's my duty."

The old skinflint shook his head, but said no more.

They were now passing in front of the widow's house. Katerina opened her door and made to cry out to them: "Courage, my lords, courage!" but she did not dare.

None of them turned his head; they even quickened their pace as if they were passing through a foul lane. They almost stopped their noses.

Only Yannakos and Kostandis stopped.

"Good morning, Katerina," said Kostandis, "did you hear the crier? Go back in."

"Have you seen Panayotaros?" Yannakos asked her under his breath, "the Agha's sent for him, too."

"It's a long time since I saw him, neighbor," replied the widow. "But he must be wandering about down there, because I just heard shouts. He was arguing with Hussein, who was trying to catch him."

"Go back," Kostandis repeated, "and shut yourself in."

They went on their way. As they came to the square, Michelis arrived running and came up to his father.

"Michelis," said the old man, "good-bye!"

"Courage, father!" said his son, and kissed his hand.

Priest Grigoris turned:

"Michelis," he said, "and you other two, go back home. We are going into the lion's den. But God is going in with us, fear nothing."

The Agha's door was wide open.

"In the name of Christ!" said the priest, and with his right foot stepped over the threshold. The others followed. Father Ladas stumbled, but the old archon held him up.

The main courtyard, with the grass growing between the flagstones, was deserted. On the left, the Agha's mare poked its head through the stable door and whinnied. A long-haired dog, which was wallowing in the dung, stretched out its neck and growled, but could not make up its mind to get up.

Hussein, the bodyguard, appeared on the doorstep. He was yellow, squinting, and his chin trembled. He had not had time to give his mustache its coat of black dye, and it was sprinkled with thick white streaks. He was wearing his full-dress costume, as though it were a day of high festival, with his yataghan hung from his wide red sash.

When he saw them he frowned.

"Take off your shoes, giaours," he growled. "The Agha is waiting."

Martha the hunchback arrived; she helped the notables to take off their shoes and laid these in a line before the doorstep.

Holding each other up, they climbed a narrow wooden staircase and reached a room, where they stopped. All the windows were hermetically closed. At first they could make out nothing. But all of them felt that a savage beast, somewhere in the depths, had its eyes fixed on them and was watching them, ready to spring.

Old Ladas gripped the archon's arm, trembling. Priest Grigoris advanced step by step, his eyes searching for the place where the Agha might be lurking. The room smelled of raki, tobacco and a heavy reek of rotten flesh.

Suddenly a terrible voice roared in the depths of the corner to the right:

"Giaours!"

They all turned; they discovered the Agha sitting on a great cushion. He was leaning against the wall, and in his belt gleamed his great silver pistols, in front of him, a tall bottle of raki.

"At your orders, Agha," answered the priest calmly.

"Giaours!" the voice roared again. "Come here, Hussein!"

The guard left the door where he had been waiting, and stood at attention in front of the Agha.

"Prepare your yataghan and wait!"

"Agha . . ." the priest began again.

But the Agha did not let him go on.

"Giaours, one of you has planted his knife in my heart. My Youssoufaki . . ."

But his voice broke. A stifled sob blocked his throat.

He wiped his eyes angrily, filled his glass with raki and drank it at one gulp. He sighed, and hurled the glass against the wall, where it smashed into a thousand pieces.

"Who's killed him, eh?" he shouted. "There are only giaours here, therefore it is a giaour who killed him! Was it you, Panayotaros, you soaker?"

From the opposite corner, behind them, there came a stifled mooing. They wheeled round and saw, in the half-dark, tethered to a ring in the wall, Panayotaros. He must have had his head broken, for the schoolmaster, who was behind the others, saw blood dripping from his forehead and neck.

The Agha addressed the notables again:

"I shall have you thrown into prison," he yelled, "and one after another, one each morning, I shall hang you from the plane tree. Until you find the assassin. I shall hang you, the leaders, first, and afterward others and then others. Next I shall hang the women, and I shall annihilate the village. Until you find me the assassin! Do you hear, white-beard? Do you hear, *raias*? What had my Youssoufaki done to you, eh? Did he ever upset anyone? Did he ever say a word against a soul? He stayed sitting on the balcony, munching his mastic and singing. Did he do any harm, giaours? Why have you killed him?"

"Agha," protested priest Grigoris afresh, "I swear by the Almighty . . ."

"Shut up! I'll pull out the hairs of your beard one by one, you, I shan't hang you, I shall impale you, great bowl of soup! What had my Youssoufaki done to you, eh?"

He began to weep.

"Agha," said old Patriarcheas, who was ashamed to let the priest bear the brunt of the squall alone, "Agha, you know I have always shown myself loyal . . ."

"Shut that, swine!" yelled the Agha. "You're too heavy for the rope, you great paunch; I shall take a rusty knife and cut you up and take a whole week about it. May my hands get pleasure out of it! I know perfectly well, you giaour, that it wasn't you who killed him, but it makes me wild to see you alive when my Youssoufaki's stretched out there, in the next room, killed. I shall rise up and set fire to the four corners of the village, I shall burn you all, curse you!"

The Agha stood up, furious.

"Who's that, at the back? Let him show himself?"

"It's me, Agha," stammered father Ladas, his knees giving way.

"Ah! Ah!" bellowed the Agha, "I shall give my Youssoufaki a royal funeral! I shall have Mohammedan imams come all the way from Constantinople to sing for him, I shall order candles from Smyrna and a cypress-wood coffin so that he may smell nice. For that I need money, lots of money. I shall open your coffers, old gold-mine, I shall sweep off all your gold pieces. Who do you think you were amassing them for, all these years, eh? For my Youssoufaki!"

Old Ladas collapsed.

"Mercy, Agha," he whined, "kill me first, before I see that horror!"

But the Agha was now addressing Hadji Nikolis:

"And you, schoolmaster, who gather the little Greeks together and open their eyes, I'll cut out your tongue and throw it to my dog. Why are you people alive, eh, why? When my Youssoufaki is dead? My heart can't stand it. It'll kill me! Hussein, bring me the whip!"

The guard ran to take down the whip from its hook and handed it to the Agha.

"Open the window, let me see their faces!"

The Agha raised the whip furiously. In the daylight his face appeared furrowed, aged, livid. In a few hours suffering had gnawed it. His mustache had gone white; it drooped and hid his mouth. He chewed it and bellowed.

He began striking the four *raias* in the face, on the hands, on the chest. Old Ladas rolled to the ground at once. The Agha trampled him; standing on his body, now weeping, now laughing, he struck without pity to right and left, uttering wild cries.

The tears flowed from the eyes of the old archon, but he kept his lips shut tight; he did not cry out. The schoolmaster leaned against the wall, his head held high, and the blood flowed from his temples and chin. The priest, in the middle, with his arms folded, received the blows of the whip, murmuring:

"Christ, Christ, let me not weaken!"

The Agha foamed at the mouth, fell upon them, lashed out like a madman. At last, when his arm was tired, he threw away the whip.

"To prison!" he shouted afresh; "the hangings will start tomorrow." He approached Panayotaros and spat in his face. "With you first, Plaster-eater!"

He turned to Hussein.

"Bring me my Youssoufaki . . ." he said in a strangled voice.

The guard opened a door and shortly afterward could be heard dragging the little iron bed in which, at dawn, the boy had been found bathed in his blood.

The Agha threw himself upon him and began to kiss him, groaning.

Hussein untied Panayotaros from the ring, picked up the whip, cracked it and shouted:

"To prison, giaours!" and he drove all five of them tumbling down the stairs.

Terror had swooped down on the village. The streets remained empty, the shops shut. The *raias,* without speaking to each other, had gone to ground in their houses; they listened to the silence and trembled. From time to time a shadow slid from door to door and spread the news: "The notables have not come out yet." After a while, another rumor went around: "The notables have been thrown into prison. Hussein has been down into the square; he was carrying a rope and a piece of soap and has placed them under the plane tree." A little later: "The Agha is threatening to set fire to the four corners of the village if the murderer isn't found; we shall all be burned!"

"We're lost! We're lost!" cried the women, clasping their children in their arms.

The men, distraught, cursed the day when they had been born *raias.*

Only mother Penelope, sitting under the trellis of her yard, knitted her sock and remained tranquil, indifferent. She had heard say that they had arrested her husband, that the Agha was going to hang him, so it was said, from the plane tree and to raze the village. She had shaken her head slightly and thought without emotion: "That too, finished," then she had set to work knitting again.

Yannakos, sitting in the stable, was chatting with his ass:

"And you, what do you say about it all, Youssoufaki? We're in a nice mess, looks to me as if things may go badly. The Agha, they say, wants to burn the village and you with it, Youssoufaki. Well, what do you think? Suppose we slipped away at evening, the two of us? No one's dependent on us, no children or dogs, why should we mind? But wouldn't it be disgraceful to let the village people drop, now they're in danger? What do you think, Youssoufaki? I've nobody but you to chat with, I've told you what's on my mind; what do you think, Youssoufaki?"

The ass had plunged his head in the manger up to the ears. He was working his jaws greedily; the voice of his master reached him only as the murmur of a spring. Believing he was still saying kind words to him, he wagged his tail joyfully.

Toward evening, discreetly, doors began to open; a few heads appeared. Michelis was the first to open his door; he made for the priest's house to console his betrothed. Kostandis also came out to open his café. But just as he was putting the key in the lock he saw, under the plane tree, a stool and, on the stool, various objects which he could not make out from a distance. He went closer and at once recoiled with terror: a rope and a cake of soap! He put the key back into his belt and returned home, keeping close to the walls.

At this mild hour of the day's ending, the Agha's habit was to sit cross-legged on his balcony; at his side Youssoufaki would pour out his drink or light his chibouk. This evening doors and windows remained closed, the balcony was deserted, the Agha was moaning; how bitter and untrue it was—the song he loved: "World and dream are but one . . ." He held in his arms the small, lifeless body. "It isn't a dream, this," he said to himself; "no, it isn't a dream," and he burst out sobbing.

Hussein, too, wiped his keen, squinting eyes, and came and went and lamented under his breath: "My Youssoufaki," and trembled lest his master should hear. Again and again he went in furiously, seized the whip, descended to the cell in the basement of the house and began lashing out with rage, bellowing like his Agha.

He would come up again somewhat relieved and wander around the little iron bedstead. Sometimes, when he found that the Agha had dropped off to sleep from grief and drunkenness over the cold body of the young boy, he would lean forward, kiss Youssoufaki ardently on the mouth, bite with rage the full, now pale, lips which still smelled of mastic, and then he, too, would roll on the floor.

Priest Grigoris sat up in the cell. He shook Panayotaros.

"Damned Judas," he said, "did you kill Youssoufaki? Confess, so we may be saved and the village too! Confess, and I'll give you my blessing, so that all your sins may be forgiven."

"Go hang, the lot of you!" the Plaster-eater brayed, wiping the blood which ran from his broken head. "Let the village go to the devil, the whole lot and me, too—it'd be a blessed relief!"

"You killed him, curse you," muttered Patriarcheas in turn, heaving his back up against the wall, breathlessly, "you, you, Judas!"

"Swine!" bellowed the saddler again, "what had I got to do with him?"

He subsided, but boiled with rage and again shouted:

"It's your fault, may curses fall on you! All of you: that one, priest with the goat's beard, you, the notables, and the schoolmaster! You and the widow, the bitch, who wouldn't let me in. You, the lot of you!"

After a moment he burst out again:

"You wanted me to be Judas, and I've become Judas!" he lowed.

"Confess you killed him and Christ will forgive you, Panayotaros," repeated the priest, making his voice gentle. "Up to now, I've been responsible for all the souls in the village; now you are, Panayotaros; rise up and save them!"

At that, Plaster-eater burst into demoniac laughter:

"Grand! What an idea you've put into my head! Hell! I wish it had been I who killed him, so I could drag you all down in my fall! But it was someone else—hallowed be his hand!—someone else got in first. That's something, anyhow! Archons, priests, schoolmasters, all with me, to the devil!"

Then old Ladas raised his head, bloody from the blows of the whip.

"Come, confess, Panayotaros," he wheezed, "and I'll give you three gold pounds. I'll sell Yannakos's ass, he owes them to me, I'll sell it and give them to you. Do you hear?"

Panayotaros cocked a snook at him, spreading out his five fingers.

"Here," he said, "old skinflint, here's five for you!"

At that moment the door opened and the Agha appeared:

"Giaours," he shouted, "the hangings will start tomorrow. I have prepared the rope, the soap and the stool under the plane tree. Tomorrow's Wednesday. I shall start with the most worthless among you: first I shall hang Panayotaros, the Plaster-eater.

On Thursday it'll be you, you dirty old skinflint. Friday you, most learned of the learned, schoolmaster. Saturday your grandeur, old dunce of a Patriarcheas. Sunday, at the hour of your Mass, you, goat-beard! That makes five necks; I've prepared five running nooses under the plane tree. That's the first ovenful. Next I'll take five more, the first that come. And then more, more and still more until the murderer is found. And I shall put my Youssoufaki under the plane tree, I shan't bury him, I shan't close his eyes, so that he may watch you and his soul may rejoice!"

This said, he slammed the door behind him furiously. He saw Hussein waiting with the whip.

"Hussein," he said, "you're weeping too, my poor friend. Wipe your eyes, it's not right that the giaours should see us weep. Go and find Yannakos the carrier, tell him to go up to the big village and bring me benjamin, the most expensive quality, and candles, and black velvet, and sweet cakes, and bring them to me here tomorrow morning first thing. Oh, and a coil of thick rope, because the priest with the beard is extra heavy, and that old goat Patriarcheas heavier still. There, go!"

But Yannakos had already decamped and Hussein drummed in vain on his door. Yannakos was not there, he had taken the mountain track and gone to warn Manolios not to come down into the village so as not to be arrested.

Manolios had milked the ewes and set the pan of milk on the fire. Near him Nikolio, armed with the great wooden spoon, was stirring the milk and humming a tune.

"What makes you always sing, Nikolio, and jump about like a goat, as if the mountain were no longer big enough for you?" Manolios often asked him, marveling at his helper's good humor and agility.

"Manolios," the little shepherd had replied, "you forget I'm fifteen! So how can you expect the world not to be too small for me?"

But Lenio did not seem to him too small. When she came secretly to meet him on the mountain, Nikolio burrowed into her arms altogether and wished never to come out.

The milk had boiled, and now Manolios was sitting near the fireplace; by the light of the fire he was turning over the pages of the little Gospel and studying it. He had no other pleasure. Often the meaning of the words escaped him, but his heart explained everything. The whole sense of them sprang forth clear and sure, grew branches in him, refreshed him within like water from the spring.

What inspiration! How it made his soul young again! As though for the first time he was meeting Christ, for the first time hearing His voice. For he did for the first time see Christ raise His eyes and look at him and say, in calm tones of enchantment: "Follow Me!" Since then Manolios, silent, happy, had walked in the footsteps of Christ, now over the fresh grass of Galilee, now on the sandy shores of Gennesareth, now on the stony tracks of Judea. In the evenings he stretched himself at the feet of Christ, under an olive tree, and through its silvered foliage watched the trees moving. How blue and deep the sky was in His company, how light the air was—like a pure spirit—and how good the earth smelled!

One day, they had gone together to a little village, Cana, to a wedding. Christ had gone into the house like a bridegroom, and all the souls there had rejoiced at the sight of Him; they had blushed like girls betrothed. The bride and bridegroom stood up and plighted troth, then the guests reclined on the couches and began to eat and drink. Christ raised his glass, pledged the new couple, said a few words—very simple, but the young pair suddenly felt that marriage is an awful mystery, that wife and husband are two pillars which support the earth and prevent it from falling in. The feast was in full swing; the wine gave out, the mother of Christ turned to her son and said to Him: "My son, there's no more wine." For the first time He moved to stretch out His hand and to order nature to change course. Like the eaglet that launches itself upon its first flight and beats its novice wings fearfully, Christ rose slowly, went out into the yard, leaned over the six jars of water and mirrored His face in them. As soon as the water had reflected His face, it changed into wine. Then Christ turned to Manolios, who had followed Him into the yard, and smiled at him.

Another time, Manolios remembered, it was very hot. Thousands of persons were gathered on the shores of the lake. Christ went up into a boat. Manolios went up after Him. Manolios gathered the good word like corn into his bosom. He could feel his heart becoming a fertile soil in which the seed grew, became blade, which in its turn became ear, and the ear bread, upon which was engraved, in deep furrows, a cross.

Yet another time they were walking through the cornfields. It
was noon and they were hungry. Christ stretched out His hand
and plucked an ear. The disciples each picked one, Manolios like
the others. They began to eat the grains of wheat, one by one.
How pleasant it was, this green corn, full of milk; how it satisfied
body and soul! Overhead, the swallows cried, they, too, following
Christ like disciples; and at their feet the humblest flowerets of the
field were arrayed more splendidly than Solomon in all his glory.

A Pharisee invited them into his house. Manolios stopped in
the doorway and watched. With what contemptuous condescension the Pharisee received Christ into his dwelling! He did not
wash His feet, poured no scented essence upon His hand, gave
Him no kiss of peace. And behold, as they were eating in silence,
the air was suddenly swept with perfumes and a woman entered,
her bosom uncovered. She had very fair hair and was carrying an
alabaster box full of myrrh. From the first, Manolios was struck.
He had seen this woman somewhere, he could not remember
where! The woman knelt down at the feet of Christ, broke the
box, poured the myrrh over the holy feet and then, undoing her hair,
wiped them, weeping. Christ leaned forward, laid His hand on the
fair head, and His voice rose melodiously: "Thy sins be forgiven,
sister, for thou hast loved much."

Manolios shut the little Gospel, his heart overflowing. He looked
around him. The fire was still bright, the hut filled with blue
shadow; Nikolio came and went, humming, busy over the dinner.

The heart of Manolios was overflowing with love, tenderness,
happiness. He could not endure it, he must share it with others.
In his impatient breast there arose a powerful longing to go and
carry the good word to the stones, to the sheep, to men.

"Hey, Nikolio," he cried, "leave the food and come and sit by
me and listen, you too, to the word of God, so as to become a man
in your turn. Up to now you're just a savage."

The shepherd boy turned to look at Manolios and burst out
laughing:

"But I don't want to, old Manolios; let me alone, I'm all right
as I am. D'you want to make me lose my good humor?"

"I'll read you a passage from the Gospel, you'll see how good it
is."

"You can read it me when I'm ill. Now I'm all right, I tell you.
I've got the table ready, sit down and let's eat."

"I'm not hungry. You eat."

With these words Manolios opened the little Gospel again, leaned over the flame and began to read:

"He that taketh not his cross, and followeth after me, is not worthy of me.

"He that findeth his life shall lose it: and he that loseth his life for my sake, shall find it.

"For what is a man profited, if he shall gain the whole world, and lose his own soul? Or what shall a man give in exchange for his soul?"

Manolios understood the meaning of that perfectly. He shut the Gospel, shut his eyes, too—why fear death, why bow before the powerful of the earth? Why tremble at the idea of losing the terrestrial life? We have an immortal soul, what is there to be afraid of?

Yannakos had been watching for a good while, on the threshold. No one had seen him. Nikolio had his back to him and was deep in his meal. He ate heartily to get strength. Lenio might come this very evening, who knows? He would have to be very strong to strive with her. Manolios had shut his eyes and was deep in an indescribable bliss.

That one's right in Paradise, thought Yannakos. If I don't say anything he won't ever come out of it. I'll speak to him!

"Hey, Manolios," he shouted, crossing the threshold, "hey, Manolios, it's good to see you!"

Manolios jumped at the sound of a human voice.

"Who's there?" he asked, opening his eyes wide.

"Have you already forgotten my voice, Manolios? I'm Yannakos."

"Forgive me, Yannakos. I was a very long way away, I didn't realize it was you. What wind has brought you up the mountain at an hour like this?"

"An ill wind, Manolios. You're in Paradise: I—forgive me—have come with news from Hell."

"From the village?"

"From the village. This morning Youssoufaki was found murdered. The Agha has gone mad with rage: he's arrested priest Grigoris, the notables and Panayotaros. He's thrown them into prison, and tomorrow the hangings start. The ropes are already tied to the plane tree; he means to start tomorrow with poor Panayotaros. Afterward, he says, he'll hang others, then others, and still more. He'll sow death until the murderer's found. It's desolation in the village. The doors are bolted. We're done for! And I've come to tell you, Manolios, not to go down to the village, for fear you'll be arrested. Here you're safe all right!"

The eyes of Manolios sparkled. "Now's the moment," he told himself, "to show you've an immortal soul!" But he took care not to let his joy be seen. He listened to his friend speaking to him and panting, while to himself he said and repeated: "Now's the moment, this is the moment. If you let it slip, you're lost!"

"Have you eaten, Yannakos?" he asked.

"No, I'm not hungry."

"I wasn't hungry either, but appetite comes with eating. We'll eat as we talk, and you'll sleep here tonight. Tomorrow, when God has given us day again, we'll see."

Yannakos looked at his friend with surprise.

"How can you speak so calmly, Manolios? Don't you understand? Our village is in danger."

"I know the murderer," replied Manolios. "Don't be afraid. The village will not be lost."

"You know the murderer?" said Yannakos, dumbfounded. "How d'you mean, you know him? Who is it? Who?"

"Don't be in too much of a hurry," said Manolios, smiling. "Why are you in a hurry? You'll know everything tomorrow. A little patience. Now we're going to eat, talk, sleep. All will be well, thanks to the power of God!

"Hey, Nikolio, make room for us, we're hungry, too!"

They sat down, crosslegged, made the sign of the cross and began to eat. From time to time Yannakos raised his eyes and looked at Manolios. In the ploughed flesh of his face he could make out sunken eyes shining calmly, happily.

I don't understand a thing. . . . I don't understand a thing, he thought.

Unable to bear this silence any longer, he asked:

"How do you spend your time all alone, Manolios?"

"But I'm not alone," replied Manolios, pointing to the Gospel; "Christ is with me."

"And your illness?"

Manolios shuddered with surprise; he had forgotten it.

"What illness? Ah, yes, I am still a sinner, Yannakos. It doesn't go away. Must mean there's still evil in my thoughts. May God in His mercy have pity on me!"

"I'm off," said Nikolio, wiping his mouth. "It's the new moon, I can't sleep. I'm going for a walk."

He picked up his crook and went off, whistling.

"Yannakos," said Manolios, "let's go to sleep; tomorrow we must get up early. Night brings counsel—I've learned that, up here alone. God speaks more often to those who sleep than to those who stay awake."

They spread out a great rug in the yard because it was cool, and lay down. The air smelled of thyme. The voice of the night rose up, stressing the silence. A quite new crescent moon was climbing up the sky.

"I keep thinking of poor Panayotaros," said Yannakos, who was not sleepy.

"So do I," said Manolios tenderly. "Him more than all the others."

"Same here. Him more than all the others. But why?"

"It's because too much love has ruined him, Yannakos. That's a proud soul, but damned. He let himself be ruled by the passions, he got entangled. That made him furious. He rushes ahead, he tries to escape. He has no luck, he only gets more tied up. He hits about him, takes to drink, swears for relief. But he gets deeper in. If he loved less . . . No, not less," Manolios corrected himself, "if he loved more, perhaps he could be saved."

"I bet my life it's he killed Youssoufaki," said Yannakos, who wanted to prolong the conversation. "Tell me, please, Manolios, to set my mind at rest. Is it Panayotaros?"

"Come on, Yannakos, go to sleep. No, it's not he."

"God be praised," said Yannakos, and closed his eyes, serene again.

Manolios did the same, impatient to be alone. These last days, even in daytime, he had preferred keeping his eyes closed. It was as though he saw his soul more distinctly that way.

For some time a phrase of Father Manasse's had kept coming back to him, sharply. One day an ascetic had come to see him and spend the day with him. He had opened his eyes for a moment, then shut them again. "Open your eyes, Father," Manasse said to

him; "open them and see the marvelous works of God." "I close
my eyes to see," the ascetic answered, "and I see Him who made
them."

So Manolios closed his eyes to see Christ and hear His voice.
He would read a phrase from the Gospel, then lower his eyelids
and go on his way. He would then distinctly see, in a cool darkness, Christ in white walking at the head of his disciples. He
would join Him, secretly and in the rear, and escort Him silently.

"Tomorrow we shall have a lot of work," he muttered, as he
shut his eyes, "difficult work; Christ, aid us!"

"Aid us, Christ," he sighed again, as though he wished to draw
Christ to him in the night.

Christ came. When, at daybreak, Manolios awoke and crossed
himself, the dream blazed in his mind, brilliant as the morning
star: it seemed to him he was walking at the tip of a lake of celestial
blue. Impatiently he parted the reeds and the willow leaves and
pressed forward in all haste. As he went forward the reeds and
willows became men and women who followed him in thousands.
A wind blew and they all began to cry out: "Kill him! Kill him!"

He tried to escape. A hand touched him on the shoulder and a
voice was heard: "Do you believe?" "I believe, Lord!" replied Manolios. Immediately the wind fell, the men and women became once
more reeds and willows. A plane tree full of swallows rose before
him, melodious. From one of its branches a hanged body was
swinging. Manolios stopped, appalled, but a voice rang out afresh:
"Don't stop, march!"

Manolios gave a cry and woke up. "Don't stop, march!" It is
the voice of God. Let's go!

At one bound he was up; he washed, combed his hair, put on
his festival clothes, slipped the Gospel into his waistcoat and
shook Yannakos.

"Hey, Yannakos," he shouted to him, gaily, "wake up, slug-
abed!"

Yannakos opened his eyes; he looked at his friend admiringly.

"You're dressed like a bridegroom, Manolios," he said, "and your
eyes are shining; what beautiful dream have you had?"

"Come," said Manolios, "don't let's waste time. Think of the
terror of Panayotaros. Think of the dread of the village. Quick
march!"

The Sacrifice

THE JOY of getting up in the morning after taking a grave decision! Manolios went down the mountain lightly like an angel. He was not touching the ground; it was suddenly as if archangels deployed their wings and helped him to fly from rock to rock. He became a cloud, a light wind was driving him.

Behind him ran Yannakos, puffing and blowing.

"I say, you must have grown wings, Manolios! Slow down a bit and let me catch up!"

But Manolios felt wings under his feet, he could not wait. How could he have said to the wings: Stop, let's wait for Yannakos!

"I'd like to, but I can't, Yannakos," he shouted; "don't stop; quick march, you too!"

They were the same ways that had sustained him when, with eyes shut, he followed Christ, journeying to sow the good word on the fertile soil or among the stones. How he had flown when he was following Christ from Gennesareth to Judea! passing in gay flight over the little, well-beloved villages with His train of faithful friends—Capernaum, Cana, Magdala, Nazareth—he crossed Samaria in a single leap and reached his favorite ground, round about Jerusalem—Bethany, Bethesda, Jericho, Emmaus. That was how Manolios flew today, as if he were again following Christ's footsteps and they led down to Lycovrissi. And as his body became lighter, he felt pricklings all over his face; scabs began falling one by one from his cheeks and mouth. His flesh seemed to him to be shaking free, to be becoming tender like the heart of bamboo.

In amazement Manolios stopped, his heart throbbing: he saw with his eyes a hand passing over his face, stroking it without haste, cool like a morning breeze.

He was sure, but dared not lift his hand to his face to make more sure.

The miracle! the miracle! he thought, trembling.

Yannakos arrived, out of breath. He raised his eyes, looked at Manolios, gave a cry:

"Manolios! Manolios!" and threw himself into his arms.

The exuded flesh had melted like wax. The burst skin had closed up, was becoming smooth again.

"God be praised!" murmured Manolios, crossing himself. "God be praised, He has forgiven me my sins."

"My Manolios," cried Yannakos, with his eyes full of tears, "let me kiss your hand. You have beaten the tempter, your soul is purified, your face is rid of Satan!"

Yannakos stretched out his rough hand and stroked his friend's face, for a long time, in silence.

"Forward!" said Manolios, "let's not waste time!"

The sun had risen, they could hear the cocks crowing and the dogs of the village barking, down below in the plain; and through a faint mist the rich little place became visible.

Manolios turned to his companion:

"Yannakos," he said, "you must accept without complaining all that I'm going to do and say now, when we get down to the village. You must realize that it's not me speaking, but Christ commanding me. I'm carrying out His orders, and no more. Do you understand, Yannakos?"

"What are you going to do? What are you going to say?" Yannakos asked, anxiously; he felt suddenly that his friend was saying good-bye to him.

"What Christ commands, I tell you. Nothing more. I don't myself know very clearly. But I'm sure of it. You must be sure too, Yannakos, and tell Michelis and Kostandis, so that they don't start crying out."

"What are you going to do? What are you going to say?" asked Yannakos again, and stopped, alarmed.

" 'Don't stop, march!'—that's what Christ called out to me last night when I was asleep. Don't stop, be confident, march, Yannakos. Haven't you just seen that the seal of Satan is no longer on me? Do you know why? Because I have heard the call of Christ and am on the march, since dawn. And not against my will, but with gladness. And you keep shouting to me: 'Stop!'

How can I stop, Yannakos? Christ is marching in front with great strides."

But Yannakos shook his head.

"I've confidence in you, Manolios," he said. "On you I've touched the miracle with my own hand. But I haven't confidence in myself. If you do something that's beyond a man's strength, I shall cry out! I shall cry out, Manolios. I'm a man, and if something's going to happen to you, I shan't leave you, I shall resist!"

"And if it's God's command?"

"I shall resist," Yannakos repeated, "God forgive me!"

"Aren't you ashamed? Aren't you afraid? Be quiet!" Manolios commanded.

They hurried on. They were not far from the village when Kostandis came up to them, running.

"Brothers," he shouted when he saw them, "where are you going? Turn back at once. I was just coming up to the mountain to tell you not to come down."

"Panayotaros?" asked Manolios.

"His rope's prepared on the plane tree. At dawn the guard sounded the trumpet. He ordered all the inhabitants to assemble in the square, men and women, round the plane tree, so they may see and be seized with terror."

"Let's go back!" exclaimed Yannakos, panic-stricken, and turning back toward the mountain: "You come too, Kostandis!"

"I've a wife and children, I can't leave them. But you, in the name of Christ, be off!"

"No," said Manolios, continuing on his way, "we must advance in the name of Christ, and advance we will! Come, Yannakos, don't be afraid. There's someone in front of us, beckoning to us. Can't you see Him? It's Christ, let's follow Him."

Then for the first time Kostandis noticed Manolios's face, clear and pure.

"Manolios," he cried, "how did the miracle happen?"

"As miracles do," answered Manolios, smiling. "Very simply, quite naturally, when you're not expecting them. But don't let's linger, brothers, let's go quickly!"

He took Kostandis by the arm; they strode forward, toward the village. Yannakos followed them, grumbling.

"Kostandis," Manolios was saying, "don't be afraid. The village won't be lost, I know the murderer. That's why I'm in a hurry."

"Who is it? who?" cried Kostandis, stopping, curious. "God showed him to you in a dream? Who is it?"

"Don't ask questions; don't stop, march!" said Manolios in a voice full of authority and love.

All three rushed ahead and soon reached the village like three horses at the trot.

Hussein's trumpet rang out angrily, urgently. The doors opened, the inhabitants, men and women, emerged. They crossed themselves and ran fearfully to the square.

"Courage, brothers!" Yannakos called to them, "God is great."

"Devil take you, crazy idiot!" growled an old man as he ran, holding his grandson by the hand. "If God is great, it's the moment for Him to show it. Let Him point to the murderer!"

Father Christofis went by, shouting:

"They're bringing Youssoufaki out under the plane tree, with candles, benjamin and sweet cakes. The widowed Agha's gone off his head."

In groups the Christians hastened up.

Michelis caught sight of his friends from afar and joined them. He was pale and despairing. But as soon as he saw the face of Manolios he gave a cry of joy and embraced his friend.

"Manolios, you're cured, you're cured! God be praised!"

"And Panayotaros?" asked Manolios.

"He'll be brought out. They've stunned him with cudgel blows, poor fellow!"

They drew near the square. The sun was a hand's breadth high in the sky, there was a little breeze blowing, delicious, and the village was radiant with a light that was all freshness. The old plane tree's tender foliage rustled gaily under the light breeze. Raising their eyes the old men looked at it with terror. How often, waking in the morning, had they not seen, swinging from its branches, Christians who had dared to lift their heads and claim liberty?

The harsh voice of the guard arose:

"Make room, make room, giaours!"

He led the way, opening a passage, with giant strides. Behind him two bearers carried the small iron bedstead on which the murdered boy was laid out. The Agha had covered him from head to foot with roses and jasmin. All that could be seen of him was his bloodless head with the curly hair, the lips scarred with bites. He had placed beside him a handful of mastic, for him to munch among the Shades.

With his hands bound behind his back, his head covered with wounds and his flesh blue from the blows of the whip, Panayotaros followed him, dragging. Only his eyes were still alive. He darted glances full of hate right and left upon the villagers.

"Haven't you any pity for the women and children, hey, you?" someone shouted at him. "Confess!"

Panayotaros stopped, furious.

"Who's got any pity for me?" he roared.

He reached the plane tree and, at the end of his strength, leaned against its old trunk, trying to wipe off with his shoulder the sweat dropping from his forehead.

Meanwhile the bearers had put down Youssoufaki in the shade, under the plane tree. They lit two great candles at his feet and threw a handful of benjamin onto some glowing coals.

Manolios and his companions cleared themselves a way through the crowd and took up position in the front, near the dead youth. In a flash, Panayotaros turned and saw them. His eyes became bloodshot. He jerked his hands as though to try and break his bonds, took a stride and suddenly yelled out:

"Curse you, Manolios!" Then he leaned against the plane tree once more, his strength exhausted.

"Courage, brother!" replied Manolios, "trust in God!"

Panayotaros was just opening his mouth again when a cry of alarm, which began at the Agha's door and grew from mouth to mouth, made the air ring with a terrified clamor:

"The Agha!"

Wearing his breeches of cloth embroidered with silver and girded with the wide red sash, silver pistols and blackhandled yataghan, his head bare, his eyes swollen from weeping, the Agha advanced alone, heavily, watching his steps, struggling not to stumble and so make himself ridiculous. All the *romnoi* had their eyes fixed on him. It would have been a disgrace to let it be seen that he was drunk or too ill now to walk. His mustache and eyebrows were thickly dyed black. From time to time he tore out a hair of his mustache with his right hand and threw it away. With his eyes and eyebrows frowning, he gazed out like a bull ready to charge. He had put musk in his hair and armpits; the strong smell of a rutting wild beast filled the air in his wake.

He did not turn to look at Youssoufaki, being afraid of not being able to control his tears: he went and took up position under the plane tree. The guard laid hands on Panayotaros, threw him brutally at the Agha's feet and held him there, motionless, with his foot.

The Agha raised his hand, and his raucous voice was heard announcing:

"Giaours! Every day I shall hang one of you. Until you denounce the murderer. The whole village shall go the way of the plane tree! In one scale of the balance there's my Youssoufaki, in the other the rest of the world. I'll hang the whole world, giaours!"

As he spoke, he grew angrier, and struck the ground with his foot like a horse. His eyes fixed the men, the women, eloquent of his haste to end them all. A steam rose from his mouth, his hair, his armpits. He stooped and began kicking Panayotaros, trampling him. A yellowish liquid foamed at his lips.

"Dirty giaour," he shouted at him, "was it you killed my Youssoufaki? Was it you, killed him? Confess!"

Panayotaros said nothing, he moaned.

The Agha, covered with sweat and no longer in control of himself, turned to Hussein:

"Hang him!" he yelled.

"Stop! Stop! I know the murderer!"

The guard let go of Panayotaros's neck, the crowd jostled and uttered cries of joy, while the Agha turned.

"Who spoke?" he shouted; "let him show himself!"

Manolios stepped forward, very calmly, and stopped before the Agha. The guard gave a bound and cocked his ear. His chin was quivering. He had gone all yellow and black.

"Are you the one who knows the murderer?" said the Agha; seizing Manolios by the arm he shook it furiously.

"Yes, I know the murderer."

"Who is it?"

"Me."

There was a great movement of relief, the women crossed themselves, faces relaxed. The village breathed again: it was saved.

"Silence, giaours!" cried the Agha, brandishing his whip.

Yannakos waved his arms, shouting: "It's not true!" "It's not true!" Kostandis and Michelis shouted, trying to reach the Agha. But the crowd threw itself upon them and stifled their voices.

"Be quiet! Be quiet! It's him, it's him! Say nothing and we'll be saved!"

Hussein was shaken with a burst of laughter. He rushed forward to take hold of Manolios and slip the rope around his neck. But the Agha pushed him back, approached Manolios and looked him in the eyes:

"You, giaour?" he roared.

"Me."

"It was you who killed him?"

"Me, I tell you. Hang me. Set Panayotaros free, he is innocent."

Panayotaros looked at Manolios with round eyes. He opened and shut his mouth, voiceless; he did not know what was happening to him. Was Manolios really the murderer? No! no! cried a voice deep down in him. It's impossible! If he's doing this to save me, may the plague choke him! I don't want to be saved. He began to cry out and to prance. The guard seized his whip.

"That's enough, giaour!" he cried.

The Agha, completely sobered, stared at Manolios, trying to understand.

"But why? What had he done to you?"

"He hadn't done anything, Agha; the Devil urged me and I killed him. In the night, when I was asleep, I heard a voice saying to me: 'Kill him!' Then I came down to the village before dawn and I killed him. Don't ask me anything more. Hang me!"

Hussein rushed forward, rope in hand. He seized Manolios by the arm. At the same moment, coming from the women's group, a voice howled piercingly:

"He's innocent, Agha, don't listen to him! He's innocent! Innocent! Innocent!"

"Shut up, whore!" cried voices all round Katerina, as the women hurled themselves on her to strangle her.

"He's doing this to save our village!" shouted the widow; "won't you have pity on him?"

But the women had already flung her to the ground and were trampling her.

"Manolios! My Manolios!" shouted the widow, fighting to free herself.

"He's innocent! innocent! innocent!" cried the three friends also, having managed to clear a way and to arrive in front of the Agha.

"Agha," said Michelis, "if this man is a murderer, I'm willing for you to cut my head off. He's our shepherd, a real saint, don't touch him!"

The Agha, exasperated, stared at Manolios, listened to the cries, saw his Youssoufaki, felt the fury growling within him; he was losing his head. Everything was confused in him, his head was reeling. "Him a murderer?" he asked himself, staring at Manolios, "or a madman? or rather, a saint? Devil take me, I can't make it out!"

He went on trying, lost his temper and, turning to Hussein, pointed to Manolios:

"To prison!" he ordered. "I'll give my decision tomorrow."

Then to the crowd:

"Go to the devil, giaours! Vanish from my sight!"

The people dispersed, frightened and relieved. Neighbors male and female gathered in knots to exchange their impressions, praising the Lord that the murderer had been found.

"Do you think it is Manolios?" they asked one another. "But he's a real saint . . ."

"Don't go straining at gnats, neighbor. What's it matter if it was him or not? He's confessed; that's good enough. He'll be hanged and we'll be saved. All the rest's frills. God keep his soul."

"But why does he go and do this? I can't understand. Because it's certain and sure he's not the murderer. Even if he says so."

"Ah, Manolios, don't you know him? Sometimes has visions, poor chap. He's doing it, he says, to save the village. No, did you ever hear of such a thing—finishing himself to save the others? If he had an ounce of brain, would he do it? Never! Well, let him, if that's what he wants."

The three friends had met in Michelis's house. Yannakos kept hitting his head with his fist.

"It's my fault, my fault! Idiot I am, it's just like me! I oughtn't to have let him come down from the mountain. Oughtn't to have told him. But how could I have thought of this?"

"He's a saint," murmured Michelis. "He's giving his life to save the village."

"We must save him!" cried Kostandis. "We must, we must!"

"If I had the strength to do what Manolios has done, I wouldn't want to be saved," said Michelis. "Did you see how his eyes shone? How his whole face sparkled? He was already in Paradise. Why bring him down to earth again? If only we could go with him!"

"We can!" exclaimed Yannakos with enthusiasm. "We've only to go at once, all three of us, and tell the Agha that we all went to his house during the night and killed his Youssoufaki. Let him hang the lot of us from the plane tree! Let's all go together, on each other's heels, to Paradise!"

Michelis shook his head:

"I haven't the strength, Yannakos," he confessed. "How could I leave Mariori?"

"Nor me," said Kostandis. "I've a wife and children."

Nor me, neither, Yannakos reflected in turn, I couldn't leave my donkey.

But he said nothing.

During this time, the four notables were waiting in the prison, leaning against the wall. In the basement where they lay heaped, they could not hear the murmur and shouting of the crowd above them. A mere thread of funereal light came in through a high round skylight.

"I'm hungry," sighed Patriarcheas.

"We're all hungry and thirsty," said priest Grigoris, "but we receive our trial with patience. God is with us in this lions' den."

"At this moment they must be hanging poor Panayotaros," the schoolmaster ventured. "Tomorrow it will be our turn. Let us show ourselves men, let us overcome hunger, thirst and fear."

Then, turning to his neighbor:

"Courage, father Ladas," he said. "Now do you see that I was right? How many times have I said to you: 'Why pile up money, father Ladas? None of your coffers of gold will follow you into the tomb. Do a good action. It alone will follow you as far as the judgment seat of God and plead for you.' What do you say now? Aren't you sorry about anything?"

Father Ladas sighed. Turning a long, completely moulted head, he stared at the schoolmaster with hatred but did not breathe a word.

"Tomorrow it will be your turn, father Ladas," said priest Grigoris then; "you will present yourself before God; you must confess. Bow yourself down, remember the evil you have done, and ask God for forgiveness. There is still time."

"I've done no evil to anyone," muttered old Ladas unwillingly,

"I have done no good to anyone, I haven't killed anyone, I'm innocent."

"Not done any evil to anyone, father Ladas?" cried old Patriarcheas. "At this moment when you're on the edge of the grave, I'm going to tell you some home truths, you old miser. I can't keep them to myself any longer. You've done no harm to anyone, eh? Who sold up the widow Anezina's house? And old Anesti's vineyards—who grabbed them at the auction? And the orphans who are now beggars—who pushed them onto the streets? You, you, by your rapacity! Today as ever is, go and give account of that to God."

Old Ladas lost his temper and came to life, suddenly leaving the wall.

"The pot calls the kettle black!" he ground out. "It suits your lordship to accuse others! But if I were to start laying out your dirty linen in public, it would be a bad look-out for you! What have you been doing on the earth, noble pig? You've guzzled up all you could, you've drunk like a wine cask, raped women, filled our village with bastards, and the neighboring ones. You've dragged your feet and idled around, all your life, billed and cooed with the Turks, humble pie on this side, presents on that. Notables, priests, even bishops, you were all the time courting the Turk. Your wife, who was a saint—wasn't it you who finished her off? She couldn't any longer bear seeing you running after women: you drove her to her death, poor thing!"

Old Patriarcheas jumped up to strangle him, but the other two intervened and separated them.

Father Ladas was beside himself. All his life he had let others say what they liked, and kept silent, had pretended not to notice; he, too, had eaten humble pie, told lies, to be on good terms with the powerful. But today, in face of death, he was bursting. He wanted to say everything, to vomit all he had swallowed and get rid of his bile, not let these people believe themselves better than he. So he went to it with a will: what need had he of them now?

He darted at the priest, and his voice whistled:

"And you, you sham, who'd make us confess, I'd like to know what sort of a face you'll wear when you present yourself before God? You come and go in the village strutting like a cock; your holiness gluts his paunch chock full, and when a poor man turns up

and knocks at the door, just as you're sitting down to stuff, you
put on the sweetest meekest voice and say to him: 'God succor
you, my brother. I, too, am hungry!' All this while the fat is
dribbling down into that goat beard of yours! Woe to the poor
fellow who dies and hasn't the cash for his burial: you let him rot!
You've always a hand stretched out for the price of spouting about
Christ. So much for a blessing, so much for a christening, so much
for a wedding, so much for the sacraments—you've even put up a
notice giving the rates, you vampire: '*Raia,* pay, or no entrance
for you!'

"The gall of your claiming to confess father Ladas, that holy
man who's been hungry all his life, who's kept himself from drinking a glass of wine when he wanted to, who's gone about in rags,
with bare feet and empty belly, like a real apostle. It's me—see?—
that's going to confess you, you fat soup-belly!"

Father Grigoris listened with his head bent in simulated Christian resignation; but inwardly he was boiling with rage. He would
have liked to twist that fleshless throat. Where had he stowed
away so much venom, the carrion? So that's what he was keeping
inside him, all these years, the old bastard. Now he was vomiting his soul and unpacking it all in public!

"Go on, go on, my dear Ladas," he said with a feigned sigh.
"Christ suffered more than sinful me. Mocked, calumniated,
scourged, crucified, He never opened His mouth. And should I
speak? Go on, go on, my dear Ladas!"

Old Ladas was about to open his gullet afresh to deal with him
roundly, but the schoolmaster intervened:

"Shame, brothers," he cried. "We have only a few hours to live
and, instead of raising our soul to God, we trail it in earthly passions. Be quiet, father Ladas, you've said enough, you've emptied
your heart. You, brothers, be quiet. The sins of men are without
limit."

Old Ladas sneered:

"Poor schoolmaster, what shall I say to you? Clean and dirty is
the same to you. Your brain's not very big, you've only managed
to do a little good and a little harm. You'd have liked to do a lot of
good, my poor friend, but you couldn't. You'd have liked to do a
lot of harm, but you couldn't. Nothing but odd jobs of no consequence. Your soul's only a small shopkeeper. She sells slates,
chalks, transfers, india rubbers, and notebooks cheap. School-

master, that's it. You also sold chalk as cheese—big words, in which you believed. You can keep them."

He was in a hurry to say everything and be relieved. Turning next to the others:

"Why are you pulling long faces at me?" he yapped, with anger in his eyes. "The hen scratches herself till she scratches out her eyes. There, you've gone too far, and you've hurt yourselves; much good may it do you!"

Priest Grigoris raised his eyes and made a sign to Patriarcheas: "Don't speak to him!" The old archon swallowed back his anger and was silent.

The schoolmaster jumped, hearing steps approaching.

"There they are . . ." he muttered: his blood stood still in his veins.

Priest Grigoris turned to father Ladas with hand stretched out to bless him.

"Be forgiven, brother," he said solemnly, "be forgiven for all you have said. You have thrown out all the foulness of your soul, it is rid of it. Without meaning to, unhappy man, you have confessed. God forgive you all the evil you have done in your life. Rise, father Ladas, your turn has come!"

But old Ladas collapsed, shaken with convulsions.

Insults, shouts and tramplings were heard. The door was barged open by the guard's shoulder, and Panayotaros and Manolios were flung into the cell so that they struck the wall. The door closed.

"Manolios," cried Patriarcheas, "what are you here for? Why've you been brought?"

"Panayotaros," said the schoolmaster, "so you're still alive? They haven't hanged you? God be praised!"

"I'm alive, curse the man whose fault it is!" roared Panayotaros and strode into a corner.

Father Ladas raised his head, stared fixedly at Panayotaros and put out a hand to touch him.

"You're still alive, really? Why didn't they hang you? Is the Agha sorry for what he's done? Can he have changed his mind?" As he asked these questions his heart beat as if to burst. Nobody replied.

"Lie down, Manolios," said priest Grigoris, "get back your breath."

"Tell us, Manolios," ordered the archon. "We can't wait any more; have they found the murderer?"

"They've found him," replied Manolios.

"Who? Who? Who?" cried all four at once, gathering around him.

"Me," replied Manolios.

"You?"

They recoiled, staring at Manolios with their mouths open. For a long time none of them said a word.

"It's impossible!" cried the old archon at last after going over in his mind the whole life of Manolios. "It's impossible! No, no, it's the end of the world!"

"I, too, can't admit it," said the schoolmaster. "Why should you have killed him? Can you kill, Manolios? You can't."

Only priest Grigoris looked at Manolios without saying anything.

"Why don't you answer, Manolios?" asked Patriarcheas.

"What for, archon?" said Manolios, wiping away the sweat which flooded over his face. "I'm the murderer, I've nothing else to say. Isn't it enough?"

"Yes!" cried father Ladas, "it's enough, my boy! They've found the murderer, we're saved, God exists!"

Manolios dragged himself into the ray of light which fell from the skylight, pulled the little Gospel out of his waistcoat pocket, opened it at random and began to read, forgetting the others around about him. He entered into the boat with Christ, mingled with the apostles, they went sailing on the lake of Gennesareth, and toward evening a violent wind came up. Christ, tired from having spoken to men all day, had gone and settled upon the nets in the stern, and had gone to sleep. But the north wind blew harder and harder, it was coming down from the mountains of Gilead, whipping up the lake, and the waves beat upon the little fishing boat with rage. The disciples were pale with fear.

"We're lost!" they kept murmuring, "we're lost! If only the Master would wake!"

But none dared interrupt the holy sleep. Peter drew near, bent over, and saw, by the light of a flash, that Christ was smiling.

"Wake him! Wake him!" cried the disciples, crowding up behind him.

Peter plucked up courage; put out his hand and lightly touched Christ on the shoulder.

"Master," he said, "awake; we shall perish!"

Christ opened His eyes, looked at the trembling disciples, shook His head and murmured bitterly:

"I have been with you a long time, and still you do not believe in me!"

He sighed, rose, stood up in the stern and, lifting His head, "Peace!" He ordered the wind.

He lowered His arm toward the angry lake:

"Be still," He said.

Immediately the wind fell silent, the waves became calm, the stars shone again, and the world once more took on its smiling look.

Manolios shook his head, and stared at his five companions. His blue eyes were shining, happy and calm, like the waters of Lake Gennesareth.

Father Ladas was coming back to life; on his feet now, he came and went, rubbing his hands.

"They've found the murderer. God be praised! we are saved. Poor Manolios, I'm sorry for you; but after all, it's not so bad. You were poor, a servant, still young. You hadn't tasted the sweetness of life. It doesn't matter your dying. Indeed, lucky you confessed and I'm saved."

He stopped, darted a sidelong glance at his companions and puckered up his lips. How the devil am I to smooth things down? he thought, how the devil, now I'm saved, smooth things down with that goat-beard and with that damned Patriarcheas whom I called "noble pig"? As for the schoolmaster, I don't care. But the others? I've been too hasty, I've cooked my goose, it's done! Still, lucky that I'm saved.

Old Patriarcheas stared at Manolios who was deep in his reading of the Gospel. He was overwhelmed. Leaning over to the priest he said, under his breath:

"Father, I've had an idea."

Priest Grigoris understood and coughed.

"Don't ask questions, archon," he said, "let be, and may the will of God."

"But if he's innocent? If he's done it to save the village? Can we let him? Isn't it a sin? Do you take responsibility?"

"God is merciful," said the priest, "He will forgive me."

"God will forgive you perhaps, priest, but will men?"

"If I am right with God," said the priest, puffing out his chest, "I have no fear of men."

"Then . . ."

The schoolmaster, who had approached and was listening, added his word:

"Don't let's search too far, let's leave it to God. He knows what He is doing. Besides, don't let's forget that Manolios is also saving his soul. That's certainly something."

"It is enormous!" the priest capped him. "He is losing the temporal life but gaining the life eternal. It's as if you gave a penny and were given back a million pounds of gold . . . Don't worry, Manolios knows what he is doing."

"He's really a clever little monkey," said the schoolmaster, looking with a smile at Manolios, whose eyes and face were radiant.

Hussein came in, rushed at Manolios and seized him by the collar.

"This way, giaour," he shouted at him, "the Agha wants to see you."

"In the name of Christ," murmured Manolios.

The Agha was seated cross-legged in his room. He was smoking his long chibouk and had Youssoufaki near him. It was noon, the heat was torrid; Youssoufaki was beginning to stink. Martha the slave entered noiselessly, with her hump sticking out. She was carrying an armful of fresh roses, jasmin and honeysuckle, which she laid in a sheaf on the half-rotted corpse, then ran out, unable to bear the smell.

Sunk in his grief, the Agha smelled nothing. He smoked his chibouk, deep in better reflections. He looked tired, he was the calmer for it. It was written, he had told himself that morning, it was written . . . and from that moment his heart had been assuaged. He threw the sin of men upon God and was appeased. Who can lay blame on God? He willed it so, He had written it. All that happens, happens by His will; bow the head and be silent. Was it not He that had written that the Agha of Lycovrissi should meet Youssoufaki at Smyrna? Was it not He, again, that had written who should kill Youssoufaki? Was it not He that had written that the murderer would be found? All is written . . .

He saw Manolios enter, laid down his chibouk on the mat on which he was crouching, and folded his arms.

"Listen to what I wish to say to you, Manolios," he said calmly. He turned to his guard.

"I don't need you any more, stay outside the door."

He looked at Manolios:

"I have dreamed that it was not you who killed my Youssoufaki. Be quiet, giaour, let me speak! You are doing this to save the village. You must be mad or a saint; that's your affair. Don't worry, it shall be done according to your desire, I shall hang you. But there is one thing I should like to know, Manolios: is it true that you murdered my Youssoufaki?"

Manolios was sorry for the Agha. Never had he seen such grief. This was no longer a wild beast let loose; suffering had made it a human being. He hesitated a moment, but recovered at once and raised his head:

"Agha," he said, "it was the Devil urged me to it, it was written, it is I who killed him."

The Agha leaned against the wall and closed his eyes. "Allah, Allah," he murmured, "the world is a dream."

He opened his eyes and clapped his hands. Hussein entered. "Take him away!" he said. "At the hour of sunset you will hang him from the plane tree."

Meanwhile the three comrades, Michelis, Kostandis and Yannakos, were going around the village, knocking at the doors and begging the villagers not to let an innocent die.

"Manolios is innocent, innocent! He's doing this to save our village!" Yannakos kept crying.

"Well, what do you expect us to do?" an old man took him up; "go and tell the Agha that Manolios isn't the murderer? And what then? The Agha will start the hangings one after the other, he'll wipe out the whole village, instead of one innocent it'll be thousands of innocents who'll die. Would that be right? Would it be any good? Isn't it better for there to be one only who dies, rather than hundreds? Besides, he himself wants it. Let him die to save us, afterward we'll make an icon to him, we'll light a candle for him and discover that he's a saint. For the moment, let him die."

The father of a large family spoke to Michelis and asked him aggressively:

"You've no children, have you, young lord?"

"No."

"Good; well you've nothing to say. Leave us in peace."

An old woman who was jumping her grandson up and down on her knees, turned to Yannakos, saying:

"Why do you stand whimpering there, Yannakos? Let a thousand Manolioses die and my grandson live."

"They're wild beasts, wolves, foxes," Yannakos moaned, wiping his eyes.

"They aren't wild beasts, Yannakos," replied Michelis, "only men. Don't let's waste our time. Let God do what He will."

"You're thinking of your father," said Yannakos with resentment. "This way the old man escapes."

Michelis looked at him with tears in his eyes.

"I'm sorry, Michelis," cried Yannakos, "I don't know what I'm saying any more."

Just as they reached the square they saw Katerina, with her hair freshly washed, and dressed in her best; she was coming straight for them, all sails set, like a royal frigate.

"Where are you going, Katerina?" said Yannakos.

"Bunch of cowards, would you let Manolios go to his death?" cried the widow, whose big eyes were filling with tears. "I won't. I'm going to see the Agha."

"Grief's driven you crazy too, Katerina," replied Yannakos.

"The Agha will kill you in his rage, poor woman, turn back," said Michelis, seized with pity.

"What would I do with my life now?" said the widow as she disappeared, her head held high, into the Agha's courtyard.

A hot, stifling odor of roses and decomposing flesh . . . The Agha, leaning his head against the small iron bedstead, had gone to sleep. He was surely dreaming that his misfortune was only a dream and that, on waking, he would once more find himself on his balcony and Youssoufaki at his side filling his glass with raki.

Two pigeons came and went on the balcony, pecking each other and cooing. Down below in the courtyard the fountain gurgled. The dog lay on the stones with its tongue hanging out and panted. A black cat, large and fat, had taken refuge in the shade; its green eyes gleamed, disquieting, fascinating.

Katerina crossed the courtyard very quickly, afraid the guard might see her or the dog start barking. But Hussein did not appear, and the dog, having sniffed and recognized her, was content to wag its tail. She knew the ins and outs of the house perfectly: Martha had several times opened the door to her secretly, to let her in at night when the Agha was alone. That was before his journey to Smyrna, when he had not yet found Youssoufaki. Since then, more than once, his bodyguard had reminded him of the widow. The Agha had laughed. "Old man," he had said to him one day, "there's a story that the pasha once invited one of his friends to drink raki with him. He served as *meze* a pot of olives and another containing black caviar. His friend touched only the caviar. 'Take some olives as well,' said the pasha to him. 'I, too, like caviar,' his friend replied. Do you understand, Hussein? My Youssoufaki is caviar." The guard held his tongue and did not mention the widow to him since that day.

The courtyard passed, Katerina penetrated into the house; she was seized with fright—the great mirror, the couches, the stools, the heavy bronze brazier, the sofa, had served as targets for the Agha; they were overturned, in fragments. Panayotaros would have done the same for me, the widow told herself, and shuddered.

Hearing footsteps, she hid behind a smashed couch. The guard appeared on the threshold. A real phantom—his cheeks were furrowed, his eyes sunk in their sockets. The saliva was running from his mouth. He paused a moment, looked about him without seeing, sighed, then went out unsteadily into the yard. He lay down beside the dog and began to cry.

The widow crossed herself. "Lord Jesus," she murmured, "You alone understand Woman and forgive her, whatever she does. I am ready to appear before You." She had put on clean underclothes and her best dress, and scented her hair with orange-blossom water. "Lord Jesus," she murmured again, "I am ready."

"Katerina, my friend, what are you doing here? Go back to your cottage at once, what are you thinking of?"

The widow turned and saw Martha carrying an armful of flowers and making ready to go up to the room. She was pale and dishevelled.

"Martha, I want to see the Agha," said the widow.

"Youssoufaki's not yet cold and you have the face . . . He'll mince you up like mincemeat, wretched creature!"

"Martha, I want to see the Agha," the widow repeated. "I've a great secret to tell him. I know the murderer!"

The old slave sneered:

"Manolios?" she said.

"No, someone else . . . You'll see . . ."

The slave laid the flowers down on a step, came up to the widow and stood on tiptoe:

"Who? who?" she breathed, and her eyes kindled; "have you thought of him, too? So've I! So've I!"

"Whom?" said the widow, dumbfounded.

The old woman looked at her attentively, shook her head, stooped and picked up the sheaf of flowers:

"Nothing," she said. "I've said nothing. I'll go and put these flowers on that damned boy; he's beginning to stink, devil take him!"

She spat on the floor, feeling sick. Suddenly her malice burst out:

"You're full of worms, you too, my pretty one," she said; "and so'm I, full of worms. Strut as much as you like, we're all the same."

But a violent blow rang out in the room and an angry voice cried:

"Who's down there? Who are you talking to, old cripple? Shut up!"

The little old woman stood up, but the widow advanced courageously to the staircase.

"It's me, Katerina, Agha."

"Bitch," yelled the Agha, "get out!"

The widow shrugged her shoulders and continued to advance. Suddenly the Agha saw her in front of him.

"Agha, forgive me, forgive me!" cried the widow, throwing herself at his feet.

The Agha, in a fury, kicked her, forced her to turn, and made a rush to throw her down the stairs. But the widow had clung to the banister and, lying face down on the ground, was crying out:

"Agha, listen to me, I couldn't keep the secret any longer, I've come to throw myself at your feet. Agha, it was I that killed him!"

"You, you whore?" roared the Agha, and his eyes swept the walls in search of his yataghan.

"Me, Agha, me, damned that I am, it was me that killed him, from love . . . from jealousy. I was jealous. Ever since he set

foot in your palace, you've not given me a look. You stopped
sending Martha to fetch me. I wept. I pined away. Day and night
I sat just inside my door, waiting. Nothing . . . nothing. You
had Youssoufaki, you forgot me. I went looking for spellbinders
of all sorts, and one night I put a spell on your door and I waited.
But you had your Youssoufaki, I was forgotten. I loved you too
much, I was too jealous, it made me crazy. The night before last,
at midnight, I took a knife . . ."

She dragged herself to the Agha's feet and embraced them:
"Agha," she howled, "Agha, kill me! What's the use of life to
me? Kill me!"

The Agha was still searching his walls for his yataghan. The
house was reeling, his eyes were going dim, he could no longer see
anything. The widow pulled a knife from her bodice.

"Here, this is the knife I killed him with." She rose to her knees
and stretched out the knife to the Agha. "Here, this is the
knife . . ." she repeated, baring her throat.

The Agha's eyes became bloodshot. He turned, saw Youssoufaki
stretched livid there, with his eyes wide and his mouth open.
Great blue and black flies were going in and out through his lips
and nostrils.

He looked in front of him again, and saw the widow. He threw
himself upon her, seized the knife she was holding out to him,
brandished it in the air and, with one blow, planted it full in her
heart, to the hilt. Then, with a kick, he sent her rolling to the
bottom of the stairs.

The Rising Path

THE WIDOW'S BLOOD revived the fury of the Agha. He saw red; he was still holding the knife. His arm was running with blood to the elbow. He called Hussein:

"Go down to the cell, take Manolios and lead him to the plane tree. Sound the trumpet, let the giaours come and watch him. Bring Youssoufaki out under the plane tree, so that he may see, too. Murderer or not, hang the wretch. Bring me the whip, I'll go down alone; I'll smash their bones. That'll relieve me! Possibly I'll hang them this morning, all five of them, one after the other. Guilty or not! I'll hang them all, all! Why should they live, when my Youssoufaki is stretched out there? Run!"

His eyes again filled with tears. Turning, he placed the bloody knife among the roses on the body of Youssoufaki.

"Take it, my Youssoufaki," he said.

He kneeled down, leaned against the little iron bedstead, and began to smoke. He shut his eyes. Through his mind passed fields, mountains, villages. He was on the road again, making again the journey from Lycovrissi to Smyrna. Now in a carriage, now on muleback, now in that devil's machine brought in by the people of the West, curse them! One morning, miracle! Palaces, mosques, bazaars, thousands of people, music, gardens, the sea! Then all vanished. There remained only a café by the waterside. Its doors were open. It was hot. The sun was setting. Seated in a circle on mats, carefully washed aghas with their clean clothes, their narghiles, their black-dyed mustaches. In the center, throned on a high stool, what does the Agha of Lycovrissi discover as he comes in? Youssoufaki singing: *"Dounia tabir, rouya tabir, aman, aman"*! The café, too, vanished, with the aghas, the mats and the

narghiles. Of all Smyrna there remained only him and his Youssoufaki. The one entreating on his knees, the other simpering
and fluttering, munching mastic the while.

Hussein entered, bringing the whip; he placed it on his master's
knees. The Agha lowered his head and gazed out under heavy
lids without a frown. Where should he go? Why leave the place
where he is, by the shore of the sea, with his Youssoufaki? He
shut his eyes and went back to Smyrna.

Outside, the guard's trumpet rang out martially. The sun was
already low, but the heat persisted. Not a leaf stirred. Motionless,
defenceless, bunched in the sun, the village scorched.

One by one the doors opened. Hearing the trumpet the villagers
assembled around the plane tree. Some, the dour ones, were
silent. Others, overexcited, came and went, arguing. Did Manolios kill him or did he not? Is he or isn't he a criminal?

"Never trust sleeping water!" said one of them, shaking his
head. "I was always suspicious of Manolios. First with the widow,
now with Youssoufaki. Ugh! disgusting! the devil take him!"

The old beadle arrived, his tongue hanging out. He was the
bearer of terrible news, and this rejoiced his heart:

"Was just passing the Agha's door, went quite close, what should
I see in the yard? Martha, the old hunchback, beating her breast
and groaning. 'What's the matter, mother?' I says to her. 'They've
killed the widow!' 'Who's they?' 'The Agha! He cut her throat
like a sheep's, then threw her right down the stairs.' Let's go and
bury the poor thing; she, too, was a Christian; she, too, had a
soul."

"Bury her? what next, beadle?" sneered a yellow-skinned old
man. "Let her go burn in Hell!"

The sun was about to set. The birds were fluttering around the
plane tree, seeking to rest there for the night, but they saw a crowd
of men assembled; from it rose a disquieting murmur, and they
took fright. They flew hither and thither, undecided, waiting for
this human gathering to disappear and let them return to their
nests.

The Agha's heavy door was heard opening. All heads turned.
Calm and smiling, Manolios appeared on the threshold with his
hands tied behind his back. Blood was dripping from his face and
arms.

He paused a moment on the threshold; but the guard was following him and with fury struck him a violent blow with the whip. Manolios crossed the threshold unperturbed. He was followed by the bearers with the little iron bedstead on which Youssoufaki lay under armfuls of flowers.

Manolios advanced with even steps. His gaze was floating slowly, for the last farewell, over the faces around him, over the houses, the trees and, in the distance, the cornfields bowing their ripe ears and glowing like gold at the final flames of sunset. God be praised, he said to himself. We shall have a good harvest this year, the poor people will get enough to eat.

Suddenly he caught sight, under the plane tree, of his three friends who were watching him and weeping. Manolios smiled to them and gave a sign with his head to greet them. He stopped for an instant, looked at the people and cried:

"Good-bye, friends, I am going."

He turned his eyes once more to his three companions:

"Brothers," he said, "Michelis, Kostandis, Yannakos, I am going. Keep well!"

"Innocent! Innocent! Innocent!" cried the three friends, though their voices were strangling.

"Haven't you then any self-respect?" flung Yannakos at the villagers, who stood watching without a word. "Won't you fall on your knees before him, you swine? It's for us he's dying, to save the village. Don't you understand? He's taking on him the sins of us all, like Christ. My brothers . . ."

He had no time to finish. The guard had rushed at him, and the whip made a double turn around his neck.

The Agha crossed the threshold. All at once fell silent. The crowd opened to let him through. Heavily, gloomily the Agha advanced, with his eyes on the ground.

When he reached the plane tree he stopped; without even turning to see Manolios, he stretched out his arm toward his guard:

"Hang him!" he ordered.

The colossus, Hussein, threw himself on Manolios and seized him by the throat. At that instant a piercing voice rang out:

"Agha! Agha!"

Old Martha came running up, breathless, bearing in her arms a bundle of clothes. Hussein turned pale, let fall the rope he was knotting, and leaned against the plane tree, trembling. The old hunchback woman collapsed at the feet of the Agha:

"Agha," she yelped, "look! look!"

She unfolded her bundle at the Agha's feet and laid in a line on the ground, spotted with blood, a jacket, breeches, leggings and a pair of Turkish slippers. The Agha stooped:

"Whose is all that?" he cried.

"Hussein's!" answered old Martha. "Your guard's."

The Agha turned and stared at Hussein. He had collapsed at the foot of the plane tree. The villagers held their breath.

With a bound, the Agha was on him, and shook him, yelling: "Hussein Moukhtar!"

The guard, bunched in a ball on the ground, hid his face in his huge hairy hands.

"Mercy," he lowed, like a calf.

The three companions drew near. Their hearts were beating as if to burst. The crowd, like a human tide, surrounded the Agha, the guard and old Martha. Yannakos stealthily approached Manolios, untied him, and seized his hand and kissed it.

The Agha raised his head, looked at the villagers, saw their faces illumined with joy and brandished the whip.

"Giaours," he shouted, "be off! Out of my sight, or look out for yourselves!"

He fell on the crowd and began striking women and men. He was foaming at the mouth.

In the flicker of an eyelid the square emptied. All stampeded to their homes. The boldest hid behind corners to see what would happen. Manolios was led away by his three friends; they went and leaned against the wall opposite.

"It was you, was it? It was you, was it?" bellowed the Agha, dancing on the guard's belly and spitting on him. He unsheathed his yataghan, and sheathed it again. He stooped, picked up pebbles and struck him on the skull with them. He had lost his head and did not know what death to choose.

Old Martha darted to and fro with a multitude of little jerks, agile, possessed. She kept gathering and dispersing the clothes of the bundle, waving them in the air, laying them out on the ground, exhibiting the great stains of blood.

Panting, she repeated ceaselessly the same words, like a refrain:

"I heard him, Agha, go upstairs in the middle of the night. I heard a tiny cry, like a bird being killed, Agha. But how could I dare open my mouth, a poor woman like me? Only you see, I found these things and this blood!"

She began again unfolding them and exhibiting them on the ground, showing the bloodstains.

Soon the Agha had had enough of her refrain and gave her a kick in the kidneys. The little old woman gave a sharp cry like a cat being killed, and trotted off limping to her master's door. She bunched herself up on the doorstep like a bat, with her piercing eyes fixed on the Agha and the guard.

"Now tear each other's eyes out, you dirty Turks!" she muttered. "I've found what I was looking for, the rest can go hang!"

The Agha had knelt down on the ground and with a blow of his fist forced the guard too to kneel opposite him. They were face to face, their noses touching. For a long time they remained like that, motionless. The sun had vanished; the birds grew bold, seeing the crowd scatter, and returned to their nests in the old plane tree.

The four companions waited, crouched against the wall and holding their breath. They could feel that something terrible was about to happen.

"I pity poor Hussein," muttered Manolios.

"Be quiet, God doesn't pity him," replied Yannakos.

The Agha suddenly stood up, and roared like a lion:

"Get up, dog!"

The guard leaped to his feet. The Agha drew his yataghan and brought it down once, twice, three times, cutting off the nose and the ears and sending them flying a long way from him. The giant made no move, gave no cry. He held himself upright like a tree that is being lopped. His blood streamed, forming a pond of mud.

The Agha brandished the whip.

"Run around the tree!" he bellowed.

Hussein began to run, staggering, around the plane tree.

"Stop!" roared the Agha again.

The guard stopped. The Agha threw himself on him, tore his breeches down, grabbed his private parts, hacked them off at one blow and flung them upon the corpse of Youssoufaki, right in the middle of the jasmines.

The brute at that gave a fearful bellow and collapsed. The Agha lifted him by the skin of his back, piled him onto the stool, strung him up with the running noose, gave the stool a kick, and the guard, covered with blood and horribly mutilated, swung in the air.

The Agha wiped the sweat from his forehead with his red hand; his whole face became daubed with blood. He let himself fall to his knees on the ground and for a long time, panting, stared at his guard, with his mouth open. Then, as if his soul had at last been sated, he stood up and, without a glance at the hanged man or at Youssoufaki, went swaying back to his dwelling, with jerky steps. He kicked open the door, but slipped and fell full length upon the stones.

"What exactly can be happening up there?" the archon Patriarcheas was at that moment asking his companions. Sitting on the ground, with their backs against the wall and their heads turned toward the low door, they were waiting.

"I'll tell you, archon," replied father Ladas, who had already set to work to patch things up again with those in power and to cosset them. "Manolios, God keep his soul! is now swinging in the air. Wrongly or rightly, what can it matter to us? The chief thing is that we're saved. In a moment the guard will turn up and say: 'Out with you, giaours, get off home!' He'll give us a kick and we shall go back up to the light and to our business. As for anything we may have said to each other, archon, and you, priest Grigoris, let bygones be bygones."

I'll have your eyes out, you dirty swine! thought priest Grigoris, but remembering that he was a Christian and a priest, he smoothed out his face and voice, and said:

"Let us be saved, old Ladas, by the help of God, and the rest we'll forget. We're men, we've been through difficult moments and said a few words too many. There! I've already forgotten."

"I shall never forget that you called me 'noble pig,'" said old Patriarcheas. This nickname, which fitted him like a glove, had pierced him to the heart.

"Did I use such a word, archon?" said father Ladas with an air of consternation. "I take back what I said. I'd lost my head with fear, poor me, I was stuttering, couldn't find my words. I meant to say 'noble lord' and said 'noble pig.'"

Panayotaros raised his bruised head.

"Go to the devil, you band of cowards!" he shouted. "You're

afraid of each other and disgusted with each other, but you daren't admit it. You want to keep together, you idlers, to plunder the poor! But me, the rotter—you can't frighten me. Priests, bishops, archons, notables, schoolmaster, I spit on you!"

The schoolmaster was opening his mouth to smooth things down when the door opened, letting in old Martha, and they could see her piercing eyes shining in the half-dark.

"Well, Martha, what have you got for us from the world above?" cried the archon, rising.

The old slave grinned and stretched out a hand.

"If you fill this with gold pieces," she replied, "I won't turn my back."

"Dirty shrew," whined old father Ladas, "haven't you any pity on us? We're poor, would you drink our blood?"

"Is it good or bad, the news you've got for us?" asked priest Grigoris. "We must know that first."

"I tell you again, I won't turn my back, priest. Isn't this the way your holiness puts out his hand before starting the *Kyrie Eleison*? Why should I be better than you? Open your purses, my lords, in the name of the good I wish you!"

The archon Patriarcheas was the first to open his purse, and brought out a gold piece. Then, to the priest:

"Father," he said, "they call you 'noble pope,' don't haggle. You too, open your wallet, father Ladas, you who call me 'noble pig.' It'll do you good to be bled a little, you might have an attack, poor man. Come, schoolmaster, you too, out with it. You aren't rich, give what you can, let's be done with it. The old woman's got good news for us, can't you see how her eyes are shining?"

The priest and the schoolmaster rummaged in their pockets. Father Ladas sighed.

"If I say I owe you them, won't that do, my good Martha?" he asked in a tone of entreaty. "I'll make you out a note."

"Isn't your life worth a miserable piece of gold, skinflint? Pluck up a little courage, loosen the pursestrings."

She turned to Panayotaros:

"Poor Plaster-eater," she sneered, "I don't want a penny from you. The widow must have cleaned you out."

"Shut your mouth, old she-ass!" yelled Panayotaros. "You wait till I can measure your hump for you and make you a saddle that won't hurt you, dirty hag!"

"Don't get excited, poor Plaster-eater, I've got a piece of news for you too: you're saved! You're saved, you unlucky lover! Widow Katerina's gone underground!"

The eyes of Panayotaros became round; he tried to speak, but could not; he began to howl.

"The Agha has just killed her. He's stuck a knife into her heart and packed her off as a present to the Devil!"

Panayotaros rolled on the floor, hurled himself head first against the wall. He kept roaring like a wild beast, calling the widow. Doubled up on the doorstep, the old hunchback goaded him:

"Who told her to be pretty? Who told her to be a whore? Who told her to go and visit the Agha? Serves her right! He planted a knife in her heart and sent her rolling right to the bottom of the stairs."

But Panayotaros was not listening to her; he was twisting, biting the ground, calling the widow.

Meanwhile old Patriarcheas had collected the money; he filled the hunchback's hand. Her tongue was immediately let loose, and she began to tell the whole story. She talked, laughed, danced, imitated the Agha, the guard; howled, sneered. Priest Grigoris crossed himself.

"Come," he said, "blessed be the name of the Lord! We entered here as simple men, we go out as heroes and martyrs of Christ!"

"My word," the old archon said in his turn. "We're well out of it."

"A gold piece it's cost me, this business," growled father Ladas. "But when I'm out I'll get my own back. And to begin with, that dog Yannakos—I'll sell his ass!"

Priest Grigoris crossed the threshold.

"Tomorrow, brethren," he said, "we must celebrate a *Te Deum*, secretly. We have behaved as heroes and Christians. We have emerged victorious from the terrible trial. The Lord's name be glorified!"

"I," said the schoolmaster, "shall set the children an essay on the sufferings and heroism of the Greek race."

Priest Grigoris emerged first, his head high, strutting like a he-goat at the head of his flock. He was followed by old Patriarcheas, grimy and famished. Then came the schoolmaster, enjoying the pride of having showed so much gallantry and not having let down the ancestors. Lastly, closing the rear, father Ladas, holding up his breeches, whose belt had again broken.

"Hey, Plaster-eater," cried the old hunchback woman, who stood, key in hand, near the door, "out you go, too, go and keep him company."

"Let the big asses leave first," growled the saddler. "I shall go alone."

He clenched his fist and stood up.

"Priests, bishops, archons, notables, schoolmaster, I spit on you!"

"Judas!" the priest flung at him, unable to restrain himself any more. Having said it, he made off rapidly.

Panayotaros rushed in pursuit to catch him by the beard, but the priest had started first; he was already outside and crossing the yard. His three companions followed him in haste.

Evening had fallen. The streets were deserted. The villagers had shut themselves up in their homes; they were drinking an extra round to celebrate this memorable day. Manolios, Hussein, the widow, the Agha, Youssoufaki, old Martha—every house was buzzing with them. Old Patriarcheas was seated before his well-stocked table. He had washed, changed, was refreshed. A dainty Lenio had boiled a chicken and prepared an egg-and-lemon soup to restore her master. Michelis, sitting opposite his father, watched him wolf it ravenously, sweating in his haste to reconstitute his rudely tried strength.

He listened to him talking, laughing, chewing; he watched him in amazement.

That's my father, he thought, that's my father.

"We're well out of it," he was saying, with his mouth full. "Now that I've seen Charon face to face, Michelis, I understand what life is. Mustn't waste time, my son; must eat, drink, go on the spree before it's too late. Just fancy if I hadn't got out, this chicken would have been wasted!"

Michelis could not take his eyes off him, and said not a word.

That's my father. That's my father, he kept thinking, appalled.

Priest Grigoris, for his part, was installed in his courtyard, under the trellis weighted with clusters of fruit. He ate and could not calm his hunger. A gentle summer breeze was blowing. The sweet basil and jasmin were balmy, and the cat came and rubbed against his legs, purring. Mariori stood holding the wine jug, and served him while tears of joy ran down her pale cheeks.

The padded priest drank, ate, gorged.

"Not for one instant did my heart weaken. I behaved like a leader, like a worthy representative of God in Lycovrissi. I spoke to the Agha with assurance, I defended Christianity; in prison I held myself upright to face death. Mariori, you can be proud of your father."

Old Ladas was seated on the bench in his yard, barefoot, beltless. He munched his barley bread, carefully chewed an olive, and talked volubly to his Penelope—he had done this, they had done to him that, he had said this, they had said to him that; the business was costing him so much.

He sighed, became angry, went back into his room, opened the chest, brought out his ledgers, drew near the stub of candle. He wetted his finger and began flicking the pages of his notebooks to see who owed him money and how much, when each one's loan fell in and how much the interest came to. He smiled with satisfaction.

"Tomorrow morning, my dear Penelope, I shall get my own back. I've escaped from the claws of death; now that I'm saved, no more favors. I owe you, you eat me; you owe me, I'll eat you. And quickly, while we're still alive. What do you think, my dear?"

Mother Penelope had her empty eyes fixed placidly on her needles and was knitting away. As though she saw Charon in front of her and was in haste to finish in time. To finish the sock. She had not even been worried by the disappearance of her husband, any more than she experienced joy at seeing him tramping the yard once more, holding up his breeches, scratching, and talking without stopping.

The conversation that evening went on for a long time; the lamps burned till midnight. Then the village put out its lights one by one, shut its eyes and began to snore.

Michelis had left his friends early, being in a hurry to go and see his father.

"Suppose we went and ate together at my house?" Kostandis

suggested to his two companions. "We could celebrate your resurrection, Manolios!"

This evening Madam Kostandis was having one of her good days. She did not, when she saw them, put on her usual frown. She lit the fire and busied herself with preparing the dinner. Then she laid the table, brought wine and put the water jug into the well to cool.

"There's no one like your sister," whispered Kostandis to Yannakos, "there's no one like her for housewife's work when she's in a good mood. There's no one like her, either, when she's in a bad mood. God be praised, we're in luck this evening. Welcome, brothers," he added aloud.

"Greetings to your house, to your wife, to your children, Kostandis!" replied the guests, and all three, famished, started to eat and drink. Standing behind them, the lady of the house served.

Yannakos and Kostandis clinked glasses with Manolios.

"Christ is risen!" they cried, looking at him tenderly.

Manolios said nothing, did not smile. Yes, certainly, he was glad to be still alive, to be eating and drinking with his friends, to feel the evening breeze pass over his sweating forehead. Yet he had expected to be elsewhere this evening, and a supraterrestrial sorrow veiled his face.

"Don't be sad, Manolios," said Yannakos, "Paradise is good, but earth has some good in it, too. You wouldn't find a Kostandis and a Yannakos in Paradise," he added with a laugh. "Because we two, Kostandis, the way things are going, are ripe to go to Hell. But not to the very bottom, just to the edge!"

They all three laughed and refilled their glasses.

"The one I'm sorry for is the widow, poor thing," said Kostandis, under his breath so that his wife should not hear. "A pity, such a royal mouthful!"

"Who knows?" said Yannakos, "perhaps this moment, as we speak, Katerina the widow is in Paradise with Mary Magdalen. The two are strolling arm-in-arm over the immortal grass and looking at the earth right down below, and laughing."

"Sighing perhaps, old Yannakos, for they both of them loved this world a lot," said Kostandis. "What do you think, Manolios?"

"I envy the widow," Manolios replied, "I envy her, I'm not sorry for her. Why should I be sorry for her? It's certain she's

at this moment walking in Paradise with the angels and has neither
sigh nor smile for earth. She's completely forgotten it. This world
has vanished for her—yes, just as the leprosy has vanished from
my face."

Kostandis's wife heard these last words. She looked then at
Manolios for the first time and saw that his face, which was said
to be swollen and covered with leprosy, was now radiant and perfectly clear. She was on the point of asking him how this miracle
had happened, but the men were talking and, as this was one of
her good days, she did not wish to meddle with the conversation.
She contented herself with cocking an ear and listening. When
the widow came into it, she growled softly, ready to bite, but she
tightened her lips and did not bite.

"And poor Hussein—what do you say of him, Manolios?" asked
Kostandis. "He was a vicious dog, but all the same . . ."

"If he'd been a Christian and had repented," Manolios replied,
"who knows, Kostandis? God might have laid His hand on his
head and said to him: 'Be forgiven, for thou hast loved much.' "

"But if it were like that," cried Yannakos, "if it were as you
say, in the end everyone would get into Paradise, sinners, robbers, murderers . . ."

"Paradise was made for sinners," murmured Manolios.

"Then let's drink to the health of Hussein!" said Kostandis,
who was beginning to be gay. "Let's drink to the health of the
Agha, poor widower, because he, too, loved much. Let's drink to
Youssoufaki who died an unjust death! Was he guilty, poor thing?
He munched mastic and sang *amanés*. What else did he do?"

"And even if he did do something else," said Yannakos, bursting out laughing, "much good may it do him!"

Kostandis made a sign with his hand and winked, to indicate
his wife, who was pretending to contemplate the stars through
the open window. Yannakos understood and was silent.

"Only don't ask me to drink to the health of father Ladas, or
priest Grigoris!" said Kostandis with emphasis; "not that!"

"Your wine is good, Kostandis," exclaimed Yannakos, who was
already tipsy. "I'd drink even their healths."

He refilled his glass:

"To the health of father Ladas, the devil take him!" and he emptied it at one go. He filled again:

"To the health of priest Grigoris, the devil take him!" and he gulped that down, too.

"Is there any other sinner to celebrate?"

Wine in abundance, hearts overflowing, their breasts had dilated and were swelling with love.

Christ is like wine, thought Manolios. Like it, He opens the heart of Man and the whole world enters in. That's how He will open Paradise, that all the sinners may find a place . . .

He contemplated his friends, who had fallen into one another's arms and were laughing.

"And Panayotaros!" said Yannakos, "we've forgotten Judas. To his health, Pater James!"

"To his health, Apostle Peter!" replied Kostandis, and they emptied their glasses.

Mother Kostandis turned. They'd drink all her wine: she was beginning to get annoyed.

"You're drinking a lot, Kostandis," she said severely.

Kostandis made himself quite small.

"It's all right," he said, "don't get angry, Wife. Bring the jug of water to cool us down."

The woman went to the well, and Kostandis laid a finger on his lips.

"Look out, clumsy," he said under his breath, "take care or she'll be getting in a temper."

"We'll go," said Yannakos, "we'll go, can't have you in trouble."

"No, no, lads, only thing is to keep quiet. We'll drink her health in water, perhaps she'll calm down. You don't know anything about women."

Mother Kostandis came back with the jug. She took the glasses, rinsed them and filled them with cold water. The men raised them and toasted her:

"Your health, little sister," said Yannakos. "God in mercy cool your soul, as you've cooled our throats this evening. A better sister than you, or a better wife, doesn't exist. Wherever Kostandis goes, he sings your praises!"

"Your health, Wife!" said Kostandis timidly. "I'd rather, on my faith, go to Hell with you than all alone to Paradise!" and as he said these words he winked at his companions.

"Your health, mother," said Manolios. "You must excuse us,

it's a great day today, our village has been saved. God repay you one day for the trouble we've given you."

They drank and felt refreshed; the flame subsided a little. Kostandis pulled out his tobacco pouch and passed it to his companions after rolling a cigarette. They got up, went out into the yard and sat down on the stone bench: the woman began to clear the table, mumbling.

From the plain came the smell of the ripe corn. There was a fig tree in the middle of the yard, and night made the figs balmy.

Someone stopped before the door and knocked. Kostandis got up, surprised.

"It's me, Kostandis, open, it's Michelis."

Full of joy, Kostandis opened, and the outline of Michelis showed in the darkness.

"I've left my old man," he said. "He's eaten and drunk, it's made him sleepy. Then I came along."

He sat down quietly beside them on the bench. He could feel the gentlest silence floating around him, and did not wish to disturb it; he remained silent.

Manolios leaned his head against the wall. He gazed at the stars, and his soul became a starry sky. Gently in the night the voice of Manolios arose:

"Man proposes and God disposes," he said. "He would not let me die this evening and leave you, brothers. Who knows? God surely had a reason; we haven't finished our time on earth; must go on working hard to save our soul; this very evening, brothers, I've made a resolution."

So saying, he raised his eyes again toward the Milky Way above him.

Yannakos and Kostandis were beginning to sober down. The fumes of the wine which had gone to their heads were now spreading throughout their bodies and irrigating them like a good thought. Michelis touched Manolios's knee as though to say to him: "I'm with you!"

They were absolutely alone in the darkness. The passing wind was very gentle. The stars above them lit their faces faintly. They could barely distinguish one another in the night.

Manolios made an effort and broke the silence:

"When I was a novice at the monastery," he said, "before archon Patriarcheas came to fetch me and throw me into the world, my Superior, Father Manasse—good luck to him if he's still alive, God rest him in the odor of sanctity if he's dead!—told me one day about an adventure which happened to a monk, one of his friends. I hadn't thought of it for years, but this evening, God knows why, it's come back to me and keeps going around in my head. Do you want to go to sleep?" he broke off, because his friends were silent and he could not make out their faces very well in the darkness.

"God preserve us!" cried Kostandis, as if he had been insulted. "Why do you say that to us, Manolios?"

"Never had our minds so wide awake, Manolios," said Yannakos in his turn. "Don't hurt our feelings so. Go on!"

"Well, this monk, my Superior's friend—the great dream of his life was that God in His mercy would let him go and bow down at the Holy Sepulcher. He went from village to village, collected alms and, after several years, when he was already old, he'd managed to put together thirty pounds, just what was needed for the journey. He did penance, obtained his Superior's permission and set off.

"Hardly had he got outside the monastery when he saw a man in rags, pale, sad, bent toward the ground, picking herbs. Hearing the pilgrim's staff ringing on the stones, the man raised his head.

" 'Where are you going, Father?' he asked him.

" 'To the Holy Sepulcher, brother, to Jerusalem. I shall go thrice around the Holy Sepulcher and bow down.'

" 'How much money have you got?'

" 'Thirty pounds.'

" 'Give me the thirty pounds, I've a wife and children and they're hungry. Give them to me, go thrice around me, fall on your knees and bow down before me; then afterward go back into your monastery.'

"The monk took the thirty pounds out of his sack, gave the whole lot to the poor man, went three times around him, fell on his knees and bowed down before him. Then, he returned to the monastery."

Manolios bent his head and fell silent. The three companions were still listening to his words within them; they remained silent. Their hearts were overwhelmed.

Manolios raised his head again.

"Later," he said, "I learned that that monk who left for the Holy Sepulcher was my Superior himself, Father Manasse; from humility he was unwilling to tell me. This evening, after so many years, I understand who the poor man was whom he met as he left the monastery."

Manolios fell silent. His voice was beginning to tremble. His friends drew nearer to him on the bench. "Who was it?" they asked, anxiously.

Manolios hesitated a moment. At last, calmly, like a ripe fruit falling at night in a garden, his word fell:

"Christ."

The three comrades jumped. As though suddenly there had appeared among them in the darkness, sad, poorly dressed, persecuted by men, with His feet bleeding from walking, a fugitive, Christ.

They felt in their midst, with terror, with gladness, the invisible presence. For a long time they could not utter a word. What would they have said? To whom should they turn? To whom speak? They saw no one. And yet, never had body seemed to them so real, so palpable, as this invisible presence which, putting on a humble human form, was there in the midst of them.

It was Yannakos who first opened his mouth. He cried out, with his eyes fixed on the darkness:

"Who's there?" as though somebody had knocked at the door. "Who's there?" he repeated, putting out his hand.

The leaves of the fig tree stirred. Again the night was filled with scents—corn, honeysuckle, ripe figs. Breathing this fragrance deeply in, all four of them felt the invisible presence descend and spread through them, from head to foot. They remembered how, when they were children with pure hearts, this same invisible being used to enter into them, take possession of them, on Good Friday, when they received Communion.

"Manolios," said Michelis, who wanted to embrace his friend but restrained himself, "Manolios, from today, from the moment I saw you come out through the Agha's doorway with your hands tied behind your back and walk calmly, serenely, out to be hanged to save the village, I felt there was about you a new air, a strange brightness; it was as if you'd grown taller, as if you'd got thinner, as if you'd become flame. From that instant I took a decision: wherever you go, I will follow you. Wherever you lead me, I will go. Whatever you tell me, I will do."

He was silent a moment and seemed to hesitate. But at once, resolutely:

"Now that I've seen," he said, half whispering, "my father eat, drink and go to sleep, I understand that I'm more bound to you than to him, Manolios. It's not to him, now, that I owe obedience, but to you."

Yannakos and Kostandis also tried to speak, but they were prevented; they began to weep.

The wife of Kostandis appeared on the threshold. She heard their sobs, shook her head and went in again. Manolios took Michelis's hand and held it clasped tight between his.

"My brother," he said, "you are better, purer, nearer to Christ than I. There are no demon voices troubling you; you find the way more simply and more surely. What I've had a hard struggle for years to reach, and haven't reached—you get there with even steps and without losing your breath. Your sacrifice is of great value. For you have a lordly house, a father who's archon, wealth, a name. I've nothing to sacrifice to God, and yet it still torments me to sacrifice that nothing.

"Just like my Superior, Father Manasse, I, too, good-for-nothing that I am, had great plans. The sheepfold was too small for me; the village, too. My desire was to go up into a great ship and travel to the end of the earth to find my salvation. I imagined that the Holy Sepulcher was a very long way away, at the end of the earth; I despised this corner of the world where God in His mercy has set me down. Now I understand. Christ is everywhere, He wanders around about our village, knocks at our door, stops in front of our heart to ask for alms. He is poor, famished, roofless, Christ is, in front of this village where live and prosper people like the Agha, Ladas, priest Grigoris. He is poor and He has children who are hungry. He begs, He knocks at the doors, He knocks at hearts and He is chased away from door to door, from heart to heart."

Manolios stood up; in the darkness his face was dazzling.

"Brothers," he cried, "we will welcome Him in, we will open to Him our doors and our hearts. Formerly I didn't see Him, I didn't hear Him. Now I see Him and hear Him. The other night, when Yannakos came up to find me in my solitude, I clearly heard Him call me by name. And I came down to the village. I thought He had called me to die. But it wasn't for that that He had called me. I know now why He called me. I have taken a resolution."

A voice rose in the night; it seemed to be that of Kostandis: "What resolution, Manolios?"

"What resolution?" said Manolios and remained in meditation for a second. "How express it in words? I can't. I think it's only in acts, if God wills, that I shall. Brothers, I have taken the decision to change my life completely, to reject the past, to welcome Christ by the wayside. I shall walk before Him with the trumpet, like His bodyguard, I shall cry—I don't know what I shall cry, I don't care. When I open my mouth, Christ will put the right words on my lips. Brothers, that's the decision I have taken."

He was silent. For a long time, nothing could be heard in the courtyard but the rustling of the fig tree's leaves. But again voices and questions arose.

"And me, me and my ass, my stock in trade, my living to earn?" asked Yannakos.

"Me with my wife, my children, my café?" Kostandis insisted.

"I've nothing to ask," said Michelis. "My resolution's made. This evening, before I came to you. I took that decision: to leave my father's house."

Manolios said nothing. By the light of the stars he could make out the faces of Yannakos and Kostandis leaning toward his, still questioning and in quest of an answer. What answer could he give? How could he decide for them and upset their lives? To each his hour of redemption. Each alone can judge and decide how and when he shall find salvation.

"Brothers," he said at last, "every resolution a man makes is like the fruit of a tree. Slowly, patiently, thanks to the sun, the rain, and the wind, the fruit ripens and falls. Be patient, brothers, don't question anyone. The blessed hour will come to you, too —and then you won't have to question any more. Calmly, without it hurting at all, you'll leave wife, children, relatives and business. You'll free yourselves of all these small pearls, and find the great pearl, Christ."

"It's you who are opening us the way, Manolios," said Yannakos. "I want to go with you."

"Don't be in a hurry, Yannakos," said Manolios, clasping the hand of his impulsive friend. "Let me struggle and suffer alone, to start with."

"You won't go away?" said Kostandis, putting out his hand as though to stop Manolios. "You won't leave us!"

"And go where, Kostandis? Have you forgotten where my Superior found the Holy Sepulcher? He who strives and suffers over a clod of earth strives and suffers over the whole earth. I shall be with you, always! Here, in Lycovrissi and on the mountain, on our land. This is where God in His mercy has placed me, this is where He has ordered me to fight. Every clod of earth is also a Holy Sepulcher."

Once more Kostandis's wife came out on the doorstep and mumbled something. Manolios stood up and gazed at the stars.

"Brothers," he said, "it must be midnight; I must get back to the mountain. Christ be with you, I'm going."

"We're leaving, too," said Yannakos. "I expect my sister wants to go to bed."

"It's past midnight," she replied.

They said good-bye to the mistress of the house, trying to mollify her by polite words. They were sorry for Kostandis, whom they were about to leave defenceless in her claws.

"See you soon, lads," said Kostandis, accompanying them to the door.

Poor Kostandis! I wouldn't be in his skin, muttered Yannakos when the door was hardly shut.

Calm, mildness of spring. The village was fast asleep. In the distance a dog barked. The stars flashed above the three friends, like swords.

They went all the way without a word. What was there to say? They had said everything.

Alone, with swift, light steps as though once more the wings of an angel bore him up, Manolios took the rising path.

The Chariot of Fire

WHILE MEN WERE, some of them, blinded by their passions and groaning in their Hell and others endeavoring to surpass their nature and rushing toward Heaven, the ears of corn, calm and docile, were ripening, leaning toward the earth their grain-filled heads and waiting for the sickle.

The young girls, with their white kerchiefs tied around their heads to protect them from the sun, had picked up their sickles at dawn and dispersed in the plain. They had already forgotten the danger which had shaken their village and were gossiping away in low voices with bursts of laughter; now they would remember the widow with a blush, now Hussein whom they had seen hanging from the plane tree half naked and shamefully mutilated. There were puffs of wind, and the horrible carrion swung creaking, biting its tongue which was hanging out, purple.

But their faces lit up as soon as they thought of Manolios. Their mothers, chased away by the Agha, had come running home that day from the square and had not tired of telling how Manolios had appeared at the Agha's door, proud and slim and fair-headed, like an archangel. "Mischief makers have been saying his face was disfigured with leprosy: lies, my dear, all lies," they said; "his face was bright like the sun."

The young girls reached the fields and got busy with the sickles; they seized the ears in handfuls, made armfuls of the corn and piled them in sheaves behind them. They never stopped chattering and exchanging sly jokes about the young men of the village, poking fun at their defects—this one was hunchbacked, that one bow-legged, another had a stammer—and laughing full-throatedly.

The wife of Panayotaros and his two daughters, Pelaghia and

Chryssoula, had gone out, too, to reap their miserable field. The poor mother, slouching, wry-faced, prematurely aged, had her head bound in a black kerchief, widow fashion. She walked in front, stricken, silent. Why had she been born, what harm had she done the good God that He punished her so? And what harm had her husband also done, to fall so low, to become the drunkard, the wreck he was, the laughing-stock of the village? He, the young man full of merit, who had spoken little and worked hard and had not even dared raise his eyes to look at her when he passed in front of her door! She had been the only daughter of a well-off family, and he a poor man. One day, her father, now dead, had sent for him: "Panayotaros," he had told him, "I like you; you're poor, but hardworking and honest. I know you love my daughter; take her, with my blessing!" And he had married her. All had gone well till the accursed day when the widow had crossed his path.

"Curse her, the bitch! she's the cause of it all! O God, can You hear the prayers of honest women? If so, hear me; throw her into Hell, let her burn with Judas!"

But hardly had she muttered that name when she shuddered. It was like asking God that even in Hell and through eternity her husband, whom everyone called Judas, should not be separated from the widow. She stood still, in consternation.

Behind her, her two daughters, dark-haired and striking, with thick dark brown on their cheeks and upper lips, and covered with sweat, chatted and grinned mockingly.

"The old woman's had one of her thoughts again; look at the way she's stopped dead!" said Chryssoula, the younger one.

"Bet you she's remembered the widow!" said Pelaghia guffawing heartily.

Barefoot, bent and thoughtful, father Ladas passed by. He turned at that moment and saw them. They were going into their scraggy field, grasping their sickles.

"That your field? Haven't you any other?" he asked the old mother.

"It's all we have, father Ladas. The others are sold, it's all over," replied the old woman with a sigh.

Father Ladas cast a glance over the patch of ground, measured it with his eye, reckoned up what grain it would yield, shook his bony head and went on his way without another word. The insults of Panayotaros were still hissing at his ears, like vipers. Every day they came back into his mind, and every day he swore to lay his hands on his remaining field and on his vineyard. "I'll teach you, I will, what honesty is, you dirty dog, and what Ladas is!"

He went on, stopping at every field and doing his sums. Every year at harvest time he went out in this way for a tour of inspection. He did it again at the vintage, then again at the picking of the olives. His brain was a regular ledger, in which he wrote down the quantity of corn, wine, and oil harvested by each villager, in order to find out whether he would have enough for the year, whether he would not find himself obliged to borrow. Father Ladas pondered whether he ought to lend, how much and at what rate.

So it was, every year. This time father Ladas had set out on his tour in a more than ever grasping mood. Since the day when he had narrowly escaped the claws of death, he had been seized by a frenzy to lay hold of the greatest possible number of fields, vineyards and olive groves, to pile up in his coffers all the gold pieces he could, while he still had time. He tightened his belt more than ever—the evening before, he had even cut out his hors d'oeuvre of olives—and he now drank only the water the good God gives. "There's not time, my Penelope," he kept repeating to his impassive companion; "I may die, I must hurry. What do you think, my dear Penelope?"

"Hullo, father Ladas, do you want to gobble the lot?" a mocking voice rang out behind him. "What's the good? What'll you be able to take with you into your hole in the ground? A length of linen, that's all. Well then, leave the poor people something to eat!"

The old close-fist wheeled round. Archon Patriarcheas was standing in front of him, big-bellied, high-colored, wearing a wide straw hat fitted with a veil of white gauze to protect his neck against a stroke. He, too, was going to his fields to look over the reaper girls. His presence prevented the sickles from resting; at the same time he could contemplate the bending women sticking their rumps out and showing damp bosoms inside their unlaced bodices. He would let fly at them some broad joke or other, to excite them and himself, too.

Taken aback, father Ladas gazed at him without replying.

Archon Patriarcheas burst out laughing at the sight of the old miser's threadbare face and ragged breeches.

"To my way of thinking, that hero, Plaster-eater, hit you off very nicely in the prison," he added, to prick him on the raw.

"And didn't I tell your lordships a few home truths, eh?" hissed father Ladas. "Have you forgotten, by any chance?"

"You mean 'noble pig'? If you want to know, old man, the more I think of it, the more it seems to me you hit a bull's eye, you old viper! Believe it or not, ever since I've left the prison, I've had the devil's own appetite, a real noble pig; I eat and I eat, Lenio hardly has the time to wring the necks of my chickens, or Nikolio to bring me sucking lambs and cheeses, or my gardener fruits and vegetables. I can't manage to be satisfied, my dear Ladas. Besides, I don't want to be; when I do feel full, I take an emetic I got from priest Grigoris, I'm sick, that empties me and I fill up again. Understand?"

"I understand," replied father Ladas, spitting. "There are little worms that poke their heads out of their holes and enjoy watching you stuffing and fattening yourself up and say to themselves: 'What a blow-out he's preparing for us!' You stuff and I starve, but in the end the Devil will get us both!"

That said, he spat again and went on his way.

While the *raias* were dispersed about the plain at their reaping, the Agha, shut up in his residence, wandered up and down his room, stumbled and fell flat, dead drunk; or else he remained without eating or drinking, cross-legged on a great cushion. He smoked his chibouk, meditated on the vanity of this world and pensively followed the smoke as it rose in spirals from the chibouk and vanished in the air.

But suddenly one morning he got up, dressed and called the old hunchback woman:

"Listen, my friend, you'll saddle my mare, put some bread and meat in my saddlebag, and don't forget a bottle of raki. I'm going to the town, and there I shall take the Devil's machine as far as Smyrna. Look after the house, don't let anyone in; above all not a cat must know I've gone. Or else, you wretch, when I come back I shall cut off your nose, too, and your ears and your hump, see?"

"I see, Agha; you can go with God's blessing!" answered old

Martha, and inwardly she clucked: He's going to bring me another Youssoufaki from Smyrna, curse him!

At nightfall, to be seen by nobody, the Agha mounted and rode stealthily out of the village.

To think I've let so many days go by before my little noddle thought of this! Why, this is what it deserves! he muttered, giving himself a slap on the face.

Some days later the reaping was ending. The peasants were raising stacks on the threshing floors and beginning to thresh, winnow and store their harvest. Panayotaros took his to the mill, had it ground, brought the flour home and ordered his wife and daughters to knead the dough and bake it. This done, he armed himself with his pistol, took up position in the middle of the yard and began firing in the air. He had heard that the Agha was away, so he was now afraid of nothing. Between shots he shouted at his wife and children:

"Out with you! Be off! Out of my sight! To the devil! I want to be left all alone!"

The women neighbors intervened and threw themselves entreating at his feet, while his wife and daughters wept. But his fury only increased: "Out with you! Be off!" he repeated, raging. He caught them by the hair, flung them out of the house, locked and bolted the door, brought out a demijohn of raki from the cellar, with some sausages and some cheese, arranged the hot loaves in a row around him and lay down under the olive tree right in the middle of the yard.

He drank, ate and, from time to time picking up his pistol, let loose a shot, then reclined on his back again, half naked, and put out his tongue at the sky: "There, you swine!" he shouted at it; "there, you swine!" and began again eating and drinking.

For days and nights on end the neighbors heard him bellowing and shooting; from time to time he would start singing. But his voice became more and more hoarse, the pistol shots became rarer. One day, the neighbors ventured an eye at the keyhole and saw him lying on his back, stark naked, with his red beard fouled with vomiting, defying Heaven by yelling in a thick voice: "There, you swine! There, you swine!"

Next morning they heard nothing more, except a pistol shot

followed by a muffled bellowing and by sighs. Then all relapsed to a heavy silence. The neighbors gathered before the door, looked through the keyhole. Panayotaros was lying there on his belly, motionless in the midst of the food and his vomit.

"Let's break open the door," proposed Andonis the barber; "if he's dead, he'll rot, and disease will spread to the village."

"Let's first warn priest Grigoris," suggested the beadle, and set off at once, running.

"Break the door open; he's surely given up the ghost and the Devil's got it; bury him; I'll have nothing to do with it," snapped priest Grigoris, who was still ruminating the insults Panayotaros had hurled at him that day in prison.

The wife and daughters of Panayotaros broke open the door, lifted him up and carried him into the house, on to the couch; he was pale as death and half melted away; he must have rolled on broken glass, for he was covered with cuts. And yet he was still alive. His wife set to work washing him as you rub down a horse. Her daughters drew water from the well, they threw buckets full over him. Gradually coming to himself again, he opened his eyes, but seeing his wife and children all round him he recovered his anger:

"Out with you! Get out!" he cried, and made a rush, all doubled up, to seize his pistol. But his strength gave out and he collapsed.

Andonis the barber offered to apply wet cups, but the neighbor women prevented him.

"What blood is there to take from him, Andonis? He's yellow as a lemon. We'll call mother Mandalenia, she'll chase out the demon he's got in his body."

An urchin ran off full tilt in search of the old healer.

Meanwhile one neighbor woman suggested making him a lemonade without sugar, another putting a hot brick on his belly. An old woman assured them that if each of them spat on him three times the fiend would be frightened and take to flight.

They had not yet made up their minds when mother Mandalenia ran up eagerly with her old wives' remedies: three little bags, one white, filled with all sorts of aromatic plants, another black, with powders and little bottles, the third blue, containing black beans, fragments of green glass, some tar, a tiny piece of the Holy Cross, some flowers from the Good Friday service and a bat's bone. She bent over Panayotaros, gazed at him attentively, shook her head and led his wife into a corner.

"You are an unlucky one, mother Panayotaros," she said under her breath, "I'm sorry for you, from the bottom of my heart. That's not a man, daughter, that's a fiend; just now he's had enough, so he's quiet and good, but as soon as he gets on his feet once more he'll start all over again. My late husband was just the same, only, God be praised, the Devil took him off quickly. I'll tell you something, but first swear you'll keep the secret. God Himself mustn't hear it!"

"I swear," said the poor woman, trembling in advance.

"Look at this," said the old woman, pointing to the black bag. "In there I've a miraculous powder. Give him a pinch of it and in a few days, without any trumpets or drums, he'll cast off. What d'you say to that? That way you'll be rid of him, my poor dear!"

"In Heaven's name don't talk of such a thing!" cried the unlucky woman.

"As you like," said the old woman, shrugging her shoulders. "I'm only trying to help you, but since you won't accept, it's too bad!"

Vexed, she slid the black bag into her bodice, pulled out the white one which contained the plants, and began preparing her medicines. She made an infusion of herbs, poured it down the sick man's throat, took oil from the Virgin's lamp, mixed pepper with it and rubbed him; then she placed a hot brick on his belly. She took a bit of tar out of the blue bag, melted it and drew a cross on the threshold. After which, having put all the company outside, she shut the door, approached the dying man and spat on him three times:

"The Devil take you, Judas!" she cried three times, and rushed out.

"Don't disturb him," she said, "I've recited the exorcism; in three days he'll be hale and hearty."

To pay for her pains she took away the bits of bread left lying in the yard and a length of sausage which was still hanging from a branch of the olive tree. Then, crossing herself, she departed warily.

Men are wild beasts, curse them! she mumbled as she went along. Ah, if I were let, I'd give the lot of them, one after the other, the powders I know, and they could go to the devil!

As she was turning the key in the lock to go into her house, Yannakos went by, holding his ass by the bridle and frowning.

"Hi! stop a minute, Yannakos, curse you!" she cried. "What's happening to my fine nephew? Haven't you any pity for him? You've turned his head, and now he stays lonely as a cuckoo up on the mountain reading the Gospel, so it seems. Did you ever? The Gospel! Instead of getting children by Lenio."

"Is that your thanks for the man who was ready to give his life to save the village?" replied Yannakos, furious. "To think there wasn't one of you was prepared to fall at his feet and kiss them! To hell with you, dirty old men, dirty old women, pack of dirty dogs!"

The old woman was already inside her house; with one bound she was out again:

"Hey, you, wait till you fall ill one day," she shouted at him, "and I've got my claws on you! Then I'll get my own back!"

And with a burst of laughter she slammed the door.

But Yannakos was in no humor to seek a quarrel; his spirit had stayed behind on the Sarakina: he had just come from there and it had wrung his heart. A few huts had been built, but the refugees were short of wood for roofing them. The thin, livid children sat at the mouths of the caves and did not even feel like playing; there they remained, serious, with vague looks, like old men. A few mothers were picking herbs around about, others lit fires, but they had no oil, no olives, nothing; the fare was herbs cooked in water. The men had gone off to look for work in the neighboring villages. Priest Fotis, armed with the Gospel and a sack, was doing the round of the villages as a beggar, collecting for his people.

"How are you getting on, uncle?" Yannakos asked an old man who was drawing water from a hollow in the rock and watering a square of vegetables which he had planted in a tiny patch of earth. "How are you getting on in your new village?"

"God be praised," replied the old man, "we're still holding out."

"The children look to me a bit sickly. Some of them have got legs like sticks."

"They'll get strong, don't you worry. Some of them'll die, more's the pity, but the men, God bless them, will get others. The seed of man's immortal, you know. You got children?"

"No."

"No? Then what are you waiting for? Go and have some, it's not women, thank God, that's lacking; take your turn throwing wood on the fire!"

Yannakos went farther on. Some of them recognized him and ran up to meet him. The women surrounded the ass, looking enviously at the full paniers. A little girl stretched out her hand, unrolled a red ribbon, gazed at it, stroked it with her fingertips, sighed. A dark young woman with a swollen belly pulled out of the basket a bone comb and stared at it, unable to take her eyes off it; she could not bear to let go of it. Her longing eyes traveled from the comb to Yannakos. For a second her brain tottered; it seemed to her that she had possessed herself of the comb, taken to her heels without anyone noticing, and was now sitting in front of her cave, combing her hair happily in the sun.

Yannakos was chatting with the men. From time to time he cast a glance at the women surrounding his ass; their hands rummaged covetously among the trinkets, then fell back empty, tired. Yannakos gave a jump; his eyes shone. He unhooked the trumpet from his belt and blew. Then, making a megaphone of his two hands, he began shouting:

"Combs, ribbons, looking-glasses, cotton, needles, hooks, stuffs! Take what you want, good ladies! I don't want any money; you'll pay me in the other world!"

The women could not believe their ears. Their first impulse was to make a rush for the paniers. They held back.

"He's joking," said one of them, "we shall look silly. Hands off."

"I don't think he's joking!" said the pregnant young woman, and she made off with the comb clasped against her bosom.

The little girl came forward again and seized hold of the red ribbon.

"I'm off, too!" she cried, bounding from stone to stone like a young goat.

Yannakos laughed at the sight. He climbed up on a rock.

"Plunder the paniers, be brave, my dears; it's true what I say; I don't want any money, you'll pay me in the other world! I trust you!"

Then the women swooped on the paniers. They did not choose now, they took the first thing that came, uttered cries and ran away as fast as their legs would carry them. In a twinkling of an eye, all was swept away.

"Are you crazy or a saint? Which are you, brother Yannakos?" a little old man shouted.

"A usurer," replied Yannakos with a laugh, "God in His mercy will pay it back with interest."

"I did hear tell, son, that when our grandfathers lent money they sometimes had a paper signed, so they'd be paid in the other world. But they had the faith."

"I've faith too," answered Yannakos, and pulling his donkey by the bridle. "Keep well," he added, and went off full of joy.

At the foot of the Sarakina, just before seeing mother Mandalenia, he met Nikolio, carrying a sheep over his shoulders.

"Hey, Nikolio," Yannakos called out, "how's Manolios?"

Nikolio turned, laughing.

"He reads," he replied, "he reads, poor chap, and he thinks. I'm taking the master a sheep and I'm going to get married." He spun around, raising a cloud of dust, and began to dance, holding the sheep around his neck. His face gleamed like bronze, his teeth were dazzling.

"I'm getting married, old man, to Lenio! Heard of Lenio?"

He laughed lustily and set off at a run toward the village.

It was the truth: day and night Manolios read the Gospel and remained plunged in interminable meditations. He sat reading, bent low over the sacred text; at first he had struggled, soaked with sweat, spelling each word laboriously before he could make out the sense. How hard it was! Each word seemed to him like a shell which he must crack to get at the almond. But gradually, with the aid of time, and above all of love, the shell of words became less hard, it slowly came open under his burning breath. Suddenly all seemed clear to him; Christ became a warm and human body, coming down upon the earth for men of simple heart; and from now onward Manolios followed Christ without any effort, step by step behind Him, from His birth all through His life. He was present, singing 'Hosanna!' at the cradle at Bethlehem, with the shepherds: he followed the footprints of Christ right to the bloodstained cross, right to the glorious day of the Resurrection when Christ, springing from the tomb, entered his heart.

From time to time he would take the piece of boxwood on which he had carved the face of Christ and would set to work scooping it out inside, so as to fit it onto his own face. Once, as he was doing this, he remembered the learned theologian who had come, when he was still a novice, to celebrate Easter in their convent. On the morning of Holy Saturday he had gone up into the pulpit with a pile of fat tomes under his arm. For two long hours he had spoken to the artless monks, using learned words to explain to them the mystery of the Resurrection. Up till then the monks had thought of the resurrection of Christ as a very natural thing; they had never asked themselves questions on the how and why. The resurrection of Christ seemed to them as simple as the rising of the sun every morning, and here was this erudite theologian, with all his books and all his science, muddling things up. When they got back to their cell, old Manasse had said to Manolios:

"God forgive me, my son; this year, for the first time, I have not felt Christ rise."

Every moment Manolios would place the carved wood over his face to see if it fitted. One day Nikolio surprised him at this, with the mask over his face; he burst out laughing:

"Know what I think, old man? You're in your second childhood. Playing with masks and dolls! You certainly aren't yourself."

Manolios was content to smile.

"No, it isn't a game," he retorted softly, "I'm not playing, Nikolio."

For several days Nikolio had been hovering around Manolios. He was trying to tell him something, but the words remained in his throat and choked him. Today he had made up his mind. He approached, sat down by his master, leaned over and looked at the wood carving, but was thinking of something else. In the end he pushed Manolios's knee violently with his own.

"Manolios, listen Manolios," he cried at the top of his voice, as though he were hailing him from the mountain opposite.

"Speak, Nikolio, but don't shout like that; speak softer, I'm not deaf."

"I've something to tell you, but don't get angry, will you?"

"I shan't get angry, Nikolio, speak out. And don't hit me on the knee, it hurts."

"I'm getting married to Lenio!" Nikolio shouted, grasping his heavy crook firmly and preparing to hit Manolios if he went for him.

Manolios smiled.

"I know," he said.

Nikolio opened his eyes wide.

"You know?" he said, "you know and you don't go for me? By the bread I eat, I should have killed you."

"Well, I give you my blessing, both of you. Health and happiness! Long may you live, live to be old and have lots of children who'll grow up into fine people."

"That . . . that's beyond me," muttered Nikolio after reflecting for a long while. "You don't want to kill me?"

Manolios stretched out his arms and embraced his little shepherd.

"Here, you don't want to kill me?" cried Nikolio again, feeling uncomfortable.

"No, no, Nikolio, I don't want to kill you," he said, laughing.

Nikolio suddenly got up, alarmed. He cast a final look at Manolios, who had set to work again, scooping out the wood.

Poor chap, he's not well, he's gone crazy, I'd better be off, he told himself. Leaping from rock to rock, he put his hands to his mouth and whistled. The dogs ran up, the sheep followed. In the midst of his animals whom he knew and who knew him, Nikolio recovered his calm.

Through the mind of Manolios for a moment Lenio passed, dimpled, fresh, appetizing. He laid the piece of wood down on his knees and remained a long while in thought.

"My blessing on them," he muttered at last; "they've taken the road which God in His mercy has traced out for Man on earth. I keep struggling to take another road—no wife, no children, no joy; I renounce the world, I shake the earth from my feet. Am I right? Christ was right, He was God, He was; but Man? Might it be overbold of him to follow in the footsteps of God?"

He could find no answer. At the grave moments he asked himself no questions, he advanced, with certainty. Never had he felt the same certainty, a purer happiness, since the day when, with his hands tied behind his back, he had walked toward death. But when his soul was no longer all on fire, he questioned himself, weighed things, hesitated.

Some days earlier he had gone to look for priest Fotis on the
Sarakina, to ask his aid. Perhaps he, too, had once passed through
the same distress and might be able to hold out to him a helping
hand. The priest was away; he was on a round of the neighboring villages to collect alms. So Manolios had returned to his solitude and taken up again the Gospel; it would answer.

He opened the little book, as on the days of great heat people
open wide a door giving on the sea. He plunged into the sacred
text and was refreshed; he forgot the questions stabbing at him.
His spirit no longer questioned; his heart was overflowing with
response.

He rose, gave the final touches to the mask of Christ, scooped
where it still needed scooping and fitted it over his face; it settled perfectly.

"God be praised," he said, "I've finished." After kissing it he
went into the hut and hung it on the wall, near the old icon of
the Crucifixion with the swallows.

This year, Katerina, the gallant widow, would be missing from
the festival of Saint Elijah. Usually on that day she would brush
her hair till it shone, having scented it the night before with laurel
oil, polish her teeth with walnut leaves, hang round her neck a
necklace of blue stones against the evil eye, and take the path
which climbed to the Prophet Elijah. She went alone—no one
went near her in public—and fell on her face like everyone else
before the icon. Terrible Elijah would look down at her in wrath,
but could not disentangle himself from the paintings and *ex voto*'s
of silver under which his worshippers had smothered him. The
widow, knowing this, could touch him with her painted lips without fear.

Now she lay under the ground and everything of her had vanished—scented hair, painted lips, red cheeks, brilliant throat. Only
her teeth still shone, like the white pebbles of a river bank.

Panayotaros too was unable, this year, to start out for the festival: he was still raging on his bed. His two daughters alone had
noiselessly opened the door and were now toiling up the mountain,
fine well-fleshed dark girls with lips shaded with black down and
armpits sweating and strongly reeking of musk. They were like
two young she-wolves whom the love season torments; they kept
darting to right and left heavy and beseeching glances in search of

a male. Had they been heifers they would have lowed, had they been lionesses they would have roared at night in the forest, had they been cats they would have rolled on their backs on the ground and mewed on the roofs. But they were women; they slyly lowered their eyes when they passed a young man, and were shaken afterwards with giggles and made fun of him.

"Look at him, poor thing, what a rounded back he's got, there's a pair of pins—a fine lad if ever there was one!" And they bore him resentment for having passed by without making a rush at them.

Andonis the barber had also started out. He had not shaved himself—he had had too many customers. He thought highly of the Prophet Elijah: all the men of the village, before going to the festival, came to him for a shave; many, when they got back, had caught a chill and come hurrying to him for cupping. It was his surest source of income; how could he help thinking highly of the Prophet Elijah? He was also good at pulling out teeth, as everyone knew, but the fellows had healthy and strong teeth, fit to crack almonds. If from time to time one of their teeth came loose, they had learned—who the devil had taught them the trick?—to tie a string to it and wrench it out. After which they would drink a big glass of raki and begin again cracking the almonds for their *meze* within the hour.

The three friends, Michelis, Kostandis, and Yannakos, made their way up slowly, discoursing peacefully at the tail end of the procession. At the start Michelis and Yannakos had walked in convoy with priest Grigoris, Yannakos to keep an eye on his donkey, which Mariori was riding, and to encourage it from time to time with an affectionate call, Michelis to be with his Mariori and exchange with her some of those looks charged with longing. He, Michelis, kept admiring the whiteness and grace of his betrothed; she, the kind and mild face of her fiancé, his dark curling hair, his proud bearing. Thus in the caressing and abetting light of this late afternoon, in the midst of this rustling crowd making its climb, the engaged couple silently savored, both of them, their future embraces.

Mariori's languorous eyes, drowned in vagueness, already saw another Mariori, clasping to her a little child and giving it the breast.

"Prophet Elijah!" she murmured as she caught sight of the

abrupt crest of the mountain, "I commend myself to your mercy, let me, too, have a child!"

Kostandis came a little behind them, with his family. His wife went in front of him, riding a mule, with her two children sitting behind her, and he walked behind. They were silent; what had they to say to each other? They had said everything over and over again, sometimes affectionately, sometimes quarrelling. She still sometimes burst out in violent scenes; he had long ago laid down his arms, he had gone, he said, into the Kingdom of Heaven, into silence.

Insensibly the three friends found themselves separated from the others, forming the tail of the procession.

"Where's Manolios? Isn't he with us?" asked Kostandis. "Won't he come to the festival?"

"I went up as far as his sheepfold yesterday afternoon and didn't find him," replied Michelis. "I called Nikolio. 'Left for the Prophet Elijah this morning at dawn, with a jug of water and an armful of laurel,' he told me; 'he's not back yet. He's a bit odd, you know, and you mark my words, master, he'll end by losing his wits. He's lost them already. I told him I'd nabbed Lenio and he didn't kill me. For the moment, he reads and sings; tomorrow he'll be throwing stones.'"

The three friends burst out laughing.

"It's true," said Yannakos, "that Manolios isn't the same. Believe me if you will, brothers, maybe I'm seeing things wrong. But one night when I was with him and he was sitting on the stone bench with his head leaning against the wall, I saw a glow around his head. It was a sort of crown of light, like the saints have in the icons. Do you believe me?"

"Yes, I believe you," said Michelis.

"So do I," said Kostandis. Then they were silent.

The little church was now in sight, newly whitewashed, wedged between enormous rocks. This was how the fierce prophet was represented in the icons, between two rocks like wings on his right hand and on his left. They had in fact become wings, those sheer rocks of his high solitude, and were carrying him off, up to the sky.

Close against the church could be still seen, now threatening to crumble in ruins, the hut where in ancient times an ascetic had done his penance. The worm-eaten stool on which he had sat was still there and, hung up on a nail in the rock, his rosary, all greasy, with a little cross of black stuff at the end. Outside, his tomb, with an iron cross upon it, and its stone bearing a rubbed-out name.

The old beadle had toiled up at dawn to put the little church in order, light the lamps and decorate it with branches of laurel. As he opened the low door he gave a cry and stopped, amazed: "*Kyrie eleison! Kyrie eleison!*" he muttered, crossing himself as hard as he could. The little church was resplendent with cleanliness, swept, dusted, the candlesticks polished, the lamps filled with oil, the icons adorned with laurel. A fire had also been lit and incense burned; the whole place smelled sweet.

The beadle wiped his forehead, not daring to go in. He was afraid the angel might be still there, hidden behind the altar. Once in the village church, one morning when he had gone to put it straight, he had seen the Archangel Michael, on the left of the iconostasis, slowly unfolding his wings, and he had fainted. Since then he had wished to see no angel, and miracles frightened him.

He sat down on the threshold, turning around from time to time to glance into the church. But the hours passed, no angel showed itself; he plucked up courage again. He was hungry. Opening his bag, he took out a slice of bread and a piece of cheese; but his throat was tight and nothing would go down. He seized his little gourd of wine, swallowed a few mouthfuls and recovered a little; his throat loosened and he began eating again. His meal over, the old beadle felt braver. He crossed himself and, arming himself with courage, crossed the threshold. He fell on his face before the Prophet Elijah, timidly pulled the curtain of the choir and looked all around the interior: nobody!

God be praised, he thought; he's been, put everything straight and gone away again. I've had a narrow escape!

He started sweeping, dusting, polishing the candlesticks all over again and arranging the dishes on the notables' pew, to kill the time. The old beadle was fond of this little church. It was bound up intimately with his life. It had been a mere ruin when his father, long dead, had promised the Prophet Elijah to restore it if his little new-born son got well again—the same who was there today, the old beadle. He had got well and his father had kept his word.

The beadle recalled the past and sighed.

Extraordinary signs had accompanied his birth. He was born seventy-five years ago, on Good Friday at noon, the exact hour when they were crucifying Christ. The midwife had at once declared that the child would be a bishop one day. From then onward his father, who was a good Christian and family man, had set himself, as his aim in life, to make his only son study in order that his destiny might be fulfilled. All went as well as could be. The future bishop did well at school, he was intelligent and pious. He had just left the high school with the mention 'Very good,' and was getting ready to set out for the big seminary in Constantinople, when, just then, on a fine evening, in a deserted lane, the Devil appeared before him; his name was Kyriakoula. Short, dark-skinned, with breasts straining her bodice and with three beauty spots at the wings of her nose and above the upper lip, she was twelve years old. The future bishop lost his head. In a giddy fit, he barred her passage. The three beauty spots, above all, had bewitched him. In vain his poor father wept, adjuring him not to stray from the path God had marked out for him. The unlucky boy declared that it was she, and none other, he would take for a wife, that he would kill himself if he did not marry her. He married her.

"God be thanked," he often said to himself, by way of consoling himself, "God be thanked, I became beadle, I haven't left the path."

The sun began to descend and the beadle came back and sat upon the threshold, watching with pleasure the pilgrims already on the path and beginning the ascent. He remained where he was, as though this were his own day and his friends were coming out to his house to wish him long life.

He could already hear distinctly the braying of the asses. He rose, took hold of the rope, and the little bell began tolling a festal tune.

The first to appear was priest Grigoris, throned upon his mule. The beadle ran to meet him, to proffer the steps and help him to get down.

"Have you swept and dusted, and polished the candlesticks?" the priest asked, even before setting foot to ground.

"All is in order, Father," the should-have-been bishop replied humbly. He did not dare tell of the miracle, for he wished to keep all the glory for himself alone.

"Did you put the dishes on the notables' pew in the way I suggested? We said three dishes: one for the priest, one for the saint, the third for the candles."

"All is in order, Father," he repeated in submissive tones.

During this time the crowd of pilgrims was arriving. They entered the church, placed a few ears of corn and a bunch of grapes on the notables' pew, then pulled out their purses, put their offerings in the dishes, bought candles and went to fall on their faces before the terrible Prophet. He was shown on the edge of a precipice, in a chariot of fire drawn by four purple horses. The robe he wore was also purple, and flames issued from his head. Hurtling out above the mountain, the chariot remained suspended in the air. An ascetic, who had fallen backward among the boulders and was shielding his eyes with his hand, gazed at him in terror.

"It's the sun!" whispered a young woman, admiring the Prophet; "it's the sun, my dear!"

"It's Saint Elijah, don't be irreverent, my good Mariori," said another.

"It comes to the same," said a third, "let's kneel down and have done."

The sun had set; the stars were not out yet, the light was still struggling desperately. She had taken the path up to the heights, but the night was climbing up from the earth and pursuing her from stone to stone, right to her last entrenchment, the little white church of the Prophet Elijah, at the very top of the mountain. At length, unable to resist any more, she leaped skyward and disappeared.

At this moment the refugees of the Sarakina were in their turn arriving at the festival, pitiable, ragged, with haggard cheeks. Priest Fotis preceded them, holding in his hand the monk's short iron staff. They were the last to enter the church. Having nothing to put in the dishes, they simply advanced, empty-handed, toward the saint and prostrated themselves.

"Forgive us, terrible Prophet," murmured priest Fotis gazing at the saint; "you, too, were poor; like us, you wore rags. You possessed only the great flame. We still have a spark from that flame, we refugees of the Sarakina. We are glad to salute you, comrade!"

Having bowed to the ground, they went out, and dispersed among the rocks after the people of Lycovrissi.

"Forgive our villagers," said Michelis, ashamed, "their bags are full."

"God will forgive them," replied fierce priest Fotis. "God, not I."

He fell silent, but his eyes darted flames. That morning he had returned with his alms sack empty. Contemplating in wrath the harvested plain from the height of the crags, he looked indeed like the Prophet Elijah astride the flames.

"The earth is theirs," said priest Fotis, "let them enjoy it; God grant we may have Heaven as our portion." He was silent.

The pilgrims spread out rugs of many colors around about the little church, opened bags stuffed with food, and their jaws went into action. The gourds were upturned; throats also. The wine gurgled; the austere solitude of the Prophet became filled with bursts of laughter and incoherent tumult.

A few oil lamps were lit among the boulders, throwing their light on the empurpled faces of the women, on girls' pliant necks, and on bushy mustaches. A great three-beaked lantern hung on the wall of the church threw up the puffy face and triple chin of archon Patriarcheas; and, close by him, a white forked beard followed the movement of jaws busy munching. The two heads of the village, the archon and the priest, were seated side by side, and at certain moments a ray of light fell on the frail and nimble hands of Mariori carving the roast and serving the two insatiable notables.

Then, one after another, the lamps went out. Shadows stole on all fours around the holy rocks, and were quickly indistinguishable. Only the laughter of girls being tickled could be heard; soon all fell back to silence. Among the stones, like scorpions, human beings were coupling, celebrating the Prophet of Fire in their fashion.

God called up the day; the sun appeared, in a chariot of fire, just like the Prophet. The human beings got to their feet, yawned, stretched, coughed, rubbed their eyes, drank coffee to wake themselves. The little silvery bell tinkled again, alert and joyful. Its slender voice was pitched from place to place on the mountainside, cascading like living water before spreading over the plain.

Leaning on his shepherd's staff, Manolios appeared in the midst of the boulders, calm and smiling. He gazed about him and caught sight of his companions, standing on a crag and looking for him uneasily in the direction of his mountain. Joyously, he stepped over the pilgrims to get to them, opened his arms and clasped them to his heart. They gave a cry.

"We waited for you all night," said Yannakos. "Why didn't you come?"

"Is everything ready?" asked Manolios.

The three companions could not believe their ears.

"What ought to be ready?" they said.

"Souls to wake up," Manolios answered, smiling, "backs to receive blows, mouths to cry."

"You've an idea in your head?" asked Yannakos, seizing his friend's arm. "I'm with you, for life or death!"

"I've nothing in my head," Manolios answered, "but perhaps God in His mercy has got something in His. Must be ready."

Then, after a gaze around:

"I love this mountain top," he said, "and that Prophet who had the conflagration as his mount and gave one kick and rose up from earth and was off. I even like the village people today, all clean, with bright eyes, and dressed in their best. They seem ready, some to catch fire, others to strike it; are we, too, ready?"

From the sanctuary, at that moment, rose the thunderous voice of priest Grigoris. Mass was beginning, they fell silent.

As many as could find room entered the little church. The less lucky ones remained standing on rocks. The singing escaped through the door and, behind, through the small window, a pathetic echo of the far-off ancestral spirits who had conceived these chants for their God.

Mass said, they all came out. The schoolmaster, rather pale, climbed onto a boulder. He began to speak in a husky voice, to sing the praises of the prophet. He went on without transition, by a prodigious leap, to the encomium of the Greek race, comparing the Prophet Elijah to Apollo, then to the light and finally to the eternal spirit of the Greeks who had routed the barbarian darkness. From that he passed, rather skillfully, to the Turkish occupation. At the beginning he was rather careful, but suddenly the reins escaped him, he let his zest run free and began, point-blank, singing the National Hymn.

Those about him were at first astonished, then felt their blood warm up, and all began singing, with emotion and with heroic discord, "Liberty, I know thee by the terrible edge of thy sword."

The Prophet Elijah had suddenly become an Armatole and a Klepht of the mountains, wearing the *tsarouchi** and carbine.

Manolios leaned toward the three friends.

"Are you ready?" he asked once more.

"Ready!" they replied as one man. "In the name of Christ, forward!"

They had no very clear notion of what Manolios meant or for what they were to be ready, but deep down in themselves they felt that their souls were up and ready.

The schoolmaster had at last come to the end and was climbing down from the rock, still boiling from his speech. Old Patriarcheas had wet eyes and priest Grigoris was raising his hand to bless his flock. Now that they had done their duty toward God, they could give themselves over to feasting.

At this very moment Manolios stepped forward, bowed before the priest, kissed his hand and asked permission to speak.

At the sight of Manolios the villagers, who had put on their Sunday souls for the day, remembered with emotion that this young man with the fair hair had dared to give his life to save the people. A delighted murmur came from all those mouths to bid him welcome.

Priest Grigoris frowned and bent toward him:

"What do you wish to say?" he asked. "Can you speak? What about?"

"About Christ," answered Manolios.

"Christ?" said the priest, taken aback; "but that is my business!"

"Christ has ordered me to speak," Manolios insisted.

"And He hasn't by chance explained to you what you are to say?" said priest Grigoris sarcastically.

"No, but He will explain it to me as soon as I begin."

Michelis took a step forward:

"Father," he said, "Manolios wants to speak to the villagers. We all beg of you, give him permission. When the whole village was in danger, Manolios came forward and offered his life that we might all be saved. So he has the right to speak."

* Beautiful leather shoes

"Give him permission, Father," said old Patriarcheas in his turn. "He's a good lad."

"He'll speak of things he knows nothing about," retorted the priest.

"That doesn't matter," Yannakos broke in; "your holiness knows them and will enlighten him."

"Let him speak! Let him speak!" cried Kostandis.

The villagers took courage. Dimitri the butcher rose, Andonis the barber and father Christofis; they began to clap their hands and shout: "Let him speak! Let him speak!"

Priest Grigoris, indignant, shrugged his shoulders.

"All right, all right," he said, "stop making that noise!"

With an ill grace he laid his hand on Manolios's head:

"May God enlighten you," he said; "speak!" Then he folded his arms to listen.

Manolios took a step forward and stood in the middle of the crowd. Yannakos and Kostandis rolled to his feet a stone on which he mounted. The villagers, men and women, surrounded him. Priest Fotis also approached with his people. He gave a slight bow with his head to salute priest Grigoris, who pretended not to see him.

Manolios, turning toward the east, made the sign of the cross and began to speak.

"Brothers, I want to speak to you of Christ; you must excuse me, I'm not educated, and I can't make fine phrases. But the other day, sitting in front of my sheepfold at the hour when the sun sets, Christ came and sat beside me on the bench, simply and quietly, like a neighbor would. He was carrying an empty sack and, giving a sigh, He let it fall to the ground. His feet were covered with dust. The four wounds the nails had made on Him were open; He was bleeding.

" 'Do you love Me?' said He to me in a sad voice.

" 'O my Master,' I replied, 'command me to die for Thee.'

"He shook His head, smiling; said nothing. We stayed like that a good while. I was frightened and didn't dare speak. And yet, after a while, I said to Him:

" 'Tired, Master? Your feet are covered with dust and blood; where've You come from?'

" 'I've done the round of the villages,' He answered me, 'I've been by Lycovrissi, too. My children are hungry. I'd taken this sack with me to collect alms. Look, here I am back and the sack is empty. I am tired.'

"He was silent again; both of us watched the sun setting. All of a sudden, His voice rose, heavy with reproach:

" 'Why do you stay here, you who say you love Me, why do you stay here, nice and quiet and with your arms folded, resting? You eat, you drink, you read at your ease the words which I have spoken, you weep at the story of My crucifixion, and then you go to bed and sleep. Aren't you ashamed? Is that how you love Me? Do you call that love? Get up!'

"I got up and I threw myself at His feet crying: 'Lord, I have sinned. Give me Your orders!'

" 'Take your shepherd's staff and go and find men, and don't be frightened, speak to them.'

" 'What shall I say to them, Lord? I'm without education, poor, timid; when I see men gathered in large numbers I'm afraid and I run away. And now You're sending me to speak to them. What shall I say to them?'

" 'Go and say to them that I am hungry, that I knock at their doors, that I am holding out My hand, crying: Charity, Christians!' "

Priest Grigoris was becoming nervous. He shifted his position. Old Patriarcheas yawned and looked to see how he could slip away. He was hungry. Father Ladas drew near the priest:

"This'll end badly, this business," he muttered; "tell him to be quiet."

But the country people were listening, open-mouthed. Emotion was gaining them and, little by little, a strange fear was taking hold of them. They really saw Christ wandering barefoot, knocking at their doors and asking for alms, while from inside they shouted at Him: "Go away, let God give you charity!" Wasn't that how they had driven priest Fotis away the other day, when he had come barefoot with a sack on his back?

Manolios drew breath. Drops of sweat were running down his forehead. He looked about him every way, stared at the villagers one by one for a long time, and there was on his face so much reproachfulness, so much bitterness and also so much nobility, that they were all stupefied. An old woman crossed herself:

"Lord, have pity on us," she murmured to her neighbor, "is it really Manolios, old Patriarcheas' shepherd, mother Mandalenia's nephew? It couldn't be, by any chance—forgive me this sin, O God —Christ Himself come down again on earth because of our sins? What do you think, neighbor?"

"Be quiet, mother Persephone, be quiet, look, he's going to speak again."

Manolios opened his arms wide to right and left.

"My brothers," he cried, "my sisters, men and women of Lycovrissi! It isn't of myself that I've come; how would I dare—I, a humble servant, a man with nothing—speak and teach lessons to rich heads of families, to eminent notables, to my elders? I haven't come of myself: it's Christ Who's sending me! I'm only repeating the words He ordered me to say to you; He is crying: 'I'm hungry! Charity, Christians!' Who gives to the poor, lends to God. The other day, one of our people went to see our brothers, the refugees of the Sarakina. They're hungry, they haven't clothes to wear or a place to sleep. He had brought with him all he had in the world, and he cried out to them: 'Come, brothers, take, share out among you all I possess. I don't want money, but I'm not giving you a present. I'm lending it to God that He may pay me back in the other world.' "

Father Ladas could stand it no longer. He was choking. He made signs to priest Grigoris to shut him up, but in vain. Then he intervened himself.

"So," he yelped, "is your lordship arguing that we should distribute all we've gained by the honest sweat of our brow, and get our I.O.U.'s paid back in the other world? What a brain! Just about good for plastering walls with! I'll tell you one thing, my lad, and you mustn't be upset: you can't have understood rightly what Christ said to you. A bird in the hand is worth two in the bush, that's what I think."

"Let him speak, father Ladas," Yannakos broke in. "You've heard Who it is that's sent him, it's Christ is speaking through his mouth."

"Is it you, Yannakos, raising your voice?" old Ladas burst out, furiously. "Don't you worry, just wait, we'll settle our accounts!"

The schoolmaster threw in his pinch of salt, anxious to smooth things down.

"All that you say is very fine and good, Manolios, but it can't be; castles in the air, my poor friend. We're not gods, we're men. You should take the measure of man to measure us by."

"That's the measure I'm taking," replied Manolios. "That's the measure by which I'm measuring. Of all of you who've taken the trouble to come to the festival today, who is Christian? All who are Christians believe in the other world. What does that mean, believing in the other world? That all our actions in this world below will be weighed in the other world; that the bad ones will be punished and the good ones rewarded. The man who shows charity to his brothers in this fleeting life will have as his reward the life eternal. So, father Ladas, two birds in the bush are worth more than one in the hand."

"You're a perfect halfwit," mumbled the old bird of prey.

"Well, what must we do?" cried several pious souls. "What has Christ told you? Speak plainly, Manolios, so we can understand and see if it's possible."

"Don't tell me to give everything away!" said an old man who was still hale and hearty. "That's impossible. Might as well face it."

"The harvest is in, my brothers," said Manolios. "God be thanked, it's been a good year. In a few days the vintage, too, will be done; very soon we shall begin the olive picking. Well, listen to the voice of Christ, which is tearing my heart: Inhabitants of Lycovrissi, right here, on our land, there have arrived persecuted brothers; winter is approaching, they'll die of hunger, cold and sorrow. Merciful God is opening His ledger, He is looking at the Lycovrissi people, He writes down the name of each one of them, the date, how much he possesses and how much he has given to the poor. He writes, let's say: Anastassios Ladas, son of Mikhael, had at such a date so much, he has given so much. He will be paid back with so much interest on the day of the Last Judgment."

Again father Ladas leered sarcastically:

"Depend upon it, nothing doing!" he growled.

"So," Manolios went on, "there you are, schoolmaster, there's the human measure you're asking for: that every proprietor, after each harvest, should take the tenth part of it and lend it to God, as Christ commands. Let us aid our brothers on the Sarakina for one year, two years, until they're set up again. There's also this: some of us have fields lying waste, so much heath, so much land we haven't had time to sow and have left untilled. Isn't that a sin before God? Let's give these to them to sow, to plough and go halves: it will mean more wealth for the village, and those who are hungry will have food. Woe to the Lycovrissi who eats his fill without thinking of the children on the Sarakina. Every human body starving on our land is tied round the neck of each one of us and drags us down to Hell. There's how many of us here, at Lycovrissi? Two thousand? All those who die of hunger on the Sarakina change into two thousand corpses and hang themselves like a necklace round our necks. It's with this necklace of corpses that we shall appear one day before the Lord."

The villagers shuddered. Some of them involuntarily raised a hand to their neck and felt it. The most exalted saw with their eyes two thousand Lycovrissi in the air, going off helter-skelter to the Last Judgment, each carrying hung round his neck like a rosary ten, fifteen, twenty corpses, and the angels escorting them were stopping up their noses for the stench.

Andonis the barber, though he had only a few vine plants and one small field, cried out:

"All right! You, too, keep a ledger, Manolios, and write down: 'I, Andonis Yunnidis, son of Thrassivoulos, barber of Lycovrissi, undertake to give the tenth part of my harvest to my brothers on the Sarakina. I am lending it to God.' Write it down, Manolios; merciful God is writing it down too, I trust Him!"

Several voices were heard and hands raised:

"I too! I too! Write, Manolios!"

There were eyes bathed in tears. Others were filled with anxiety. Yet others stared at Manolios with hatred. Old Patriarcheas had managed to slip away. Sitting now behind the little church, he had opened his bag and was laying out on lemon leaves the roast sucking pig he had left over from the night before.

"He's hopeless, that poor Manolios," he muttered, munching noisily; "before long they'll be chasing him with rotten tomatoes."

At this moment priest Grigoris raised his hand angrily, with his eyebrows working up and down; if one had touched them with one's fingertip sparks would have come from them.

"Hey, my sons of Lycovrissi," he shouted, "listen to me; don't fall into the snare of this wheedler, take care! The world, remember, rests on four pillars. Along with faith, country and honor, the

fourth great pillar is property: don't lay hands on it! God dis-
tributes wealth in accordance with hidden laws which are His
own. The justice of God is one thing, that of men is another. God
has made the rich and the poor. Woe to him who dares disturb
order; he is infringing the will of God! Impertinent Manolios,
I repent of having given you permission to speak. Come down
from there! Go and look after your sheep. That is the place God
has assigned to you; do not try to go higher. Do not grow where
you were not sown. All this nonsense you have talked is against
the will of God. He it is who decides, and all that happens in
the world happens because He wills it."

He began to be carried away and turned toward priest Fotis,
who had been listening all this time with bent head.

"Priest Fotis," he cried, "we were all right till now in our village,
order and concord reigned there; then you came with your band
and since that day our peace has been over. There's nothing now
but grievances, scandals, thefts. The poor have grown bold and
wish to raise their heads, the rich cannot sleep. But don't worry,
the Agha will return and the Council of Elders will throw itself at
his feet, that he may chase you away and we may have peace
again. Go somewhere else, with the grace of God, but let it be far
from us. I have spoken!"

Priest Fotis raised his head.

"Father," he said, serenely, "you are right. All that happens
in the world happens by the will of God. Manolios has spoken,
he has uttered the words he had in his heart, because God willed
it. Some Lycovrissi hearts have felt pain when they heard of our
sufferings, some Lycovrissi eyes have filled with tears, some storerooms have opened, because God willed it. And if we have come,
as your holiness says, to bring trouble to your peaceful village,
that also has happened because God has willed it. For water which
remains too long stagnant grows foul. God grant that we may be
the wind that rouses the storm and makes the waters live again;
makes souls live again!"

He turned toward the Lycovrissi:

"My brothers, we too were once property owners; now we are
reduced to begging. I have done a round of the villages, knocking
at all doors, one after the other, and I have come back to my
people with empty hands. For me, I do not mind; let me die!
For the old men, I do not mind, they've had their time, let them

die. But I am sorry for the children; every day there is one who dies of hunger. Those that are still alive can hardly stand on their feet. What is it they lack? A crust of bread, a drop of oil, a rag to dress in. If they had these trifles, which you throw to the dogs or into the rubbish heap, they would live. It's for these children that I'm begging. It's for them that I, too, hold out my hand and cry: 'Show charity, Christians!' "

Priest Fotis bent his head again and was silent. His face was yellow as wax, his eyes had grown huge, his hands, now folded on his breast, shone, and the bones were clearly visible under the transparent skin.

This time sobs burst out from all sides. Mariori began to weep, trying to hide it; a young married woman took off her necklace of gold pieces, as ashamed as if she had stolen it. In the breast of the enormous Dimitri, the butcher, God made Himself heard.

"I have a fat calf," he said, "which I was planning to kill next Sunday for the village; now I'll go and share it out on the Sarakina; you're right, Manolios; it makes me ashamed to see us eating while our brothers are dying of hunger."

Andonis the barber took fire:

"I'll go up also to the Sarakina on Saturday evening and shave them all free. I'll pull out their bad teeth free!"

The schoolmaster, carried away in his turn, overcame his fear:

"And I've got some alphabets and books for the children, I've some slates, pencils and a map of Greater Greece; I put them at the disposal of the community of the Sarakina."

"The devil take you!" muttered father Ladas furiously.

Priest Grigoris threw a fierce glance at his brother, but did not open his mouth.

Manolios approached priest Fotis and kissed his hand.

"Father, you see, you mustn't despair. Christ is still alive, He is still walking on the earth, hearts have opened and have welcomed Him; courage!"

The three friends approached them, followed timidly by Dimitri the butcher and Andonis the barber; other villagers came in turn, rather hesitantly, and at last the schoolmaster, half frightened, half resolved.

Priest Fotis, turning, saw them and crossed himself:

"Let us go, my sons," he said. "We, too, have our little chapel, in an old grotto which has already served as a church. Let us all go together and glorify God. Today is a great day: the heart of Man has trembled."

He turned toward the people, now dispersing and opening heavy bags:

"Health to you, Lycovrissi, good appetite! Your blessing, priest Grigoris!"

"My curses, rebels!" roared the well-padded priest; "cursed be all who follow you, you criminal!"

"May God who separates the sheep from the goats," retorted priest Fotis calmly, "be judge. It is in Him that we put our trust!"

So saying, with his scraggy finger he pointed to the sky.

The Priest's Curse

Priest Fotis and the four friends were sitting in front of the grotto, now a chapel, on stone benches hewn by the Christians of ancient times who, pursued by the idolaters, had taken refuge in these caves.

The mountain smelled of mint and thyme; night was flowing forward, blue and translucent. Now and then they could hear a night bird howling as it hunted caterpillars, mice or snails. The stars, that evening, had come down so low that they could be distinctly seen suspended between heaven and earth.

For a long time the five companions remained silent; deep in ecstasy they contemplated the night. They were quivering, that evening, with a strange emotion, as if, driven out from everywhere, they had taken refuge there, in front of that grotto, and were conspiring. What was their conspiracy? They did not themselves know: what would these five simple souls do, what were they capable of overthrowing? What new world could they have constructed? And yet the air around them was vibrant and on fire; they all felt, in their midst, a supreme invisible presence.

"A fine night, tonight," ventured Yannakos, to hide his emotion.

They all trembled at the sound of a human voice; the souls rushed back, each into the breast where it lived, the charm was broken.

Growing bold, Kostandis spoke:

"Father, it's already nearly four months since the Council of Elders summoned us and allotted us our parts in the acting of the Mystery under the church porch; up to now our everyday worries have turned us aside from the road, we've forgotten our goal. It's time we pulled ourselves together. But what are we to do, and how? Your holiness must know; help us!"

Priest Fotis smiled:

"What ought you to do, Kostandis? Go on with what you are doing, there; nothing else. You have taken, my sons, the straight path which leads to the Passion and to the Crucifixion of Christ."

"But what are we doing? We're doing nothing, Father," protested Manolios, with humility.

"Nothing, nothing, nothing!" sighed Michelis.

"You're forgetting the baskets, Michelis," replied the priest, pressing the young archon's hand affectionately; "Yannakos, are you forgetting that only the other day you called the poor together, gaily, to pillage your wares? And you, Kostandis, the simple man, who yesterday were only a humble café proprietor, didn't you leave your work and rise up to resist injustice? Didn't Manolios take upon him all the sins of the people and walk to death to save the village? Even Panayotaros, poor fellow—what else is he doing but prepare himself for the terrible part of Judas? You are preparing yourselves, my sons, you are preparing yourselves without knowing; that is the right way."

A long silence followed. Manolios sighed, staring at a star which was smiling and dancing in the sky. The shepherd knew that star well; how often, when he was a shepherd boy, had it not laughed at him, making him believe that it was the morning star, so much so that he brought out the sheep to pasture!

Kostandis bent his head. A great sadness was invading him. He was the only one to have done nothing, absolutely nothing; he suffered at being the last; even Judas had got ahead of him.

Yannakos, on his side, shook an overwhelmed head. I've done nothing, he told himself. Giving money, making a present of one's wares, all that is nothing at all. To give my Youssoufaki—that would be a sacrifice! There's where I'm waiting for you, Yannakos! Are you capable of doing it? All the rest is wind!

Once more the spirit of priest Fotis had traveled far away. It went home to familiar places, then returned on its tracks till it came to a solitary mountain named Sarakina. It was night, and he could barely make out, by the wan light of the stars, four beloved faces against the background of rock.

The priest's voice rose, grave, full of tenderness:

"My sons, sometimes the human soul seems to me to be like that flower they call Marvel of Peru. All day it keeps shut; it only opens and spreads in the shelter of the night. So this evening, more guessing than seeing you there in the darkness, I can feel my soul unfolding. One day, on the mountain where Manolios lives, I promised you—do you remember?—to tell you the story of my life. This evening I'm ashamed at your bowing and kissing my hand when you don't even know who I am or what hand you are kissing."

"Our souls, Father, are open this evening," said Manolios, moved; "we are listening."

Priest Fotis began slowly, as story tellers do:

"Near the Sea of Marmora, opposite Constantinople, there is a charming small village, gay with gardens strung out along the shore. It is called Artaki. That is where I was born. My father was priest; a severe, taciturn, fierce man with the kind of face the ascetics have on the walls of the old churches. My grandfather was also a priest; both of them wanted me to become a priest in my turn. I hated the idea; my dream was only of travels and trade, of filling my coffers with gold to buy rifles, arm men and liberate Artaki from the Turk. I was born a rebel, you see: my brain was filled with wind.

"In all my life I've been afraid of no one, except my father. I was terrified of him, and if I went to school regularly and was the best pupil, that was not from love, but from fear. School over, my mother (she's dead now), a holy woman, packed my trunk. She put into it my linen, an icon of the Baptism of Christ, biscuits, nuts, raisins, and figs sprinkled with sesame, and I was sent to Constantinople, to the big seminary.

"But, alas, no patience, no love of God to make me apply myself to theology! I was an incurable rebel; I ran all over Constantinople like one possessed, my eyes dazzled by its beauty. I had only one idea in my head—to liberate these lands and sacred waters from the Turk. One day the accursed war of '97 broke out. My brain caught fire and set me crying out: The moment has come to chase the Turk to Hell! I managed to embark secretly in a boat; I landed on a Greek coast, dressed as a rebel, armed myself with a rifle, girded on a cartridge pouch, got my feet into *tsarouchi* and set out to fight Turkey!"

Priest Fotis sighed, his voice had grown bitter and sarcastic:

"Ugh! We were seven goat-stealers setting out to overthrow an empire! Cursed be the state, my sons, cursed be it; it is the cause of the ruin of our race."

He was silent again for a moment; then, after a gesture with his hand, as though to throw off that national shame behind him, he resumed:

"To get to my own adventures. Greece is immortal, she can afford to risk adventures; she has before her the time needed for repairing the damage. But can I, poor ephemeral fly that I am? So, to cut a long story short, one day when, with my *tsarouchi* gaping and my stomach hollow, limp as a pricked balloon, I was wandering about the quays of the Piraeus in search of a boat that would take me back to Artaki, I saw some Jewish refugees landing from a caïque. A son and grandson of priests, I couldn't see a Jew without remembering that it was they who had crucified Christ, and the blood mounted to my head. Nonetheless, that day, I remained on the mole and enjoyed watching those Jews, with their hooked noses, sparse red beards, prying and burning eyes, and cloaks gone green with wear. They kept shouting all at the same time, pushing one another, jostling, in the struggle to be first off. Suddenly a piercing cry: a young Jewish girl slipped, fell into the sea and sank like a stone. No one made the least move to save her; I couldn't bear it any more. I said to myself: She's a human being, Jewess though she is, she too has a soul, and I threw myself into the water just as I was, seized her by the hair and hauled her out on to the mole. Immediately the women rushed to help and rubbed her to bring her back to herself. As I was drying myself in the sun I turned my eyes toward her. She was red-haired, with an extremely hooked nose and a freckled skin. She opened big blue-green eyes and looked at me, as someone told her that it was to me she owed her life. I saw her eyes and terror laid hold of me; in my turn I was falling into a blue-green sea and drowning there."

The priest's voice broke; he shook his head.

"The world is a mystery," he said after a while. "The motions of God's will seem complicated to Man's narrow brain; salvation or ruin comes by ways so unexpected that we can never know which road leads to Hell and which to Paradise. It seemed to me I had done a good action: I had saved a human being; yet, from that moment, I was off on the direct path to Hell.

"Up to then I had never defiled myself with a woman. You are younger than I, I'm ashamed to speak of the sin of the flesh in front of you; I will simply confess this: I sinned with that young girl. From then on, everything changed its taste: water, wine, bread, day, night took on for me a new savor. God disappeared. With God disappeared my father, my mother, and virtue and hope. A man of my village, seeing the state I was in, went and told my father, and the old priest sent me a letter with its four corners burned in sign of anger: 'If you sin with this Jewess, my curse upon you, and may I never see you again before my eyes!' We read this letter with the Jewess and laughed our heads off.

"One day—I've told you this—we had gone to a small village where we had friends, to celebrate Easter. The Jewess was with me. We were eating and drinking among the gardens. As I seized the knife to cut up the sheep I shouted, by way of a joke: 'If I had a priest in front of me, I'd cut his throat!' 'There's one behind you,' cried someone from the neighboring group. I turned, I saw the priest, I flung myself upon him, I cut his throat. Why? Because the Jewess was with me and I was ashamed to appear a braggart in her eyes.

"I was thrown into prison. The Jewess came to see me every day, washed my linen, brought me food and cigarettes. Through the bars she stroked my face and hair, weeping. She grew thin, she pined away before my eyes. One day she didn't come, nor the next day either, nor the next. Then I had a dream in which I saw the Holy Virgin dressed in black. It seemed to me I saw her a very long way off, quite small, then getting bigger as she approached. Her lips were moving, she was murmuring something, but she was still too far away; I couldn't hear. I listened hard. Her voice became more and more loud, and the Virgin still grew bigger. At length she was standing before me, and I heard distinctly: 'She's going to die, she's going to die, she's going to die . . . she's dead!' I woke up with a start. I had understood.

"It was dead of night. It was raining. I squeezed out, into the prison yard; I didn't know what I was doing. The limits of human power were abolished in me; I was sure I could climb the prison wall at one go and escape, passing in front of the sentinel without being seen; if he saw me and fired, he wouldn't be able to hit me. Love and grief had made me lose my head. Some days ago I had memorized the lie of the land, and chosen the part of the wall where a madman or a man in desperation like me might try to climb over. I found this bit of wall in the dark and, clinging to the stones, I started to climb like a wildcat. In daylight I should have been terrified, but I repeat, I had forgotten how far human strength will reach. Having managed my climb, I let myself drop down the other side. It was raining in torrents. No one there to see me; I made off as fast as I could run.

"Day was breaking as I reached her home. I knocked, but how could anyone have heard in the midst of that deluge? I jumped over the wall, crossed the courtyard, went furtively up the stairs, opened the door of her room. I called her softly. Silence! I struck a match. Pale, with her mouth twisted and her eyes wide open and the whites showing, the Jewess was stretched on her bed. She had taken poison, that very night; unable to bear the separation any longer, she had killed herself."

Priest Fotis stood up, looking about him, as if he wanted to flee. He sat down again, exhausted, as though coming back from very far away, from the end of the world. For a long time he remained without speaking.

"And then, Father?" the four friends asked, breathing hard.

"I've finished," said the priest.

"What became of you?" Manolios asked. "How did you return into the way of God?"

"The soul of man is a mystery! Love had parted me from God; grief, blessed be it, brought me back to Him. I went to Mount Athos. At first the solitude did me good. My soul was calmed a little. But gradually my solitude became peopled again with Jewesses, cries of joy and sobs. Unable to bear it, I went and announced to the Superior that I had changed my mind and wanted to re-enter the world; he gave me his blessing and I left. I walked for a long while. I reached a little village. A voice arose in me: 'Stay here!' and I stayed. I married, I was ordained priest. I had decided to throw myself into the torments of the world in order to forget, and I did so. Sickness came, my wife died, my children died, I found myself once more alone, standing, wounded, face to face with the Lord. Then the Greeks came, then the Turks. The rest you know. God be praised for all the evil and all the good He has given me!"

The four friends bowed down to kiss that martyr hand.

"I'm tired," murmured priest Fotis, sighing, "I'm tired. I've lived my life over again. What a punishment, what a desolation, how bitter it is, the honey of the earth! I say to myself sometimes: 'O God, what a Hell this life would be if there were not the great hope, the Kingdom of Heaven!' "

None of them said another word. Priest Fotis rose, looked toward the east and crossed himself; day was breaking.

All that night, seated on his bed, old Patriarcheas kept watch for the sound of the front door and the steps of his son in the courtyard. He listened; when footsteps rang on the road he got up and leaned against the window. Nobody! He smoked a cigarette, then another, and let himself fall heavily onto his bed again. At dawn sleep took possession of him: he saw a falcon swoop into the courtyard and seize his white cock, his favorite, the one he kept for breeding. The falcon clutched it in its claws and carried it off into the sky, while the cock gave cries of joy as though the day were breaking.

He leaped up terrified, a shiver passed down his back.

"May this evil omen be averted!" he muttered, crossing himself.

He clapped his hands and called Lenio. She arrived half awake, scantily clad, with hair in disorder and eyes shining; her breasts jumped about, trying to dart out of her white slip.

"Here, Lenio, has Michelis come in? Where's he been all night? Where did he sleep?"

"He isn't back, master. I looked into his room as I passed, and saw no one. His bed's not been slept in."

After a moment she added with a knowing laugh:

"The widow's dead; God knows where they go now, the lads who sleep out."

"As soon as he arrives, tell him I want to see him. Don't go! What became of you yesterday during the festival? I lost sight of you."

Lenio blushed, giggled, but did not answer.

"You shameless bitch! Can't you hold yourself in for a few days? We've decided you're to be married next Sunday, and to have done with it. That way you'll have peace, my poor girl; Nikolio won't, any more. . . . Do you hear what I'm saying to you? Your eyes are far away. Where's that spirit of yours gone wandering, eh, harum-scarum?"

Lenio burst out laughing, and made as if she were rubbing lovingly against someone.

"In the mountains," she replied.

In truth her spirit was up on the mountain, under the big holm oak. Nikolio had bleated yesterday like the ram when he had turned and seen her arriving, covered with sweat, her cheeks on fire. Silently, brutally, he had caught her by the neck and flung her to the ground. Dassos, the bellwether, had come up, sniffed at her, recognized her. He had bleated like his master and stayed near them, licking himself. Suddenly Lenio heard the aged master's rough voice. She jumped.

"What are you thinking of, you blessed female in heat? I speak to you and you don't hear me. Is your spirit gadding on the mountain?"

"At your service, master," said Lenio, back from the mountain. "Excuse me, I didn't hear."

"I was telling you to get me a strong coffee, well sweetened. My head's going around, I'm not well. Perhaps I'm hungry."

Lenio was already out of the door and tumbling down the stairs, making a clatter with her heels.

The old man closed his eyes and recalled his dream. "The falcon—that means what?" he muttered. "I don't understand. May the good God protect my house!"

The sun was already high; the village lanes rang with men's cries, bleatings and brayings. Men and beasts were off to work and were greeting the new day.

Lenio brought the cup of well-sweetened coffee. The old archon sat down near the window and savored the magic drink, drop by drop. His brain grew clearer. He began to smoke, keeping his eyes fixed on the front door. Every moment he twisted his mustache and groaned piteously. Last evening priest Grigoris had gone for him, telling him that while he had been quietly enjoying his sucking pig, Manolios had been rousing the peasants, proclaiming that Christ commands each of us to give a tenth of his income to the people on the Sarakina; and what was worse, some hot-heads had believed him. That fox of a priest Fotis, that bag of lice playing the ascetic, had joined in and spread discord. "Wait, wait, there's worse yet: your son, Michelis, was the very first to take their side, threatening the village! And here we are, now, with that cursed Manolios, that little hypocrite, raising the standard of revolt; do you hear me, archon? Please God to take the matter in hand, otherwise we're done for!"

"My friend, if I don't take it in hand myself," archon Patriarcheas had muttered, "the good God won't exactly put Himself out. Besides, has He the time to look after everyone? I'm the one who'll put things in order here, in Lycovrissi. And I'm off now to give the ear of my fine fellow of a son a twisting. Afterward it'll be the turn of that idiot Manolios."

At this moment the outer door opened and Michelis stole in. The old man jumped and leaned out of the window:

"A happy awakening to you, my young spark," he cried; "be so good as to come up and let us too see something of you!"

Careful, Michelis, hold your tongue, said the young man to himself; he's your father, don't forget.

"I'm coming, Father," he replied.

He climbed the stone staircase and wished good morning to the old man, who did not even glance at him: he was trying to make himself angry. Up to this minute, he had been swearing at his son, but now that he had seen him coming in furtively, just as he himself had used to slip in at his age, into this same house, his father's, coming back from his women, the old man felt his heart melt in him. I was the same, he thought. But I used to spend the night out because I was sowing my wild oats; with him it's to yarn about the good God with his crazy friends. Heavens, who knows, that's a kind of wild oats, too, he's young, he'll get over it. As he thought, with his back turned to his son, he kept on trying to get up his anger. Seeing that the wrath was slow in coming, he turned suddenly, annoyed at not having managed to lose his temper, and cried:

"What's this I hear now, eh? Aren't you ashamed? Haven't you more respect for your position? Are you forgetting whose son and whose grandson you are?"

He was happy to notice that as he spoke he warmed up; he raised his voice still more:

"I forbid you to see Manolios any more!"

Michelis hesitated to answer: He's your father, he said to himself, be patient; it's not the one that explodes who is the stronger, it's the one that controls himself. Control yourself!

"Why don't you answer? Where've you been gallivanting all night this time? On the Sarakina? With that ragamuffin priest of yours and that revivalist of a Manolios, the servant? Fine company! Have you sunk to that, my poor fellow?"

"Father," replied Michelis calmly, "don't insult men who are better than we."

This time the old archon jumped up and lost his temper properly:

"What's that you say? Look here, have you lost your wits altogether? Better than we? The priest in rags, and our lackey!"

"That priest in rags, as you call him, is a saint. We are not even worthy, any of us archons Patriarcheas, to undo the strings of his shoes!"

The old man threw away his cigarette, the blood was rising to his heavy head.

"As for Manolios, if you want to know," continued Michelis quietly, pitilessly, "you know quite well that when all you notables, archons, priests and schoolmasters were crouching and trembling in the prison, thinking of nothing but how to save not the village but your skins, the lackey Manolios rose up to save the people. Who showed himself the true archon of the village? You, archon Patriarcheas, or perhaps his holiness priest Grigoris? No, no! It was Manolios; from that moment it's we who are the lackeys, and he the archon!"

The old man fell backward on his bed, winded. He was choking.

Michelis fell silent, ashamed at having forgotten the lessons he had given himself and at having, in spite of himself, answered his father back. He drew near and arranged his pillows for him.

"Is there anything you want, Father?" he asked. "Would you like Lenio to make you a lemonade?"

"You're just like your mother," muttered the old man, staring at his son in stupefaction, "you're just like your mother. All honey outside, all poison inside."

Michelis's eyes blinked. Between him and his father the air thickened, and all of a sudden his mother rose, pale, sorrowful, full of nobility and humility. Mother! murmured Michelis, staring at the sudden apparition. A breath passed by, the light quivered and the holy form vanished.

"What are you thinking of?" asked the old man.

"My mother," replied the son. "My mother. You treated her very harshly, Father."

"I'm a man," retorted the old man angrily, "I do treat females roughly. It's what they want. But how can you know? You've still got your mother's milk on your lips."

"God grant I may always have that milk on my lips."

Again his mother rose between them, fierce this time. She shook her head, looking at her son, and stretched out her hand to give him her blessing. A voice, the voice of his mother, arose from the deepest depths of Michelis. "Raise your head, my son, you're a man, don't be afraid of him as I was. What I was afraid of saying to him, Michelis, avenge your mother and say it to him."

Resolute now, the son leaned his elbow on the windowsill and waited.

The old man got up, sighing, and also approached the window. "Listen," he said.

"I'm listening," replied the son, looking his father in the eyes.

"I've decided, and you can decide, too: either me or Manolios, choose. Either you'll leave Manolios and his band, or else you'll leave my house."

"I shall leave your house," replied Michelis.

The old man rolled his eyes with amazement.

"You love the valet more than me, your father?" he cried.

"I don't love Manolios more, no; what has Manolios got to do with it? It's Christ I am choosing. That's what you've asked me, without realizing. And you have my answer."

The old man was silent, strode the length of the room and stopped again in front of his son.

"What have you got against me?" he said in a voice heavy with reproach.

"Nothing, but you've forced me to choose, and I've chosen. I can't help it."

The old man collapsed again with all his weight on the bed and feverishly clutched his head in his hands. He felt his entrails torn apart.

"Go," he said in the end, "go, let me never see you again!"

The son turned. He saw the old man prostrate, he was sorry for him; but inside him an imperious voice was crying out to him: "Go!"

He came close to his father and fell on his knees.

"Father," he said, "I'm going. Can you give me your blessing?"

"No," answered the old man, "no, I can't."

Michelis rose and made for the door. His father was on the point of crying: "My child!" but he was ashamed to humiliate himself and was silent.

The son opened the door, turned once again:

"Father," he said, "good-bye!" Then crossed the threshold.

A long while afterward Lenio, hearing no more sounds of argument, went up stealthily and put her ear to the keyhole. She heard a deep snoring, broken by sighs. The bed groaned.

The old man's asleep and having nightmares, she whispered; the row's over. At noon he'll get up, hungry as a wolf; I'll go and wring a chicken's neck. Talk of a belly, I can't manage to fill it. No good glutting it, it's never satisfied. A regular pit!

She went downstairs again and into the chickenhouse to choose the chicken she would kill. With scarlet crest, the white cock strutted boastfully; around him the hens pecked and clucked. Lenio stopped for a moment, burning with desire to see a hen crouch down and the white cock leap upon her; for years she had watched this, gasping with delight; it was she who was crouching down and could feel a weight, very agreeable, like a man's. What man's? At first, when she was very young, this invisible male had had no face; later he had taken that of Manolios, then that of Nikolio, and for some months had not changed.

She looked about and chose an old hen, the speckled one; but just as she was stretching out her hand to grab her, the speckled hen crouched down and, spreading his wings, the cock covered her. Lenio had pity on the hen and chose another.

Toward noon she laid the table, threw an egg into the soup and waited for the master to call her; he was late.

"He's taking his time, the old glutton," Lenio murmured, "next thing he'll be off to another world."

She became anxious.

"Provided he lasts till Sunday evening, or best, Monday morning. Otherwise when'll we get married? I can't wait any longer."

She went up again, opened the door softly and scanned the room. The archon was stretched on the bed, motionless. His open eyes were staring at the ceiling. He no longer moved, no longer sighed. Lenio went right in, terrified: could he be dead? But the old man blinked his eyelids.

"Master," said Lenio, reassured, "I've put the egg in the soup, time to come down."

"I'm not hungry," he groaned, "I don't feel well, you know, Lenio. Call priest Grigoris."

The old man sat up; his face was blueish, striped with purplish streaks; Lenio gave a cry.

"Don't be afraid, I'm not dead yet. I merely want to have a talk with the priest. Is Michelis downstairs?"

"No. He went to his room to change; he put on his everyday clothes again and went off carrying a bundle."

"He said nothing?"

"Nothing."

"Send someone to the mountain to fetch Manolios, the devil take him! He's to come and see me as quickly as possible, before sundown. Do you hear? There, off with you!"

"Aren't you going to eat?"

The old man thought for a moment:

"What have you got ready?"

"Your favorite boiled chicken."

"Put plenty of lemon in the soup, I'm coming down."

Lenio bundled down the stairs joyously. "He'll certainly hold out till Monday morning. His face worries me. I'll go and ask Andonis to cup him. Can't have him dying too soon."

Meanwhile Michelis had arrived up on the mountain, with his bundle under his arm. He did not find Manolios at the sheepfold, and sat down on the bench by the door. The shadows were contracting, noon was near. On the mountain opposite, the little church of the Prophet Elijah seemed dissolved in the vertical light.

Michelis shut his eyes. He was exhausted, his heart was overflowing with bitterness. "It's the end of everything," he muttered, "and the beginning of everything. Christ, You have marked out the path, help me to go to the end of it. You are there, I know, at the end of the path and are waiting for me."

He opened his bundle and pulled out the Gospel book left him by his mother. It was bound in thick pigskin and closed with a chain clasp. One of its pages had in it a laurel leaf as bookmark. Bending his head over the sacred text he read:

If any man come to me and hate not his father and mother and wife and children and brethren and sisters, yea, and his own life also, he cannot be my disciple.

And whosoever does not bear his cross and come after me cannot be my disciple.

For several days he had been reading and rereading these words of Christ and trying to understand them. At first they had seemed to him hard, inhuman. Isn't there, he asked himself, a way more in harmony with the human heart? Must a man then pay for his salvation in blood? Why are the father and mother such an obstacle? Can't we both love them and raise ourselves toward God?

Michelis asked more and more questions, but he was unable to find any answer. But behold, gradually, he felt his heart lighten itself of the weight of the earth, and slowly rise. Already, since the other evening, he had come to feel suspended between heaven and earth.

Shortly after noon, Manolios came back from the pasture. He was surprised to find his friend on the mountain at such an hour.

"I've left my father's house, Manolios. The old man gave me the choice. I've chosen the way of Christ."

"It is a hard way, Michelis," said Manolios thoughtfully. "Hard above all for the rich. Welcome!"

He served the meal on the low table. Michelis told of what had happened with his father and the decision he had taken.

"I couldn't go on any longer, Manolios, my life was too easy, I was ashamed."

"Welcome," repeated Manolios. "The road is rocky, the rise is steep, at first one hurts one's feet, Michelis. But gradually you grow wings, angels take you under the arms and you climb the sheer mountain of God gaily, singing."

He stood up and took his shepherd's staff.

"Your father," he said, "has sent me a message to appear before him immediately. I can guess what he wants of me. Till this evening!"

"God go with you!"

Lenio, on her knees in the courtyard, crimson and with her sleeves rolled up, was polishing the copper utensils which the old man, her master, had generously given her as dowry. Lenio rubbed with all her might, singing as she did so. Her voice flew up toward the mountain, and Nikolio, standing in the shadow of the holm oak, cocked his pointed ears, took his long flute and replied.

Manolios appeared at the turning of the road. He heard Lenio's warbling and smiled.

A wild mare, this Lenio, he thought, a real wild mare; only a little child will be able to tame her.

Lenio raised a fiery face and saw Manolios as he crossed the threshold.

"Health and joy, Lenio," said her one-time betrothed; "I see you're getting ready. Good luck to you!"

"Same to you!" answered Lenio mockingly; "may some nice girl carry you off! Come, hurry up, poor chap, the master's waiting for you."

So saying she returned to her singing with even more zest, wishing to show her ancient swain that she did not care a pin for him since she had found a better fiancé: That'll make him burst with fury!

Old Patriarcheas had been rolling cigarette after cigarette, smoking away and digesting his chicken while waiting for Manolios. He had put on his long archon's robe, and was barefoot. He was hot. His face had taken on an aubergine color and the veins on his neck were starting out. He came and went about the room, foaming with anger and from time to time threw himself on his bed, exhausted.

It's my fault . . . it's my fault, he repeated to himself without ceasing. My fault for having had pity on him and brought him out of the monastery, where he was living like a eunuch, to make him into a real man. A fine job I've done! That skinflint Ladas is right; how many times he's told me: "Do evil, and people fear and respect you; do good and you have nothing but trouble!" I used to make fun of him. Well, here's the trouble all right!

In the end Lenio's singing got on his nerves.

To the devil with that blessed female, for heaven's sake let her marry, that'll calm her. Otherwise she'll turn the village upside down. He rushed to the window to shout to her to shut up, when at the same moment the door opened. He turned. Manolios appeared on the threshold. He jumped, and rage lit up his eyes.

"Come in," he shouted; "come in!" He slammed the door violently behind Manolios and pushed him against the wall.

"Is that the thanks I get, eh? I let you into my household and you've brought misfortune upon it! We were all right before you came, we were quiet in my house, quiet in the village. You came, you dirty prophet, to upset order. Why? By what right did you put yourself forward the other day to save the village? That was my business. Why must you put in your pinch of salt and meddle in things that don't concern you? I'll tell you why, I will: to pass yourself off as a saint, make the fools believe you and proclaim revolution at the feast of the Prophet Elijah."

"Revolution!" said Manolios, dumbfounded.

"What else was all that impudent nonsense you spouted to us on the mountain the day before yesterday? How we ought to pay a tithe to the lice-carriers, how we're all to be equal, all brothers, all lousy, hey! That what you mean? Give them our fields, too, half-and-half—by what right? But they're ours, they are, they're our patrimony, our blood! In that case ought we to share our flesh with them too, give them part of it to eat? It's the end of everything!"

He shook Manolios by the collar, furiously.

"Are we to make this place a second Russia? Country where they eat each other, where everyone tramples on his neighbor, where there's no difference any more between masters and lackeys, where the louse—Lord have mercy on us!—has grown as big as the tortoise? And that louse—would you come bringing it to my bed to feed on me?"

Seized with alarm at the idea of this louse, he stared at Manolios with horror.

"One day—hasn't anybody ever told you this, you head without a brain?—the belly had raised the standard of revolt and climbed into the head to take command. Then the man's filth came out of him through the nose, the mouth and the eyes, so that he died of it. So don't disturb God's order. Let the belly stay in its place and the head in its, to command. I'm the head!"

He was pacing up and down like a wild beast in its cage, hitting the walls with his stick, and spitting on the floor.

"There ought to be no more rich, says he! But if there are no more rich, who'll give alms to the poor? Thought of that? To whose house will your aunt Mandalenia go to find work? And in whose will your lordship be servant?"

He exploded.

"Scurfy, lousy scoundrel," he shouted, "you haven't even an inch of land and you cry: 'We're brothers!' Why? So we can share and share like brothers, as you put it, and you can gobble up half our possessions. Who put those ideas into your head, eh, you vagabond?"

"Christ," answered Manolios.

"The devil take you! What Christ, eh? Yours, not mine. You've invented a Christ Who's the spit and image of you, a lousy, famished rebel; a bolshevik, that's it! You've put into His mouth whatever pleased you and then raised Him up like the church's banner, howling: 'We all have the same Father, so down with inheritance, let's share it out. We are all brothers, so bring the roast and let's all eat it!' Well, no, you shan't eat it!"

He threw his cigarette out of the window, spat into the courtyard, then, coming back toward Manolios, seized him by the collar:

"You will leave my service, and double quick!" he shouted at him. "At once! This evening! Go and join the beggars, your like! Share your scurf, your lice, your Kingdom of Heaven!"

At these words the door opened and, majestic as a bishop, priest Grigoris appeared.

"Archon," he said, "excuse me; I'm late because Mariori, my daughter, is not well."

Turning, he saw Manolios and frowned.

"Most reverend," said old Patriarcheas, "nothing here is right any more, the world's upside down, archon Manolios has proclaimed revolt, he wants to set the world on fire. And that fine bird of a son of mine has raised the standard, too. This morning he declared to me: 'I'm leaving the house, I'm leaving you, old Patriarcheas, I'm choosing the way of Christ.' As though my way was the way of Antichrist! It's the end of all things! Lucky you've come, Father, time we got things straight."

Priest Grigoris stretched out his arm, pointing at Manolios:

"Here is Antichrist! He it is that is sowing discord among us. He it is who is filling the people's heads with hazy ideas. What was all that stuff and nonsense you poured out before us at the festival, you knave? Upon my word, it's the rebellion of the feet against the head!"

"The words of Christ," replied Manolios. "Be charitable to the poor, let him who possesses two shirts give one, we are all brothers. Nothing else."

The bile rose to the eyes of priest Grigoris. Disdaining to argue with a servant, he addressed himself to the old archon:

"This man is dangerous. It is essential you should drive him out, he should be driven out of the village, to stop him contaminating us! It's he who's turned your son's head. With his intrigues he's managing to appear important, and he'll have the lot of us. Let him get out! That's no shepherd, that's no sheep, that's a wolf!"

Manolios left the wall and put his hand up to his chest:

"Good-bye, archons and reverends, I am going."

"Get out, with the curse of God!" roared the priest, raising his hand.

"The curse of the notables and priests," replied Manolios. "It is you, the priests, who crucified Christ. If He came down upon earth again, you would crucify Him afresh. Good-bye."

He went quietly to the door, opened it, turned and repeated calmly:

"Good-bye."

He went down the stairs, feeling light and gay, carried by angels.

The Muscovite

When Manolios set out for the mountain it was already dark. Clouds were piled in the sky, a warm east wind was blowing, a few drops of rain fell on his hands, on his face and on the parched earth. The flesh of Manolios, as thirsty as the earth, rejoiced.

What a miracle this world is! he soliloquized as he climbed. If I open my eyes I see the mountains, the clouds and the rain falling; if I close my eyes, I see God, Who created the mountains, the clouds and the falling rain. Everywhere, by the light of day and in the darkness, the grace of God is around us!

He had already forgotten archons and priests, got rid of vain cares, passed beyond petty joys, petty sufferings; he had attained the greatest joy and the greatest suffering, that which is above all joy and all suffering; he was face to face with his God.

Dismissed by the master he had served so faithfully, he would say good-bye, tomorrow at dawn, to the mountain he so loved. He would put his bundle on his back, take his shepherd's staff and go off alone, defenseless, on the lonely route which climbs unceasingly.

The rain became thicker, in the distance claps of thunder rumbled dully, and Manolios quickened his pace. The wind was at his back, pushing him forward; it seemed to him as if the wind had hands and a human breath.

He caught sight, far off, of a feeble light. He recognized the little window of the shepherd's hut. By now, he thought, Nikolio has finished milking, had his dinner, gone to bed. The light must be Michelis waiting. His heart thudded hard at the thought of his friend.

"He won't be able to stand it," he muttered; "he has an archon's ways, he's used to good food, sleeping in a soft bed, living in the warmth and shelter of a house; he'd much better go home. Let him be patient; his hour has not come yet. Whether he likes it or not, wealth does weigh down the soul, stops it from walking freely. There's also Mariori to keep him on earth in spite of himself."

He remembered the hard, clear words of Christ. "It is easier for a camel to pass through the eye of a needle than for a rich man to enter the Kingdom of Heaven."

He found Michelis sitting in front of the fireplace, staring at the fire.

"Greetings to the young archon of the mountain," he said joyfully, wiping his hair and his running face. "Tomorrow morning I shall say good-bye to this dear hut and go away; your father's dismissed me."

He sat down on the ground in front of the fire and in an even voice told of how he had found the old archon boiling with rage; how the archon had used harsh words to him and dismissed him, and how the priest had placed his curse on him.

"It all happened," he concluded, "as I expected, as it was bound to happen; I've no regrets. Your father was bound to dismiss me, the priest was bound to curse me, and I was bound to leave."

"Where will you go now?" said Michelis, pressing his friend's hand with anxious affection.

"Night will bring counsel. God often comes down to us in our sleep and shows us the way in the form of dreams. I've not taken any decision yet; He will take it. We shall see; don't be anxious."

"Do you remember the evening in Kostandis's yard?" said Michelis. "I told you—remember?—that wherever you went, Manolios, I'd go with you; I say it again this evening."

"Don't be in too much of a hurry, Michelis, don't be in too much of a hurry; we'll see, tomorrow."

They both of them lay down, tired. The rain redoubled, violently, joyfully; the dry grasses of the mountain were refreshed and balmy, the wind brought in soft gusts, from a long way away, the resinous smell of pines; the earth exhaled its fragrance. Manolios's brain, like a clod of earth, welcomed the rain and drew from it refreshment.

Was that God's answer? Was He coming down this evening in the form of a beneficent rain? Manolios welcomed God and felt happy from head to foot. The night birds also, as they huddled in the rocks and in the hollows of the trees, felt God descending upon their soaked wings.

Michelis listened to the rain falling, he sniffed the scent of the damp earth, he could not sleep. Mariori rose up in his mind, and his heart began to flutter anxiously along, flush with the soaking earth. The last time he had seen her he had found her without make-up, pale and worn out. She kept coughing, with her handkerchief held to her mouth, but this time the handkerchief was no longer white, it was a red one, to prevent the blood from showing. "Michelis," she had said, "I'm going away, my father's taking me to see the doctors in the town; I'm not well."

As he sniffed the scent of the earth, Michelis felt his heart shudder. I'm still attached to the earth, he thought, still . . .

Gently, in the midst of this rainy night, sleep enfolded Michelis and Manolios, and in the morning, when they opened their eyes, the freshly washed mountain was smiling at the first rays of the sun; clouds like fleeces were rising in the sky, and drops hanging on the branches shone and quivered.

Manolios took down from the wall the icon Michelis had given him, the Crucifixion with the swallows. He then took down the mask of Christ which he had carved, gathered up some clothes, made a bundle of the lot and laid it on the stone bench.

Michelis watched him without a word. They sat down and drank some milk in silence, then Manolios stood up. His gaze lingered on the hut, on the bench, on the rocks around about, on the mountain, for a mute farewell. He picked up his shepherd's staff from a corner. Michelis had stood up.

"It's decided, Manolios? You're leaving? Where are you going?"

"Fare you well, Michelis."

"Tell me, where are you going?"

"To the Sarakina. I'm going to share hunger with them."

"Don't you want me to go with you?"

"Not yet. Be patient. You've your father and a betrothed. I've nothing. It's easier."

"Yes, but it is written: 'He who hateth not his father, his wife and his children, is not worthy to be called my disciple.' "

"I know, Michelis. But has your heart uprooted all the roots that attach it to earth, to father, to wife? Not yet. So have patience; your hour will come, don't be in too much of a hurry. It will come like the partridge, walking without a sound."

"I don't want to go back to my father."

"All right, don't go back. Stay here, between the Sarakina and

Lycovrissi, wait for the partridge, your own hour. See you soon!"

He held out his hand to Michelis, who pressed it impulsively.

"Manolios," he said, "it won't be long before I come and join you, I swear. See you soon!"

Manolios took his little bundle under his left arm, crossed himself and set off. The angel's wings came again, and Manolios flew from stone to stone. The little church of the Prophet Elijah was getting nearer and nearer, glittering among the crags on the peak of the mountain. At the sight of it, Manolios raised his staff and uttered a wild cry.

Old Patriarcheas waited for his son all day long. Two, three days passed in vain; in desperation the old archon sent relatives to talk to him, despatched the schoolmaster, in the end called Yannakos:

"Do me this favor, Yannakos, go and see my son; you too, talk to him. You're of the same band, perhaps he'll listen to you."

Yannakos shook his head.

"I think, the way things are going, it won't be long before I, too, take to the mountain, archon," he said. "Send someone else."

Panayotaros came to see him.

"Archon, I've got some details. Manolios has made his lair on the Sarakina. He calls together the refugees, makes speeches to them, works them up. He declares that the hungry have the right to strip all those who have enough to eat. Remember this that I'm telling you—the day when hunger drives them to it, they'll come down on the village like wolves."

He stopped a moment, seemed to hesitate, sighed, looked about him and leaned toward the old man's ear.

"I've a suspicion, archon," he insinuated in a whisper.

"Speak out, Panayotaros, I'm listening. As you don't love anyone, you've clear sight. So speak out!"

"Manolios is a bolshevik!"

"Bolshevik?" said the archon, scratching his head, "and that means—?"

"That means: if you want to eat, you help yourself, and if you want anything, you grab it! It's a band of brigands that's been plowing up the world for some time now."

"And you think . . . "

"Sure and certain. Those people have their men in every country, in the smallest village, and to the far end of the world. Go to the desert and you'll find them; into each family and you'll find them; lift up any stone and you'll find them. Well, to Lycovrissi they've sent Manolios."

"That's a fine yarn you're spinning me, Panayotaros! You're giving me the creeps, I shall die of it. Speak out clearly!"

"It's true, it is a dying matter. The skill they go to work with, those sons of the fiend! Have you watched Manolios? He plays the saint. Doesn't want any meat, so he says, never tells a lie, doesn't go after women, and even, lately, never lets go of a little Gospel book—every time he sees anyone coming, there he is, with the book open, making believe he's reading. All sham! T'other day, when he was going to be hanged, know what they tell me he did? Listen to this, it'll give you gooseflesh: he fixed up with old Martha, who'd found Hussein's blood-stained clothes, so she'd only show them at the last moment. Why? So the folks would believe that Manolios is ready to give his life for the village—a way to make himself a name, have the people with him; and then, when the moment comes, at orders from Moscow, drive them to slit the throats of the archons and notables."

Old Patriarcheas collapsed on a chair and buried his head in his hands.

"Mercy of God," he muttered, "mercy of God, it's the end of all things!"

He jumped up, almost at once, his bloated eyes wide:

"But in that case, my son . . . ?" he stuttered with his mouth all twisted.

"Manolios has got around him, archon, he's worked on his feelings, and he, too, has gone bolshevik, without realizing it. Don't you see, he left your house to go and join him on the mountain? It won't be long before Yannakos goes, too, you'll see, and Kostandis after him—he'll leave his house and go off to join them. It's like infectious diseases, archon. One person gives it to another. Andonis the barber looks like catching it too. And fat Dimitri the butcher. And if you want to know what I think, even the schoolmaster."

"What's that you're saying, Panayotaros? It's the end of all things! I'll go and look for priest Grigoris, and we'll put all straight!"

"As for priest Fotis and the ragged lot he drags around after him, if you want to know, it's the men in Moscow sent them straight to Lycovrissi. They say the Turks drove them out. They sacrificed themselves for the country. Ever hear such nonsense? It's the fiends in Moscow sent them, I tell you! Manolios had got a message to them, saying: 'Here in Lycovrissi there's no lack of bread, there's everything in profusion here, come and we'll sack the village! The archon here's a complete dotard, he'll put up no resistance. And you saw, that's why Manolios and priest Fotis got on at once, like thieves at a fair. In a twinkling of an eye they understood each other. That's why the other day when you kicked him out—where d'you suppose he went? Straight to the Sarakina! It's clear, archon!'"

Old Patriarcheas was pacing up and down the length of his room. Suddenly he stopped, having made up his mind:

"Go and tell priest Grigoris I've absolutely got to see him. This very evening!"

"Priest Grigoris is off this evening with his daughter to the town. He'll be back tomorrow. He's taking her to see a doctor or two; she coughs, she spits blood; in fact, she's badly ill."

"Devil take you!" fulminated the old man, furiously. "Haven't you anything but calamities to report today, from crack of dawn?"

"Archon, I'm only telling you what I know. Believe it or not, as you like, that's your affair. I've bothered you long enough, I'm sorry, I'm off."

"To blazes with you, Judas Iscariot!" swore the old man, inwardly. Then, aloud:

"Good-bye for the present, Panayotaros. And anything you hear . . ."

"Don't worry, archon, I'm around."

He went out with a heavy bear's gait; an evil smile lit his pitted face.

Old Patriarcheas slumped down on the bed, full length, ruminating strenuously the things Panayotaros had said to him. But it was no use, he could not digest them.

"God damn it, it looks to me as if we'd nearly fallen into a fine old mess! The good God had made us all blind, I swear, not one of us had seen through it—neither the priest, the old fox, nor the schoolmaster, with all his books, not even me. To think I've had a spy in my service! It was from my house that they meant to light the fuse which was to set fire to the village! Old man, as an archon you're not brilliant! Waiting for that bear, that brute, to come and unseal our eyes! Must drive that swine Manolios right away and

dislodge those lousy devils from the Sarakina, the dirty bolsheviks; must clean up the neighborhood and make honor and
justice reign once more in the village! Tomorrow, when the priest
comes, we'll put all this straight."

This thought calmed him; he shut his eyes and tried to sleep.
But sleep would not come. Down below Lenio was singing, cooing
away like a dove. Unable to keep still, she kept wandering all
over the place, waiting for friends to whom she could show off her
trousseau; she was busy displaying all the items skillfully in the
long gallery, that there might seem to be more than there were; and
the marriage garlands woven of lemon blossom were there, between
the sugared almonds and the big white candles.

This evening Nikolio would come down from the mountain,
dressed in his new suit, the master's wedding present, and with
his black hair bound in the red handkerchief Lenio had given him.
Tomorrow, Sunday, the marriage would be celebrated and the
bride, dame Nikolina, would ride on a mule with a red sumpter-
cloth up to their future domain, the mountain and the sheepfold.

Lying on his bed, the old man listened to Lenio's singing, to the
gay exclamations of her friends as they arrived, the laughter of
the girls. It reminded him of his own wedding, when as a young
man of twenty-two, slim and handsome as Saint George, he had
rushed out on his white horse to fetch his betrothed. He could see
her again on the threshold of his father's house, white-veiled as
custom required, that her face might not be seen. Impatiently
he, the bridegroom, kept shouting to her parents: "Take away the
cloud, let the sun show!" Then her old mother, with wet eyes,
stood on tiptoe and pulled the veil aside. Immediately the whole
procession—bride and bridegroom, parents, friends, horses, mules,
shawls of many colors—shone as if indeed the sun were rising at
that instant.

Then, with a great sweep of its wings, the thought of old Patriarcheas crossed time.

The years went by, the sun had darkened; Saint George
had put on weight, a great deal of weight. But his blood was still
seething. There was, in his archon's residence, a certain servant,
a robust girl called Garoufou. He could see again her erect, firm
breasts, her haunches that seemed to embrace the world, her heels
like red apples. One night the archon had gone noiselessly downstairs, taking care not to make the stairs creak, not to let the lady

Patriarcheas, aged before her time, hear him. He had slid into the tiny room where Garoufou slept, had lain in her bed and had produced Lenio.

Now Lenio was getting married.

The old archon smiled. He had forgotten what Panayotaros had said, forgotten that his son had left the house; the dead years revived in his mind and reawakened bygone pleasures, escapades, banquets that had been a succession of hares, partridges, mullets, chickens, sucking pigs, lambs on the spit, pilaffs, pâtés, skewersful of meat, oysters, tarts, brioches, wafers, sherbets, old wines, caviar—all of which he had put away ravenously.

"God be praised," he murmured, "I've certainly had a good time."

His brain grew fuddled and he closed his eyes and slept.

Meanwhile priest Grigoris on his gray mule and Mariori on Yannakos's ass were making for the mountain to which Michelis had withdrawn. The girl had begged her father to grant her this favor.

"I must see him, Father, I must see him; I don't know if I shall come back from where I'm going."

"Don't say things like that, my child," exclaimed her father in a voice broken by sobs. "God is great, you will get well; at Christmas we'll be celebrating your wedding. That day I'll dance to give you pleasure."

"Let's go by the mountain, so I may see him once more," the girl begged.

"As you wish, my child. Have I ever refused you anything?"

With these words, he steered the mule toward the mountain. Michelis was sitting on the bench, alone. Nikolio, dressed for his wedding, with his curled and perfectly clean hair carefully bound up in the red silk handkerchief, and his staff held behind his neck, between his shoulders, appeared against the mountain and set out on his way.

"Good evening, master," he shouted to Michelis, who was admiring him in silence, "good evening; going to get married; give my greetings to the owls!" and his laughter rang about the mountain.

He passed close to the flock and put his two forefingers to his mouth to give the sheep a parting whistle. But seeing Dassos, the bellwether with the spiral horns, get up to watch him, he could not resist the temptation to seize him by the horns and have a bout with him.

"There, old pair of horns," he shouted at him, once his desire was satisfied, "go and look for your ewes. I'm going to look for Lenio! See you Monday morning. Give me your blessing, friend Dassos!"

Then he scrambled down the slope, and his heels made a gallant clatter.

Hearing sounds of voices approaching, Michelis stood up. Between the rocks he saw priest Grigoris advancing and, behind him, Mariori, the girl he loved. His heart began throbbing anxiously.

Where are they going? Why are they coming here? Something bad must have happened! he muttered, rushing to meet them.

"My dear Michelis," said the priest, "we are happy to find you in your solitude. We are off to the town, and Mariori didn't want us to leave without saying good-bye to you. She's not very well, we're going to see what's the matter with her."

"Good-bye, Michelis," said the young girl softly, blushing as she looked at the man she loved.

Michelis helped them to dismount, and they all three sat down on the bench. The sun was still high, but in the distance a mist was already spreading in the plain, bathed till then in light. Two crows passed overhead noisily. Seeing them, the priest frowned, but said nothing. The two young people had not noticed. Michelis had taken the slender fingers of his betrothed, on which the gold ring glittered.

"I'm going to visit your palace," said the priest, and went into the hut to leave the engaged pair alone.

"My little Mariori," Michelis asked, "aren't you well? God is great, my darling, put trust in Him. You'll get well, it's nothing, be brave, the months pass quickly, Christmas is coming."

"Yes," said Mariori softly, "Christmas is coming."

Then, after a little:

"Have you quarrelled with your father?"

"Forget my father, the subject's too painful, don't let's talk about it, Mariori. I love you, I don't want to lose you. You alone bind me to earth, no one else. Only you; understand?"

"If I weren't there any more what would you do?"

Michelis closed her mouth with his hand.

"Be quiet," he said.

Mariori had time to place a kiss in Michelis's palm.

"My love," she murmured, while tears flowed from her fine despairing eyes.

Priest Grigoris reappeared on the threshold.

"Mariori," he said, "we mustn't linger. Come, may God be with us!"

And to Michelis:

"I'd have liked to have a talk with you, Michelis; but that will be for our return. When are you going back to your father's?"

"When God wills, Father," answered Michelis, bending to kiss his hand.

"God sometimes waits for the heart of man to give Him a sign, Michelis," said the priest, looking at him severely.

He would have liked to say more, but refrained.

"Good-bye!" cried Michelis, "God go with you!"

He held Mariori's tiny hand in his for an instant.

"Mariori," he whispered, "only you! Don't forget."

He turned his face away that she might not see tears there, climbed onto an abrupt crag and watched them going down. Yes, he muttered, my heart is still attached to earth.

He wandered about the mountain, then went down toward the plain. The vintage had begun, and the singing of the women harvesters drunk with the fumes of the grapes could be heard clearly. They were choosing the ripe bunches and throwing them into the baskets. Their hands were dripping with the blood of the vine. As they watched the young men who carried away the baskets, some of them sighed, others grew lively, all found relief in humming tunes.

Michelis stopped; his heart was heavy with an insurmountable sadness; no, those were not vintage songs, but funeral lamentations.

Standing there, without stirring, he felt life turning on and on, inexorably, never stopping. The wheel of the earth was turning. It had now reached the vintage. The turn of the olives would come; then that of the birth of Christ. The almond trees would blossom afresh, the corn would be sown again, the harvest would come around. It all went on as if Michelis were tied to that

wheel and rose and fell with it under the sun, under the rain. Tied
to it with him, day and night also rose and fell. Christ new born with
them, grew, became a man, went forth resolutely to spread the
word of God, was crucified, rose again, came down again from
Heaven the next year, was again crucified.

Michelis, with his temples humming, felt his head seized by
giddiness. He clung to a rock as though to stop the wheel, prevent
it from turning. He slid to the ground and suddenly, for no ap-
parent reason, burst into tears.

Next day, Sunday, old Patriarcheas did not get up. He had not
closed an eye all night. When sleep did come to him for a moment,
nightmares assailed him, the blood rose to his head and he found
himself stifling. He had sent word to his son to come to Lenio's
wedding, but his son had answered: "For a death I would have
come; for a wedding, no." The old man had received this answer
like a stab to the heart.

What have I done to him? But what have I done to him? the
poor man murmured, with his eyes full of tears; he's the only
person in the world I love, why does he refuse to come? What
can I have done to him?

He went over his whole life, remembered his father who, in his
old age, in a fit of anger, had decided not to open his mouth again.
He would not unclench his teeth, but went about whip in hand,
striking the men- and maidservants, or else picking up stones and
throwing them at the young girls on the way to the fountain and
smashing their pitchers. He ate like an ogre, drank like a fish; no
sickness could get a hold on him. He grew new teeth, to the stupefaction of everybody. One fine day he fell over a precipice and
was killed. Even now, at the memory of this, old Patriarcheas was
filled with terror. When they had come to him with the news:
"Your father's killed himself!" he had been seized with nervous
laughter; the whole village had been horrified at this filial heart-
lessness. But he had felt relief at having laughed. It had seemed to
him as if he had been crushed till then under a rock and it had
suddenly rolled away. Now the son could breathe freely, and how
good it was! He could not repress his joy.

Remembering that laugh, the old archon shuddered.

Mightn't Michelis, too, be feeling crushed by a rock which prevented his breathing? Could it be true that everything has to be paid for in this world—and would Michelis start laughing in his turn?

He rolled terrified eyes.

And yet I loved my father, I did. Michelis also loves me, no doubt. Well then? I don't understand! Is it then written that all sons shall in the end come to the point of feeling disgust at the man who's brought them into the world, and hating him? Why? Why? I don't understand.

Old Patriarcheas reflected on all this and sighed, turning over again and again on his bed so that the floor trembled under his weight. Toward evening the doors of the house were opened to let in the guests. Priest Grigoris arrived and the marriage ceremony was about to begin. Then only did the archon rise, wash, dress and adorn himself, puffing like an ox and taking a deal of trouble: he dyed his mustache and eyebrows, sprinkled his hair with orange-blossom water and came down to appear at his daughter's wedding.

The engaged pair were resplendent, well washed, richly dressed. Both of them sweating freely, they gave out that smell which horses have when they emerge from the sea. You could feel that if these two bodies were alone left on earth, it would soon be peopled afresh with a new humanity.

The old archon took his place beside them. He was to give her away and to carry out the exchange of coronets. Priest Grigoris had already begun intoning the psalm, the beadle was swinging the silver censer in time, the guests stood ranged all around the room, proud to be there. Two little girls were in attendance, bearing dishes piled with sweetmeats.

Priest Grigoris was hurrying so much that he stumbled. He was not himself, his thoughts kept flying off toward his daughter, whom the doctors had examined that morning, shaking their heads. He hustled the singing, swallowed half the words in his haste to be done. The bride and bridegroom were also impatient to be alone, not understanding what use all this could very well be to them. As for old Patriarcheas, he was longing for it to be over, for his legs were giving way. But pride made him clench his teeth and stiffened him.

"My friends," he said when the ceremony was over, "this evening

Lenio and Nikolio are celebrating their wedding; welcome to my house! Eat and drink your fill, we've slaughtered plenty of sheep and, God be praised, there's no lack of wine. As the vintage has begun, the barrels will soon be full to the brim again, so unbutton your middles and drink."

He turned toward the young couple.

"Long life, my children," he wished them; "grow old together, have children, people the earth; let the race of men multiply, don't allow the hearth to go out. Mustn't lower the flag in face of Charon. We sow, he reaps, we shall see who wins. D'you hear, eh, you blessed Nikolio? Fire the powder! Sow all you can!

"I, my friends, you'll excuse me, I'm going up to bed. I'm not feeling very well. But you—get down to it! Eat and drink, today's a holiday, amuse yourselves till daybreak!

"You, young maidens, and you young lads who haven't yet got a hair on your chin, my wish for you is—may it soon be your turn and, to celebrate your weddings, and may I become once more a young Saint George to bring you wine by the demijohn!"

There was general laughter. The archon raised his right hand to salute them, a young girl ran to open the door for him; on the threshold he stopped and, turning to priest Grigoris, who was silently folding his stole:

"Father," he said, "when you've had a bite, come up and let's have a chat."

The priest rose at once.

"I'll come with you, archon," he said. "God be with you, friends!" And to the bride and bridegroom: "Keep your coronets clean and fruitful!"

The old notables gone, the company took a deep breath and made for the festal table.

The two village bigwigs locked themselves into the room. Down below the festivities were in full swing, meat and wine were being turned to song and dance, bursts of laughter and gasps of desire. Upstairs two old men heard nothing, being tormented by grave cares.

Stretched on his bed, old Patriarcheas discoursed abundantly. He had got going. He was speaking of the bolsheviks, whom his imagination presented as half men, half beasts, flooding down from the north in clogs with iron studs. At their passage the stones spat

sparks and the villages caught fire. At the head ran Manolios, who
had also become half monster. Flames were coming from his mouth,
and with outstretched arm he was pointing at Lycovrissi.

"Fotis, that excommunicated priest, is also with them," said priest
Grigoris; "he's the head!"

"Priest Fotis, too, Father, with all his band of ragamuffins on
the Sarakina. The whole Sarakina is on the march to swoop down
on our village. You were indeed right when you said: 'The feet
have revolted against the head.' That's why I wanted to see you,
Father. We will examine, the two of us here, what it's best to do
to put things straight again."

Priest Grigoris listened. From time to time his anger was re-
born, but immediately his thoughts returned to Mariori, his eyes
became veiled, his ears were humming, he heard no more.

They talked till midnight. In the end weariness overcame them;
they had had enough of each other and looked at each other with
hatred. "Couldn't he grow a boil on his tongue and be quiet?"
thought priest Grigoris. "Won't he soon take himself off?" said
Patriarcheas to himself; "he bores me to death, the fat pig!"

Priest Grigoris again thought of Mariori, left behind alone at
the clinic in a small room giving on a narrow courtyard. The heat
there must be stifling. "She must stay here for a time," the doctors had declared, "under observation; we will let you know." "Is
there danger?" the poor father had asked, trembling; "is there
danger?" "There is danger and there is hope, Father. We must
wait. At present two beasts are fighting one another in your daughter's blood; we shall see which wins." "Tell me the whole truth,"
the priest implored. "We have told you, Father. Come back in a
month." "I will pray to God," said the priest. "Do all you can on
your side; we on ours will do all we can. Come, good-bye; may
God aid us!" They were in a hurry to get rid of him, having other
patients to visit.

The priest stood up briskly and held out his hand to Patriarcheas.

"Good night, archon," he said with a sigh. "Tomorrow we'll
speak of all this again."

"Won't you stay a little longer, Father? Why are you in such
a hurry? Excuse me, I forgot to ask you for news of Mariori.
What did the doctors say?"

"She's nothing the matter with her, apparently. She's a girl, she's languishing. According to them, she ought to get married soon."

And to change the subject:

"And Michelis—how's he? I'm worried about him, archon."

"No need for you to worry," replied the old man angrily. "He's young, he has bees in his bonnet, it'll pass. Must get rid of Manolios, then everything'll come right. Good night, Father!"

With these words, he turned sharply and faced the wall.

He listened to the priest going heavily down the stairs.

The goat-beard, he growled; he's worried, says he! I'm worried about your Mariori, old man! If my son's to marry a consumptive and contaminate my race, it'd be better if your daughter died, then we'd have peace. I'm sorry for her, poor thing, sorry, God's my witness, but it'd be better if she died!

At the time when the notables of Lycovrissi were deciding to get rid of Manolios, he was with priest Fotis, trying to think of a way for the Sarakina refugees to get through the winter without dying of cold and hunger.

"Only work can save us," said priest Fotis; "work and love."

They gathered the men and women capable of working, divided them into separate teams—brotherhoods—and appointed to each brotherhood a responsible leader, an elder brother or mother. Then they sent them out to look for work in the neighboring villages. They dispersed in different directions, leaving on the Sarakina only the old men and women to look after the children.

"With the grace of God, my children," priest Fotis wished them, as he accompanied them a little on their way; "work, set aside all you can, fruit, oil, wine, clothes, have our new home always in your minds. When the bees have their hives and spread over the mountains and in the plains to gather honey, do they not come back laden to their little wax cells and to the nurslings they left behind? Do as they do, my children. Go, the grace of God be with you!"

Manolios often went with them. On the way he encouraged them, pointed out the villages around about, told them what they would need most and at what doors they should knock. He got them work, then returned to the Sarakina. Priest Fotis and he gathered the children together, and, using the slates given by Hadji Nikolis the schoolmaster, taught them the alphabet.

When night came, the two of them lingered talking on the stone bench by the church.

"Even in the smallest pebble," said priest Fotis one evening, "even in the humblest animal, in the thickest soul, God is present fully, Manolios. Let us do what we can to make our little village, our hive, shine all through with the divine presence and be industrious, prosperous and united. For mark this: a good action, even if it is done in the remotest desert, has its repercussions throughout the world."

Manolios raised his eyes and looked at priest Fotis. He seemed to see his emaciated, intrepid countenance glow in the dark. His hands, stretched toward the sky, waved like flames.

"Yes, every man," Manolios responded ardently, "can himself save the whole world. I've often had that thought, Father, and it makes me tremble. Have we then such a great responsibility? What must we do, then, before we die? What way must we follow?"

He was silent. Night was deep, the old women had lit fires and prepared the meal; famished, the children waited, squatting around them.

Manolios placed his hand on the knee of priest Fotis, who, absorbed in his meditations, said nothing.

"How ought we to love God, Father?" he asked in a whisper.

"By loving men, my son."

"And how ought we to love men?"

"By trying to guide them along the right path."

"And what is the right path?"

"The one that rises."

You Killed Him—You

Next day, about midday, the Agha arrived from Smyrna. Not alone; behind him advanced, on a chestnut colt, a new Turkish boy, the sly looks, the surly manner of a wild young male animal. He munched no mastic; he did not sing that the world is a dream, but he shouted, cursed, threw his weight about and gave orders. His poor lover, the Agha, drank him in with his eyes and put up with all his fancies. His name was Brahimaki. Fifteen years old, with full lips shadowed with thick elfish down.

The Agha had unearthed him in a narrow, ill-famed Smyrna street where every house has the red lantern for its sign. He was selling grilled sunflower seeds, rubber sheaths, roasted crabs and jasmin flowers, all mixed up pellmell in one basket. Every evening, from twilight onward, the alley was the scene of a procession of men, young and old, Jews, Moslems and Christians, come from all the corners of the town in search of a moment of pleasure in which to forget the troubles of the day. Before their doors, half-naked women waited, with a bestial smile on appallingly made-up lips.

As soon as the Agha had caught sight of Brahimaki he had been attracted. He had approached and bargained for a while. They had agreed in the end. He bought him a small chestnut horse, a new suit of fine cloth, a silver watch and chain, a jar of musk and a bag of cloves and cinnamon flowers. He then took him to the *hamam*, where he bathed and the water became covered with a layer of oil. From there he took him to the barber, who cut his hair and scented him with lavender water; finally to a *hodza,* an old friend of his, a sack and cord man, to have him taught a few tricks.

In this way the Agha took delivery of a clean, scented and

skilled Brahimaki. Martha received the new favorite with grumbles; but after looking him over thoroughly she gave a mocking, satisfied laugh. With that bastard, she thought, you're for it, Agha!

"What news, old Martha?" asked the Agha as he dismounted in the courtyard. "Any deaths? any marriages? Have the harvest and the vintage been good? Are father Patriarcheas and priest Grigoris, the old goat-beard, still in this world? Haven't the *romnoi* come to blows? haven't they torn out each other's eyes? I seem to have been away for years."

And turning toward Brahimaki:

"This is mother Martha, our faithful slave," he said. "A good woman, excellent housewife, doesn't talk, honest. A bit hunchbacked, I agree, but you get used to it. Do as you like with her, beat her, kill her, sleep with her, she's yours."

Brahimaki made a face, laid his hand on the old woman's hump and laughed.

"What should I do with her?" he said. "She's a camel, you can keep her!" and he strode in to take possession of the house.

"Take no notice, Martha," said the Agha, "he's a colt not yet broken in; he rushes about, he bites, but you keep quiet. I shall keep quiet, too. Patience, Martha, patience; he'll learn."

Brahimaki came back into the yard:

"Any birds in this hole of yours?" he asked the Agha. "You'll have them dance one day, so I can see them and make my choice."

The Agha jumped:

"You listen to me; none of that. See? They're all Greeks here. I don't want any trouble; you stay sitting on your eggs."

"They'll do the sitting," said the shameless colt, with a loud laugh. "Here, old hunchback, lay the table and let's eat, I'm hungry."

The Agha sighed. He remembered his Youssoufaki. He had had a mouth, but no words. You told him: "Sing," and he sang. "Light me my chibouk," and he lit it. "Let's go to bed," and he came. This one's the Devil in person; but what's to be done? The animal's got such charm!

"All right, Brahimaki," he said. "Everything in its time, be patient! Run along, my poor Martha, and wring a chicken's neck."

An hour later the Agha and his colt, having eaten and drunk copiously, locked themselves into his room. What happened there nobody knows, but toward evening, when the Agha emerged exhausted, with swollen eyes, he called Martha:

"Go and tell Patriarcheas to come, I want a word with him. Brahimaki insists on seeing the women dance; can we refuse him anything? Come, take your shawl, run along!"

Martha found the home of Patriarcheas all upside down. Dogs wandered into the courtyard as if it belonged to them, two or three servants were picking up the scraps from the feast, washing up, wiping the tables, sweeping the house. Lenio and the new husband had already gone off to take possession of Manolios's sheepfold. Today mother Mandalenia had command over the house; she was keeping an eye on the servants and giving orders. She held a sack, into which she stuffed all she could, sometimes surreptitiously, sometimes openly, and from time to time she went upstairs to see how the master was.

In fact the old archon was not at all well. He had waked up half paralyzed, unable to move his right leg or arm, and with his mouth twisted to one side.

"It's nothing," mother Mandalenia kept telling him; "it's nothing, don't you get worked up, archon; I'll give you a rubbing and it'll pass. It's a chill."

But the old archon gazed dully at the window opposite the bed, and the saliva dribbled from his mouth.

As soon as mother Mandalenia saw old Martha come in, she ran to stop her; she could not bear the sight of the old hunchback.

"What do you want, Martha? Is there some fresh misfortune fallen on the village? Has the Agha come back? Speak out, I'm going to burst!"

"Hi, wait a bit, you're strangling me, you dirty witch! I want to see the archon, I must."

"You can't see him, no, you can't see him, I tell you. He's very ill, paralyzed. He's sent for his son. A stroke, that's what he's had. He can hardly talk, he stammers, he slobbers. You can't see him!"

"Let me see him with my own eyes, get out of my way! It's the Agha has sent me!"

"I won't let you!"

"Yes, you will. Paws off!"

They came to blows. The servants ran up and separated them. The hunchback managed to reach the staircase and started up it, huddled in a ball and darting at full speed like a spider. She opened the door and slipped into the room. The old archon opened his eyes, saw her, but did not stir.

"Archon," said the little old woman, "it's me, Martha. The Agha sends you his greetings. He asks you to have the goodness to come and see him, he would like a word with you."

This time the old man slowly turned his head; his lips moved but nothing came out. Martha was drawing near when mother Mandalenia entered, beside herself, pushed her away and bent over the old man:

"What did you say, my archon?"

The old man moved his lips again, stammered something; turning toward the hunchback, mother Mandalenia said:

"Go to the devil, that's what he says."

"What am I to tell the Agha, archon?" the little old woman insisted.

The old man's lips moved yet again, and mother Mandalenia went to him a second time:

"He says that he can go to the devil too."

The little old woman shook her head, then coming up to the bed she leaned over:

"Archon," she whispered, "the Agha's planning mischief, do you hear? He's brought back from Smyrna a new demon who's going to cause trouble among us. The blackguard wants all the young girls of the village to come and dance in the square, under the plane tree, so he can take his pick. You've chosen a bad moment to fall ill, archon."

The old man opened his eyes wide, the blood rose to his face. Gathering all his strength, he cried:

"Never!" then fell back on the pillow.

"You'll kill him, hunchback, curse you; you go to blazes!" yelped mother Mandalenia. She seized Martha by the hump and threw her out.

Coming back to the bed, she began rubbing the old man with oil and camphor. This relieved him somewhat, and he opened his eyes.

"Send someone to tell priest Grigoris to come!" he stuttered with great difficulty. Then he shut his eyes again.

That instant the door opened and Michelis entered.

"Go away!" he said to the old woman as he approached the bed. She gathered up her remedies and disappeared.

Michelis stood still, gazing at his father, with tears in his eyes. The old man's face was swollen and waxen. His triple chin had emptied, it lay flabbily on his throat and covered it. The right side of his mouth was sagging.

The old man opened his eyes and smiled at the sight of his son.

"Welcome!" he murmured, holding out to him his left hand.

Michelis, leaning over, kissed it. The old man fixed his eyes on his son with a deep, despairing gaze, as though saying good-bye.

"Good-bye, I'm going," he murmured, putting out his hand again.

He gathered up his strength and spoke as best he could:

"My son, I'm off. I'm leaving the table; I'm folding up my napkin; it's over. If ever I said a bitter word to you forgive me. I'm a father and I love you. Often love doesn't know what it's saying. I've one thing to ask you."

"Say it, Father."

"Mariori . . ."

He fell silent. The sweat was beading on his forehead. His son leaned toward him, wiped his face with his handkerchief.

"Mariori—listen—has a bad disease; don't take her as your wife. Our blood would be contaminated, do you hear?"

"I hear, Father."

"You'll do as I say?"

Michelis was silent.

"It's the only favor I ask of you. You'll do it? Say yes so that I can die in peace."

A few seconds went by. The old man was looking at his son fearfully.

"Yes," Michelis muttered at last.

The old man shut his eyes.

"That's all," he breathed, "all!"

Michelis went to the window and looked out. Evening was falling; the peasants were coming in from their vineyards, tired out. Two young girls passed by, chattering, their pitchers on their shoulders. Old Ladas crossed the road, bent, barefoot, his hands smeared with grapejuice . . . He was at his vintage.

The old man stirred slightly and sighed. Michelis turned. His father signed to him.

"Don't go," he said, "wait."

"I'm not going. Go to sleep, Father."

Far away, close by Saint Basil's Well, a girl's voice rose. She was singing, giving vent to a monotonous love lament. It was haunting. As though no man and woman had ever before been united, ever before known the relief of the embrace. The girl continued, inconsolable. Michelis thought of his betrothed; he, too, wanted to give vent to a cry which would unite with the girl's lament.

Suddenly he caught sight, down below, at the entrance to the courtyard, of the forked white beard of priest Grigoris. Walking on tiptoe he opened the door slowly so as not to wake his father, and waited on the top step.

"What did the doctors say, Father?" Michelis asked anxiously, when at last, with slow and solemn gait, the priest had reached the top of the stairs.

"She's got nothing the matter with her, my son; in a month she'll be as fit as a fiddle."

He peered through the open door.

"Seems the archon isn't well; he sent for me."

"It looks bad, Father. Go in. Softly, so as not to wake him."

The old archon was not asleep. Hearing whispering, he opened his eyes.

"Welcome, Father," he murmured.

"What's happened to you, archon? It's nothing, courage!"

"It's nothing, Father, I'm going to die. Sit down, I've something to say to you. Approach, Michelis."

Spluttering, stuttering, deforming the words, he began to tell them how the Agha had sent for him; apparently the new Youssoufaki wanted all the young girls of the village to go and dance before him so that he might make his choice.

"Never!" cried priest Grigoris, rising abruptly. "Better they should all die!"

"Better we should all die!" Michelis corrected. He, too, was indignant.

"Do your duty," said the dying man. "I shan't be with you any more; Michelis will take my place."

He closed his eyes, exhausted; then, taking priest Grigoris's hand:

"Come tonight and give me Communion," he said.

Priest Grigoris started for the door and Michelis followed.

"Don't leave him, Michelis; your father's not well at all, may God protect him."

He reflected a moment, then:

"The Agha—I'll go and see him at once; I'll speak to him. God spare us such shame!"

Michelis went back and sat by his father's bedside. All night he watched, with his eyes fixed on the poor face with its twisted lips, sagging cheeks, sweat-soaked hair.

This was my father, he muttered, this was my father. This was the great archon Patriarcheas, slim and gallant as Saint George in his youth; even on foot he seemed to be on horseback. He has eaten the finest viands and drunk the best wines, embraced ladies and maidservants, two nuns and an abbess, filled the houses of others with sons and daughters.

The hours went by, the village was asleep. The priest returned, confessed the old archon, gave him the absolution, administered Communion, and once again Michelis was left alone with the heavy and motionless body that had been his father. At break of day, a dog in the neighborhood began to howl; Michelis rose and went over to the window. Already the sky was becoming tinged with rose; trees, birds and men were asleep still. Everything was profoundly calm; only the dog howled, alarmed.

Old Patriarcheas heard it, opened his eyes. The Archangel with the black wings was above his bed. He uttered a cry and gave up the ghost.

The door opened. Priest Grigoris appeared on the threshold. He approached the bed and laid his hand on the old archon's heart; it was no longer beating. Fiercely he turned toward Michelis.

"You killed him," he cried in a strangled voice, "you!"

Michelis started up in terror; he looked the priest in the eyes; he tried to open his mouth; he could not.

One of the pillars which upheld Lycovrissi had just collapsed. The whole village was shaken as the news ran from door to door: "The old archon's dead!" The Agha himself, who had only just

waked up and was sitting on his balcony with his eyes half closed,
going over in his mind all that he had seen and done in dreams
during the night, turned in stupefaction toward old Martha who
brought him the news:

"He's dead, quite dead? Has the tower collapsed? That makes
the village a cripple! Indeed I must have been sleeping deeply,
not to have heard the crash!"

"All the dogs of the village kept barking last night, Agha," the
little old woman assured him. "I knew what it was, at once. I says
to myself, the Archangel must have come into this village to take
away a prime soul. The dogs saw him and they were frightened."

"He was a fine man," said the Agha, sniffing his coffee, "a fine
man, the kind that go to Paradise: he liked good living, knew how
to revel and wench. Pity he wasn't a Moslem, he'd have gone
straight to our Paradise where pilaff, boys and women abound.
That's where you should have had your place, my poor Patriarcheas; now it's too late!"

Brahimaki arrived, with hair tousled, eyes heavy, shirt open;
a beauty spot was visible at the springing of his throat; the Agha
stretched out his hand greedily, fondled the black curls, the warm
neck, and lingered over the beauty spot; he felt he was entering
Paradise.

"When are the women going to dance?" asked the savage boy,
seizing the Agha's hand and flinging it from him angrily.

"Don't be in too much of a hurry, please. I'll do what you ask,
but I don't want to rouse the whole village. Yesterday evening
their priest came to see me: 'Don't inflict this indignity on us,
Agha,' he said to me; 'you'll let loose a storm. A little patience,
we'll find a way.' So be patient, my Brahimaki, there's sure to
be a festival when they'll dance of their own accord, without being forced; then you'll see."

But as he spoke he warmed up:

"And besides, after all," he shouted, "I didn't bring you here
for you to get married!"

Meanwhile the gate of Patriarcheas' house had been thrown
open wide. The dead man had been placed in the middle of the
courtyard, and the whole village was filing past to bid him good-
bye. They had forgotten his defects to remember only his kind-
nesses, and were busy praising the virtues of the deceased untiringly.

Panayotaros even, when he came to give him the farewell kiss, could not hold back a tear: "Forgive me, and may God forgive you," he muttered, laying his coarse lips on the frozen brow of the dead man.

Father Ladas also came, kissed him in his turn, then ran his eyes over the archon's residence. Through his mind there filed, in a rich funeral procession, the vineyards, fields, olive orchards and gardens of the deceased, and he sighed: "Pity, all this wealth! Michelis will make short work of ruining it, I must keep my eyes open. It's the priest I'm afraid of!"

Mother Mandalenia wanted to let herself go in a lament; she had already thrown back her kerchief and loosened her hair; but Michelis pushed her aside with his hand: "No cries!" he said to her, "be quiet!"

Before the open grave, the schoolmaster made a speech. He went right back to ancient Greece, to Miltiades, to Themistocles, to the Persian Wars, before coming on to Alexander the Great and to the time of Christ. He passed in review the Byzantine Empire and arrived, distraught and soaked with sweat, at the taking of Constantinople by the Turks. There he could not control his lamentations. And all the company, distraught, heard him cry, beside himself: "Courage, brothers, Constantinople will be ours once more; once more we shall celebrate Mass in Saint Sophia!" He drew breath, wiped his face, and passing hastily over the years of slavery, arrived at 1821, whence, in a single audacious bound, he leaped and alighted before today's open tomb. In it he saw the archon Patriarcheas.

He stopped for a moment to recover breath and to wipe his misted glasses; then, gathering up his strength, he began the panegyric of the dead man:

"George Patriarcheas, whose memory we shall ever keep, was an authentic descendant of the ancient Greeks, an authentic grandson of the great Byzantine Empire, an authentic son of the heroes of 1821. This great archon has indomitably pursued the mission of the Hellenic race: Man's struggle for liberty!

"In the hour of danger, he was the first to proffer his breast, ever ready to make the sacrifice of his life. Just like Alexander the Great, George Patriarcheas kept alight, in this village in the heart of Asia, the torch of the spirit, never allowing the barbarians to snuff out the light of Greece.

"The death of George Patriarcheas would be an irreparable

national misfortune, were it not that he leaves behind him a son
worthy of him, Michelis. He will continue, in his turn, the heroic
tradition of his glorious father."

At the moment, all believed the schoolmaster's words. They saw,
for the first time, what a remarkable hero they had lost, and began to weep. Yannakos and Kostandis led away Michelis who,
motionless in front of the grave, was watching the coffin as it was
lowered into the earth. He had only one thing in his head—the
priest's sentence: "You killed him, you . . ." They led him away
and started in silence on the way back.

When they had reached the big house, now empty, and had
closed the door behind them, Michelis went to the middle of the
yard and let himself fall to the ground, where, that morning, the
corpse of his father had been laid out. He put his head down,
kissed the ground, and suddenly leaped to his feet; he felt, deep
down in him, in the most obscure recesses of his being, an inhuman joy, unacknowledgeable. Of course, he had a human heart
which loved and regretted his dead father; of course, his eyes were
big with tears; but deep down in him he was experiencing an inhuman joy.

He called Mandalenia.

"Make us some coffee, bring us some wine; wring the white
cock's neck and get us a meal ready, quick!"

The friends looked at him in astonishment; his eyes were full
of tears, but his voice was clear and joyful. He began running
about the house in all directions, as though he were seeing it for
the first time, pushed into the storerooms, took the lids off the
jars, tapped the barrels to see if they were full, opened the chests.
Then he came and sat down at the table, which was now ready,
placed Yannakos on his right, Kostandis on his left, poured wine
into the glasses and raised his:

"All that stuff the schoolmaster spouted about my father at the
cemetery was nonsense," he said. "My father wasn't a hero, he
never proffered his breast to danger, he never took a manly decision. He was just a fine fellow who loved life and dreaded death:
that's all. God keep his soul!

"But all that that good schoolmaster said about our Greek race
was true. Every Greek in this world, down to the humblest and
most ignorant, is, without knowing it, a great archon. He has a
heavy responsibility. Every Greek who doesn't take, if only once

in his life, a heroic decision, betrays his race. While that poor
pedant was talking, I saw with terror how I was running the risk
of taking the same road as my father, the most even, the most
convenient one; but all of a sudden I was ashamed; before the
grave of my father I swore to myself to take the noble precipitous
road my race followed, thousands of years ago."

"What road?" asked Yannakos, who was listening with emotion
to his friend's words, "what road, Michelis?"

"The one that rises. That's why I'm going to ask you a favor,
my comrades, my friends. When night comes we'll go up to the
Sarakina to look for Manolios and priest Fotis. During the night
I spent watching my father dying, and again just now at the cemetery, I made a resolution. This evening, when we're all five of us
together, I'll tell you. Brothers, I want your help."

"With you even to death, Michelis," declared the two friends;
they drank his health and began to make short work of the chicken.

At fall of day, priest Fotis and Manolios were sitting in front
of their grotto in peaceful conversation. They had only just come
in from neighboring villages, where they had gone to help their
companions to find work. They had done the journey on foot;
the heat and dust had exhausted them. On the way back they
had met old Christofis and learned from him that old Patriarcheas
was dead and already buried.

"Pity that machine for turning out dung and bastards has
stopped working!" said the foul-mouthed mule driver. "He's left
a lot of widows in villages round about. Long life to us!"

"When? How did he die?"

"Well, he'd eaten, so they say, two sucking pigs the evening before, at his daughter's wedding. Seems he wanted to put away a
stuffed turkey as well, but lo and behold, his right arm was paralyzed and he was put to bed. In the morning he was found stone
dead. The schoolmaster made a speech and told a lot of true
things about him, but the devil if I could understand a damned
word. Still I cried, so as to do like the others. Afterward I took a
handful of earth and chucked it on top of his belly; that was the
last mouthful of sucking pig he bolted. God Almighty rest his
paunch!"

With that, he set off again. When he had gone a little way, a
thought struck him and with a burst of laughter he shouted:

"I've heard say, priest Fotis, that the gate of Paradise is as narrow as can be. Fat people can't get through, so it seems. But the three of us will get through, no question. Long live poverty!"

"He has a crude way of putting things, father Christofis has," said priest Fotis, "crude, but true. Yes, it is hard for a rich man to be saved. It isn't enough for a man to be a fine chap, when he knows there are people who are hungry and doesn't share out his wealth with them. He pretends not to see anything, his bad habits deprive him of all courage. Now it remains to be seen what Michelis will do; this is where I shall wait and see!"

"I've confidence in him," said Manolios.

"May God hear you; but I've seen so many in my life . . ."

He had not finished his sentence when the three friends came up to the grotto. The priest and Manolios rose.

"God keep his soul, and long life to you, Michelis," they said.

All five sat down and remained a long while silent. At last Michelis began:

"Father," he said, "my brothers, I wept for my old father, I was part of his flesh, I was very sad at his death. All the same I felt—God forgive me!—that I'd been set free, it was as if I was relieved of a great weight. From today, I realize, I am alone responsible for each of my actions. Two roads lie open before me: the one along which my father was drawing me and that other, much more difficult one, along which Christ draws me. Which am I to choose? This morning, at the cemetery, I decided. This evening I've come to tell you what my resolution is and to ask you, Father, and you, my comrades, to help me carry it out."

He fell silent, and laid his hand on priest Fotis's knee as though to say: Help me!

Priest Fotis took Michelis's hand and clasped it between his bony palms:

"My child," he said, "we are with you in this difficult hour. Speak, you can trust us!"

"My father inherited from his father, and he from his ancestors, a great deal of land and a great many trees. They all enjoyed this wealth to the full; from time to time they threw a crumb to the poor, and they died content at having done their duty. Or so they believed. I, too, believed it. Up to the moment when, thanks to Manolios and thanks to you, priest Fotis, God unsealed my eyes. I saw. He opened my heart. This is the decision I have taken: all that I possess I will distribute to the poor. I shall not even keep the crumb my fathers used to throw to the starving. I shall give it all to your community, to the Sarakina. Accept it, Father!"

They were all listening, heads bent. When Michelis had finished, none raised his head. Nothing was heard in the night except the stifled sobs of priest Fotis.

Unable to control himself any longer, Yannakos rushed to Michelis; he took him in his arms and pressed him to his heart. He tried to speak, but the words would not come; so he began to laugh and dance.

Priest Fotis rose and laid both hands on the bent head of Michelis:

"My son," he said, "my life has been forced to drink at bitter waters; you have now made me forget them. Thanks be given to you, Michelis, in this world and in the other! You have just saved from shame and death some thousands of souls, these refugees and their children and their children's children. Blessings on you!"

Manolios, with his head hidden, was weeping. He had never felt a deeper joy. Not even when he had come out from the Agha's door and seen the plane tree where they were going to hang him. For he could see at last that the word of Christ was all powerful, stronger than all the good things of the earth. When a man has nothing, to sacrifice this nothing to God is easy; when a man has everything, the sacrifice is a very hard one. Michelis was sacrificing everything. Manolios was overcome and could not raise his head to speak. He stood up at last, embraced Michelis and wept.

Kostandis watched and listened with a tightening of the heart: I've given nothing, he thought, I've done nothing, I've left nothing for the love of Christ. Not my children, not my wife, nothing, nothing . . .

The night was fine, the moon was rising slowly in the sky and pouring its intoxicating honey upon the Sarakina.

In silence Michelis watched the moon softening the mountain. There was a tightening at his heart, too: I'm worth nothing, nothing, he thought; everything I do is done not from kindness but from fear. I'm afraid I may have killed my father, I'm loaded with a terrible sin. I'm giving everything away to get relief, to forget, to be able to sleep, to stop hearing those terrible words: "You killed him, you!"

Next day the news burst like a bomb in the village. Michelis was giving up his whole fortune to the ragamuffins of the Sarakina! Priest Grigoris bounded into the street in down-at-heel slippers, without his belt, without his cap, and with his hair in disorder. He ran to see Michelis in his father's house.

The door was open. He rushed up the stairs and found Michelis busy writing, close by the window. He was writing to Mariori; for a long time already he had been struggling over a sentence in which he would have liked to tell her how much he loved her, but also how necessary it was that he should leave her. Already he had begun again several times, but the words which came under his pen seemed to him too cruel. The same phrase could not express both the sweetness of love and the bitterness of separation. "Always" and "never" were two distinct words, and what Michelis was looking for was precisely the word that would contain these two terrible abysses of the heart.

At this moment priest Grigoris's storming cassock burst into the room.

"What fresh calamity is this I hear of, Michelis?" he cried breathlessly. "There's a rumor that you're giving away all you possess to the ragamuffins of the Sarakina. It's a crime! A crime, d'you hear? a shame!"

Michelis had the letter he was writing. He gazed at the maddened priest without replying.

"Have you no respect even for the memory of your father? Not content with having killed him, you must now go and hack him to pieces and share him out, bit by bit, to these beggars, these reprobates! Haven't you any fear of God?"

"But Father, it's because I fear God that I'm doing it. Christ says: 'What shall it profit thee to obey all the commandments? That is not sufficient. Sell thy goods and give to the poor if thou wouldst enter the Kingdom of Heaven.' Well, I have done what Christ commands, Father. So why should you seem so shocked?"

Priest Grigoris, beside himself, strode up and down in his down-at-heel slippers. He bit his fists with rage.

"Why don't you answer, Father? Have I done what Christ commands, yes or no? Yes or no? Answer!"

"You're shaking the foundations of society, that's all I know about it. I give you back my daughter's ring, and there's my answer; I won't have this marriage any more. Soon I'll be seeing you trailing about the village streets, begging with a sack on your back!"

"What can that matter since I shall reach the Kingdom of Heaven?" replied Michelis calmly. "What is this life worth, Father?"

"You're mad, you don't any longer know what you're saying!"

"No, merely a Christian, Father."

"I shall excommunicate you from the pulpit, you and Manolios! You're traitors, yes, traitors, both of you, indeed all three of you, you and that goat-beard of a priest Fotis! Yes, yes, no use rolling your eyes, I know your secret!"

"Our secret?" said Michelis, dumbfounded. "What secret?"

"Bolsheviks! You receive orders from Moscow to overthrow religion, country, the family and property, the four great pillars of the world! Manolios, curse him, is your leader. And priest Fotis has come from the other end of the world bringing, by way of a new Gospel, Moscow's orders!"

"That's as much as to say that Christ is a bolshevik!" Michelis protested.

"What Christ? The one you've fashioned in your image, you bandits? That's not Christ, it's the Antichrist!"

Unable to control himself any longer, Michelis leaped to his feet.

"It's you who've altered Him to your image, you, the priests, the bishops, the notables! You have made of Christ a hypocritical, twisted, lying, cowardly father Ladas, a usurer with coffers full of Turkish and English gold. Your Christ—you've made him the accomplice of all the princes of this world to save his skin and his purse!"

"Are you declaring war on us, my lord Michelis?" roared the priest, projecting a jet of saliva onto the wall.

"I'm not proclaiming war, I'm proclaiming justice. But be careful; if you attack us we shall defend ourselves. The true Christ is with us, He is our leader, and one day, you'll see, Sarakina the ragged will get the better of your rich Lycovrissi."

The priest jumped. He struck his forehead violently, as if he suddenly understood:

"So that's why you've given your fields and your houses to the people of the Sarakina, that they may introduce themselves into Lycovrissi and one day have us in their power! No, no! Never shall they penetrate into our village, never. They shan't get by. If they come, they shall be driven away. And meanwhile, your olive orchards, your gardens, your fields shall not be dug or watered. They'll all go to rack and ruin. I raise my hand and I swear: next Sunday I shall go into the pulpit and pronounce the anathema against the lot of you, renegades!"

With these words he went out, slamming the door. Michelis watched him as he crossed the courtyard, dragging his old slippers. His flying cassock blocked the door as he went through. Then all Michelis could hear was the barking of dogs, alarmed at the sight of him.

He sat down again by the window and began his letter to Mariori once more. This time the words flowed, as from a spring; he told her how her father had just left him and, furious at learning that he, Michelis, following the teachings of Christ, had shared out his goods among the poor, had given him back their engagement ring.

He went on to tell her how much he loved her, how much, day and night, she filled his thoughts and heart, and that life without her would be a rough, sad road. As he wrote, this love grew, and filled his heart with an unexpected warmth. It was as though each one of the words of love, which he summoned up to console Mariori, created the feeling, which had not existed before it was expressed. In the end, life without Mariori appeared to him as an unendurable martyrdom, and he burst into tears.

I didn't know I loved her as much as this, he whispered, I didn't know.

Meanwhile priest Grigoris was on his way to seek out his brother the schoolmaster, next father Ladas and then the other biggest wigs of the village. When he had explained matters to them, they all agreed with him in recognizing that the danger was great, that all the honest folk must unite to strike the Antichrist on the head and that they must act quickly, before the evil could spread and contaminate the whole village. Only the schoolmaster ventured a few timid objections, but his brother raised such a clamor that he hastily went back into his shell.

It was agreed that, when the people of the Sarakina came to take possession of the Patriarcheas properties, force should be used to drive them away, and that on Sunday, after Mass, priest Grigoris should pronounce the excommunication. To begin with, it would be enough to strike at Manolios, their leader. Later on, if the lousy crew did not return to their senses, it would be the turn of his accomplices, Michelis, Yannakos and the rest. The tares, thundered priest Grigoris, must be uprooted from the village and only the good grain kept! He went off in all haste to write to his daughter and let her know of the noble deeds of that fancy fiancé of hers, and tell her that the best she could do, God bless her, would be to expel him from her heart. He felt sure he could find her a husband with some ballast, and more God-fearing into the bargain, when with God's help she came back to the village, well again. Indeed they must give thanks to Heaven that Michelis had thrown off his mask before the wedding and shown himself for the villain he was.

Then he sent for Panayotaros:

"Keep your eyes open, Panayotaros. Go from time to time and have a look at what's happening on the Sarakina, manage somehow to find out what they're doing and what they're saying, and let us know. We have the same enemies, and as you're no weakling we may soon need you."

"I'm disgusted at the lot of you," Panayotaros replied, "but even more at that swine Manolios and his acolytes trying to pass themselves off as Christ and his Apostles. That's why I'm working for you: it doesn't stop me being disgusted at you."

The priest gave him his hand to kiss, but Panayotaros turned his back on him and made for the door:

"I've never kissed any mucky hands or skirts," he said as he went out.

Next morning, Sunday, all the village, men and women, were early at the church, some worried, others delighted. Even the sick and the small children had been brought, so that they might see and remember the fate which awaits those who deny Christ.

The church was humming like a hive when a hornet has got in. Old Ladas was standing posed in the notables' pew. For this solemn day he had pushed luxury so far as to don the shoes he had bought in the town when he was engaged to be married and now wore only once a year, at Easter. As they had become too narrow for him and hurt him, they gave him the hopping gait of a crow. He carried them in his hand when he left his house, and only put them on in front of the church. When Mass was over he would take them off, tuck them under his arm and carry them preciously home.

Panayotaros, who had not set foot in church for months, was also seen approaching. His pocked face was radiant, and he had slipped a cigarette behind his ear, to smoke it after the excommunication to show his pleasure.

Mother Mandalenia, in black and nervous, came, too, to be present at the downfall of her nephew the Antichrist, who was bringing shame upon her honorable house. She had foretold that that good-for-nothing would damn himself with too much study, and she was delighted today at seeing herself proved right and him marked out for Hell.

Michelis arrived, pale, sad, dressed in black from head to foot. Not one night had he managed to shut an eye, and every time that, at dawn, sleep at last took hold of him, he saw his father staring at him and shaking his head, as though to curse him. Yannakos and Kostandis had arrived at the same time as him, closely followed by Andonis the barber and fat Dimitri the butcher.

"I'm going to kill a sheep," he confided to the barber; "I'm going to kill a sheep and take it to the Sarakina to celebrate the excommunication. Come with me and have a bite."

"I thought of going there too, to trim Manolios's beard and sprinkle it with some of the good lavender water," declared the barber. "I've got razors and the bottle already in my pocket."

The schoolmaster took his place near the first choir stall to intone the responses. He was frowning, as he did on his bad days. This inhuman ceremony was not at all to his liking. In his opinion it was an injustice, an affair of personal animosity, mean interests; but he dared not take a stand against it. From childhood he had been afraid of priest Grigoris, his elder brother, who used to beat him unmercifully when they were children. He had never managed to get over this fear, even though he was now a bachelor of sixty.

Priest Grigoris appeared, ferocious, with his prophet's forked beard. He got through the Mass smartly; he was in a hurry and so were the villagers. Then he climbed into the pulpit, and the whole village, raising its head, stared at him in apprehension. The bell rang the knell; a soul was being lost.

From up there the priest let his eyes roam over his flock, assumed an air of wrath and swelled his voice:

"Brother Christians," he thundered, making the vault of the church ring, "brother Christians, the church is a sheepfold, whose sheep are the faithful and whose shepherd is Christ. The priest is the representative of Christ on earth. When a sheep has an infectious disease, the shepherd drives it out of the sheepfold that the others may not catch the disease. It is sent to die as far away as possible, among the precipices. It is painful to the priest to see a contaminated soul, but his duty is to be inexorable in order to save the healthy souls.

"There is, in our Christian sheepfold, a scabby sheep. Brother Christians, it is Manolios. He has rebelled against Christ, it is our duty to strike him a straight blow. He has rebelled against our country, the family and property, he has raised the standard of revolt, a red standard, to plunge us all into bloodshed. He is receiving the orders of Moscow. The faith, our country and honor are in danger. He's a bolshevik! Our duty is to excommunicate him: that is to say, to separate him from the healthy sheep and drive him toward the precipices of Satan, that he may fall down then and we may be saved. I am now coming down from the pulpit to drive him away!"

He came down, and the beadle ran to bring him the holy water. He dipped the sprinkler in the stoup, sprinkled the air, and pronounced in a thunderous voice:

"Out from here, out from here, excommunicated!"

He took a step forward, sprinkled the air afresh and cried once more: "Out from here, out from here, excommunicated!"

It was as if Manolios were there, in the air, invisible, and the minister of God were advancing upon him to drive him away. Sprinkling the air untiringly he arrived at the church door. The villagers drew aside in terror as though afraid of being touched by the accursed soul as it recoiled and recoiled, driven out of the church.

On the threshold the priest gave a vigorous lunge with the sprinkler and, turning toward the villagers:

"Cry out three times, brother Christians, cry out all together: 'Manolios is excommunicated.'"

An immense din arose; the church trembled with it. All present raised their hands and cried out three times: "Manolios is excommunicated!"

The priest brandished his sprinkler for a final sprinkling and cried once more: "Out from here, out from here, excommunicated!" as he shut the door violently. Everyone breathed deeply as if the demon had gone and the air had been purified.

Back in the center of the church, the priest stopped:

"Brother Christians, let no one henceforth approach him, let no one stretch out a hand to him, to give him a piece of bread or a glass of wine! Let no one open his mouth to wish him good day! Anyone who meets him will spit on the ground three times and turn away from him. He has denied Christ, Christ denies him! He has denied religion, country, the family, property; they in their turn deny him. Be he vowed to the eternal fire! Amen!"

"Amen!" cried the crowd with hatred and relief.

"Amen!" thundered the voice of Panayotaros, louder than all the rest.

And behold, at this moment, a calm voice rang out in the middle of the church:

"Father, Manolios is not alone; I am with him. I wish to be excommunicated, too—I, Michelis Patriarcheas."

Immediately another voice, an angry one:

"And I, Yannakos the carrier and postman; I'm with him, too!"

"And I, Kostandis, I'm with him, I, too!"

There was a stir. The villagers drew aside, and the three friends were left alone in the middle of the nave.

The voice of priest Grigoris growled:

"Your turn will come, emissaries of Satan, you wait! But the Church of Christ, which is all forbearance and mercy, leaves you time for repentance. The thunderbolt of Christ waits suspended in serenity over the heads of men. I command you to the grace of God."

"God will be our judge, Father," said Yannakos. "Our trust is in Him. God, not you!"

"God has judged you by my voice!" roared the priest, and his eyes went bloodshot. "I, the priest in Lycovrissi—I am the mouth of God."

"Only the pure heart is the mouth of God!" retorted Michelis; "our heart is pure, Father."

And addressing his two companions:

"Let us go, brothers; let us shake the dust of Lycovrissi from our feet. Good-bye, you others!"

No one replied. The women crossed themselves in horror and spat into their bosoms, murmuring: *"Kyrie eleison! Kyrie eleison!"*

"Good-bye, you others!" Michelis repeated. "Our Christ is poor, persecuted; He knocks at doors and no one opens to Him. Your Christ is a rich notable, who hobnobs with the Agha. He barricades his door that he may eat and not give anyone a crumb. Your Christ has a full belly, and proclaims: 'This world is just, honest, softhearted, just right for me. Excommunicated to anyone who stirs a finger to disturb its order!' Our Christ is a beggar who looks at the bodies of the starving and the souls of those in fear and cries out: 'This world is unjust, dishonest, without pity; let it perish!' "

Priest Grigoris gathered up his cassock and rushed at them:

"Bolsheviks!" he roared, "get out of the house of God!"

The crowd grew stormy, father Ladas leaped from his pew, Panayotaros shook his fist, cries of rage arose:

"Out! Out! Out!"

Yannakos bounded forward, ready to strike, but Michelis seized his arm.

"Let us go," he said. "God will judge."

He crossed the threshold of the church. Behind him Yannakos and Kostandis slid furtively through the crowd, and at some distance Andonis the barber and fat Dimitri the butcher followed on their heels.

"Do you mean you're deserting us, Kostandis?" said a strident voice behind them, all of a sudden; "are you deserting your wife and children, excommunicated?"

Kostandis turned and saw his wife running toward him, all dishevelled. He stopped for a second, but Yannakos dragged him on by force:

"Come, don't look back!"

Initial Skirmish

Priest Grigoris went home on fire from head to foot, mad with anger, as though his hands had just hurled the thunderbolt.

A priest's word ought to have power to kill, he thought; when he says; "Be accursed!" the men whom he is cursing should fall dead on the spot. Then the world would be rid of all the enemies of God; peace and justice would reign.

In his mind there formed a procession of the men he would have killed if he could: first of all, Manolios. He was the most dangerous because no fault could be found in him; he didn't get drunk, he didn't steal, never was he heard to swear or lie; he didn't run after women. Well, him first. Immediately afterward, or rather at the same time, that criminal priest Fotis. He hated that one so much that he would have enjoyed tearing his eyes out. Everything about him got on his nerves—his ascetic's face, his flaming eyes, his deep voice. On top of all that, he ate hardly at all, never got drunk, he too had no failing, and all his people adored him. Ah, if he could make him bite the dust, tear out his beard, cut off his nose! The more priest Grigoris thought about him, the more his rage increased; so much so that he no longer knew which of them—priest Fotis or Manolios—he would exterminate first.

Then he would kill Yannakos and Kostandis. Those two had taken the bad road, they were setting the bad example, it would be better to suppress them. As for Michelis! He reflected a moment. "Let's still wait a little . . ." he muttered. But as for father Ladas, no doubt was possible. He would kill him. Not because he was a miser, guilty of having thrown a throng of orphans onto the streets, but because he had called him goat-beard in the prison.

Those five would make the first batch; afterward, day after day, he would do away with all who resisted him. He had still some accounts to settle with the bishop's palace in the town—some archimandrites, some arch-priests, and the bishop himself. He would exterminate them all. And certain little ruffians who had played dirty tricks on him when he was a student—if they were still alive he'd settle them like the others. . . .

Priest Grigoris sighed.

Yes, a priest ought to have that power, he ought, he kept telling himself.

The villagers had scattered, some in the square, some in the churchyard, and tongues were going full tilt. They were excited, full of zest. Their life had just taken on a meaning—they had seen hangings, the death of famous notables, the murder of a young Turkish boy, a widow's throat slit, and now today it was given them to be present at an excommunication! Panayotaros had lit his cigarette and was sitting under the plane tree, smoking away in perfect bliss. It's working, he thought, the maneuver's successful, I'll have them all, yes, all, Christ and Apostles and all, the devil take them! He inhaled the last puffs voluptuously, blew the smoke out through his nostrils, spat and got up to go and spy on the Sarakina and see something of what was happening there.

He took a path known only to him, and came across a little old man from the Sarakina busy picking up wood and twigs to light fires with.

"Good morning, old fellow," said Panayotaros, "how are things?"

"Getting along, getting along, son; don't you know? Seems we've been given some fields and vineyards to stop all us poor wretches starving. God be praised! Tomorrow we're going down to Lycovrissi to harvest the grapes."

"You mean some of your people are going grape harvesting, grandfather?"

"That's sure, we too got lads and girls that can work; you'll have a chance to admire them tomorrow."

Panayotaros went on his way. Lucky I found that out, he said to himself, I'll go and tell goat-beard that.

He reached the rock he had adopted as his watch tower. From it he could see what went on among the caves. He lay down on his belly and watched closely.

Priest Fotis must have finished his Mass, for a crowd of old men, old women and children were assembled in front of the

grotto church: priest Fotis and Manolios were speaking to them.
Panayotaros strained to try and hear; the few isolated words which
reached him now and then were not very clear, but by putting the
jumble together he got this sense out of them: Manolios was
speaking and saying: "It isn't God that has excommunicated me,
it's priest Grigoris, and that's not at all the same thing!"

A little farther on there was a fire lit, and fat Dimitri, on his
knees, was roasting a sheep on the spit, while Yannakos, standing
at his side with a knife in his hand, pricked the meat from time
to time to see if it were cooked. They were exchanging jokes and
laughing. Beside them, Andonis was lathering his soap and shav-
ing an old man. The children had run up to have their hair cut
and were waiting for their turn, playing about his legs. Kostandis
and two or three old women came and went, carrying water.

They're having a good time, they are, growled Panayotaros; they
aren't worrying. Look here, priest Grigoris, where's it got to—what
you called the thunderbolt? And the fires of Hell, where are they?
Devil take you!

He crawled a bit nearer to hear better and craned his head over
the tip of the rock.

Hi, and where's Michelis? he wondered; I don't see him. He
must be somewhere or other, groaning over his fate, the idiot. Everything's going wrong for him: he's lost his father, that noble pig,
he's given away his fortune, the crazy fellow, and the priest has
chucked his ring in his face—so there he is, orphan, pauper and
widower!

Cries and laughter were heard. One of the refugees must have
brought a mandolin; he had begun tuning it. Yannakos and the
huge Dimitri drew the sheep away from the fire and laid it on
some stones. The starving band of the Sarakina ran up and formed
a circle around the roast. Some of them began banging old pots
and pans and danced a few steps. Priest Fotis approached in his
turn. He crossed himself, blessed the sheep and set to work sharing
it out in small portions, like consecrated bread. Everyone sat on
the ground, bursts of laughter arose, and the mandolin twittered.
Suddenly Manolios stood up and looked about him anxiously.

"Michelis!" he called, "hey, Michelis!" But in vain: no one replied.

Priest Fotis was making wide gestures. He was in a joyful mood
and talking loudly. Now Panayotaros could hear distinctly.

"My children," he was saying, "this day is blessed; all that Christ prophesied for His disciples is today befalling us as a benediction! Christ said: 'Blessed are ye, when men shall revile you, and persecute you, and shall say all manner of evil against you, falsely for My sake. Rejoice and be exceeding glad, for great is your reward in Heaven, for so persecuted they the prophets which came before you.' Those, my children, are the words of Christ. You see: today men are insulting us, reviling us and persecuting us because we love Christ. Our comrade Manolios was excommunicated this morning by the priest with the pot belly. God be praised, we are on the right road. Christ marches before us and we are following Him. Rejoice and be exceeding glad, my children. Christ is risen!"

So saying, he filled an earthenware cup with water and drank it at one gulp.

It's true, those people aren't men, they're wild beasts! Panayotaros growled. The bells have rung the knell, they've been excommunicated, driven out of the church, and there they are, laughing for all they're worth and swanking about it. How do they manage to be so cheerful? On my faith, they're possessed by the Devil. Damn me if I understand a thing!

He craned his head to hear better, but immediately felt a hand grip his neck like a pair of pincers. Furiously he shook himself. Michelis was there, leaning over him and gazing at him with a smile.

"What are you doing there, watching, Panayotaros?" he asked gently. "Why don't you come down and have a bite with us? Here, come with me," and he took him by the arm.

But Panayotaros curled up like a hedgehog.

"No, I won't come!" he cried. "I don't want any of your *mezes*, I don't want any of your company, renegade! Leave me in peace in my corner, all alone!"

"Aren't you ashamed, Panayotaros?—a good man like you, open and honest—to go along with the swine? Was it they who sent you here to spy?"

"I don't go along with anyone, I'm all alone, Michelis, alone in my skin and in my carcase, like a wolf; don't you realize that? I'm disgusted with everyone—you and the others. Be quiet, don't talk to me, I bite!"

"What's happened to you, poor Panayotaros?" said Michelis, sitting down near him; "for several months you've been unrecognizable. You were always a rough one, but not mischievous. Someone's injured you, Panayotaros? Who? What's happened to you?"

"Lots of things, devil take me, lots of things, and you know very well. So why ask me? You know very well!"

"Is it because you were chosen to act Judas?" Michelis asked shyly; "but it's a play, a sacred play but only a play, not real. Is Manolios Christ once and for all? Am I really John, His beloved disciple? How did you come to get an idea like that into your head? It's a real sin! It was simply that you had a red beard . . ."

"I'll cut her off!" cried Panayotaros in fury, "I'll cut her off, the bitch!"

Michelis burst out laughing.

"Here, come along, we've got the barber with us. Come, he'll cut it off for you; that'll calm you."

"I'll burn her myself with an ember! I'll set fire to her and pack her off home to the devil!" said Panayotaros, jumping up, as though he had just made a resolution; "here, I'll do it straightaway!"

"Come with us," begged Michelis again, gently, "come with us; you'll see, everyone'll welcome you with open arms. You're all that's lacking to make us perfectly happy."

But Panayotaros had already decamped from the rock and gained the path down. He turned for a second, and saw Michelis watching him from above, sadly.

"Go to the devil, all of you!" he shouted, "you and the others!" and with his huge hand he indicated the Sarakina on one side and Lycovrissi on the other.

That night Michelis had a bad dream. He was lying in the same grotto as Manolios; he had brought from his father's house all he could in the way of mattresses and clothes, had distributed them to all who were without, keeping hardly anything for himself, and then had declared to priest Fotis:

"Father, from today I'm leaving Lycovrissi and taking refuge under your roof. I shall work, too. I shall struggle; I shall win or lose with you. The air of the plain doesn't suit me any longer."

"Welcome to our army, my son," the priest replied; "together we shall climb the hill and at the top we shall find God. You are used to well being, but you've a valiant soul and a big heart; in the fight you'll be the best of us all. Welcome!"

"Come, Michelis," said Manolios, "you'll share my place, the cave just by our church; you'll find there the Crucifixion you gave me, the one with the swallows."

Michelis carried his stuff and his large silver Gospel book to the cave. So that night he slept there, and had a dream which terrified him: he saw Mariori prisoner in a high tower guarded by enormous black dogs which prevented her from escaping. Michelis was at the foot of the tower; he was singing her a song to make her appear at the sound of his voice. And now he saw the iron doors of the tower open and Mariori come out, dressed in a sea-colored robe whose long train swept the ground; three roses adorned it, one over the heart, one at the waist, the third at the knee. Silent and with tongues hanging out, the black dogs ran in front of her and at her sides. Mariori was holding her little white handkerchief, and kept wiping her mouth. There was a caïque at the foot of the tower, long and narrow like a coffin; Mariori went aboard the caïque and it cast off. Just as she was moving away, she turned and saw him. She waved her little handkerchief covered with red spots, and gave a great piercing cry. Michelis, at this cry, awoke with a start.

"What is it, Michelis?" asked Manolios, awakened roughly.

"I had a nightmare, Manolios; I saw black dogs, a boat, and Mariori going away."

Manolios shuddered, but said nothing; he heard flying in the air the wings of the Archangel Michael.

The weak light coming into the grotto gently stroked their faces and, in a hollow of the rock, the silver Gospel book.

"We've a lot of work today," said Manolios jumping up. "Some twenty comrades who are working outside have been warned to come and harvest the vineyards you have given to the community, God bless you. You've saved a lot of souls, Michelis."

"It didn't cost me anything to give what I had; so I don't think that's enough to save my soul, Manolios. Only sacrifice is worth anything, and I've made no sacrifice. Yannakos has made a much bigger one by giving his ass."

For a moment Manolios weighed his friend's words in his mind.

"I believe you are right, Michelis," he said after a while.

About ten comrades and as many women had arrived and were chattering gaily in front of the cave. When they saw Michelis come out they ran to shake him by the hand.

"You've made us poor people property holders again," they said to him. "God sanctify your father's bones!"

For a moment the kindly fresh, rosy face of his father appeared to him; with eyes full of tears it looked at him reproachfully. Its twisted mouth moved as though to speak, as though to say to him: "Why did you kill me? Why?" But it had pity and was silent.

It's for his soul that I've done it, murmured Michelis, bending his head, for his soul! God give him rest . . .

He hesitated a moment:

"Besides, it was his last will," he said at last; "it's he who ordered me to share out all his goods among the poor."

. Manolios turned, looked at his friend, went up to him and clasped his hand. Michelis shook his head and turned away to hide his tears.

Priest Fotis had arrived.

"My children," he said, "make your sign of the cross and go with God's blessing and harvest our vineyards; Manolios will guide you. We are beginning, my children, to have land and to plant firm roots in it. What was up to now only a dream is beginning to come to life. We now have lands and trees, and we will all work them together and all enjoy them together. None of us will be rich, none will be poor. We will form a united family. God grant we may show how men ought to live together and how justice can reign on earth. With the grace of God and of the Virgin, success to this beginning! Go with them, Manolios, show them the way; you know where the vineyards are. I shall go with Michelis to the town to fill in the official papers that will make our community proprietor of the goods of archon Patriarcheas."

The companions crossed themselves, Manolio took the lead of the little band, and they set out. They went joyfully, singing vintage songs in advance, in no way suspecting what awaited them at Lycovrissi.

The evening before, as soon as he was back from the Sarakina, Panayotaros had run to priest Grigoris's house.

"It's tomorrow those people are coming to do the vintage," he announced, "get busy!"

Priest Grigoris was at table; he dropped his fork, such was the fury this news produced in him.

"I won't have them come into the village," he shouted. "They're not going to do any vintage, no! I won't let them; I'm going to see the Agha!"

He put on the cassock he wore on festal days, hung his heavy silver cross round his neck, took his long ivory-handled stick and made for the Agha's dwelling with slow and solemn step.

The Agha had just finished his meal; he was drinking his coffee. Beside him sat Brahimaki with his back turned to him, rolling a cigarette. They had certainly had yet another quarrel, for the poor Agha, as he drank his coffee, made a face as though he were swallowing poison.

Priest Grigoris appeared in the doorway bowing and scraping. "Salutations, Agha!"

The Agha did not bother to turn his head.

"I realize it's you by your voice, priest," he said unpleasantly. "What fresh worries are you bringing me? Come in front of me, so I can see you. Take a stool and sit down."

He clapped his hands and the old hunchback woman appeared.

"A coffee for the priest effendi," he ordered. Then to the priest: "Speak."

"Agha," the other began, "as your lordship is well aware, the world hangs by a thread. If this thread is cut, the world falls and breaks in a thousand pieces."

"Even Martha the hunchback knows that," said the Agha, testily. "Go on."

"Well, Agha, somebody's trying to cut that thread."

The Agha put his hand to the hilt of his yataghan; he half stood up, ready to spring.

"Who is it?" he shouted, "so I can cut off his head. Yes, by Mahomet, confess who it is, priest, and you shall see!"

"The Muscovite," replied the priest.

The Agha let his yataghan fall back into place.

"How do you expect me to leave Lycovrissi, leave Brahimaki, abandon my ease and go to the devil with a following wind, to look for the Muscovite in the snow and cut his throat?"

The priest swallowed his cupful of coffee at one gulp, and sighed.

"He's too far away, that scoundrel is, you blessed priest; don't let's talk of him, he's too far away, how d'you expect me to go that far! You have only to play the innocent priest—believe me, I've your welfare at heart—and I shall do the same, just long enough to last out our lifetime in peace; after us, the deluge!"

"But there's no need for you to stir from Lycovrissi, Agha. The Muscovite has already sent some of his men to us. It's here, at Ly-

covrissi, they mean to start cutting the thread. I did my duty this
morning at the church; you've only to do yours in your turn; there!"

"Yes, the hunchback did mumble something to me about it, I
didn't understand at all."

"I have excommunicated Manolios, Patriarcheas's shepherd; I
have driven him out from the sheepfold of Christ."

"And why, priest? He's a good lad, poor chap, only a bit crazy.
Wasn't he ready to save the village? It isn't easy to do that, priest,
it isn't easy!"

"Hypocrisy the whole thing, Agha; lies! You know, he did it on
purpose, to deceive the people."

The Agha scratched his head; his nerves were beginning
to jangle.

"That's enough, shut up, priest!" he cried. "You'd put horseshoes
on fleas, you Greeks! How d'you expect a man of sense to understand what you want? Your actions say one thing, your words another, and what's in your head is a third! There, priest, don't make
me giddy, leave me alone. I'm not myself this morning. And besides, I've Brahimaki, the demon, into the bargain," he added,
pointing at the boy.

Brahimaki had smoked and said nothing, sending puffs up to the
ceiling and uncovering teeth that were white and sharp as a dog's.
But when he heard his name he turned furiously toward the Agha.

"Tell the priest you know what; otherwise I'm going; I'm off
back to Smyrna. This place'll be the death of me!"

He made as though to rise, but the Agha seized him by the
shoulder.

"Sit down, demon, I tell you. Sit down, once more!" Then, to
priest Grigoris:

"Priest effendi, what d'you want me to do? You came to ask a
favor. What favor? Speak out, and we'll bargain. But clearly, eh,
and make it short, so I can understand. Don't muddle everything
up, see? My brain isn't an ant heap. It's simple and straightforward;
come, go ahead! I'm listening."

"Agha," priest Grigoris resumed, drawing his stool up closer;
"that simpleton the son of the late Patriarcheas has given away all
his fortune to the beggars on the Sarakina."

"Well, he has a perfect right to," the Agha interrupted; "it's his,
isn't it? He's doing what he likes with it."

"Yes, but all those rascals, you must realize, are the Muscovite's men; he's sent them here to cut the thread."

"Eh, what's that you're saying, priest? Speak clearly, priest. All?"

"All. Their leaders are priest Fotis and Manolios. Tomorrow they're coming to harvest their vineyards, as they put it. Do you see what that means? They have a foothold in our village—in your village, Agha; and little by little they'll have the lot of us out; and it'll be all over with the thread!"

"Well? What do you want?"

"Tomorrow, when the Muscovites come, you must place yourself at the entrance to the village and drive them away."

"But why do you want me to drive them away, priest? Aren't the vineyards theirs?"

"No!"

"How 'no'? My head's going to burst, I can feel it. Hasn't Michelis given them to them? Aren't they theirs now?"

"I tell you no, Agha! We're going to declare that Michelis is unbalanced."

"Unbalanced? And what's that mean, now? Explain things clearly, I tell you!"

"Well, that he's not all there, that he doesn't know what he's doing, that the gift is not valid."

"But is he really mad? Faith, I think he's got all his wits."

"Folly and sense join on to one another, Agha; no one knows where one ends and the other begins. So we shall find a way of proving that Michelis is mad."

The Agha clutched his head between his hands and suddenly he burst out laughing.

"I see," he said. "I see! You blessed Greeks, you're clever as monkeys. One of these days you'll make the world into a pellet and swallow it!"

"Well, Agha?"

"Listen to me, priest Grigoris, cards on the table; give and take. I'll go and take up position at the entry of the village, as you desire, and I'll drive away those poor devils of the Sarakina; but on your side, you . . . give and take, you know what I mean?"

The priest, who had understood, blenched.

"Understand? I'll do what you ask, priest; but you, too, will do what I ask."

"Say what it is, Agha," said the priest with the edge of his lips, "and if it's in my power . . ."

"Nothing could be simpler; don't get in a state. Brahimaki, here present, is set on having the girls of the village dance one day so that he can make his choice."

"That is grave, Agha."

"Grave or not, there's nothing else to be done. Can't you see? A strapping fellow of fifteen. Who could hold him in? You? Me? Just try! He'd make one mouthful of the two of us. Only a woman can check him. Well, some female who'll tame him must be found. For the moment he's like an unbroken colt. Try to get on him, he throws you. But as soon as he's been broken in, you'll get on him and he'll wag his tail into the bargain!"

Brahimaki, when he heard this, began clucking as though he were being tickled.

"A pity the widow's dead," muttered the priest.

"Let's find another, priest."

But Brahimaki gave a bound:

"I want her to be young, plump and not a hunchback!" he shouted, "white as bread, and she must resist, so that I can fight her and up end her while she screams and weeps and tears her hair; that would be fun. Well, priest?"

The priest was reflecting.

"Have to find an orphan girl, one that has no protector in the village, to avoid scandal," said the priest; "it's the scandal I'm afraid of, Agha, the scandal, nothing else. Give me time, Agha."

"What? what's he want?" interrupted Brahimaki, on edge.

"A few days' respite so that he can find you the woman you want, you bastard! Old Cassock's quite right. D'you think he keeps them in his chicken run, d'you imagine they're chickens and he's only got to catch you the one you want? And another thing: none of your sulks, see, or by Mahomet I'll have you castrated! Then we'll be rid of you and there'll be some peace for us, too! Hear what I'm saying? Keep it shut! And if you're in too much of a hurry, you've got Martha."

"Ugh!" said Brahimaki, spitting against the wall, "I don't want her!"

"All right, priest, don't you worry about him, I'll give you a few days. You've heard the sort he wants—young, well-fleshed, white-skinned, and innocent."

The priest sighed.

"Agreed, Agha," he conceded, rising; "and tomorrow, as soon as the Muscovites come in sight . . ."

"All right, agreed. And on your side—"

"I'll try to find . . . May God forgive me . . ."

"Don't you worry, priest, he'll forgive you surely; there, he's a broad back, God has; he's seen life!" said the Agha with a laugh.

The priest left the Agha's worried. This business was not to his liking, but it had to be gone through. Anything rather than let the village be doomed and fall into the hands of priest Fotis. Religion, country, honor and private property in danger . . .

He therefore called together the village bigwigs and spoke to them in these terms:

"Tomorrow those louse carriers will turn up to harvest the vineyards of that poor madman Michelis. But all of us here can bear witness—and even swear if necessary—that Michelis, from a small child, was never normal, understand? That he sees things, he's crazy, how shall I put it? unbalanced. A cunning man—priest Fotis, for instance—could easily entangle him and make him sign anything he wanted. In consequence, the gift is not valid, the vineyards do not belong to the Sarakina vagabonds, no more do the fields, the gardens and the houses. Patriarcheas had no other children, so all his goods will go to the community, to us. Agreed?"

"Agreed!" replied the bigwigs, admiring the astuteness of their priest.

"I've just come from the Agha's and have reached an understanding with him. After a bit of toing and froing I've persuaded him to show himself, armed and on horseback, at the entry to the village. He won't let the lousy folk, the bolsheviks, in. And you—gather, all of you, with your servants, your dogs, your sticks, to give the Agha courage. Only be careful, no bloodshed, not even a scratched nose. Don't forget we are Christians and we ought to love our enemies."

He then sent for Panayotaros. He appeared toward evening, unrecognizable. He had set fire to his beard with a coal and had burned his cheeks so that they were covered with blisters. He had also cut his hair with the big scissors used for shearing sheep.

In spite of all his cares, the priest could not help laughing.

"Here, you idiot, do you realize the state you've got yourself into?"

"That's my business!" growled Panayotaros. "Don't ask too many questions, priest, or I'll go away and leave you high and dry. And I know you need me."

"Don't be angry, Panayotaros, it's not as if someone had called you hunchback! Listen, tomorrow I'm going to need you. Take your big stick and, if Manolios comes with them, fall on him. He's excommunicated and no one can bring you to book; you can even kill him. Go, and God be with you."

"Leave God out of it, priest, don't mix Him up in our arrangements. You're scared of priest Fotis, and I hate Manolios, that's all there is to it. Don't mix in the Gods and the Holy Virgins, that doesn't work with me. You're sly enough to know what I mean. See you tomorrow!"

He made for the door; he stopped for a second on the threshold:

"We're a couple of old scoundrels, that's a fact!" he said with a guffaw.

So down came the Sarakini from the mountain, singing; deep in thought, Manolios marched in front. God grant, he kept saying to himself, there's no resistance; no bloodshed.

But as they approached the village, they saw men assembled around Saint Basil's Well; some were sitting on the ground, others were striding about with big sticks, and their cries and oaths could be distinctly heard.

Manolios stopped and turned to his companions:

"I think, friends, they're going to resist us. Let the women stay here and wait; we men will go on and may God come to our aid. We shall go forward, be confident, right is on our side. But if they want a fight at all costs we'll not come to blows with them; they're our brothers in spite of everything; we'll go and find the Agha; he's the governor of the village; he will judge. There's no possible doubt; the vineyards are ours now, he will support us. So forward, brothers, in the name of Christ!"

The women sat down in a circle among the boulders; the men continued on their way. They had not gone a hundred paces before a stone whistled over Manolios's head. Another followed, more still; the attack had been let loose. A group of men left the well and moved out to meet them; at its head, with burned beard and hair, Panayotaros advanced with his heavy bear's gait.

"What do we do now?" bellowed Loukas the giant banner bearer; "we can't let them use us as targets without answering back! Pick up stones, my friends, up and at the pot bellies!"

But Manolios intervened:

"Stop, don't shed blood, brothers!"

From Saint Basil's Well came a burst of furious cries: "Back! Back, you lousy lot! No one's to come in! Back!"

Manolios advanced with his hands up, to show that he wished to parley.

"Brothers, brothers, listen to me!"

"Excommunicated! Bandit! Assassin! Bolshevik!"

Foaming with fury, the Lycovrissi rushed at him. Panayotaros held out his great arms.

"No one's to touch him! He's mine; I'm the one who's going to do him in!" he bellowed, hurling himself upon Manolios.

But the Sarakini had already surrounded their leader.

"If anyone touches Manolios," cried Loukas, picking up a huge stone, "I'll smash his skull like a watermelon!"

The beadle, to whom priest Grigoris had given his instructions, ran up and down, yelping:

"He's excommunicated, strike him down, Panayotaros, your hand will be sanctified!"

The schoolmaster arrived, out of breath:

"In the name of Christ, what's happening, friends? Stop!"

"They're trying to invade our village and occupy it," the beadle shouted.

"We're trying to harvest our vineyards!" cried the Sarakini. "They're ours, Michelis has given them to us."

"Michelis has been proclaimed mad, the gift is invalid," yelled father Ladas stridently, hiding behind the schoolmaster.

"The gift is invalid! Out with you, out with you, bolsheviks, bandits, scoundrels!"

Just then Panayotaros, with head lowered, charged Manolios like a bull. But Loukas, who had a huge stone in his hand, hurled it at him with all his strength. It hit him on the knee; he staggered. Loukas flung himself upon him, bowled him over and, sitting on his back, began hitting him furiously. Panayotaros, using his full strength, shook free and caught Loukas by the waist. They wrestled, bellowing and rolling, now one on top and now the other.

The beadle picked up a stone and aimed at Manolios.

"Excommunicated!" he yelled, "bolshevik!"

The stone flew and hit Manolios on the forehead; blood spurted out and flooded over his face.

"They're killing our Manolios! At them!" cried the friends, and attacked.

Sarakini and Lycovrissi came to grips. Father Ladas took to his heels. The schoolmaster, trying to intervene, got himself mercilessly knocked about by both sides.

An urchin ran to the village, shouting at the top of his voice, joyously:

"Manolios, the excommunicated, has been killed! Manolios, the bolshevik, has been killed! Rejoice!"

Kostandis heard it, rushed out of his café, grabbing his stick, and set off running.

"Where? where?" he shouted to the urchin as he passed.

"At Saint Basil's Well."

Kostandis made for it, hell for leather. On his way he met Yannakos. Without a word, they ran together.

Around the well, Sarakini and Lycovrissi were now only an inextricable mass rolling about among the boulders and roaring. The women from the Sarakina had come up to the rescue, beside themselves; inured to war, with arms hardened by country labor, they gave and received blows like men.

"Manolios! Manolios!" cried two voices raucous with anguish.

Manolios, who had sat down on a rock to bandage his wound, recognized the voices and looked up.

"Here I am, brothers," he shouted, "don't worry!"

At the same time father Ladas, who had climbed on to a rock, yelled joyfully:

"Here's the Agha! Here's the Agha!"

The whinnying of a mare was heard, sparks flew from the pebbles of the track, and the Agha appeared before the well, with his silver pistols, his long yataghan, his big red fez, completely drunk. He tugged the reins so sharply that the mare reared. He managed to keep in the saddle by clinging to the mane. He took his pistol, fired into the air, and his voice rang out, thunderous:

"Giaours!"

In an instant the melee came untied, the Sarakini grouped themselves on one side, the Lycovrissi on the other, their clothes in strips, covered with dust and blood. Only the schoolmaster remained stretched on the ground right in the middle, rather badly hurt and making vain efforts to stand up and salute the Agha.

"Giaours!" yelled the Agha afresh, looking at the Sarakini with bloodshot eyes. "What have you come to my village for, eh? Back, back, vagabonds!"

Manolios stepped forward and spoke:

"Agha, we have vineyards at Lycovrissi and we have come to harvest them; they are ours!"

"Go and be hanged! Since when are they yours, eh? Where did you pick them up, you lousy lot?"

On his rock, father Ladas craned his neck and leered.

"Michelis has given them to us!" replied Manolios.

"That means nothing, you poor fools, his signature means nothing, he's not reached the age of reason," said the Agha.

"It's not the age he lacks," corrected father Ladas from his perch, "it's the reason!"

"Same thing, old skinflint, shut up!"

He pulled out his pistol and aimed at father Ladas.

"Mercy! Mercy!" cried the old man, collapsing behind the rock. "You're right, Agha, he's not old enough!"

The Agha burst out laughing and put back his pistol in his belt. Then, to the Sarakini:

"Which of you is Manolios? It's cloudy; I can't see very clearly. Let him come forward!"

"I am," said Manolios, drawing near the Agha's mare.

"Well, you're a good lad, you are, Manolios, whatever they may say. Here, tell me frankly what's meant by bolshevik. They keep dinning it into my ears without stopping. Is it a man, tell me, or an animal, or a disease like cholera? I really don't know. Do you know?"

"Yes, Agha," Manolios answered, "I know."

"Well, speak out, by your God, so I may know too!"

"The first Christians, Agha . . ."

"Leave the first Christians where they are, giaour, don't muddle me up, there's plenty of raki to do that! What have I got to do with the first Christians? I'm asking you what 'bolshevik' means."

"I'll explain it, Agha," said the nasal voice of father Ladas; "they

want there to be no rich and poor any more; only poor. To be no
masters and *raias* any more; only *raias*. There! No your wife and
mine any more; all free for all!"

"No Aghas and *raias* any more?" roared the Agha. "Does that
mean they want to upset God's order? Here, turn that mug of
yours this way!"

He spread out his fingers and made a long nose at Manolios.

"Light up your lamps and look: are all the fingers equal? There
are little ones and big ones, God made them like that. And that's
how He's made men too, some little, the others big. Some masters,
the others slaves. That's how He's made fishes—the big eat the little.
In the same way God has placed the sheep alongside the wolves:
for the wolves to eat the sheep. This is God's order, and now you
come, you bolsheviks . . . To blazes with you!"

With these words he unsheathed his yataghan, spurred the mare
and charged the Sarakini.

The women gave piercing cries and took to the path, running;
the men drew back, dumbfounded. Only Manolios remained, stead-
fast.

"You, giaour," the Agha shouted to him, "be off with you or I'll
cut off your head. Aren't you afraid?"

"Yes, I'm afraid," said Manolios, "but only of God; of men not
at all."

"Faith, you're stark mad!" said the Agha, bursting out laughing.
"You're a damned funny fellow: come home with me and help me
pass the time. In our religion idiots and saints are all one, it doesn't
distinguish. You're mad and a saint, you're a holy joke, I'm telling
you. There, come along, I'll take you with me, I'll give you food
and drink, I'll clothe you, I'll make you a happy man. You won't?
Go and be hanged, idiot; go, be off, I've changed my mind, I shan't
kill you."

He turned to the Lycovrissi who were listening delightedly to
the Agha taking up their defence:

"You, giaours, you aren't either mad or saints; go to the devil!
Stuffed bellies, idlers, get out of my sight!"

In alarm the Lycovrissi made themselves scarce. Yannakos and
Kostandis picked up the schoolmaster and supported him and
helped him home. The poor man was limping; he was in great
pain.

"Serves me right," he confessed. "I'm neither sheep nor wolf,

I'm a bastard, the wolves bite me and the sheep vomit me. I know very well what's right, my friends, I haven't the force to do it. I know very well where the truth lies, but I keep silent. I'm afraid. How shall I raise my head, poor wretch that I am? I'm afraid. . . . Lycovrissi and Sarakini have thrashed me without mercy. They're right! They're quite right, by my faith, it serves me right!"

He looked at the two companions, who were helping him to walk:

"Aren't you afraid?" he asked admiringly.

"Yes, we're afraid, too," replied Yannakos, "but we pretend to be brave, there you are! How can I explain it to you when it's all muddled up in my head? Look here: I pretend to be brave and my heart beats like mad. But little by little—it's curious!—by dint of pretending to be brave, I get there! See what I mean, old man? What have your books got to say about it? To tell you the truth, I don't understand too well! I'm an ass!"

The schoolmaser smiled in spite of his pain:

"I'd give all I know to be like you, Yannakos," he said. "And you, Kostandis?"

"Me? Worse than Yannakos; yes, I assure you, worse. I'm frightened, I shiver and shake, my heart beats fit to burst, but I'm ashamed. If one day I let everything drop so as to follow Christ, it won't be from goodness, or from bravery, but from self-respect. I shall tremble and be frightened, but I shan't retreat. Understand?"

"Manolios is better than all of us," Yannakos added. "He doesn't have to pretend to be brave. He is."

Barefooted Journey

NEXT MORNING, at the crack of dawn, Michelis was on his way down from the mountain, boiling with rage. I'm going to the priest's house, he said to himself, and I'll tear out his beard, I'll go and tell the notables where they belong, I'll have the church bell rung and get all the village to come and listen to me.

Warming up and calming down by turns, he sought the hardest words he could find. He had not been able to sleep all night. At dawn—and this time his eyes were certainly open—he had seen him again; the dead man had once more appeared to him. He had paused by his bed, looking at him reproachfully and shaking his head. His lips moved; he could hear his voice, a feeble, extinguished voice from the other world: "Why? Why? Why?" Nothing more.

Michelis had jumped up and, taking his stick, made for the village, trembling.

He went straight to the priest's house, pushed the door, entered. He crossed the courtyard and found him sitting near the window, bent over a letter, tears flowing from his eyes as he read it.

As soon as he saw Michelis he hastily hid the letter under his cassock; but Michelis had time to recognize the writing. He understood; his anger vanished. He saw death in the air; his heart tightened. The priest pulled himself together; he dried his eyes and looked at Michelis.

"What brings you here, young man?" he said mockingly. "Had enough of the Sarakina already? A monk's life is hard, so go back to your house, come back to the village, enjoy your wealth, poor lad. You haven't, by any chance, signed any papers?" he added anxiously.

"I've nothing now, nothing; I'm free."

"You have signed papers?" repeated the priest, worried.

"Yes."

"You're mad!" roared the priest, banging the window sill with his fist. "You're lost, you poor wretch. Here you are now, the slave of the swindler priest! More's the pity for all that fortune!"

"Free, you mean," Michelis repeated, feeling anger rumbling within him. "You are the slave, Father. More the pity for the holy habit which you wear!"

"It was for your good I was taking to much trouble, and for the good of my daughter," said the priest in a wan voice full of rancor. "Now it's all over!"

"What's in her letter?"

"Here, read it!" he said, pulling it out.

Michelis seized it. It was covered with tears. The father's? The daughter's? How could he know? He read it slowly, with difficulty: tears misted his eyes.

"I'm not at all well, Father, forgive me, not at all well. I get a little worse each day; I'm wasting away. The doctors now go past my bed without stopping. They don't even glance at me any more. They've already struck me off their list. And I lie here with my eyes fixed on the ceiling, as if it were the sky; it's the only sky left to me. I should be calm, perhaps even happy at dying, if it weren't for you, Father, left there all alone after I've gone, and with no one to bring you even a glass of water. It's because of you I grieve, and also because of the man to whom I was betrothed. Perhaps he doesn't grieve at seeing me go, but I can't stop weeping when I think of him. Why? Why? What have I done? I only wanted a house and a child . . . and now . . ."

Michelis could not read any more. He laid the letter on the window sill and made for the door.

"All right," he said, "I'm going."

"What did you want? What did you come for?"

"Nothing. I didn't want anything. What could I ask you for? Keep well!"

"God is cruel, He strikes men without mercy. What have I done to Him?"

Michelis was already on the threshold. He turned, tensely:

"It's you He should have struck, you, priest, who are full of passions, not your daughter!"

"He knew where He should strike me; He has done so," mumbled the priest, and his eyes filled with tears again.

Suddenly, in an access of rage, he bounded into the middle of the courtyard, barefoot.

"It's your fault, all of you," he moaned: "Manolios, the Sarakina goat-beard, and you! You are the cause of everything, with your trickery and your treason! Before that, we were all right here, everything was going on in the Lord's way, my daughter would have recovered her health, you would not have killed your father by your bad conduct, and I, in a year's time, would have been holding a grandson in my arms. Alas, that scoundrel good-for-nothing Manolios put ideas in your head. Then there arrived that goat-beard, that old fox, curse him! Then your father died of grief, and now you've smashed your fortune to bits, and I've thrown the engagement ring at your head. My daughter's condition worsened when she heard. Now it's all over, she's lost. You are responsible for her death too, wretched boy! You have killed her, as you killed your father; she had the courage to fight against her illness, poor thing, but now . . ."

He strode up and down the courtyard, swearing and sighing. He was seized by a fresh access of fury.

"I was indeed right to proclaim it everywhere: you're unbalanced, a madman, your signature is worth nothing. I shall take everything from you and give it to the community. The Sarakina, curse it, shan't eat a single grape! Not an olive, not a grain of wheat! No, no, things shall not go the way you want! I'll do for you, I swear, as you've done for your father, as you've done for my daughter. You'll see, you'll see, it's no laughing matter. I'll go and find the bishop and tell him the whole story. I've all the people of the village to witness; even the Agha is with me. I'll have the lot of you!"

"You have everyone with you," said Michelis, his heart torn by the sight of the priest's sorrow and hate, "you have everyone with you, except God. Will you have the heart to let so many people die of hunger on the Sarakina? Have you no fear of God?"

"If Mariori dies I shall become savage; I shall have no pity for anyone! I shall throw my cassock into the nettles, take my gun and kill people. Why should God kill my Mariori? What has she done to Him? Has there ever been on earth a better, more innocent, more delightful creature? And first of all I shall kill Manolios. That cur is the cause of all. The Agha didn't hang him; I shall. He plays the saint, martyr and hero before us and he's sold himself to the Muscovite, the traitor, the renegade, the bolshevik!"

Mad with rage, brandishing his fists above Michelis's head, he roared:

"Go away! Let me never set eyes on you again! Go away if you don't want me to smash my head against the wall!"

He collapsed on the gravel of the courtyard, with his mouth wide open.

There was no one in the house. Michelis bent down and, gathering his strength, picked up the heavy old man. He carried him into the house and laid him on the sofa. He went into the kitchen, filled a glass with water and brought it to him. The priest seized the glass, drank in small gulps, and opened his eyes.

"Michelis," he murmured, "I am a broken man. God has struck me right to the heart, but I can't repent, I can't. I can't forgive anyone, anyone! Go away, I don't want to set eyes on you any more!"

He revived, stood up, crossed the courtyard and opened the door:

"Get out, and never again set foot in my house!"

With these words he shut the door brutally on Michelis.

Michelis passed through the village lanes as if he had fallen into some unknown place, as if he were walking in a dream and seeing these houses, these shops and the plane tree for the first time. When he passed before the family house, he stopped for a good while to stare at it; it was as though he were making an effort to remember. He wanted to cross the threshold and go in, but was seized with terror at the thought that he might see in the courtyard a tall dead man draped in grass torn up from the soil and with arms outstretched to bar his entrance. He shuddered and hastened away; it seemed to him that the priest's accusing words: "You killed him, you . . ." had become dead people, a long series of dead people, pursuing him.

He stopped at the end of the village. Why did I come? he asked himself, yes, why? I was angry, and my anger has died down, so why? Suddenly the image of Mariori took shape; he saw her stretched out before him, pale, with eyes wide open, pressing a small red handkerchief to her mouth. This village is full of dead, he muttered, full of ghosts. I must go!

The sky became covered with clouds, the sun darkened, a sudden wind sprang up; the trees shuddered, some dead leaves fell, strewing the ground with yellowish patches.

Two or three villagers passed along the road and, pretending not to see him, hastened their steps and disappeared. A child started crying at the sight of him. An old woman appeared on the doorstep, saw him, crossed herself and at once shut the door. She went over to her husband, who was wandering about the yard in search of a ray of sunshine to warm his old bones.

"Outside," she whispered to him, "there's the son of our old archon, Michelis. If only you could see him! He's pitiful. The state he's in, God-a-mercy! thin, pale, with his eyes dead . . ."

The old man shook his head.

"Serves him right," he said maliciously; "he's given away his wealth, the idiot, and now he's wandering the streets. Is he barefoot?"

"No, he's still got his old shoes. Poor thing, they're right when they say he's lost his wits."

"The end of the race of the Patriarcheases!" the old man sneered. "They ate everything, drank everything, embraced everything, and that's where they are today! Faith, the good God is just, say what you like! Listen, wife; one of these days when he comes knocking at doors, give him a bit of bread, so they can say that we, too, have given alms to the Patriarcheases!"

He crossed himself:

"God be praised!" he muttered, satisfied.

The thunder rumbled in the distance. The wind had grown colder and brought a smell of rain. Michelis shook himself.

"I'll go and find Yannakos," he decided suddenly. He went back into the village.

Big drops of rain were now falling, the lanes were empty. As he passed in front of the widow's house he stopped, and pushed open the door. The courtyard was deserted, the red carnations faded. He went in. The bedding, stools and chest had been stolen. The wooden bed frame was lying about in pieces, the shutters had been torn away. There was only one left, hanging lamentably on its hinges, banging against the wall and creaking lugubriously as the wind shook it. Passers-by had been in and befouled the corners and walls. . . .

"Poor Katerina!" muttered Michelis. "What a lot of pleasure you gave and received! The things she must have heard and seen in this room, now so desolate. Ugh! the misery of this world!"

A mouse could be heard nibbling. She had nested in the rush ceiling and was hard at work, unrestingly, as if the good God had engaged her by the day to devour the widow's ceiling.

He shut the door behind him and made for Yannakos's house. "In spite of all her follies, Katerina is more sure of entering Paradise than priest Grigoris with all his cassocks," he thought, on the way. "Perhaps she's there already, sitting at the side of Mary Magdalen!"

With his heart a little lightened, he knocked at Yannakos's door.

Yannakos had been in the stable since daybreak. He was saying good-bye to his donkey. He had promised to give him to the Sarakina, but yesterday evening he had received a message from father Ladas: "Either you'll give me back the three pounds or I shall take your donkey. So think it over, if you don't want to go to prison."

He put his arms around the sturdy warm neck of his beloved companion. He sobbed as he spoke to him, and what affectionate words he found to say to him!

"My Youssoufaki, people are wicked; they're jealous of us; they want to separate us. Who'll come every morning to talk to you, stroke you, fill your bucket with fresh water and your manger with fodder? Who'll go to the fields to find you tender grass to refresh you, my Youssoufaki? You're all I had in the world; I didn't care a fig for anything people could do or say to me, I smiled as I listened because I knew that, when I got back home, I'd find you there waiting for me, and you'd turn those good eyes of yours toward me and wag your tail. And that we'd go off, the two of us, you in front, me behind, to do the round of the villages, buying and selling; earning our bread honestly, by the sweat of our two brows. What's going to become of you now, in the hands of the old skinflint who's spoiling to separate us? And me, what'll become of me, alone in the world? We're done for, my Youssoufaki; cursed be the wicked and their gold pieces, cursed be the unjust fate which made us poor. Good-bye, good-bye, my Youssoufaki . . ."

He bent down to embrace the velvety neck, passed his hand slowly, tenderly over the white and downy belly, reached the rump, pulled the tail and wept.

Youssoufaki, happy at his master's caresses, shook his head, raised his neck, lifted his tail and began braying softly.

There was a knock at the door; Yannakos jumped. But when he saw Michelis, fear vanished.

"Greetings, Michelis," he said, reassured. His eyes were red.

"What's the matter, Yannakos, are you crying?"

Yannakos, ashamed, wiped his eyes with the back of his hand.

"Must be second childhood," he said. "I was saying good-bye to my donkey. Father Ladas is claiming him, devil take him!"

"Got anything to eat?" asked Michelis; "I'm hungry. I left the mountain at dawn and it's nearly noon. After that—listen, Yannakos—I'll go straight off and find father Ladas. The donkey belongs to the Sarakini, he shan't take it!"

Yannakos shook his head; he had heard that the priest had already reached an understanding with the Agha, that he had written to the bishop and would not let Michelis touch the inheritance until a judgment had decided whether his signature was valid or not. The whole village was ready to bear false witness and say that the son of Patriarcheas was wanting in his wits.

"If he takes him from me," he said suddenly, "by the faith of Yannakos, I'll set fire to his place!"

He went into the house, prepared some poached eggs, brought bread, cheese and grapes. The rain had stopped; they sat down to eat in the courtyard, in front of the stable; beside them the ass, too, ate, well content.

"How nicely off we are here, the three of us!" sighed Yannakos. "And that old robber wants to separate us."

"I'm off to see him now," said Michelis, rising and wiping his mouth; "he shan't have him!"

Father Ladas and his wife were sitting cross-legged in front of the low table, lunching. Old Penelope had left the sock she was knitting on the stool close by her. She threw tiny mouthfuls into her mouth as into a hole, and chewed them slowly, dully, without a word. The old man was in a good humor; he pursued his monologue:

"All's going well, my dear, God be praised! The priest's a regular Devil in a cassock. He's got hold of the Agha and he's written to the bishop. You'll see, it won't be long before old Patriarcheas's properties fall into my hands. It's the community will have them, so they say! Pff! Don't you believe it, mother Penelope. I've fixed up everything with the priest. They'll be put up to auction; the priest will have his share; the swine, wanted to keep it all for himself, but you can imagine I didn't let him get away with that. We reached a compromise. In a few days, too, we shall have the ass that belongs to excommunicated Yannakos. He'll be yours, my Penelope, you'll get on his back to go pottering round our land. He's docile, well-trained and you must have seen his saddle, all covered with down—you'll sit on it like a queen! Being all alone—no children, no dogs—we've no overhead, my Penelope, we're king and queen. O dear, O dear, if I could live another hundred years or two, the whole of Lycovrissi would fall into my hands. And why do you think? Because they're all a lot of pretentious imbeciles, they all buy new clothes and shoes, they have children. All that costs a lot of money, and as money's round, it rolls. Whereas we . . . Your health, my Penelope!"

He filled his bowl with fresh water, emptied it, and smacked his tongue with pleasure.

"What's wine, compared with the water given by the good God?" he added.

Michelis pushed open the door without knocking and came in. At the sight of him, father Ladas frowned. He must be looking for a row, he told himself; I don't like the look of him. I'll act stupid.

"Welcome, my lord Michelis," he said. "Take a seat. I expect you've eaten."

Mother Penelope got up, cleared the table, picked up her sock and, sitting down in the corner, resumed her knitting.

"Old gobble-all," said Michelis, "what'll you do with all those fields, vineyards, olive orchards, houses and full coffers you've amassed? Take them with you into the tomb? With a foot in the grave already are you still not satisfied? And you now want to lay hands on poor Yannakos's ass as well. Have you no fear of God? Have you no shame before men?"

Faith, the old man said to himself, scratching his sugar-loaf head, I really do think he's already lost his wits. Still mixing up God in my affairs! I'll talk to him gently, or he might have a fit and let fly at me with his fist.

"My dear Michelis," he replied with sickly sweetness, "what can I do? Justice is justice. He owes me three gold pounds, what can I do? I, too, have needs."

"And if I made you out a paper saying that I owe them to you, and signed it?"

The old man coughed.

"The ill-natured gossips, my young archon, are saying, with all respect to you, that, for the moment, your signature . . . Don't get angry, in Christ's name! I don't believe a word of it, but we're only men—delicate machines, if a screw comes loose . . ."

Michelis leaped up. He picked up the stool he had been sitting on and threw it down. At this rate, he said to himself, they'll drive me really mad. He came close to the old man, and stared at him with eyes of flame.

Father Ladas cowered into a corner, clung to a window and looked into the yard. God be praised, he said to himself, the street door's open; if things go badly I'll slip past and out . . .

"If you could pay me in kind . . ." he whimpered.

"I'll go home and find you something, old scoundrel!" cried Michelis, hemming the old man in still closer. "Skinflint! Usurer! Swine!"

"Your father's house has had seals set on it today by the Agha," said the old man. He immediately bit his tongue. I've made a blunder, shouldn't have said that. He'll be furious! Here it comes, I'm done for!

Michelis clutched his head in his hands; he could feel it ready to burst.

"In the name of Christ," he cried, "you're driving me mad! Speak clearly, father Ladas; are they chasing me out of my father's house? Upon my word, I'll take a can of petrol, soak the village and set fire to it! Don't go, skinflint, where are you going? Come here, you swine!"

He rushed to lay hands on him, but the old man, with one bound, was already at the door. Michelis darted and caught him by the neck. The old man fell on his knees, squealing.

"Who did that? The priest? The Agha? You?"

"No, not me, it wasn't me, Michelis! Ask mother Penelope, I was shut up in my house. I just heard. Ask mother Penelope. Seems the Agha went there this morning with priest Grigoris. I was told the bishop's coming, too, from the town and bringing doctors."

"Doctors?" cried Michelis, his hair standing on end, "doctors?"

"Let me go, Michelis, don't grip me so tight. I'll tell you everything. Don't strangle me!"

Michelis lifted him by the scruff of the neck and set him on his feet again.

"Speak, old filth, tell me everything, everything!"

"Penelope, give me a bowl of water . . . I'm choking!"

But mother Penelope went on knitting, she heard nothing; she did not stir. She knitted and smiled, calm, motionless, dead.

"Let me shut the door, so the neighbors mayn't hear us," said the old man, and bounded out onto the road, where he set off running as fast as his legs could carry him, shouting:

"Help, villagers, help! Michelis is trying to strangle me!"

The terrified neighbors bolted their doors. Father Ladas went on running and shouting. The village was soon upside-down. He arrived at priest Grigoris's house; the priest appeared on his doorstep.

"Help, Father, he's having a fit, Michelis wants to strangle me! Let me in!"

But the priest, barring the door with his arms, kept him out.

"Run," he said, "call out, give the alarm to the whole village! There, go, father Ladas, let everyone hear, then they'll believe. There, off with you, run!"

And he shut the door in his face.

The rain had begun again. Father Ladas, alive to the priest's trick, ran all over the place, stopping at every corner and uttering shrill cries. He had picked up a piece of rope off the ground and displayed it:

"Michelis came to strangle me, here's the rope! Help, brothers! Someone open his door and let me in! Michelis is coming, he's got a can of petrol!"

As soon as a door opened, he went off at a run and did his shouting a bit farther on.

"He's taken a can of petrol to set everything on fire! Help! Help!"

The village was soon in an uproar. Some took down their old guns, posted themselves behind their door and waited. The Agha emerged onto his balcony.

"Let two robust men go and arrest him! Where's Panayotaros?"

Panayotaros came hurrying:

"At your service, Agha!"

The Agha threw him a rope.

"Here, go and tie him up and bring him to me! And wait, listen:

from today I'm taking you into my service, Panayotaros. You're fiery, robust, snarling like a mastiff. Just what I need. Wait while I throw you down the fez my old guard used to wear, curse him! You will wear it from now on. Go, and good luck!"

He turned, took down the fez from its hook and threw it.

"There, my friend, may it bring you luck!"

Then, to Brahimaki, who was sitting behind, smoking lazily and blowing out clouds of smoke through his nose:

"My little Brahimaki, it looks to me as if they've driven him mad in good earnest, the poor fellow!"

"When are they bringing me the women?" said the colt, warming up. "By Mahomet, I'm not far from going crazy myself!"

Panayotaros caught the rope and the fez, then made for father Ladas's house.

But Michelis had left long ago. He ran through the least frequented lanes, afraid of being seen by the inhabitants. The doors closed as he passed; the women screamed with fear.

When he reached the path to the mountain, he slowed down, out of breath. Rain was still falling, fine and close. The mountain was enveloped in a light mist, the plain covered with water. Michelis slid under a rock to wait for it to clear. His mouth was parched. He stared at the rain and listened to the murmur of the water flowing and cascading from rock to rock. Gradually his thought began running with the water and descended to the plain. It, too, rolled, increased, swelled, received tributaries from all sides, became a cataract, flooded the village. Michelis's breast dilated. Living and dead emerged from the earth under the rain, covered with mud; they left the plain with solemn step and climbed straight toward him. At their head was marching a dead man, tall in stature and very fat, with his belly swollen like a gourd, greenish blue: the archon. It was like a Last Judgment. The angels had sounded the trumpet; the human worms were emerging from the mire.

A few days before, Michelis had read the Apocalypse, and his mind was peopled with angels, trumpets, prostitutes sailing the waters of seas with foaming shores, horsemen on black, green, red and white horses swimming in blood. Michelis stared at the rain, listened to the water; his temples throbbed; it seemed to him that the earth was crumbling away. It was beginning to get dark, the rain went on, sad and regular, determined to drown the world and gnaw away the earth.

"O God, Thou only art immovable," murmured Michelis, and his eyes filled with tears. "If Thou didst not exist, to what should a man cling when everything is disappearing, dissolving and lapsing away? The woman he loves? The father who begot him? Men? Everything withers, crumbles, slides. Thou alone, O God, remainest there, stable. Let me lean upon Thee! Hold me tight, O God, my reason is tottering!"

In the grotto priest Fotis and Manolios had been anxiously waiting for Michelis for long hours.

"It will be a hard struggle to win this, Father," said Manolios. "Is it worth while to waste so much time over this life here below?"

"It is worth while, it is worth while, Manolios!" replied priest Fotis decidedly. "There was a time when I, too, used to say: 'Why struggle for this life here below? What does this world matter to me? I am an exile from Heaven and I yearn to go home to my country? But later I understood. No one can go to heaven unless he has first been victorious upon earth, and no one can be victorious upon earth if he does not struggle against it with fire, with patience, without resting. Man has only earth for a springboard if he would fly up to Heaven. All the priest Grigorises, the Ladases, the Aghas, the big proprietors, are the forces of evil which it has been allotted us to combat. If we throw down our arms, we're lost, here below on earth and up there in the sky."

"Michelis is too delicate, too used to an easy life, he will not be able . . . "

"He can. Let us wait for the news he'll bring us this evening. If it's bad, I'll go off tomorrow and find the bishop and ask him to give us justice. Winter's coming, it mustn't catch us naked, starving and without shelter."

"If I could give my blood to save the souls in peril . . ." Manolios murmured.

"It is easier to give it once for all than drop by drop in the daily struggle. If I were asked what is the way that leads to Heaven, I would answer: 'The hardest.' So take it, Manolios; courage!"

Manolios said nothing. He felt that the priest was right, but he was impatient. He could not forget the superhuman joy he had experienced as he went, that day, to give his life. That flame had not gone out, it was still there in him, distant as a Paradise lost. The daily struggle seemed to him slow and dull.

Both of them listened in silence to the rain falling. Sometimes a flash tore the dusk, penetrated the grotto, and lit up two pale faces, a neck, an arm; then all returned to darkness.

Suddenly they heard hurried steps on the stones.

"It's Michelis!" cried Manolios, darting out.

The two friends embraced in the dusk and went into the grotto.

"Welcome, our Michelis," said priest Fotis; "what news are you bringing us from Lycovrissi?"

"That my signature is worth nothing, that the Agha has had seals put on my father's house, that doctors are coming to pronounce that I am mad. Lastly, that Mariori is dying. There's my news! You've no call for complaint! I've brought you your money's worth, God be praised!"

He slid to the ground and leaned his back against the rock. After a short silence, he resumed, trying to joke:

"You've no call to complain, I've not come empty-handed."

"We're not complaining," priest Fotis answered, rising. "That's what it means to be a *man*: to suffer, undergo injustices and struggle without giving ground! We shall not give ground, Michelis. Tomorrow I'll go to the town and struggle."

Michelis shook his head.

"Do as God inspires you, Father. I'm giving up, I can't do any more. For a moment, down there, rage took hold of me. I wanted to strangle father Ladas, flood the village with petrol and set fire to it. But immediately, as if I'd done it, I felt tired, discouraged. I was frightened, and I fled."

"Let us do the struggling, Michelis," said Manolios, gripping his friend's arm in the shadow. He could feel it was burning hot.

The rain had stopped and priest Fotis stood up.

"Good night," he said. "I shall retire and prepare for tomorrow. We'll leave early, Manolios."

He disappeared in the night.

"How painful life is," sighed Michelis. "Do me a favor, Manolios. Tomorrow, since you are going to the town, go and see Mariori and take her my greetings. That's all."

He lay down on his mattress and shut his eyes, expecting again to see his father appear.

Next day, all the way there, priest Fotis and Manolios exchanged only a few words. The sky was overcast, but it was no longer raining. Nonetheless, after yesterday's deluge, they waded in mud, barefoot; they made headway painfully, in single file.

They went through fertile lands covered with trees and vines, sometimes spread out in a wide plain, sometimes undulating. Finally the clouds ravelled out, the sun returned, a band of tender blue sky appeared, sparkling with freshness. On an eminence two ancient marble columns shone out white.

"All these lands belonged to us Greeks once," sighed Manolios.

Priest Fotis stopped a moment, gazed at the two broken columns and crossed himself as though he were passing in front of the ruins of a church. His spirit flared up, but he said nothing.

They went on in silence with their poor wallets on their shoulders, the priest in a patched cassock, Manolios in clothes of coarse cloth.

Where they went through a village the dogs barked at their passing, doors opened, heads appeared, eyes stared at them, people now and then addressed them a kind word, a "Welcome! where are you going? good luck!" Then at once the doors shut and the two emissaries of poverty found themselves once again alone on the deserted road.

At midday they stopped at the foot of a poplar to have something to eat and restore their strength. They came up to two stones, they sat down. Aromatic plants—savory, thyme, peppermint, pennyroyal, sage—had been beaten by yesterday's strong rain and were fragrant. It cleared and a huge rainbow hung in the sky.

Priest Fotis contemplated the splendor of earth and heaven after the rain, and a broad smile relaxed his pale, grave face.

"One day," he said, "at the Holy Mountain, I asked an ascetic, Father Sofronios, who lived in a hermitage a long way from his monastery, on the top of a precipice: 'How did you find the way of salvation, Father Sofronios?' 'Do I know, my son?' he replied; 'it happened like that, without my noticing it. I got up one morning; it had rained during the night; I looked out of the window. That's all.' 'Is that all, Father Sofronios?' 'What more do you want, my son? I saw God from my window.' Since then, every time I get up early and see the earth after the rain, I remember the old ascetic with emotion. He must have rendered his soul to God a long time ago and be walking about in Paradise. Perhaps, for his pleasure, God even makes it rain at night in Paradise."

Manolios shivered: these words of priest Fotis's gave to the

soaked earth the highest meaning it can take on, and Manolios's
heart was all refreshed.

"Thank you, Father," he said, after some seconds of deep
silence. "I look for God in the great difficult moments; you show
Him to me in each moment that passes. I seek Him in violent
death; you make me see Him in the humble struggle of every day.
I have only just understood why we are going to the town and with
whom we are going to struggle when we get there."

"One never finds what one is seeking, my son. We shall find God
where we are going. And we shall find Him not as He is represented
by those who have never seen Him—a rosy-cheeked old man,
sitting blissfully on woolly clouds—but in the form of a voice
sprung from our inmost being to declare war: yesterday it was
against priest Grigoris and against Ladas, today it's against the
bishop, tomorrow we shall see. War always, the holy war, my son."

They started walking again and reached the town at twilight.
From afar they saw domes, mosques and two minarets soaring
skyward, full of strength and grace. As they passed through the
gate in the ramparts, they heard the voice of the muezzin calling,
imperatively and gently, the faithful to prayer.

The moslem town spread out before them—narghiles; beys
squatting on mats; chubby boys with young girls' slender voices,
playing the tambourine and singing *amanés*; women with long
veils; fat barefoot Turks crying their merchandise; cakes fried
in oil and grilled grains of maize.

The two travelers lodged in a Christian *khan*,* full to bursting—
on the ground floor, with donkeys and mules, on the first floor,
a great room with straw mattresses ranged in two long rows.
Priest Fotis knew the innkeeper, father Yerassimos, boisterous
and shrewd as the devil; he was an old sea captain; he had anchored
in this land-locked town and married late in life a fine slip of a girl
of Asia Minor, had children by her and opened this *khan*. His wife
did the cooking, and he busied himself with the men and animals,
with a blow here and a joke there, jovially. He was bald, and had an
enormous belly which, he said, prevented him from bending over
and knowing whether he was man or woman.

As soon as he caught sight of priest Fotis, he left his counter
and ran to meet him.

"What good wind?" he shouted joyfully; "just the man I was

* Inn

needing, priest. I've again committed a grave sin; there's a carrier forgot his purse here the other day, full of gold pieces, and I returned it to him. And ever since that day my soul's been upset; that means she's sinned, poor thing, and is dying of grief!"

But priest Fotis was not in a mood for joking.

"We shall stay here two days, father Yerassimos. Serve us something to eat and give us two clean mattresses to sleep on. We haven't any money; you'll note down what we spend; I'll pay you some day, captain, don't worry."

"Who spoke to you of money, Father?" said the old sailor with a loud laugh. "If you haven't any, the fat traders who come and lodge at the *khan* have. I'll take twice as much off them: that way I'll be paid, and handsomely. And besides, if I find a purse I won't give it back. Welcome to you both! This evening we'll eat together. You're not my customers, you're my guests. Hey, Kronstallenia!"

A robust Oriental woman with big blue-ringed eyes, came out from the kitchen with a pan in her hand.

"Kiss the priest's hand," father Yerassimos ordered; "I shall be eating with him and his friend this evening. You know what that means, eh? Pork cutlets!"

Dame Kronstallenia swaggered up, kissed the priest's hand and went back toward the kitchen.

"And where are you off to, wife?" cried the joyful husband; "no one's going to eat you, stay a little and let's have a look at you!"

He added, with a wink at priest Fotis:

"Tell us, how many pears will go into a bag?"

"Aren't you ashamed, at your age!" said the innkeeper's pretty wife, laughing and disappearing into her kitchen.

Yerassimos laughed loudly.

"Well, well, what a thing woman is, Father, all the same! I don't know what the Holy Scriptures say, but I'm sure, myself, of one thing: God made Man and the Devil made Woman. And if you want to know why: I asked everyone how many pears would go into the bag, and no one knew. My wife, the sly hussy, knew: 'Two,' she answered me, 'two!' Hear that? Devil's own female! She got the bull's eye!"

Next morning priest Fotis, having crossed himself, set off barefoot for the bishop's palace. A plump young peasant girl **opened** the door to him; she looked at his empty hands and made a face. "You're too early," she said; "my lord isn't awake yet." Priest Fotis sat down on a bench in the courtyard and waited.

Gradually other visitors turned up: men and women, each bringing an offering—a basket of eggs, a rabbit, a bowl of cheese, a cock. The young peasant girl took them, smiling, and carrried them into the house. Then she offered a chair or a stool, according to the importance of the present.

"It's his niece," whispered a little old man sitting next to priest Fotis.

After an hour the news went from mouth to mouth that the bishop had awakened. One person had heard him cough, another thought he could make out the gurgling of his morning gargle.

All turned furtive eyes toward the window with the closed shutters. A loud cough rang out; then came the noise of impressive ablutions; then dull groans; finally a clatter of water being emptied out.

"Now he's washing," said the old man. All were silent, to listen to the sacred beast washing.

A quarter of an hour later there was a din of cups, plates, forks, knives and chairs being dragged about.

"Now he's having his coffee . . ."

Another half hour went by, then shrill cries rang out, accompanied by sobs.

"Now he's punishing his niece . . ."

Not long afterward the creaking of stairs could be heard, and someone blowing his nose violently.

"He's coming down!" the old man said at last, rising. All did the same and turned their gaze toward the door. A powerful bass voice shouted:

"Anghelika, have the first comer in!"

The door opened and the young peasant appeared, with red eyes. She signed to priest Fotis, who stepped forward and went into the house. The door closed behind him.

The bishop was seated before a round table. He was a thickset, vigorous man with a short, gray finely curled beard and a wart on his nose. He looked like a rhinoceros.

"I'm listening," he said, "be brief. I think I've seen you before; aren't you the refugee? Speak."

For a second priest Fotis felt a desire to go out, slamming the door. Was that the representative of Christ? Was it that creature who taught men justice and love? Could he expect him to recognize his rights? But he controlled himself, thought of the children on the Sarakina and the coming winter, and opened his mouth to speak; but the bishop stopped him with a gesture.

"Another time, when you come to the bishop's palace, you will wear shoes."

"I haven't any," priest Fotis answered; "I had, but I haven't now; excuse me. Christ also walked barefoot, my lord."

The bishop frowned.

"Priest Grigoris has spoken to me of you," he growled, shaking his head threateningly. "It seems you want to play Jesus Christ before us, establish equality and justice in this world. Aren't you ashamed? There's to be no rich and poor any more, and of course no bishops. Rebel!"

The priest's temples began to throb, he clenched his fist; but once more he remembered, kept calm and remained mute.

"Did you pass out of the Constantinople Seminary?"

"No, my lord."

"Then you've a right to speak! I shall not argue with you, priest. You came to ask me a favor, what do you want? Be quick about it, there are others waiting. And mind what you say."

"I've not come to ask any favor, my lord. I've come to ask for justice."

"You've a very insolent look on your face. Lower your eyes when you speak to me."

Priest Fotis looked about him. He saw behind the bishop's back an icon of Christ on the cross, then a bookcase with books in gilt bindings. A picture, larger than the icon, portrayed my lord in his gold-figured bishop's robe, with a glittering miter on his head and a gilded cross in his hand. The bishop showed annoyance at his silence.

"Priest," he said, "either you speak, or you go. I've no time to waste."

"Neither have I, my lord; I'm going. I meant to ask for justice, but now I understand and I shall appeal to Him!" he said, pointing to Christ crucified.

"To whom?" said the bishop, turning.

"To Christ crucified."

This time the bishop came off his hinges. He banged the table with his fist:

"He's right, priest Grigoris is: you're a bolshevik!"

"Yes, if He is, too!" retorted the priest, pointing again to the crucified.

"Anghelika!" the bishop called.

The niece appeared.

"Another time, if this priest comes back—take a good look at him—you will not let him in."

"God will judge us, my lord bishop, do not worry. On that day we shall appear both of us before Him barefoot," said priest Fotis, unperturbed. He opened the door and went out without a work of leave taking.

For hours he wandered through the streets; he went into the mat-shaded market, paused in the courtyard of a mosque, crossed a donkey-back bridge, lost his way in some gardens and once more slipped in among the lanes. He looked about him but saw nothing. His boiling brain exhaled vapors which confused his sight. He thought of the bishop, of the children on the Sarakina, and of the approaching winter.

He was surprised to find himself in front of father Yerassimos's *khan*. He went in. Manolios was not there.

"The bird's flown!" announced the innkeeper; "he went out early to take a walk."

Priest Fotis sat down, as exhausted as if he were back from the other end of the world. Leaning his back against the wall, he shut his eyes and sighed.

Manolios, faithful to his promise, had gone to Mariori's bedside. He looked at her. She was asleep, and he waited, motionless, for her to wake up. The more he looked at her, the more his heart tightened. She was only the shadow of herself; two great blue rings surrounded her eyelids; her stretched and parchment skin stuck to her bones; one could feel that Death had already begun to lick her face.

Mariori heaved a sigh, opened her eyes; she recognized Manolios.

"Good day, Manolios," she said; "did he send you?"

"Yes, Mariori, Michelis did."

"Have you a message for me from him?"

"Yes, Mariori, his greetings."

"Is that all?"

"That's all."

Mariori smiled bitterly.

"What else could I expect, now?" she said; "greetings will do for me."

She turned her head away to hide her tears.

"Manolios, I've got a message, too," she said, "for him."

Groping under her pillow, she found a pair of scissors.

"Help me up."

Manolios raised her in his arms, arranged the pillow behind her and laid her carefully on her back again.

Mariori took off her kerchief, untied the black silk ribbon which bound her chestnut tresses, and made ready to cut them; but her strength failed her, she could not manage it.

"I can't," she said, "I can't, Manolios. Help me."

"You want to cut them?" said Manolios in alarm.

"Cut them off!" she said, feebly.

Manolios, trembling, took the young girl's warm tresses in his hand.

"Cut them off!" Mariori repeated.

Manolios cut the first tress, then the second, shuddering as if he were carving into living flesh.

Mariori took the long tresses and stared at them for a long time. They filled her hands. She shook her despoiled head painfully. She could control herself no longer: she was shaken with sobs. She bent over them, wiped her eyes upon them, then wrapped them gently in her kerchief as though she were swaddling the corpse of a beloved child, knotted the corners and handed them to Manolios.

"Take them," she said, "you will give them to him and say to him: 'Mariori sends greetings.' That is all."

But the Flesh . . .

A LL'S GOING WELL, very well," soliloquized priest Fotis on the
return journey, as he waded through the mud; "all's going perfectly, God be praised!"

Behind him came Manolios, bent double with the burden of the
two tresses in his sack, just as if he had been carrying a dead
woman on his back.

The sky darkened, there were claps of thunder, and heavy rain
began to fall.

"All's going well, couldn't be better!" priest Fotis still muttered,
as he hastened his pace.

He said not a word more. With his face lashed by the rain, he
went on, almost at a run. A flock of cranes passed overhead; he did
not even raise his eyes to look at them; he began running.

It was not until, at the approach of evening, the sharp crest of
the Sarakina came in sight, that he turned to Manolios.

"We'll struggle, Manolios," he said in tones of decision. "On
one side, all men—bishops, priests, notables, a blind tribe. On the
other, us, two or three beggars with Christ in front. Hold firm,
Manolios, we shall conquer!"

He resumed his stride, wading through the mud, and laughed.

"Why wasn't I wearing shoes! I bet Caiaphas put the same
question to Christ."

They were beginning to climb the slopes of the Sarakina.

Michelis, during those two days, had been wandering like a soul
in agony. He dared not go and lie down. Sleep had only to lay hold
of him for his father to appear to him, completely naked, with
reproachful gaze.

"If I stay here alone a few days longer I believe I shall lose my
reason once and for all," he told himself in alarm.

He took his great Gospel book and opened it, hoping to chase away the atrocious vision by reading; but the letters danced, he could not stop them. Shutting the book, he began once more striding up and down the grotto from end to end.

That day, at twilight, the schoolmaster had paid him a visit. He had come, so he said, to keep him company. He had spoken to him of his father, of his fiancée, of the approaching winter, of the luckless people on the Sarakina, wondering how they would stand the bad season. Then he had got into severer subjects—what is life, what is death, what is man's duty. Michelis answered him reluctantly, absently, impatient to be alone once more. The schoolmaster looked him in the eyes. Suddenly Michelis realized, and leaped up furiously.

"Schoolmaster," he said, "did you come to verify whether I am mad?"

"What do you mean, Michelis?" the schoolmaster protested, blushing.

"I know: you're an honest man, and your conscience no longer lets you rest; you came this evening to make sure whether your brother, the priest, is a liar and a criminal? What's your conclusion, your own, Hadji Nikolis, the honest man?"

The schoolmaster was silent.

"In all honesty, coward soul," Michelis muttered, looking at the schoolmaster with compassion, "in all honesty you daren't reply, soft soul."

"No, no," said the schoolmaster in a low voice, "I daren't . . ."

"If they insist, will you tell the truth?"

"Yes, I think; but they're sure not to ask me anything."

"And if they don't ask you, won't you stand up of your own accord, to cry out the truth?"

The schoolmaster coughed, but remained silent.

"No," he answered in the end, full of shame.

Michelis was sorry for him, but his anger still possessed him.

"Is that what you teach the children?" he shouted at him, "are you what's been found for forming the new generation?"

The schoolmaster rose; he seemed extremely tired.

"The spirit is willing," he said, "but the flesh . . ."

"If the spirit were really willing, it wouldn't worry about the flesh. Doesn't it do what it likes with it?"

Michelis felt, deep down inside himself, that the reason why he had got into such a rage was that he was like the schoolmaster. He was only speaking to him with this harshness the better to scourge and cover with shame his own soul.

"Why are the wicked the more powerful in this world?" Michelis went on, "why are the good so weak? Can you explain me that, wise man?"

"No, I can't."

After a moment he added: "You've covered me with shame, Michelis, and you had a right to do so. But my brother, the priest, is stronger than I. He's always been the stronger; he used to beat me when we were little. Even now I haven't the strength to resist him. If he weren't there, perhaps . . ."

Michelis hesitated a moment.

"Listen," he said to him, dully, "doesn't there ever come into your mind, Hadji Nikolis, a horrible temptation—to kill him?"

The schoolmaster jumped with terror.

"Sometimes . . . sometimes," he whispered; "not often, only in dreams."

Hardly had he pronounced those words when he regretted it bitterly. Put out at having had his secret guessed, he made for the opening of the grotto. It was still raining; the darkness was profound.

"I'm going," he said, "good evening."

"It's pitch dark, schoolmaster," said Michelis sarcastically, "go, have no fear, no one will see that you've been to the Sarakina to bring back a report to the priest, your brother. Keep well!"

As he reached the foot of the mountain the schoolmaster thought he saw two men coming up. He quickly hid behind a rock. As soon as they had gone by, he staggered back onto the path.

Michelis is right, he told himself, exasperated against himself; yes, yes, my brother is an impostor; and I'm only a poor little whipster, honest, oh, yes, but a coward . . . But I'm going to take my courage in both hands; I shall go and find the priest this very evening. I shall shout out the truth to his face, and may God come to my aid!

In front of the grotto Michelis waited dully and anxiously for priest Fotis and Manolios. As soon as he saw them his heart became firmer. He was not alone, the world was again at peace, and the dead man had disappeared.

"Welcome," he said, "the solitude was heavy."

"The journey, too, was heavy, my son," said priest Fotis, "but God was with us and lent us wings."

In a few words he told how he had seen the bishop and what they had said to each other.

"So it's war?" said Michelis, frightened.

"War!" priest Fotis asserted; "the holy war First it was the Turks and their aghas; now it's our own people, the rich ones and the notables. They are the more mischievous. But Christ, the supreme beggar, is with us."

He turned toward Manolios.

"For Christ, believe me, is not always as you carved Him in the wood one day, Manolios: kindly, easy, pacific, turning the other cheek when He receives a blow. He is also a resolute warrior, who advances followed by all the disinherited of the earth. 'Think not that I am come to send peace on earth: I came not to send peace, but a sword!' Whose words are those? Christ's. Henceforward the face of our Christ is like that, Manolios!"

The priest's eyes burned in the depths of the grotto, like two red-hot coals.

After a pause he resumed:

"I am happy, my children, happy that we have such a leader. It's good to be a sheep, but when you are hemmed in by wolves, it's better to be a lion."

Someone called at the entrance of the grotto; they could see the glow of a face and two outstretched hands.

"Who's there?" cried Michelis, in alarm.

Under the rain, in the dark, full of anger and grief, the voice of Yannakos arose:

"Me, brothers! I've left that dirty village, I've come to take refuge on your mountain."

"Welcome, Yannakos!" cried all three, their arms wide open.

"What's happened to you, Yannakos?" Manolios asked him, "what brings you here at such an hour, through the pouring rain?"

Yannakos seized the hand of priest Fotis and kissed it tenderly.

"I heard your last words, Father, and I agree! 'It's good to be a sheep, but when you're hemmed in by wolves it's better to be a lion.' "

He twisted his dripping hair, put his bundle on the ground and sat down on top of it. They all fell silent.

At last Yannakos said:

"This evening Panayotaros, the new bodyguard, came to see me, bearing a paper with the Agha's seal; he's taken away my ass on the excuse that I owed something to that swine Ladas . . ."

He could not help crying, but quickly pulled himself together and, rising to his feet:

"One night I'll go and set fire to his damned house; yes, by Christ, fire!" he shouted.

"No, not all alone; be patient, Yannakos," said the priest. "We'll all go down together!"

"Has the hour come?" asked Yannakos impatiently.

"It is not far off, it is approaching. That is why I propose that from tomorrow the women and children should learn how to use a sling. We must be prepared."

So saying he went to the opening.

"That's sufficient for this evening, my sons," he said. "Today, men have made us drink all kinds of poison. That's enough of that. It's time to go and sleep; let slumber heal our wounds so that we may be ready to receive others tomorrow. Come, Yannakos, you shall share my poor cell with me; I'm glad to see you among us!"

Yannakos picked up his bundle again and followed the priest.

The two friends were left alone. Michelis turned to Manolios and took his hand:

"Well?" he asked in a low voice.

Manolios pulled the girl's kerchief out of his sack.

"With Mariori's greetings."

Michelis gazed at the sad present and felt it with a trembling hand; he understood. He untied the two long tresses, buried his face in them and began to weep abundantly and to cover them with kisses.

He remained like this a long time; then, raising his head:

"She is dying?" he asked.

Manolios did not answer.

The schoolmaster, having taken his heart in both hands, had gone to find priest Grigoris. Michelis's words had increased his shame and raised his courage. For the first time in his life he was resolved to resist his brother.

The priest was at table; he had dined well, the cooking had been good, the wine excellent; having lit a cigarette he was smoking blissfully. The day before, the Agha had sent word to him that his request had been fulfilled—he had driven away the Sarakini and had seals placed on the house of Patriarcheas. It was only right that, in his turn, he should grant the favor which Brahimaki was asking. For some days and nights the priest had been vainly turning the position over and over in his mind: he could think of no young girl who could be suggested to the Agha without provoking a scandal. And lo and behold, this evening he had found the solution, as he smoked his cigarette.

The thing's in the bag, he muttered, pouring himself out a drop of wine. A divine inspiration! Upon my faith, the girl will do very well, she'll ask nothing better, no one will say a word, the Agha will be pleased, we shall have him on our side. God be praised!

At this moment the schoolmaster came in.

"Good evening, Nikolis," said the priest without getting up. "Where've you come from? You're all covered with mud."

"From the Sarakina!" replied the schoolmaster bravely.

The priest moved uneasily in his chair.

"What did you want to go into that frightful wasps' nest for? Don't you know that Sarakina and Lycovrissi are at daggers drawn?"

Courage, schoolmaster! said Hadji Nikolis to himself; now's the moment! Show that you are a worthy son of Alexander the Great!

"I went to see Michelis," he said, taking the plunge. "I wanted to see for myself whether he was really mad, yes or no."

"Ah!" growled the priest, "you wanted to see for yourself! Well?"

"I talked with him for an hour on all sorts of subjects, big and little."

"Well?"

"He's perfectly sane."

At these words the priest jumped up.

"Mind your own business, schoolmaster," he shouted, "don't meddle in other people's affairs! Did I tell you to go there? What's bitten you?"

"I had a weight on my conscience," the schoolmaster murmured, "I was doubtful, it's not right."

"Is it for you to tell me what's right, idiot! Michelis is mad, that's what's right!"

"But he isn't," ventured the schoolmaster.

"He is, I tell you! You see no farther than the end of your nose, you can't see beyond individuals; I don't bother about individuals, I only care for the whole; I am the leader of a people, I am. Understand, triple dolt?"

The schoolmaster said nothing.

"When an individual suffers an injustice and this injustice is profitable to the whole, then it is just that he should suffer this injustice! But your brain's much too small to take that in!"

He paused in front of his brother, who was listening with bent head.

"If you're asked, that is what you must say. If you can't, then keep quiet!"

"I'll keep quiet," said the schoolmaster, rising, "but deep down inside myself . . ."

The priest gave a sardonic laugh.

"Inside you, whatever you like, I don't care a fig; inside you, absolute liberty. But outside, look out for yourself!"

In a milder voice he added:

"You're my younger brother; we're brothers, Nikolis; remember that in front of people we must be of the same opinion—mine, d'you hear?"

The schoolmaster wanted to cry out: "Till when? I, too, have a soul, I can't agree with you, I won't subscribe to injustice, I'll go to the village square and shout at the top of my voice!" But, in place of all that, he made for the door and said:

"Good night!"

"The gall! Him!" grumbled the priest as he emptied his glass; "An opinion of his own, the nincompoop!"

He folded his napkin, crossed himself, thanked God for giving men food and drink in such abundance, then went to bed, saying to himself:

"Tomorrow, at crack of dawn, I'll send for Martha."

Early next morning Martha arrived, bent double and cursing. What can that goat-beard want with me at peep of dawn, just the moment when that cursed bastard will be waking up and shouting: "I want this, I want that," without knowing in the least what he does want, like a woman with child. Be on your guard, old woman; don't forget, you poor wretch, that the Devil's behind everything the goat-beard says, and you mustn't fall into the trap!

When she came in, the priest was sitting cross-legged on his little sofa, sipping his coffee. His eyes were still swollen with slumber.

Martha bowed to the ground, kissed the priest's hand and, withdrawing into a corner, folded her arms.

The priest was turning over and over in his mind what he wanted to say to her, not knowing where to begin.

"You, mother Martha," he said at last, "will one day enter Paradise with your body fashioned straight as a candle. Through all the years you've been in the service of the Turk, you've still not forgotten Christianity, and when we Christians are in a great difficulty, it's you we call for. That's why I've summoned you today, my good Martha."

Devil's own priest, said the hunchback to herself, there he goes, preparing his trap. He's already put the cheese in and set the spring. Eyes open, my poor Martha, don't walk in!

"Father," she said, "your words are the words of God; at your orders."

"You know that Brahimaki is demanding a woman; he wants the young girls of the village to dance before him so that he may take his pick, the hound! That is a great shame, death would be better. Isn't that so, Martha?"

"Death would be better!" the old hunchback confirmed.

"Yet on the other hand one must not quarrel with the Agha," the priest went on; "in the interest of the community it is better to have him with us. Well, the Agha has declared explicitly: 'If you do not find a woman for Brahimaki, I shall declare war on the community! Do you understand, mother Martha? We should be ruined! So what's to be done? Find a woman for Brahimaki or condemn the community to ruin? What do you think, mother Martha?"

"Let the community go to its ruin!" replied the old woman, sure in advance that that was also the priest's opinion.

"What did you say, Martha? God preserve us! Let the community go to its ruin? Let Christianity be ruined! Lord, have mercy on us! No, no, my good Martha, come, think it over!"

"I've thought it over," said Martha immediately. "Let a woman be found for him!"

"Bravo, that's what I expected of you, my child. You know the kind he wants? Well-fleshed, white as the best bread, and innocent."

"Well-fleshed, white as the best bread, innocent. Hm, what do you expect me to say, Father? I don't know any."

"Come, think a little, my daughter, if you want to oblige me."

"What am I to say, Father? I've been through the lot of them in my mind; one's fat and innocent, but not white, another's white and innocent, but not fat . . ."

"D'you know who I thought of? Pelaghia, Panayotaros's elder daughter, and I'll tell you why . . ."

"But she's not white, Father; if you want to know, they call her 'Darkie,' or even 'Blackie' . . ."

"That doesn't matter, my good woman. That'll be all right. I'll give you a box of powder, she'll rub her face with it morning and evening and become as white as the best bread."

"In that case, Father, it'll go quite smoothly."

"But she—do you think she'll be willing?"

"She? But, Father, nothing can stop her! She's a female Brahimaki; only Brahimaki's a man, he shows it, while Pelaghia's a woman and hides it. Whatever will happen when those two fetch up together in bed! They'll bring the house down on my head!"

The old hunchback woman grinned and wiped her running nose with the back of her sleeve.

"That'll do. There," said the priest severely; "don't go jumping to the worst. We'd do better, both of us, to think what's the best way of arranging things. Panayotaros has become the Agha's guard. So nobody will be astonished if Pelaghia comes to the Agha's, under color of visiting her father. You'll be able to manage, Martha; you're an expert on that sort of thing. When she comes, of course, Brahimaki must see her. But before he does, you must have taken her the powder."

He rose and opened a small cupboard, from which he took out a box of powder.

"There!" he said, placing it in Martha's outstretched hands. "Tell her she can mix it with a little flour, for economy."

The old woman shook her head. She saw what the priest was pushing her into, and hesitated.

She made up her mind at last and retorted:

"All that's very well, Father, but one thing's been forgotten, the most important . . ."

"What, Martha?"

"Suppose Panayotaros found out? First, he'd kill me; then Brahimaki; after that, your holiness. And to end up, he'd set fire to the village, you'd better realize!"

The priest scratched his head.

"You're right," he said. "He might kill me, too. But since it's got to be done, what are we to do? Ah! I've got an idea! I'll tell the Agha to send Panayotaros on a round."

"And suppose she became pregnant?"

"Who?"

"Who d'you suppose, Father? Pelaghia . . ."

"That'll do! you talk of nothing but misfortunes, you dirty old woman!" cried the priest, exasperated. "She won't."

"How do you know?"

"God is great," replied the priest, who did not know what to answer.

"Hm . . ." said the old hunchback, "do you think the good God busies Himself with such dirty doings, Father?"

"All right; well, you will fix it up with Mandalenia. She knows herbs."

Get thee behind me, Satan, muttered the old hunchback in an aside, is the blessed priest God's representative or the Devil's?

"What are you thinking, my child?"

"You are God's representative, Father; that's all I want to say. Do what you think best."

"I am striving for the food of Christianity, mother Martha. God knows. He will bring us His aid and all will go well. Come, courage, child, your pains will not remain unrewarded."

The old woman opened her round eyes wide: Goat-beard, she thought, that's how you should have started.

"Very good," she concluded, "it's as much as my life's worth, but I'll do what I can. On your side, let your holiness do all you can. I'm a poor, miserable woman, all alone."

"Don't worry, mother, you shan't lose by it. Run along now, and good luck, we'll talk again. I'm there, trust me!"

The old woman bowed and kissed the priest's hand.

"Give me your blessing, Father," said she. "I understand what you want; and you understand what I want. I'll go, today as ever is, and see Pelaghia. She'll jump with joy, the holy female."

"God be with you, run along and hurry up and bring me good news."

He patted her on the shoulder, then on the hump, protectively.

"And to your wedding, mother Martha," he said, "I'll unearth a good lad for you, too—but for the good reason, eh, ending in marriage, and let you escape from the hands of the Turk. Run along!"

"Do the best you can, Father, be kind to me, I'm alone in the world," said the old woman with emotion; "do, Father, and may God reward you!"

With these words she went out, wiping her nose, which was beginning to run again.

The old fool, muttered the priest, as soon as she had shut the door; she believed it! What a mystery Woman is, God preserve us!

He waited a day, two days, on tenterhooks. On the third day the door opened. Panayotaros entered, wearing his new scarlet fez. At the sight of him the priest started.

"What's happening, Panayotaros?" he said, rising.

"The Agha's sent me, Father."

"What did he bid you tell me?"

"It beats me. I don't understand. He sends his greetings and I'm to tell you that Brahimaki's become quieter than a lamb."

The Wolves Do Their Own Hunting

WINTER ARRIVED SUDDENLY. Nature took on a hostile air. The rain began to fall, an icy wind blew from the mountains, the leaves grew yellow and strewed the ground. In the earth the seeds were bathed in water, swelled, filled with juice, prepared to put forth their shoots in the spring. The lizards lodged in their holes, the bees shut themselves up in their hives, the bats hung in clusters in the eaves. All creation withdrew to wait.

The Lycovrissi came home early to warm themselves at the corner of the hearth. They brought out from their store rooms the corn, oil and wine which they had harvested and which enabled them all through the winter to have abundance of food and drink. The oil lamps gave light to the women spinning or knitting and to pass the time, telling each other legends old as the world or wanton stories.

Nikolio had brought his sheep into the fold and now remained near the fireplace, knee to knee beside Lenio. She had already spun a great pile of wool and was busy on clothes and bonnets for the baby; her belly was growing round and Nikolio looked at her as peasants look when rain comes to land well plowed and well sown.

"We'll call him George," said Lenio, "George, after his grandfather, old Patriarcheas."

"No, we'll call him Haridimos, after my father," insisted Nikolio.

"No, I tell you, we'll call him George."

"It's the husband to command, we'll call him Haridimos."

And about this they quarrelled for fun, tumbled on the bed, near the fire, and embraced to their hearts' content.

Every time it cleared, priest Grigoris got on his mule and went to see Mariori in the town. He came back each time more taciturn and more discouraged. His face had become more somber and his heart harder than stone. One day, as he returned, he met Pelaghia wading barefoot through the mud; her chubby cheeks were rosy as the April rose. He blamed the good God.

"Why art Thou so hard on me, Lord?" he exclaimed. "Where is Thy justice? Thou makest Mariori to waste away like a candle and to the bad girls Thou givest rosy cheeks."

Brahimaki, too, was warming himself at the fireside; a thinner and sager Brahimaki, who docilely lit the Agha's chibouk and filled his cup for him with raki; without a word . . . The Agha watched him out of the corner of his eye and smiled maliciously.

"How do you find life here, Brahimaki? Want to go back to Smyrna?"

"I'm all right at Lycovrissi; I'm not stirring!"

"The woman's got you, you poor devil. I told you so: beware of women! But you—it was no good. 'I want a woman! I want her at once!' Look at the state you're in now; it serves you right!"

Father Ladas, dried up by his avarice, walked barefoot among his vines when the sun showed itself, and his elderly mate went before him, riding on Yannakos's ass.

"You see, my good Penelope," he told her, "God is just. He's a good moneylender like me. He understands business. We didn't lose the three pounds as you feared; we've now got our donkey and you can contemplate the world from on high. Ah! how right I was when I said that, if I lived a couple of hundred years more, I'd make you queen!"

At Kostandis's café the villagers drank sage, sucked the narghile, played draughts, and the youngest played backgammon. The air smelled of tisane and tobacco. Every Saturday evening the schoolmaster came; they made him sit in the middle and he told stories of the deeds of their ancestors. As he spoke he came alight, waved his arms and raised his voice. He would put the chairs with the narghiles on one side and the tables with the games of backgammon on the other.

"Here, on the right," he would cry, "the Persians are drawn up in order of battle; on the left, the Greeks. Suppose I am Miltiades. How many Persians are there? A million. How many of us Greeks are there? Ten thousand; one against a hundred. Attention! The attack is beginning."

The schoolmaster hurled himself upon the chairs and upset

them, putting the narghiles in great peril. In the midst of the battle, Kostandis would intervene and pick them up.

"They're beaten hollow!" shouted the schoolmaster, streaming with sweat. "We've thrown them into the sea, at Marathon. Long live Greece!"

When the game started, the villagers laughed and poked fun; but gradually they, too, were drawn in and warmed up. No one was willing to stand on the right with the Persians; they all ran to take their places behind Hadji Nikolis, the Miltiades.

"Bravo, Miltiades!" they shouted, when the battle was won, and ordered a hot tisane for the victorious hero.

One day Yannakos came down from the mountain and entered Lycovrissi, Wolf's Fountain. Sleet was falling, the streets were deserted. He gazed at the smoke-capped chimneys, sniffed the fragrance of the food the housewives were cooking, and recognized each dish by the smell—here, fried potatoes, here they're cooking sausages in the embers, there pilaff is being soaked with melted butter. They don't stint themselves, the swine, he muttered; they stuff their paunches full, the devil take them! Farther on, the scent of hot bread being taken out of the oven tickled his nostrils. Bread . . . bread . . . he sighed, with saliva on his lips.

He hastened his pace and arrived at father Ladas's house. He walked round it once, then a second time, reconnoitring carefully the position of the walls, the windows and the patch of garden behind the house. Here, he muttered, the wall's lower; good . . . All of a sudden he stood still and his heart beat fit to burst: he had heard, from the patch of garden, Youssoufaki braying, his beloved Youssoufaki. It was as if he had caught the scent of his master.

Yannakos leaned against the wall, cocked an ear and listened, troubled. Never had he heard a sweeter voice, never had Youssoufaki uttered a tenderer bray. He remembered how, when young, he too had sung serenades under the window of the damsel he loved—his wife now dead; but what he heard now was altogether more passionate and more sorrowful!

Don't worry, my Youssoufaki, he whispered, and his eyes were full of tears, don't worry, my Youssoufaki, I shall deliver you!

It was already dark when he returned to the mountain. He was cold and hungry. He made a round of the caves where the women were gathered, clasping their children against them to warm them. Yannakos would go in, say a kind word—"Courage, friends, grit your teeth, this, too, will pass!" The men growled without looking up and the women shook their heads and sighed.

"Trust in God, ladies!"

"Till when, Yannakos?"

Not knowing what to say, he left them and went farther on.

"What are they doing down below in Lycovrissi? Isn't that where you've been, Yannakos?"

"Their chimneys are smoking; they're eating, curse them! They've harvested our vines and are drinking our wine. They've gathered our olives and are stuffing themselves with our oil. But God has eyes and sees."

"When'll he turn His eyes for a moment in this direction and see us too, Yannakos?"

Yannakos again went farther on.

Three men were sitting in a grotto, conversing in the darkness, huddled against each other for warmth. The one in the middle was Loukas, that huge devil of a banner bearer.

"Have you seen the children?" said one of them, "they're beginning to swell with hunger. Mine can't stand on his little legs any longer."

"Up to now we placed our hope in God, but . . ."

"God helps those who help themselves; if you don't stir, God doesn't stir either," said Loukas. "It's time we placed our hope in ourselves. We've only got to go down to the village and steal what we can. Who was that, came in?"

"Me, lads," said Yannakos.

"Greetings, brother. Come and huddle against us and get yourself warm."

"I'm boiling, I'm burning," replied Yannakos. "I'm not cold, I've just come from Lycovrissi."

"When are we going to do what we said?"

"Perhaps tonight," said Yannakos; "agreed, lads?"

"We're ready!" they cried, all three. "Strike while the iron's hot."

"All right, tonight, that's fine. It's dark as an oven, there's a damned cold rain falling, the people'll be at home with all the chinks stopped, and as they'll have their bellies full they'll be sleeping like tops. We won't meet a living soul in the streets."

"We're ready!" they repeated. "We'll wait here. Come by and pick us up."

"Good. Get ready the bottles and sacks, and you, Loukas, the dark lantern."

"It's all here, Yannakos. Hurry up."

Yannakos went out and made for Manolios's grotto. On the way he caught sight of Michelis, holding something in his arms and looking at it by the light of a small wood fire which he had lit.

Yannakos came up on tiptoe. These last days Michelis had remained taciturn, plunged in deep meditation. He kept wandering alone from cave to cave, looking at the people without speaking to them.

Yannakos bent over his shoulder and saw that he was holding a little child about three years old, all skin and bones, with swollen belly and limbs as thin as reeds. On its chin long hairs had grown.

"Michelis . . ." said Yannakos, very softly so as not to alarm his friend, "don't look."

Michelis turned.

"Look, Yannakos," he muttered, "it's growing a beard. It's only three years old and famine has made it grow a beard! I found it on the road."

"Don't look," Yannakos repeated.

"I found it on the road," said Michelis again, "I can't stand it any more, I can't stand it any more, Yannakos. Can you?"

"Come," said Yannakos, taking him by the arm.

"Wait. Don't you see? It's going to die."

The child tried to cry but had not the strength. It kept opening and shutting its mouth, like a fish thrown on the beach. It moved its little hands, and suddenly stiffened in Michelis's arms.

"Come," said Yannakos. "Leave it there, tomorrow we'll dig a grave."

"I can't stand it any more, Yannakos. Can you?"

But Yannakos had seized him forcibly by the arm and was dragging him along.

They found Manolios sitting in a corner of his grotto, with head bent.

"What news, Manolios?" Yannakos asked.

"Bad, Yannakos. The comrades who work round about have

brought a little bread, but it's not enough by a long way. We've sent men to Lycovrissi and father Ladas has sent back answer that we can just die. Priest Grigoris's answer was: 'Let your priest Fotis do a miracle!' There's Dimitri the butcher has sent us a little meat and Kostandis has emptied his modest storeroom. But that doesn't make even one mouthful per child."

"Where's the priest?"

"Here!"

Priest Fotis entered and sat down without a word. He had just buried two little brothers, who had died of hunger together, in each other's arms. Their father had brought them in a bucket, wrapped in grass, having no linen for their burial. The priest had picked them up with care to avoid separating them, laid them on the ground and recited the prayer for the dead. Meanwhile, a few paces away, their father was digging a little grave.

All were silent. The priest was the first to speak.

"Woe to the man who would measure God by the measure of his heart," he said. "He is lost. It can lead him to lose his wits, blaspheme, deny God . . ."

He fell silent once more, appalled at the words he still had on his tongue, but he could not hold himself back.

"What is this God Who lets the children die?" he cried out, rising to his feet.

"Father," said Yannakos, "I don't measure God, I do measure men. I've measured the Lycovrissiots, I've judged them, I've condemned them, and I'm going down this evening to take what they refuse to give."

The priest reflected for a moment. The two little corpses embracing came back to his mind.

"With my blessing," he murmured at length; "go to it; I take the sin upon me."

"I take it upon myself, Father," Yannakos protested, "I'm not leaving it to you."

He got up.

"The lads are waiting for me," he said. "I'm off!"

"God bless you! Soon we shall all go down together, in daylight."

"I'm going with you!" said Michelis, opening his mouth for the first time.

"Come, Michelis, it'll get the rust off you!"

He took him by the hand; the night was ink; they groped their way. Yannakos was now in an excellent humor.

"It's a good start, Michelis; we've got to get some of the rust off! Up to now we were content to say: 'Come a little this way, good things, and I'll eat you!' But they're not so simple. So put out your hand and catch them! Mustn't count on God for everything; He is good, but He, too, has His worries, can't be everywhere! We've got to stir ourselves a bit. 'Wolf, why is your throat so fat?' 'Because I do my own hunting!' Well, we, too, are going to do our own hunting, tonight. Hey, friends, we're starting!"

He had come in sight of the companions in the grotto, sitting waiting around a small fire. They sprang to their feet.

"Forward, in the name of Christ!" said Yannakos. "We've got the priest's blessing too. Come on! Don't wear your heavy shoes and boots, hey, they'd make a row and we'd have them after us."

They burst out laughing. Where would they have found shoes? Their feet were wrapped in rags.

"Got the dark lantern, Loukas?"

"Don't worry, here she is!"

Yannakos looked at it and grinned.

"It was a present from poor Captain Fortounas," he said. "I expect he can see it from Hell and is having a good laugh."

Yannakos and Loukas led the way and the two companions followed him. Michelis went off on his own.

"Do your business, lads," he said to them. "Don't bother about me, I'm going to have a look around the village."

They could not see two steps ahead; the rain continued. Trickles of water ran down, gathered and cascaded among the rocks. At intervals, in the hollows of the mountain, a night bird uttered a plaintive cry. Suddenly, on the Prophet Elijah's peak, there rose a long, far-off howl; the four men stopped.

"A wolf," said Yannakos; "he's starving, too."

"Perhaps it's Saint Elijah," said Loukas, "and he too is hungry."

"May Saint Wolf aid us!" said Yannakos. "Come on, lads, the sheep are waiting for us."

They resumed their march. Loukas took Yannakos by the arm.

"Decided where we're going to strike first?"

"Of course! The richest, the dirtiest, the worst miser of the lot. Father Ladas. We'll fill our sacks and bottles brim full! So the poor Sarakina may have something to eat and stop howling."

Then, after a moment:

"One night we'll go down and steal some petrol as well," he added.

"Bread and petrol! You're right, Yannakos. That's what men need nowadays, to keep alive and get their own back. Because it isn't enough just to keep alive."

At the edge of the village Yannakos stopped and, turning to his companions:

"I'll go in front," he said to them, "I know the ground. Follow me, one behind the other, single file. I'll climb over first."

They entered the lanes. These were deserted. It was not far off midnight, and the whole village was in its first slumber.

Provided my Youssoufaki doesn't scent me again and start braying . . . said Yannakos to himself, just as they reached father Ladas's house. God grant he's asleep . . .

He flattened himself against the wall and waited for the others. They came up one by one.

"Let's slip around behind the garden," said Yannakos under his breath. "The wall's less high that side. Give me the lantern, Loukas. Here, come, careful!"

"Is there a dog?" someone asked.

"How would he have a dog, the old miser! A dog eats," answered Yannakos.

And to Loukas:

"You, lamppost, you'll stay outside and act as the ladder. We'll climb on your shoulders and jump down inside. If you see danger coming you just hoot like an owl. Ready, lads?"

"Ready!"

The tall devil leaned against the wall, caught hold of Yannakos and hoisted him on to his back.

"In the name of Saint Wolf," he said, "jump!"

Yannakos bestrode the wall, then jumped down into the garden. He waited for his companions, who jumped down too, one by one, with the sacks and bottles on their backs.

"Follow me, I know the way. Attention."

They crossed the garden, found the back door open and entered the house. They heard the snores of the owner coming from the upper room.

"He's asleep," said Yannakos. "We're in luck."

He lit the lantern, found the still-room door and pushed it open; they went in.

It smelled of oil, wine, dried figs, quinces. The lantern flashed around the room, lighting up the rows of fat-bellied jars and the barrels of wine.

"Hurry up, lads, work fast," Yannakos whispered; "come on, fill up!"

One of them tapped a barrel and ran the wine into his leathern bottle, another poured corn into his sack. Yannakos lifted the can of oil and filled a bottle; then he stuffed a second sack with corn.

Glancing about, he saw a ladder against the wall. "God be praised," he said, "there's a ladder also; otherwise how would we have got all this up? The God of thieves is with us; come on, lads, let's be off!"

Laden like bandits, they crossed the garden once more, put the ladder against the wall and climbed up with their heavy and precious booty. Loukas opened his arms to receive sacks and bottles and laid them out on the ground. Then each of the companions, using his broad shoulder for support, jumped down. Yannakos was the last and stayed astride the wall. He did not want to come down.

"Here, lads, one minute, while I go and see my donkey, and I'll be back," he said.

"Let the donkey be, Yannakos," protested Loukas, "and come along. There's no knowing what may happen."

"I can't," muttered Yannakos, "I can't; only a minute, lads, and I'll be here."

With these words he went down again into the garden.

His companions frowned but said nothing and, with straining ears, kept watch in case anyone should come along the road or open a door.

"Go on ahead, you two," said Loukas to his comrades; "it's better we should be dispersed. I'll wait."

He helped them load the two sacks on to their backs and they made off.

Left alone, Loukas crouched in the rain and waited. Suddenly a bray rang out, joyous, triumphal, like the trumpet of the Last Judgment. "Devil take that donkey of his," growled Loukas; "he'll wake the whole neighborhood."

A window opened in the house and a voice called; it was father Ladas's:

"Mother Penelope, are you asleep? Hey, mother Penelope, why's the ass braying like that?"

But no one answered. The braying stopped, and once more nothing was heard except the rain pattering in the courtyard. Loukas raised his head and saw a shadow astride the wall.

He stood up to his full height and caught Yannakos by the feet.

"Let's be off, Loukas, let's be off! I think the old man's awakened."

Putting the leather bottles on their backs, they took to their heels.

"You've done what you wanted," said Loukas when they emerged from the village; "you've seen your ass."

"Yes," said Yannakos with a sigh; "if I could have got him up the ladder, upon my word I'd have brought him with me. And Michelis?" he added, a little later, anxiously.

"He must have had his look round and come back. Let's get on!"

Priest Fotis and Manolios had not gone to bed. They were waiting. Day was breaking already. The east was lightening faintly; the rain had stopped, but the sky remained threatening. Suddenly whistles and joyful voices were heard.

"There they are!" said Manolios, running out.

The four robbers appeared, heavily laden. They had lit the lantern to show their way and their faces could be seen glowing. Yannakos was leading, with the wineskin on his back.

"Many greetings from old Ladas, that good and charitable man! It isn't much, he says, but my heart goes with it. He sends you this wine to drink his health in!"

"And here is oil to lubricate your innards," said Loukas, laying down the other skin at the priest's feet. "If you want more, his jars are full of it, he says."

"Here, there's corn, so the poor little children, for whom he's full of pity, may have bread to eat!" said the other two, laying down their full sacks.

"Thanks be given to him," answered priest Fotis, laughing, "and may God pay him for them with interest! I'll go at once and write him a letter saying that four angels have entered his house by night, that they have taken the precious gifts and, loading them on their wings, have brought them to us on the Sarakina. That everything may be in order, I'll enclose an I.O.U. valid in the life to come."

"Write also, Father," said Yannakos, laughing, "that one of the angels wanted to smash his jars and his barrels and spill the oil and wine, but that at the last moment he had pity, not on him, but on the wine and on the oil."

"Manolios," said priest Fotis, "bring a glass and let's offer the angels a drink! Come in and shake out your soaked wings, my lords!"

"To the health of father Ladas, that good man!" said the priest, emptying his glass.

"To the health of the angels," said Manolios.

"To the health of Saint Wolf," said Loukas. "You know, as we started, he began to howl on the top of Sarakina, and that gave us courage."

"And Michelis?" said Yannakos; "we didn't see him."

"He's come back," Manolios answered. "He was covered with mud and said nothing. He's asleep."

Next morning, when father Ladas came down into his garden, the sight of the ladder placed against the wall made him uneasy. Turning, he called to his wife, who was up already and sitting by the window, gazing at the world with her dull eyes.

"Hey, mother Penelope, who put the ladder against the wall? Did you?"

But mother Penelope had already picked up her sock and was knitting. She did not even look in his direction.

The old man put the ladder on his back and carried it to the still-room. He gave a glance around to see if everything was in place: the jars, the barrels, the dried figs, the quinces.

"God be praised," he muttered. "Luckily no thieves came. She doesn't know what she's doing any longer, poor woman; I must keep an eye on things. She's quite capable of setting fire to the house one day."

Then he went into the stable. The ass too was in his place.

"Here, what was the matter with you last night, waking me up with your hee-haws?" he said, furiously, giving him a kick.

But the donkey did not turn, either. His big eyes were strangely lost in the void. He had the impression of having dreamed that during the night his real master had come and tenderly, as he always did, stroked his neck, belly and back. He had then lifted his tail happily and let out a bray, and his master had caught him by the muzzle to make him be quiet, and had kissed his ears and neck. And he had vanished through the little round window.

The ass bent his head, shut his eyes and prayed to his own God— a God with an enormous bushy tail, a huge pure-white ass's head, a velvet and gold pack-saddle and red harness embroidered with silver spangles, glittering like stars:

"O God, make my last night's dream come true!" he prayed.

Early in the morning the news of the miracle spread over the whole of the Sarakina: four angels, during the night, had brought corn, oil and wine to the starving! The simple among them believed and crossed themselves; the more shrewd glanced with smiles at Yannakos and Loukas. The women fell upon the corn and at once began to sift it, singing softly as though to lull a baby to sleep, as though they were dandling the Child Jesus. Did a grain fall to the ground? They quickly stooped to pick it up; was it not a precious part of the God, which must not be allowed to be sullied by contact with the soil? In a twinkling they crushed a certain quantity on the stones, fashioned a flat cake and baked it in the embers, moistening it with a little oil to make it more tasty; then they gave everyone a mouthful, sharing it out like the consecrated bread; and straightaway they felt comforted in flesh and blood, as though that bread were really the Body of Christ.

After that, all drank a drop of wine, and the women could not keep back their tears.

"O God," they sighed, "a mouthful of bread, a sip of wine— that's all that's needed to make the soul feel it's growing wings!"

In the afternoon, two men loaded the corn onto their backs to carry it to the mill. The women escorted the precious cargo part of the way as though afraid it would never come back.

"When'll it be back?" they cried to the bearers.

"Tomorrow morning, don't you worry, ladies!" they answered laughing.

Yannakos had become the Sarakina storekeeper. He it was who kept the victuals and shared out to the women, each morning, what they needed for the day's meals.

"Spin it out, friends," he would cry; "tighten your belts till winter's over. The angels have other things to do, they can't bring us some every day."

A little bread and a little oil was enough to revive the flame which had been on the point of going out. The children began to lose their swellings and to get some color back into their cheeks. The women had milk, and the sucklings no longer complained all night. The men, too, grew cheerful again; their arms recovered strength. They transported stores to finish the huts they had begun. From time to time even a laugh was heard, a joke, and in the out-of-the-way grottoes it was now possible to stumble on a couple who had the strength to kiss and embrace.

"All this corn, this oil, this wine must become blood and we must gather the strength for an expedition," said priest Fotis to Manolios that day. "We can't always be hungry and steal. We shall have to go down to the village and take possession, by force if need be, of the lands which belong to us. They alone will enable us to live on this barren mountain."

"Soon," said Manolios, "the vines will have to be pruned, the olives lopped, the fields dunged. Are we going to let them go neglected? It would be a year lost. What are you waiting for, Father?"

"I'm waiting for the sign in me, Manolios. I'm waiting for the voice which will give me the order. You know, never have I taken an important decision without hearing that voice. And the decision you mention, Manolios, is a grave one; blood will be shed."

"I know, Father. But in a world like this, without honor and unjust, can anything be done without blood being shed? I used to tell myself: the Lycovrissi will see the state our children are in, they'll see their swollen bellies, their hollow cheeks, their skinny legs; they'll have pity on them. So the day before yesterday I sent some of them to the village. Do you know how they were received? Some people took up sticks and chased them away from their doors, others threw them a bit of dry bread, as though they were dogs. Only one had pity on them. Do you know who, Father? The Agha! He saw them from his balcony, scratching at the ground to find a few grains, a few bits of potato peel, a few lemon skins, and he shouted out: 'What's that? little monkeys? little men?' He came down, opened his door to them, and had them come in. Then he called Martha. 'Lay the table, Martha, bring them something to eat. They're little monkeys, give them something to eat and let's turn them into men.'"

"I didn't know. You didn't tell me, Manolios!" cried the priest, his eyes shining through his tears.

"I kept it from you, Father, to spare you. Your heart's full of poison which men keep pouring into it; what was the good of adding this?"

"You should have told me, Manolios; my heart's got to overflow! If man's heart doesn't overflow either with love or with anger, nothing gets done in the world, you can take it from me!"

He fell silent; suddenly exhausted, he sat down on a rock, with his head bowed on his chest, as though listening. Manolios sat down facing him, gazing at the plain. It was no longer raining, and the earth was brimming with winter, glutted. A light wind was blowing and the olive trees were waving, now silver, now dusky green. The vineyards, too, were steeped in water and looked quite black. A falcon launched into flight from Saint Elijah's crest and wheeled above the plain.

Priest Fotis stood up.

"My heart has overflowed," he said, "I'm going."

Manolios said nothing; he was aware of the priest's body taut to the breaking point. "Better not speak to him," he told himself, "better not . . ."

Priest Fotis clambered up the rocks and took the path leading to the peak of the mountain. Saint Elijah was gleaming up there, perfectly white.

The priest kept on up, holding himself upright like a sword; sometimes he disappeared behind the rocks, only to reappear farther on, still advancing. He had taken off his monk's skullcap and his hair was floating in the wind.

Soon Manolios saw his silhouette in front of the little chapel, cut out against the white wall and no larger than a falcon's. Immediately afterward the door yawned, dead black. The priest entered and disappeared.

Manolios at once went back into his grotto, took a big oak log, and began to carve the new face of Christ.

The Savage Face of Christ

NIGHT WAS FALLING and the priest had not returned. A violent wind had arisen, the sky turned threatening. The howl of the wolf rang out again, far off, in the night.

"Let's go and see what's become of him, something may have happened to him," said Michelis.

They were the first words to issue from his mouth for many days. He had been more and more deeply plunged in bitter meditations, sometimes sighing, sometimes raising his eyes toward the little mountain church—and smiling, then, at peace. He kept the tresses of Mariori clasped against his chest, next to the skin, and trembled and clutched them at every moment as though afraid he had lost them. At night he would awake with a cry, start up, and be unable to get to sleep again.

Manolios was sitting quietly with him in the grotto. It was perhaps midnight.

"Nothing can happen to him," Manolios answered. "From the way I saw him stand up and take that path, Michelis, nothing can happen to him. For a moment I thought he was immortal."

"He's a long time . . . a long time . . . what's he doing?" muttered Michelis, not reassured by his friend's words.

"They are in consultation, they're having a secret conversation, the two of them, they're making plans, Michelis—Saint Elijah and he. No one can come between them. They're taking decisions."

"But will he have anything to eat this evening? How will he get any sleep? It's freezing."

"He won't eat, he won't sleep, and he won't be cold. In the state he's in now, I assure you, he needs nothing. He's as though dead, as though deathless, I don't know. He needs nothing."

At this moment Yannakos appeared. He was morose, grumbling and cursing.

"There you are in a bad temper again, what's the matter with you, Yannakos?" Manolios asked. "How's business, storekeeper to the Sarakina?"

" 'How are your little ones, Mr. Crow?' 'They're getting blacker and blacker,' " was Yannakos's answer.

He added, a moment later:

"We're getting to the end of the victuals, that's what the matter is; we shall soon be seeing the bottom. What's to be done? Take the lads down again, for a descent to the plain? This time it's priest Grigoris's turn."

"It's Lycovrissi's turn; you wait!" said Manolios.

Yannakos shivered and clapped his hands with joy.

"Has the hour come?" he cried. "Has the priest said so?"

"He hasn't said anything yet, but I think the hour's getting near. He said his heart had overflowed."

And he began to tell of his conversation with the priest.

"If only he could wait a bit longer, give me time to get ready," muttered Yannakos this time; "I'm not ready."

The two friends turned toward him to try and make out his face in the darkness.

"Something missing, Yannakos?" asked Manolios.

"Yes, indeed."

"What?"

"The petrol. I gave the good God my word to burn father Ladas's house."

"You are savage," said Michelis, making up his mind to speak.

"I'm just," retorted Yannakos. "If Christ came down on earth to-day, on an earth like this one, what do you think He'd have on his shoulders? A cross? No, a can of petrol."

Manolios jumped up, and leaned against the wall of the grotto to listen.

"What do you think, Manolios?" asked Yannakos, "you don't say anything."

"How do you know, Yannakos?" Manolios muttered, trembling.

"I don't know, I wasn't taught it, nobody told me, I'm sure of it."

After a silence, he went on:

"In a few days' time our children will be wandering in the streets of Lycovrissi again with their crutches, poking in the rubbish bins to find peel and filth to eat, while the fat pigs watch them and laugh. Well, that's how our children see Christ in their dreams. That's the way they ask Him to come down on earth. But in the morning, when they wake up, they forget—they're children, aren't they?—and they go back to poking the rubbish heaps."

Manolios listened, breathlessly, without a word. But his heart was leaping. That was exactly how he had seen Christ in a dream the other night, but he had not dared reveal it. He had seen Him coming down from a sunlit, bald mountain just like the Sarakina, barefoot and carrying on His shoulder not a cross but a can of petrol. His hard, sad, wrathful face was turned toward Lycovrissi.

Looking at Yannakos, he said to him:

"You're right, comrade; not a cross; petrol."

"I'm off to find my zebras. There's no time to lose."

At the opening of the grotto he stopped and laughed:

"Priest Grigoris," he said, "has a petrol lamp, so he must have a can in his storeroom. Perhaps two, even. I'll take Loukas with me; he makes a fine ladder. See you tomorrow!"

It was already broad daylight when Manolios made out priest Fotis coming down from the top of the mountain. He was leaping from boulder to boulder, with his cassock flying like two black wings; his hair was straggling over his shoulders. He really looked like the Prophet Elijah in person, especially as, behind him, the sky in the east was red with a more than customary brilliance. The priest seemed to be coming down ringed with flames.

Several women who had gone to fill their pitchers with water caught sight of him, were terrified and set up a cry:

"God, mercy! Saint Elijah's escaped from the mountain—he's coming down!"

The men rushed out and went off to meet him with Manolios at their head; they had suddenly all had the presentiment that the priest was bringing them great news.

"What's he got in his hands, lads?" said Yannakos, who, not having slept all night, had tingling eyes. He had not even washed, and his hands reeked of petrol.

"It's true, what is it he's carrying?" said Michelis, trying to make it out.

"An icon! An icon!" cried Loukas who was in front. He, too, gave out a smell of petrol.

"He's taken Saint Elijah and is bringing him to us!" Manolios said to himself, "it's a good sign!"

Now they could make out the priest's face clearly, a severe, somber face. He seemed not to see them, not to hear their calling, as if his spirit had not yet left the Prophet's burning solitude.

"Let's draw aside and let him pass, friends," said Manolios. "Don't let anyone speak to him; he's still conversing with God."

The priest was coming down with great strides, he was hurrying, sending the stones rolling. Everyone could now recognize that he was carrying, held upright in his arms, the miraculous icon of the Prophet.

"I believe I smell powder," said Yannakos to Loukas, his companion of the night's work, "look at his face!"

"Lucky we've done our business in time!" said Loukas. "Most of the houses are wood; our two cans will be enough."

The women had climbed the slope and were arriving, babbling and chattering about miracles, saints, dreams. With craning necks they gazed at the priest descending. One saw that he had black wings and was flying, another that they were not wings but his cassock; only there was a raven which had perched on his shoulder and was holding in its beak a burning coal and making him eat it. All of a sudden they fell silent: the priest was coming past.

"Come with me!" he ordered the men, without stopping.

"And you too, women," he flung at the group of women, as he marched on with huge strides, holding the Prophet dead straight in his arms.

All were taken aback, as though some bird of prey had just passed through them, brushing them with its harsh wings. In great excitement, men first, the women behind, they followed in silence.

The sun, already high and shining through light clouds, was a mere white-hot ball. Below, the plain was still drowned in a thick mist. A few old women, late comers, emerged from the grottoes, shielded their eyes with their hands and gazed in amazement at the crowd descending.

When he reached the caves, priest Fotis stopped. He placed the icon on a rock, and they all—men, women and children—gathered in a circle around him.

Stretching out his arms, he began to speak. At first his voice was hoarse. his throat tight. The words hastened, jostled, trying all to get out at the same time; none got through. But gradually his throat untied itself, his voice grew firm, the words fell into line.

"Men," he cried, "listen. Women, take your children in your arms, let them hear, too! I come down from a chariot of fire. I will lead you where it has led me. What it has confided to me, I will reveal to you! Life is not a sleeping water; submission and resignation are not the most virile virtues, nor those most pleasing to God! A good man cannot see children fall and die of hunger before his eyes without rising up and demanding an account even from God!

"I went up to that peak to talk with the patron saint of our mountain, that our decision might lead to a remedy for the evil. For our children are also his, he is responsible for them!"

With outstretched arms he addressed the icon:

"You are responsible for them, Prophet of the fire; that is why, to be honest, I went right up to your eyrie. And like the tenant farmer who goes to render his yearly accounts to his landlord, loaded with presents drawn from his vineyards and his gardens, I, too, took with me the sufferings and mourning of the people, and I have laid them at your feet.

"All night, my children, I remained standing before that Prophet and spoke to him. I told him who we are, whence we have come and how we arrived upon his mountain, seeking refuge beneath his roof. All that, he knew—I had told him already—but it was good that he should hear it afresh. He listened and said nothing.

"Then I spoke to him of our neighbors, down below, in Lycovrissi, telling him how they have treated us, how they have driven us away, all without exception, priest, notables, inhabitants, how they have despoiled us, not allowing us to work the lands which Michelis, our benefactor, has given us. I told him all, I lightened myself of my bile. Still he listened and said nothing.

"Then I spoke to him of the martyrdom being suffered by his people, of the hunger, of the cold, of the sickness. 'The insolence of the rich passes all bounds, patron,' I cried to him, 'the gullet of the sated is swollen to excess, the knife is touching the bones; do you hear, fierce charioteer of the fire? Arise, harness your horses, descend!' And still he listened to me and said nothing.

"I grew white hot, and I gazed at him, saying within myself: 'Won't his heart then burst? How can he contain so much suffering, accept so much injustice, tolerate so much insolence? Won't he dart out from the icon? Won't he harness the flames, seize me by the nape of the neck and seat me by his side that we may go down to Lycovrissi?'

"I clung to the icon and, leaning close to his ear: 'Elijah, hey, Captain Elijah,' I cried to him, 'listen to this as well: our children can't any longer stand on their legs, so hungry they are; some on crutches, others with sticks, they have gone down, limping like crows, to beg in Lycovrissi. You know this, surely, you must have heard; you leaned down from your peak, I saw you; your beard swept the roofs of Lycovrissi and you saw our children weeping in front of the doors.'

"Under my gaze I felt the body of the Prophet grow warm, come to life and, taking new courage:

" 'Yes,' I cried to him, 'you consented to lean out of your chariot of fire, to look down below and see how the Lycovrissi received them! Listen: there are some who took up sticks to drive them from their doors; others—did you see?—beat them unmercifully!'

"Hardly had I uttered these last words when I recoiled, terrified. It seemed to me as if the icon struck me, as if the four horses of fire came to life, as if the lips of the Prophet were moving and as if I heard a great cry: 'Let me go!'

"At that, the icon leaped into my arms."

All were overcome, gasping. The women, with cries, fell on their knees before the miraculous icon; the men, exalted by the priest's words, raised their heads and saw the Prophet, ringed with flames, descending from the peak of the mountain.

"Welcome, Prophet Elijah!" the women greeted him.

"Give the signal, Father," cried Yannakos, "while we've still a mouthful of bread to eat and while we've strength. The victuals are giving out!"

Manolios approached the priest and, kissing his hand:

"Raise your arm, Father. Has the hour come? We are ready."

Priest Fotis raised his arm toward his people:

"In three days," he cried, "in three days, my children, on the twenty-second of December, on the birthday of light, the birthday of the Prophet Elijah. That will be the great day! Prepare, companions, men and women; we shall descend!"

All passed in procession before the icon and bowed to the ground. In their eyes the Prophet was alive, his mantle was simply a brazier crackling in the wind. The women saw drops of sweat welling from his forehead and the children, as they pressed their lips to the icon, felt the Prophet move under their mouth.

Exhausted, priest Fotis went and lay down in his cave. He closed his eyes, that sleep might come and God might descend in a dream and speak. Manolios bore away the icon of the Prophet of fire and placed it at the back of the grotto, in the darkness, beside the Crucifixion with the swallows.

From that moment the Sarakina began to hum like a martial camp. Those who had no stick went off into the mountain in search of holm oaks whose branches they could cut. Those who knew how to handle a sling taught the women and children to use one. Priest Fotis, having distributed to the bravest the arms that were available, ran indefatigably from one to the other, giving instructions.

Toward evening Kostandis, arriving from the village, was struck with amazement at hearing this noise, at seeing the men busy showing the women how to hurl stones from the sling or how to cut branches for clubs, as though they were preparing, every man and woman among them, for war. He found Manolios carving hastily the new face of Christ; it was his own weapon, and he was in a hurry to finish it that all might be ready.

Kostandis sat down beside him, dismayed.

"Manolios," he said, "if you've the time, raise your head a moment and listen to me. I've brought bad news."

"Welcome to it, Kostandis; the mountains are used to snow, they aren't afraid of it, speak."

"Mariori is dead."

Manolios dropped the piece of wood he was carving. His eyes grew big with alarm.

"Dead?" he said, stupefied, as if he were hearing of death for the first time.

"The news came yesterday, at midday. Her old father gave a cry that shook the village. He at once got on his mule and went off groaning. When he reached the town, she was already buried; he wasn't able to close her eyes. This morning he came back. You wouldn't know him. Grief has set his wits tottering. I saw him knocking at people's doors in the village and I was frightened. I was sorry for him. He was walking barefoot, with his long hair in the wind. He kept knocking at doors, calling everyone to church. He wanted to speak to them. He had the beadle ring the knell.

Everyone left work and went. He gathered us together in the churchyard and stood on a stone bench. His chin was trembling so that he couldn't speak. But his bloodshot eyes were shooting flames. In the end he managed to pull his strength together and a hoarse voice came out of his throat.

" 'My sons, I shall only say two words to you, I can't say more, my heart would break: the Sarakina will have us all! The Sarakina will have us all!'

"He stops, draws breath. After a long while, he begins again: 'Rise, arm yourselves, I shall be at your head; up, my children, they must be driven away, the brutes! It's they who've cast the evil eye upon our village, which was so prosperous. Ever since the cursed hour when they set foot here, misfortune and death have rained blows on us without respite. The first and most to blame is Manolios, the excommunicated! He put ideas into Michelis's head and made him mad. He was the cause of the breaking-off of his engagement with my Mariori; he it is too, who's killed her, killed my daughter!'

"He tried to go on speaking, but he was taken with giddiness. He stretched out his arms to steady himself against the walls, but he couldn't see and lost his balance and fell heavily on the stone pavement."

Kostandis fell silent. Manolios tugged the end of the handkerchief he was wearing around his head like a turban, and bit it so as not to cry out. "Mariori is dead, dead . . . dead . . ." he repeated to himself without managing to give these words a meaning.

He turned toward Kostandis:

"Well?" he asked, his mind wandering, "well?"

"I came to tell you, Manolios, so that you might be on your guard. The villagers are beside themselves after what the priest has said to them, and they're preparing to come and attack you. They were looking for a pretext and now they've found one. The rich are frightened of you because they believe you're bolsheviks; the poor hate you because the rich have blinded them; so they'll hit out when they can. There's a lot of them and they've arms; also, the Agha's with them; be careful."

"Kostandis, go and find poor Michelis, tell him the news. I can't. Break it to him gently, because lately our young archon hasn't been himself. He comes and goes without a word, he looks at you and his mind's somewhere else; you speak to him, he doesn't answer. At night he trembles at going to bed, he's afraid to go to sleep. One day I asked him: 'What are you afraid of, Michelis?' He had trouble in opening his mouth: 'The dead man . . . the dead man . . .' was his answer. Come, courage, Kostandis, go and find him. I'm going to speak to the priest."

"It's all over now," muttered Michelis, closing the silver Gospel book which he had been reading. "I don't need anything any more, Kostandis. God has taken a knife and cut my life in two. He'd already thrown the first half into the earth; now He's thrown the second. All of me is now under the earth."

Kostandis was troubled at seeing with what calm Michelis received the terrible news; behind Michelis's serene face he could feel the world crumbling.

"All is over," said the man who had once been a young archon, again, and stood up. He took a rope from a hollow in the rock and tightened it around the Gospel book, as though he were muzzling a wild animal to prevent it from biting.

He looked at Kostandis and shook his head.

"Which way am I to turn, Kostandis? Toward man? That's dirty and stinks. Toward God? He lets father Ladas live and prosper and kills Mariori. Toward myself? An earthworm twisting in the sunshine and crushed by a boot at the very moment when he was telling himself: 'I'm all right, I'm all right in the sunshine, it's warm.' Can you understand it at all, Kostandis?"

But Kostandis had children, how could he understand? He got up.

"I'll go and see Yannakos," he said.

In the cave which he had transformed into a storeroom, Yannakos was measuring what was left in the way of oil and flour. For several days there had been no wine.

"Two days more," he muttered, "three at most. We shall just do it. After that, war. Then, we shall see! Life's a curable disease. Here, as long as I'm alive, as long as I can say to myself I'm alive and my Youssoufaki's alive, I've courage. One day we shall be together again. Death's the only thing that can't be cured."

"Hullo, Yannakos!" cried a voice behind him. "What's become of you, old one? D'you never come down to the village now?"

Yannakos turned and saw Kostandis.

"Hullo, Kostandis, friend," he said joyfully. "Yes, I do still go down to your blessed village, but how'd you see me? At the hour when I go there, it's black as pitch."

He told him, laughingly, how he had twice been into the village, like a wolf, to carry out a raid on the two houses.

"Look here," he said in conclusion, "the victuals we got away with are saying good-bye to us, but here's the petrol, see, in the corner; no one's touched it yet. It's waiting for the moment to do its miracle!"

"What miracle?" asked Kostandis, agog.

"Turning into fire, Kostandis. Isn't that its job? If not, why has God sent it down to earth?"

He thought for a moment and struck his forehead.

"You did well to come," he said, "it's the good God sent you. Want to do something for me? Today's Sunday. The day after to-morrow—Tuesday—can you take my ass from father Ladas's? You'll tell him you need it. If you pay the old skinflint, he'll let you have him; you'll keep him all day at your place? Understand? Not a hair of his must be burned. At your place he'll be safe."

"So you're planning to set fire to father Ladas's house?" said Kostandis, appalled.

"Well, what else have we been talking of, all this time? Isn't that petrol's job? The good God knows what he's doing."

"Weigh up the pros and cons, Yannakos; this will get you into terrible trouble."

"I've weighed them again and again, Kostandis, the weight's just right for me, as if I'd ordered it. I've told our Prophet Elijah too—Captain Elijah, as our priest calls him. He says yes."

Kostandis scratched his head.

"I don't understand," he said.

"You don't understand because you've got a café, a wife and children. If you're hungry, you manage somehow. How could you understand? So you act stupid, you kiss the Agha's dirty hand and priest Grigoris's and all the rest! But the man who hasn't anything, Kostandis, doesn't kiss any hands; there's the whole secret. Don't frown, old one; your hour will come, you'll see, be patient."

"I'm on your side, Yannakos, so don't go for me," said Kostandis after a while, with a deep sigh. "I often talk it over with Andonis and fat Dimitri the butcher. What can we do?"

"Go and ask priest Fotis, he'll tell you. All I ask is one thing:

for my Youssoufaki to be at your place on Tuesday; there! And watch out, not a word about it, eh?"

Sunday passed and Monday came. Toward midday, thick snow began to fall; soon the top of the mountain was all white. The Prophet Elijah muffled himself in his white; famished, the ravens flew off toward the plain. The sky was of red copper.

Manolios, bent over the oak log since early morning, was concentrating all his force and carving the wood. His soul had become a graving tool, cutting, gouging, hollowing, endeavoring to set free the face of Christ imprisoned in the wood. The divine face rose up within him, as he had seen it the other night in his dream, hard, sad, wrathful. A deep weal gashed it from the right temple to the chin; it had a drooping mustache and bushy eyebrows.

Since dawn he had been trying to reproduce this austere image faithfully; he must be quick. As evening approached, the divine countenance emerged at last from the wood; Manolios jumped back, appalled.

At that moment Michelis came in, tired, despairing. He looked at the carved wood and recoiled.

"What is it?" he cried; "it's War!"

"No, it's Christ," replied Manolios, wiping the sweat from his forehead.

"But in that case, what's the difference between Him and War?"

"None," replied Manolios.

It had grown dusk. The flakes were falling thickly, silently, covering everything. Down below, the plain had disappeared.

Manolios lit the oil lamp, took down from its hook the old face of Christ which he had carved, and placed it side by side with the new one.

"What a difference!" muttered Michelis, fearfully. "Is it the same?"

"The same. Then, He was patient, meek, serene; now, He is hardened. Can you understand, Michelis?"

Michelis was silent. But after a moment:

"In the past, I couldn't have," he said; "now, I can." Then he fell silent again.

On the Tuesday, day had scarcely broken when the Sarakini were already afoot. The peak of the mountain was sparkling white. The

Prophet was hidden under a thick hood. But as soon as the first rays of the sun fell on him he came to life and awoke in a rosy glow.

Priest Fotis assembled his people:

"My children," he said, "this day will decide our fate. We have been patient as long as we could. We have reached the edge of the abyss. If we had waited a little longer we should have fallen in. The children first, then the men and the women. We had to choose between dying or fighting for life. We have chosen the fight. Is everyone agreed?"

"Agreed, priest, all of us!"

"I have questioned the watchman who is stationed up there above us, Captain Elijah. He, too, agrees. Then I questioned my heart. Agreed, likewise. All our today's undertaking is undertaken not blindly but with open eyes, with clear minds, like free men. We shall be going to demand what is our due, not charity, but justice! In the plain we have gardens, vineyards, fields; we have olive trees and houses. Let them give them to us! We are not seeking to lay hands on the fields belonging to the others; we are asking that we may work our own, and so live. We are not the army of violence; we are the army of the victims of injustice who have had enough of injustice.

"We shall not be the first to strike. But if they strike us, we have the hands God has given us and we shall strike back. What can justice do, how can it impose itself in an unjust and dishonest world, if it is not armed? We are going to arm justice. They have armed injustice, they have! We are going to show, today, that virtue, too, has heads. Christ is not only a sheep, He is also a lion. And it is as a lion that He will come with us today.

"Manolios has carved His face in wood. There it is! That is the Christ who will march at our head and be our leader!"

With these words he lifted the savage face high. In the morning air, above the heads of the crowd, the image of Christ swayed, menacingly. At the last moment Manolios had painted red the wound which went from the temple to the chin. So Christ appeared to the gripped people like some great Combatant wounded in the wars and sallying out afresh to combat.

"Here is our leader!" cried the priest. "Raise your hands, salute Him!"

Then, to Loukas, the banner bearer:

"Loukas, fix this holy face on the top of the banner, and let it go before us and blaze our march! And now, everyone to his place, God's day has dawned, forward! First, Loukas with the banner; then the men with arms, then, closing the rear, the women and the children with slings!"

The troop formed, all crossed themselves, priest Fotis took the icon of the Prophet Elijah in his arms, Manolios moved to the van with his men; Yannakos took up position behind them, with the petrol can under his arm. Michelis had climbed onto a rock and watched them set out.

"I shan't go with you, Father," he had declared to priest Fotis; "my arms—see?—have no strength in them. Good luck!"

He watched them go. Their rags were fluttering in the wind; many of them were barefoot, others shod with sheepskin or clouts. Their cheeks were hollow, their bones stuck out and glinted at cheek and chin, their eyes looked like black holes. They were hungry, they were cold, they began running to get warm.

Yannakos put the can of petrol down for a moment and rubbed his frozen hands.

"Aren't we going to sing, lads?" he cried. "Do people go to a festival with their mouths sewn up? Come on! A marching song, an *amané*, a psalm, anything you like; let's sing, lads, and get warm!"

And suddenly breasts swelled, mouths opened; priest Fotis gave the signal and all the people intoned triumphantly the ancient warlike canticle their ancestors had sung when going out to war against the barbarians:

> *Lord, save Thy people and bless Thine inheritance;*
> *Lord, aid us to drive out the barbarians.*

No Other Way

It was the hour when Lycovrissi was beginning to stretch and wake. It was freezing hard. The mountains around about were all white; the men of the village had stayed huddled in their nice warm beds, spinning out their laziness. The night before they had killed the pigs and, having singed off the hides and emptied them out, had turned them over, properly clean, to their wives and daughters, who today would busy themselves with preparing the jelly, stuffing the bowels to make sausages, filling small pots and jars with the pâté, the bacon, the salted breast.

That day, therefore, the housewives had got up first and, rolling up their sleeves, had placed cauldrons on the fire, then set to work, from dawn onward, grinding the pepper and caraway for the sausages, pressing bitter oranges and lemons for the jelly. Fat, all pink, freshly washed and hairless, hanging head downward from the hooks in the kitchen, the pig was waiting.

"Woe to you, mother Martha, if you introduce any of that unclean meat into my house!" the Agha had told his servant the evening before. All day he had heard the squeals of the pigs being killed in the yards. "Ugh! giaours!" he kept saying, aloud, "you people who soil yourselves with pig's flesh and poison the air with your grilling sausages!"

But secretly the Agha was mad on pork sausages; he knew of no better *meze* to go with raki. The sly hunchback served them to him every year, pretending they were made with camel's meat. The Agha knew perfectly well they were not, but he feigned innocence. In that way he could eat them and lick his fingers, all the while keeping the law of the Prophet. To the depths of his being he was determined not to know that the savory meat which he tasted as a connoisseur was pork. So every year, on the day they killed the pigs, he would arraign the old hunchback:

"Woe to you, mother Martha, if you introduce any of that unclean meat into my house!"

Which meant: Go and buy me all the sausages you can, as you would if it were for you. And bring me them and swear that it's camel.

"Don't worry, Agha," replied the hunchback, without even venturing to smile, "I'll find you plenty of camel sausages again this year, never fear. Brahimaki shall have some, too."

Meanwhile the starvelings in rags were coming down from the mountain at the double. Yannakos at one moment said to those next to him:

"It's a good day the priest has chosen for marching on the village, brothers. Today the pigs are hung on the hooks, all ready. The wives have lit the fires and are getting them ready for us. At last the time's come for greasing the insides of the poor."

But his comrades, gripped by the war hymn, did not hear.

The troop had reached the foot of the mountain and was coming out into the plain. The village lay in front of them with its houses covered in snow; all the chimneys were smoking. The nostrils of the starvelings quivered as they scented the fragrance of the pigs already being boiled to make the jelly. The women remembered their homes laid waste, they recalled what they, too, used to do at this time of year, on the same day, and they sighed.

Before they reached Saint Basil's Well, priest Fotis halted and signed that he wished to speak.

"My children," he cried, "attention! We'll go first to the house of old Patriarcheas and entrench ourselves there. If the door is shut, we'll break it open; the house is ours, we will enter it. Then we will split up and go to our gardens, our vineyards, our fields, and occupy them. God grant they may not come and attack us. But if we are attacked, we will reply. It's war. We are claiming our right, God forgive us! The village is awake, I can see men assembling in the distance, I can hear the bell ringing, take care. Forward, in the name of Christ!"

The bell was, in fact, ringing for all it was worth. The village was upside down. Panayotaros, who had been unable to get to sleep, had got wind of something and, going out at break of day on to the Agha's balcony, had looked out toward the mountain. And behold, in the dawn half-light, he had seen the Sarakina descending. Hurtling down the staircase, he had come out into the square, run to the church, seized the bell rope and begun to ring the tocsin furiously.

At the same moment old Mandalenia, who had gone with her pitcher to Saint Basil's Well, had seen in the distance the beggar people coming down with a roar. As fast as her legs would carry her she had made for the village again, screaming:

"They're coming, the bolsheviks! The bolsheviks! To arms, villagers!"

The inhabitants, who were still lying in bed, jumped up when they heard the bell ringing. The cries of mother Mandalenia reached their ears. They bounded out of bed, opened their doors and, wrapped in their blankets, began running to the church. Housewives, abandoning their kitchens, shouted from doorstep or window to the men as they passed in disorder:

"Hullo, what's happening? Why's the bell being rung?"

But they ran breathlessly on without answering.

Priest Grigoris had already reached the church and was standing before the door, gasping.

"To arms, friends!" he shouted. "Here are the bolsheviks coming down from the Sarakina. Don't let them get into the village! Go home, arm yourselves, and to Saint Basil's Well, all of you!"

He turned to Panayotaros who was tugging the bell rope like a madman:

"Panayotaros, go and wake the Agha! Tell him to get on his mare and rush to Saint Basil's Well, the bolsheviks are coming down!"

The schoolmaster arrived, breathless. He had forgotten his glasses and kept knocking into things right and left.

"Don't arm, brothers," he begged, "I'll go and parley with them. I'll get them by persuasion! We're brothers, don't plunge the village into bloodshed!"

"Mind your own business, idiot!" roared the priest, furiously. "No compromise now! The hour has come to wipe them out! At them, lads! Arm, brothers! Death to the lice-carriers!"

Brains caught fire; the villagers ran to their homes, armed themselves with clubs, pistols, scythes; many of them seized the knives with which they had killed the pigs the evening before. All tumbled, yelling, in the direction of Saint Basil's Well.

Panayotaros arrived running and placed himself at the priest's side; he brandished his pistol, and fired into the air. "Forward, hearties, the Devil take them!"

The Agha heard the pistol shot in his sleep: he struck the floor with his whip; Martha appeared.

"Here, what's that pistol shot?"

"The bolsheviks are coming down, Agha!"

"What bolsheviks, you misshapen hag? Speak! The ones from Russia?"

"No, Agha, the ones from the Sarakina; get on your mare, the Christians want you to, on your mare and go and help them!"

The Agha burst out laughing; he still felt like sleeping; he turned over on his other side, toward Brahimaki:

"You'll wake me up when the ones from Russia come; for the moment, be off with you!"

Priest Fotis, seeing the Lycovrissi fiercely advancing, left his people and came forward, unarmed, with the icon of the Prophet Elijah in his arms.

"Brothers," he cried, "I've something to say to you; halt! For the love of Christ, listen to me; let no drop of blood be shed."

For an instant, the two rival troops halted and waited; priest Fotis took a few more steps forward.

"It's to you, priest Grigoris, to your reverence, Father," he cried, "that I wish to speak; come nearer."

"What do you want with me, goat-beard?" replied the priest, coming toward him with a rush; "here I am!"

The two priests were now face to face, between the two troops; the one tall, thick set, shining with fat, like a bull; the other with his skin sticking to his bones, his cheeks hollow, his bare feet covered with blood, like an old raw-boned, wounded horse.

"Father," said priest Fotis in a powerful voice, that all might hear; "Father, it is a great sin to foment war between brothers; the blood that would be shed would fall upon our two heads. I've something to say to you, Father; listen to it, and you, too, all of you, my brothers! Lay down our arms, don't come to blows, wait; we two leaders, priest Grigoris and I, each representing his people, will fight it out here in front of you, disarmed; we will take an oath: if priest Grigoris throws me, and my back touches the ground, we will go back up to the Sarakina peaceably, empty-handed; if I throw priest Grigoris and make him touch the ground, we shall go and take possession of the goods which Michelis has given to our community; between us two, above us, God will judge."

The Lycovrissiots exulted when they heard the words of priest Fotis; at the sight of his livid face, his cricket's feet and hands, they roared with laughter.

"Blow on him, priest Grigoris, blow on him and he'll fall over backward!"

The people of the Sarakina were alarmed:

"No, no, Father," shouted Loukas; "let the bravest of them come and wrestle with me; that fire-eater Panayotaros, who struts about with his pistols and his great red fez, the dirty Turk! Let him step out in front of me, if he dares!"

He handed the banner over to a companion and rolled up his sleeves.

"I'm coming, scum! Here I am, bolshevik!" roared Panayotaros rushing forward: "I'll break your neck, you swine!"

He drew his pistol from his belt and bounded forward; but priest Grigoris raised his hand:

"Stop! Leave us alone, it's for us priests, us two alone, to give judgment. I accept your challenge, lousy priest; I swear before God: if you throw me, I shall not oppose your taking possession of the goods the witless Michelis made you a present of; but if I win, go away the lot of you and leave us in peace! I invoke God: let Him come and stand between us and let Him judge!"

"In the name of Christ," said priest Fotis, crossing himself.

He turned, signed to an old man and gave the icon of the Prophet into his arms. Then he took off his threadbare cassock, folded it carefully and laid it on a stone; his black shirt appeared, in rags, likewise his tattered trousers; his spindle shanks were covered with wounds.

Priest Grigoris waited with his legs apart and hands folded; he tapped the ground with his foot like a mettled horse; he was in a hurry to be done. But seeing priest Fotis suddenly standing before him, like a skeleton, in rags, with deep black eyes like wells, he shivered: he thought he had before him the scarecrow Death.

"Make the sign of the cross, Father," said priest Fotis calmly; "I am ready."

Priest Grigoris crossed himself mechanically, and disdainfully stayed where he was.

"Come here, vile grasshopper!" he bawled; "come here and let me twist your neck!"

"Can't you open your mouth, Father, without uttering an insult? Is it with such lips that you sing the praises of the Lord? Are those the hands that elevate the holy Chalice?"

"They are the hands that will break a goat-beard's bones," yelled priest Grigoris, and he charged his opponent with lowered head, like a bull.

He raised his fist and struck; but priest Fotis stepped lightly aside and the fist fell on empty air; priest Grigoris, carried along by his momentum, all but fell and rolled on the ground. Seized with rage, he charged priest Fotis again; he caught a tuft of his beard and pulled it out in his fury; priest Fotis in turn, gathering all his strength, brought down his knotty fist in a terrible blow on the buxom belly of priest Grigoris; the old man bellowed with pain; his eyes turned; he blenched; but he quickly recovered himself; fury increased his strength tenfold; he leaped upon priest Fotis and began biting his neck, nose, ears. Nothing could be heard but the screams of priest Grigoris, like some wild beast devouring his prey.

The Sarakini, terrified, held their breath; with craning necks they watched, breathlessly, their priest in danger.

"Our priest's done for," muttered Yannakos in despair; "that brute will strangle him."

"Have no fear, my Yannakos," answered Manolios; "can't you see God? there, just above them? Trust Him."

Manolios had not finished speaking when priest Fotis, getting a grip on priest Grigoris's forked beard with an iron hand, struck him with the other a powerful blow on the jaw; howling with pain priest Grigoris doubled up, spitting teeth and blood; before he had time to recover, priest Fotis caught him by the waist, shook him to right and left, then hurled himself upon him and, with the whole weight of his body, made him bite the dust.

With his knee he was preparing to hold priest Grigoris down, but he did not have time: Panayotaros had rushed upon him and was striking him in a mad frenzy. Then Loukas darted forward, next Yannakos and Manolios; the two camps mingled, the slings began to whistle and for a long time nothing was heard but blows of sticks and pistol shots, while knives, too, were plunged into flesh. At first there were cries and insults; but gradually there were only gasps and muffled groans.

Kostandis, Andonis the barber, the fat Dimitri, the butcher, ran up armed with clubs and flung themselves into the combat. Yannakos, seeing his friends, detached himself from the melee and shouted to Kostandis:

"Hey, Kostandis, did you do what I asked you?"

Kostandis gazed at him open-mouthed; he could not remember.

"My ass . . ."

"Don't worry, Yannakos, he's at my place."

"Fire, then!" cried Yannakos, hoisting one of the two cans of petrol on to his shoulder.

"Courage, lads," thundered Loukas, laying about him blindly right and left with his club; "courage, we've got them, the swine."

In fact, the Lycovrissi were giving ground; they recoiled gradually and took refuge in the village; several had already barricaded themselves in their houses. Meanwhile the Sarakini had picked up priest Fotis, stretched him out near the well, and were washing his wounds; blood was running from his broken head.

"Courage, brothers!" shouted Manolios, rushing forward. He had snatched from Panayotaros one of his pistols, and was firing into the air as he chased the retreating villagers.

The alarmed voice of the schoolmaster again made itself heard:

"Stop, brothers, don't kill each other; we shall reach a compromise, trust me; we are all Hellenes, Christians, brothers!"

But he was quickly caught between the two camps; friends and enemies hurled him to the ground and trampled him frenziedly; someone threw a huge stone at him, and the poor peacemaker rolled into a ditch, unconscious.

The Lycovrissi were now all retreating toward the village; Loukas then seized the second can of petrol, darted forward, and began throwing petrol on to the doors, windows and walls.

"At them, women, follow me; set them on fire!" he cried, as he advanced.

Soon the flames began to lick the houses; the Lycovrissi women, shut up in their homes, began uttering shrill cries.

Before Priest Grigoris had yet recovered consciousness, he had been carried to old Mandalenia's house, close by, and laid out in the middle of the yard; the old woman brought her herbs and unguents, washed his wounds and anointed them with balm. The poor priest had no pride left and was roaring with pain.

Meanwhile Manolios went ahead, followed by his men; they arrived before the spacious house of Patriarcheas, broke open the door and entered.

"Here, my braves, we'll barricade ourselves!" Manolios declared; "let two of you bring our priest here; you others, go in quickly; we're at home!"

Andonis the barber and Kostandis volunteered to bring priest Fotis; the villagers were busy with buckets of water, trying to put out the fire; the whole village was howling. Suddenly terrified voices rang out:

"Old Ladas's house is burning!"

"They've smashed his jars, the oil's running down the road; they've stove in his barrels, the wine's spilling in floods!"

In the fight Panayotaros had lost his fez; he ran limping this way and that, firing with the pistol he still had and summoning Manolios to appear. But Manolios, full of anxiety, was bending over priest Fotis, who had been brought in and laid on Patriarcheas's bed. The women had bandaged his wounds, and now he opened his eyes, looked at his companions and smiled.

"They broke their oath," he murmured, "God will punish them! I rolled their priest over, I'm happy."

"Are you in pain, Father?"

"Of course, my Manolios, my wounds are hurting me, but I'm happy, I tell you; God has given His judgment; we have won!"

Joyful shouts rang out in the courtyard; Loukas and his companions, having set fire to the houses, had gone in and taken three newly-killed and beautifully cleaned pigs; they brought them with jubilation into the house of archon Patriarcheas.

"Light a big fire, women," they cried, "we've plenty of wood; open the storerooms, take flour, make bread; roast the pigs, the fight's sharpened our appetite, we're hungry!"

"It's Advent, it's a fast, even oil's forbidden!" protested an old woman; "have you no fear of God, you?"

"Let's consult our priest!" Loukas suggested.

"I take the sin upon me," replied priest Fotis; "eat!"

Yannakos arrived, with his beard scorched and his clothes reeking of wine and oil.

"I've done what I wanted, brothers!" he cried triumphantly;

"my soul's satisfied; the old skinflint's house is blazing; God be praised!"

There was a knock at the door; the voice of Kostandis could be heard outside.

"Open, open, brothers; the schoolmaster's been killed!"

They opened the door, and Kostandis, the barber and the butcher brought in the schoolmaster's lifeless body. His brain was leaking out of his open head; his wide-open eyes were glassy; his jaw was hanging.

"We found him in a ditch," said Kostandis; "both villagers had been over him."

Men and women bent over him in silence; they kissed him; a few meager flowers were picked in the courtyard and put into his hands.

"He wanted to reconcile us and we've killed him," said Manolios, wiping away tears.

The Agha, stretched on his soft couch, listened to the pistol shots, smoking his chibouk and caressing Brahimaki. But the wild boy sniffed the smell of powder and his blood flared up; he gave his Agha several kicks and tried with all his strength to rush off into the road and take part in the fight; but the Agha held him back by the foot and would not let go.

"Don't be a fool, my Brahimaki," he told him, "leave the giaours to break each other's bones. Won't the dirty vermin ever disappear? How many years have we been sweating blood and water to finish them off? And what's the result? A hole in the water. You cut off one *romnoi* head and lo and behold, ten more rear up. If they don't kill each other, I'm telling you, no one will manage to wipe them out. So I'm letting them be; when they're knocked out, I shall get on my mare and restore order. D'you understand, thickhead? I'm telling you so that if one day you have the luck to become agha of a Greek village, you'll know how to deal with giaours."

"Let me kill one or two!" cried Brahimaki; "my hand's itching."

"Don't bother, I'm telling you, let them kill each other of their own accord. If we get mixed up in it, we shall have trouble; the vessels of the Franks will anchor in front of Smyrna once more and proclaim the blockade, and then you'll have hell to pay! Here we are, nice and comfortable, my Brahimaki; it's cold outside, I won't let you go out. The old woman'll bring some honey and nuts, you'll see."

He clapped his hands, and old Martha appeared.

"What's happening outside, old thing?"

"They're cutting each other's throats, Agha. The two priests have torn each other's beards out, Panayotaros has lost his fez and had his knee broken, old Ladas's house has been set on fire and the oil and wine are running in floods down the road!"

The Agha roared with laughter:

"Bravo, giaours; go to it, my lads; the plague take the lot of you! Bring us some honey and nuts, old Martha, quick!"

He turned toward Brahimaki, who was cursing and wanted to go out.

"Don't be a fool, I tell you, don't mix yourself up in the *romnoi* affairs! That cursed race, a real blunder of Allah's. Listen to what my late grandfather used to say to me: pay attention and try to understand, lout! All that Allah had created was perfect; but one day he was not himself: he took fire and dung and out of them he kneaded the *romnios*. As soon as he'd seen what he'd done, he was sorry—the blessed scum had an eye that went through you like a gimlet. 'I've made a blunder,' Allah muttered with a sigh; 'how'm I going to put it right? Let's roll up our sleeves now and knead the Turk; he'll kill off the *romnoi* and everything will be in order again.' He took honey and gunpowder, kneaded them well and fashioned the Turk. Without losing a minute he put the Turk and the *romnios* on a dish together, they started fighting straightaway. They fought and they fought, from morning to evening, and neither could manage to bring the other down; but as soon as night came that artful *romnios,* in the darkness, tripped the Turk up, and he fell. 'Devil take me,' muttered Allah, incensed, 'I'm in a fine mess! These *romnoi* are going to make one mouthful of this world I've created; what's to be done?' He didn't close an eye all night, poor devil; but next morning he jumped out of bed, full of joy: 'I've got it! I've got it!' he exclaimed. Once more he took fire and dung, he kneaded another *romnios* and set the two of them on the dish. The fight began again straightaway; one gets tripped up, then the other; one gets knifed, then the other. They fought day and night, fell, got up again;

came to blows afresh, fell yet again, got up again at once, and the fight went on; it's going on still! That, my Brahimaki, is how the world found peace . . ."

Old Martha came in with the honey and nuts.

"Open the window, open it wide, Martha," the Agha commanded, "let me hear their cries and the pistol shots and rejoice my heart. Fill the bottle with raki! Keep a look out, and when they've all been killed come and let me know; I'll get on my mare and go and impose order!"

Toward evening, at length, the shots ceased; the villagers were in their houses, washing their wounds and anointing them with oil, letting themselves be cupped and having tisanes prepared for them. They lit the oil lamps and inspected the damage: an ear hanging in strips, some teeth missing, a finger cut off, two or three ribs broken. They also visited the village: several shutters burned, some doors smashed in, three pigs which had been hanging from the hooks had disappeared, old Ladas's house was still blazing, the oil and wine still flowing into the road and the corn strewn about the courtyard, charred.

"And his poor wife, you know, mother Penelope, that real saint," asked old Mandalenia, "what's become of her?"

"All praise to the neighbors' wives—they dashed into the flames and saved her. She was sitting on her stool, poor old thing, paralyzed and screaming. She hadn't got up to try and escape; she was frantically clutching to her bosom the sock she had been knitting, and jabbering something."

"Hadn't her swine of a husband dashed into the flames to save her?"

"What next? The old skinflint did dash into the flames, of course, but not to save his wife, oh no; to save his coffer with the gold in it; he grabbed it up in his arms, rushed into the road, put it on the ground, sat down on it and started whimpering. Soon they brought mother Penelope to him and—would you believe it?—she sat down on the ground and at once started knitting again. You're right, my dear Mandalenia, what a saint the poor woman is!"

Old Mandalenia was busy cupping the wounded. As she went to bring help farther on, rating the men under her breath (curse them, the good-for-nothing rascals!), a door opened suddenly and a hand caught her by the skirt.

"Seen my man, you old witch? The Devil's got into him once more, he's picked up his pistols and turned the village upside down, so they tell me; is all that true, mother Mandalenia?"

"I haven't caught sight of your man, mother Garoufilia, all I've seen is his big fez, close by Saint Basil's Well. His head, my poor woman, must have gone one way and his fez the other. There! let go my skirt!"

"Plague take him!" said mother Garoufilia, and slammed her door noisily.

The old healer set off as fast as her legs would carry her, in haste to reach the house of priest Grigoris, who had been taken home; his neighbors were coming and going, bringing him coffee, lemonade, tisanes.

"There's nothing wrong with you, Father," a little old woman in rags whispered in his ear. Snot dripped from her hooked nose on to his venerable beard. "There's nothing wrong with you, you mustn't worry. You've had nothing to eat since morning and you're hungry. That's all it is, Reverend Father."

And a moment later, with a sigh:

"All illnesses, believe me, come from hunger," added the poor little old woman who was always hungry; "eat and you'll get well."

They brought him food—lenten fare, since it was Advent. The priest sat up and began munching, painfully, fretting and fuming; that accursed priest Fotis had smashed his front teeth, and he swallowed each mouthful precipitately, half-chewed; blood was flowing from his broken head. He waited for mother Mandalenia and her drugs. His aches and pains had indeed calmed down a little, but his heart was boiling with rage.

"Tell me, old girl," he whispered to his hooked-nosed neighbor, "tell me, I must know: did anyone see when that damned priest threw me? Move away a little, please, your nose is running."

"What's that you're saying, Father? Is such a thing possible? Could a mosquito like that ever knock down your holiness? God preserve you from it! Don't say such a thing! No, my lord, no one saw, no one, I swear!"

But the suspicious heart of priest Grigoris remained inconsolable. He clenched his fists and once more rage gripped his chest. "That bandit Manolios, that pervert, is the cause of everything! He's the one has put himself at the head of the Sarakina and invaded the village; he's the one has kindled fire and burned down houses. He's the one—the traitor, the reprobate, the bolshevik! I'll tear his eyes out!"

He signed to the neighbors and they drew near.

"Pity it's Advent," he sighed; "I mustn't eat meat."

"But you're ill, Father," protested the little old woman, "as you're ill, it's all right."

"I am the priest, God's representative: it must not be!" declared the priest in a sententious voice. "Bring some more bread, olives, and vegetables without any oil. I'm hungry."

They brought him the tray, loaded; they filled his glass with wine.

The priest began eating again, greedily.

I must eat a lot, he told himself, I must drink a lot, to get back some strength. Tomorrow I must get up early and go and see the Agha; he must send an urgent despatch to the pasha of Smyrna and get Turkish soldiers post-haste with guns: the bolsheviks have invaded Lycovrissi, let them be quick and drive them out! It's time order and justice reigned again on earth!

The door opened and the priest turned.

"Welcome, mother Mandalenia," he said, relieved, "come close, a word in your ear."

The old woman drew near and bent over the priest.

"Get rid of the neighbors," he whispered to her, "and kill me a chicken."

In Vain, My Christ, in Vain

Next morning the Agha woke early. He listened hard: no cries, no pistol shots; all was calm. He became anxious.

"The giaours," he rumbled, "aren't they fighting any more; why the devil have they stopped killing each other?"

He called Martha.

"Here, you dirty Christian, aren't they fighting any more? Is it all over?"

"It's all over, Agha; they're not fighting any more. But the bolsheviks are occupying the house of Patriarcheas, they won't clear out; 'The house is ours,' they say, and the poor schoolmaster—well, he's been killed."

"Killed!" exclaimed the Agha, enraptured; "bravo, that's what I like to hear; one less. And the priests?"

"They're still alive, Agha."

"Both of them?"

"Both of them. You know, priests are like cats; each one has nine lives. They've only got their faces knocked about and half their beards torn out; but they're all right; they're not dying."

"A pity," muttered the Agha, "a pity they're still alive! But patience; there's sure to be another fight soon. Saddle my mare."

The old hunchback went to the door, but the Agha called her back:

"Where's Brahimaki? He slipped away before dawn."

"That trollop Pelaghia must have turned up before dawn; that's it!"

"Devil take her! Hasn't he yet had enough of her? To hell with him, the young rake! Go and saddle my mare!"

Priest Fotis, too, had waked up early; he was still in pain, but he bit his lips; he uttered no cries; he would have been ashamed. He called Manolios.

"Dear Manolios," he said, "let's hurry, let's lose no time. Send our people quickly, men and women, to take possession of our gardens, our vineyards and our olive orchards. Let them put up huts there and remain on guard so that no one may come and expel us. I shall stay here with a few companions. Go, in the name of Christ."

"Are you still in pain, Father?"

"What does it matter whether I'm in pain or not, dear Manolios? Our community is in danger, and are you still thinking of me? Go, call our men, get out among our property; any minute the Agha will appear."

Manolios went down to the courtyard; the schoolmaster was still stretched out on the stones, right in the middle of the yard. His eyelids were stiff, it was no longer possible to close his eyes; they stared at the sky.

The women had cut laurel branches and covered the corpse with them; a few old women were squatting about him and weeping softly; a mother had placed in his hands a sprig of basil, that he might take it to her child who had died of hunger; he had been going to the Lycovrissi school these last months, and Hadji Nikolis had been very fond of him.

Manolios called the companions and divided them into three groups. They armed themselves with their sticks, took with them food fetched from the storerooms in the house, and set forth: one of the groups make for the gardens of old Patriarcheas, another for his vineyards, the third for the olive orchards.

The village was still asleep. They passed in haste through the deserted streets. Old Ladas's house was still smoking; the snow had melted in the plain, the sky was limpid; the Prophet Elijah's peak smiled, bathed in light and covered with snow.

The beadle heard footsteps, opened his window, saw the Sarakini and immediately understood. He dressed hastily and hurried to bring the bad news to priest Grigoris. He was delighted.

"I'll put some gunpowder in his ears," he muttered, grinning; "I ought to have been bishop and him beadle; but destiny is blind."

He ran up the road which climbed to the priest's house; several doors opened timidly, the cocks began to crow. He arrived, pushed open the priest's door and entered. The old man was sitting on his bed, watching the day breaking. He had dined well last evening, the chicken had been succulent, he had gone into it up to the ears; old Mandalenia had spread balm on his wound and bandaged his head with care; he felt no more pain. Only his beard was rather sparser, and the right half of his mustache had been almost completely pulled out. The well-padded priest had emerged from the combat decidedly the worse for wear, toothless, seedy, like a scalded cat.

But he no longer felt either pain or shame; he had only one idea in his head, only one desire: to finish off Manolios. The anathema he had hurled at him was not enough; he wanted to tear out his eyes and eat them; ancient cannibal atavisms, wild prehuman instincts had awaked within him. Ah, to roll Manolios on the ground, fall on top of him, bite the knot of his throat and drink his blood! A wolf, come from the depths of the ages, had exploded the crust of his soul; it gazed at Manolios and howled. Christian love, Christian kindness, fear of God, Hell, Paradise—all had deserted the heart of priest Grigoris; nothing was left in the inhuman gulf of his entrails but the wolf.

The beadle approached, swallowing his saliva, not knowing what sequence to give to his words, to make them hurt the priest most cruelly.

"Father," he began, with feigned humility, "forgive me— The great vessels are subject to the greatest tempests; the highest peaks are struck by the lightning. You are a great vessel, Father; you are a high peak . . ."

"Speak out, old fox, don't play the innocent!" cried the priest, exasperated, "I know you well, come! You had the gall to want to be bishop, you didn't manage it and your lips distil poison. Drop those two-edged hints of yours, and speak out clearly. What's the matter?"

The beadle boiled inwardly but controlled himself; he set to work to pour him out the poison drop by drop.

"Priest Fotis," he said in a tearful voice, "has come out of the fight safe and sound; he's alive and he's triumphant."

"Drop that, you scoundrel, you're getting at something else; up with that bile of yours!"

"The Sarakini—I've seen them with my own eyes—have gone out early and spread over old Patriarcheas's property; by now they must have taken possession of it; we're done for!"

"Plague on you, rogue! That's enough!"

"There's more, alas, Father, forgive me."

"Speak!"

"The whole village is amusing itself with the story of how priest Fotis knocked you down and got his knee onto your venerable chest."

Priest Grigoris became purple with anger.

"Come closer, scum, approach!"

But the beadle was frightened and took refuge in a corner.

"And what's worse still . . ." he continued.

"Worse still? Speak, viper's tongue, empty your sack. D'you want to be the death of me?"

"What's worse, Father . . . Hey, courage, we're mortals, you know . . . poor mortals . . . We shall all die . . ."

The priest seized his steel snuffbox and hurled it at his head; but the beadle had time to avoid it by ducking and the snuffbox went through a pane of the window, which smashed into smithereens.

"Speak, or I shall get up, you blackguard, and beat you black and blue. What's worse . . .?"

"What? Didn't you know, Father? How am I to tell you? I shall faint. Your brother . . ."

The priest could no longer control himself; he threw off the bedclothes, leaped out of bed and flung himself toward the beadle. But the beadle took care to put the table and two chairs between him and the priest and barricaded himself in behind them.

"Your brother . . . has been killed," he whimpered.

"Who has killed him? Who?" roared the priest, and the blood began to flow from the swollen veins on his forehead. "Who? when? where?"

"I don't know, Father, how d'you expect me to know? Poor man, he was found in a ditch with his head smashed in. At present he's laid out, stiff, in Patriarcheas's yard, surrounded by those bandits."

"Don't you suspect anyone, beadle, damn you? Come, think and answer!"

"How d'you expect me to answer, Father. No one. But . . .

now I come to think of it . . . who knows? . . . perhaps it might be . . ."

"Might be? Think properly, my good friend. Out with it straight, don't be afraid. You're a man with a lot of sense, you must know . . . Well?"

He pushed aside the table and chairs and laid a protective hand on the beadle's shoulder.

"Surely you must know," he wheedled. "It might be . . ."

"Hm . . . I was there, for a moment I thought I saw . . . But I can't be sure of anything, I'm afraid of sinning, I'm afraid of Hell, Father . . ."

"Reassure yourself, my son, have no fear of Hell; I am there to protect you, speak freely! I too suspected the same person immediately. The cursed bolshevik! You saw him with your own eyes, didn't you, my friend?"

The poor beadle was silent; he was afraid of Hell, but he was also afraid of the priest; he became giddy.

The priest shook him roughly.

"Can I take you as witness? Come, help me dress, you know how fond I am of you; I'll go and see the Agha, I'll ask him for vengeance! So you saw him, didn't you? You saw him with your own eyes, my dear son?"

"What am I to say, Father? I thought I saw . . . but I can't tell you for sure that I saw . . ."

The priest brandished his arm menacingly; the beadle cowered.

"You saw him, yes, you saw him," he shouted at him; "why deny it? Can you be in league with him, with the bolshevik, you too, wretch?"

The beadle raised his eyes and saw the priest's fist suspended over his head.

"Father," he entreated, "give me time to gather my thoughts together, to remember . . ."

"All right, I am waiting."

I said I had seen, thought the beadle, but whom? that I won't say. That I won't say. In that way I shan't be committing a sin . . .

He found relief:

"I saw him," he cried, "I saw him, Father! I remember now. I saw him at the moment when the priest of the Sarakina had just thrown you and was planting his knee on your venerable chest . . ."

"Shut up! Help me dress, I tell you. I'm glad you saw him—the Antichrist—and will be able to bear witness. You don't know what an immense service you are rendering to Christendom, my friend!"

The beadle picked up the priest's drawers, socks, shirt and cassock and set to work dressing that sacerdotal bulk; he put on his shoes for him, his belt, his priest's cap, then helped him to reach the door.

"Give me your arm, don't go, beadle; help me as far as the Agha's house. Quietly, don't go too fast. Then, see that the body is brought to the church. Above all, don't forget that you saw him!"

The Agha was preparing to mount his mare; he saw priest Grigoris come in, tottering, hobbling, with his head bandaged, and he burst out laughing.

"How did you get into that state, priest?" he exclaimed. "Who's been damaging that face of yours?"

"Justice, Agha!" cried the priest, with outstretched arms; "justice, vengeance! Who? Manolios! He it is who roused the Sarakini; he it is, brought the bolsheviks into your village, set fire to the houses, has broken my head and killed my brother, the schoolmaster. I have witnesses. You are the representative of the Turkish Government at Lycovrissi: I come to you, I stretch out my arms—justice, vengeance, Agha! Deliver up to me Manolios, that I may judge him; the whole village implores you through my voice!"

"Don't shout like that, you blessed priest; you're splitting my ears. Sit down; Martha will make you a cup of coffee, to set you up again, you poor old thing. It's nothing, don't worry; you're *romnoi*, you've *romnios* heads, they bang against each other like eggs and break, that's all; so don't shout!"

"Deliver up to me Manolios!" repeated the priest, leaning against the wall to prevent himself from falling.

Martha ran up, brought him a chair, helped him to sit down. The Agha meanwhile was slowly buckling on his yataghan, thrusting his silver pistols into his broad red sash and tucking his whip under his arm.

The door opened, and a little old man entered, barefoot, bent, with his hair and beard half-burned and with large burns on his cheeks and hands. He advanced hopping into the yard and collapsed at the feet of the Agha.

"Agha," he cried, "pity."

"Heavens, aren't you old Ladas?" said the Agha, giving him a poke with his foot; "what's this carnival mask? where did you dig it up?"

"They've my house on fire, Agha. They've broken my jars, my barrels, my coffers, my furniture, my heart!"

"Who? who? Did you see them?"

"Manolios! Manolios! the bolshevik!"

"We have witnesses, Agha," cried priest Grigoris triumphantly; "Panayotaros saw him, the beadle saw him. I saw him, too!"

"Burn him, Agha, burn him as he's burned me! Pity, Agha!" bleated the old miser. "We'll pile up wood in the middle of the square, soak it with pitch and burn him up!"

The Agha scratched his head and spat, perplexed.

"Trouble . . . trouble . . ." he grumbled. "Devil take you, *romnoi!*"

He strode nervously up and down the yard, whipping the air, and the more he played with his whip the angrier he became.

"By the prophet Mahomet," he roared, "I'll catch the lot of you, priests, notables, bolsheviks, and I'll hang you one after the other from the plane tree!"

Hearing the door open, he turned. Panayotaros came in, hobbling, without fez and with only one pistol now in his belt; his clothes were torn, spotted with blood, covered with mud; and his face was bloated and quite purple.

The Agha could not help laughing.

"What's this poor devil with neither horns nor tail? What name am I to give you, eh? plucked bear, mangy camel, or Panayotaros?"

Panayotaros leaned against the wall, growled, but did not answer; his knee was hurting, he could not stand; he collapsed slowly and rolled on the stones of the courtyard.

The Agha gazed in turn at his three visitors: the priest, doubled up in his chair, was groaning, his hand was trembling, and he had upset his cup of coffee on his cassock; old Ladas, sunk at the Agha's feet, was wagging his head slowly, opening and closing his mouth, in a stupor; and Panayotaros was now only a heap of rags and mud.

"Well I never, what shipwrecked vessels are these!" cried the Agha jubilantly: "torn banners, admirals who've pissed in their bags! But it's the whole of Christendom that's infesting my courtyard! Come, old Martha, bring a dishcloth and wipe them!"

The priest felt the insult and raised his head:

"Agha," he said, "remember you will have to give account to your august Government! Here, to Lycovrissi, there has come an envoy of the Muscovite, his mission being to sack, to set blaze the Turkish Empire! Don't laugh, don't amuse yourself; raise your fist and strike! What does one do when a wolf gets into a sheepfold? One kills him! Deliver up to us Manolios! Don't get mixed up in it yourself, leave the dirty work to us Christians. The whole village will come before your door today crying out for justice. Voice of the people, voice of God! Listen, the people are crying out: 'You are Agha of the village, give justice!' "

The Agha fell into profound thought; his head was whirling; with it, the courtyard and the village. Panayotaros raised his head:

"Why are you hesitating, Agha?" he ventured; "decide. I saw Manolios with my own eyes smash in the schoolmaster's head with a huge stone. I saw him, saw him with these eyes, give the can of petrol to Yannakos; I heard him say to him: 'Set fire first of all, Yannakos, to the Agha's house; burn him too, the dog; let our village be set free from the yoke of the Turks!' "

"You swear it, eh, you swear it, Panayotaros?" roared the Agha, his eyes going bloodshot.

"I swear it, Agha!"

"Manolios is a dangerous bolshevik, Agha," priest Grigoris took him up, struggling to rise from his chair; "he has one aim only: to overthrow the Ottoman Empire. Behind him stands the Muscovite, pushing him on. If we let him live, he'll have us all!"

"Always back to that, you damned priest," retorted the Agha, scratching his head. "No, it isn't true," he muttered after a few moments. Nonetheless he had ended by becoming uneasy.

The priest had stood up; he gathered his strength and approached the Agha:

"It isn't true?" he whispered; "is that what you think, Agha? But the thing's clear, clear as daylight! Remember what Manolios was to begin with, in our village—a low shepherd, Patriarcheas's lackey, without a sheep to his name, without the least clod of land, a wretch, a lousy fellow. In a few months, by his tricks and with the help of the Muscovite, look what he's become: a monster! He has raised a banner of his own, he has killed men, he has broken up families, he has brought in from the other end of the world this rogue priest Fotis, with his ragged band, he has taken possession

of the Sarakina and begun to build, under our noses, a new village
peopled by bolsheviks! He has sworn to burn down your house and
to kill you, Agha, to sack our village and to call in the Muscovite
to take possession of it. You are staking your neck, Agha; look
out! The wolf has got into your sheepfold; kill him!"

"Kill him! Kill him!" cried the other two in unison. The Agha
again scratched his head. Up to now he had taken the thing
lightly. "These are *romnoi* manias," he had told himself, "let them
shift for themselves; I smoke my chibouk, I sip my raki, and I
don't care a fig! But now the Ottoman Empire's becoming mixed
up in it, the Muscovite is there, things are getting out of hand.
Yes, yes, if I let that abortion Manolios live, the Ottoman Empire
is in danger. I've got myself saddled with a bad business! That
goat-beard is right: the wolf's got into the sheepfold, and if I don't
kill him, he'll kill me!"

He opened his mouth, exasperated:

"Get out, all three of you, leave me alone; the matter is grave, I
shall think it over. Off with you, to blazes!"

He raised his whip and began to strike heads and backs.

Terrified, all three, with their heads sunk between their shoulders, dashed for the door, huddling against one another; behind
them the whip whistled. With a kick the Agha slammed the door
upon them, and was alone.

"Bring the bottle of raki," he shouted to Martha, "I have a decision to take!"

Priest Grigoris and father Ladas moved about the village and
the beadle was ordered to ring the knell. The villagers at once assembled in the square; all cried vengeance; they could not get over
the shame of having been beaten by those beggars. The priest stood
up in the midst of them; he had recovered his strength, and
shouted:

"My children, we have covered ourselves with shame, we must
avenge ourselves! I've spoken with the Agha, and we are in agreement. Who is the cause of all our misfortunes? One person only,
Manolios the excommunicated! But now his hour is come; the
Agha is going to deliver him up to us, and we shall judge him,
we shall condemn him, we shall drink his blood! Fall upon him,
my children; arise and go, all of you, to the Agha's house, assemble
before his door, raise your hands and shout: 'Manolios! Manolios! Give us Manolios!'—only that; the rest I will look after."

He made for the church, bent over the body of his brother, gave him the last kiss, read over him the prayers for the dead, hastily; his mind was on Manolios. The villagers lifted the body and bore it to the cemetery. The priest, as he saw his brother lowered into the grave, remembered their childhood years, and tears filled his eyes. The villagers threw each a handful of earth on the dead man; the beadle poured them out a glass of raki to drink to his memory, and distributed to each a piece of bread and a handful of olives; immediately all went back to the village in haste and took up their positions before the Agha's door.

Toward midday the Agha was completely drunk; he had come to a decision; he called Panayotaros, who had remained squatting outside on the threshold and was waiting like a beaten dog.

"Come here, you damned blusterer; can you still walk or are you a complete cripple, you poor fool?"

"If it's for Manolios I can walk."

"I can see that head of yours, but not your fez; what have you done with your fez, giaour?"

"I left it yesterday, Agha, at Saint Basil's Well; mother Manda-lenia's found it, I'm told; I'll send for it."

"Put on your fez, choose two stout men from the village, if you can't manage alone, and go and get me Manolios. Off with you! Gallop!"

"Dead or alive?"

"Alive!"

Panayotaros, transported with delight, forgot that he was wounded in the knee; he set off running for all he was worth.

"Your hour is come, your hour is come, my Manolios!" he muttered, rubbing his hands. "Bravo, Judas Panayotaros, my gallant, you've got him!"

Manolios and his men had put up a hut in the big Patriarcheas garden, outside the village, near Lake Voidomata. Manolios had chosen those who were to keep watch, while he would go back into the village toward nightfall to see what was becoming of priest Fotis and to consult with him; he had heard the knell ringing and was worried.

Shortly after midday Kostandis arrived running, bearing news:

"Priest Grigoris is rousing the village afresh; he's running about the village with his head bandaged, exciting the villagers, urging them to assemble in front of the Agha's door and to shout: 'Give us Manolios! Give us Manolios! Death to Manolios!' They want to arrest you, my Manolios, shove everyone's crimes onto you and condemn you as robber, incendiary, murderer; and, above all, as bolshevik! Hide, take refuge on the Sarakina, or further away still; your life's at stake; they're all after you!"

"My post is here, with my brothers in danger!" replied Manolios; "flight would be desertion, my dear Kostandis. What's become of our other companions? Have you seen them?"

"Yannakos found his ass at my place and has hidden him in the big olive orchard; he's barricaded himself in there with his men. Priest Fotis is better; tomorrow, he declares he'll get up and go and see the Agha; 'He's a brute,' he says, 'but not wicked at bottom; he'll recognize our right, all will come straight; Christ is with us!' All the same, I'm frightened, I am, my Manolios; they've all sworn to have your blood."

"God grant that all the crimes may fall on me, Kostandis, and that they may make an end of me; then our companions will be left in peace. To all their accusations I shall answer: 'Yes. It's I who robbed, I alone; it's I who killed, who set things on fire; yes, I am a bolshevik.' All, all, if only the community may be saved . . . I shall go of my own accord and give myself up to the Agha; and at once."

Kostandis opened his eyes wide; the face of Manolios was sparkling; his stature seemed magnified; he stood in the midst of the trees of the garden like a column of light. Kostandis's eyes blinked; they were dazzled.

"Dear Manolios," he said, "it's not for me to give you advice. My soul can reach as far as Kostandis and his family; at the very most, as far as a few friends; farther she can't go; your soul stretches to a whole people. What you run to meet, I tremble as I see it coming. You can follow in the footsteps of Christ: do as God inspires you, my Manolios!"

"Come," said Manolios, making for the gate of the garden.

Kostandis followed him, with bent head.

They went out of the garden and skirted the lake; the sky was cloudless on that winter day, the air translucent. The dark green lake gleamed in the sun; all around it, reeds and a few willows looked at themselves in it; a stork, standing on one leg, gazed impassively; two more, with their feet folded under their bellies, flew off noiselessly, staring into the water: they were hungry.

Manolios took a long look around, said farewell to the lake, to the trees now growing quite bare, to the Sarakina with its tender violet shade; his gaze descended into the plain and crossed the olives; the medlar trees were already in blossom, the lemons were shining among the dark leaves, an almond tree was foretelling the spring and its buds were on the point of bursting.

"How beautiful the world is . . ." murmured Manolios under his breath.

The human soul is even more beautiful, sometimes, thought Kostandis, but he said nothing.

They made for the village; the bell was still sounding the knell; in the distance a confused noise of voices and barking could be heard; a cock crowed.

"The weather's going to change," said Manolios; "listen to that cock crowing."

Kostandis compressed his lips; he was afraid he might burst out sobbing; he followed Manolios with his head bowed, silent.

Just as they were approaching Saint Basil's Well, they saw Panayotaros and two other stalwarts dash out from a bush, brandishing huge clubs. Panayotaros was now wearing his fez. Kostandis blenched and recoiled.

They're going to lay hold of Manolios, he said to himself. His first impulse was to flee as fast as his legs would carry him; but he was ashamed; he stood still, transfixed with fear.

Panayotaros advanced in front of his two companions with an air of decision.

"Where are you going, curse you?" he bellowed, stretching out toward Manolios a threatening arm.

"I'm going to see the Agha, my poor Panayotaros; don't get excited; I heard he was looking for me, I'm going to give myself up."

Panayotaros stared at him, open-mouthed.

"Aren't you afraid? Aren't you afraid of the Agha, of priest Grigoris, of the village? Might you be the Devil in person?"

"The man who's not afraid of death isn't afraid of anyone, Panayotaros; there's my secret. Let's go!"

"Walk in front, I don't want you to escape me!"

He turned toward his two stalwarts:

"Get along with you, you two, I'll manage this rogue by myself. Be off too, you, Kostandis, dirty bolshevik!"

Kostandis hesitated; he looked at Manolios.

"Go, my Kostandis," said Manolios; "go home, go to your children; leave me alone."

Kostandis did not need to be told twice; he went off at the run.

Manolios and Panayotaros were left alone; for a good while they walked in silence.

"Panayotaros," said Manolios at length in a calm voice, "do you then hate me so much that you want my death? Why? What have I done to you?"

"Don't talk to me in that tone of voice," growled Panayotaros; "you tore my heart to bits, you know very well."

The widow reappeared before his eyes, with her fresh laughter, her rouged mouth, her brilliant teeth, her hair fair as honey; Panayotaros felt a tearing of his entrails.

"When I've killed you, Manolios," he bellowed, "I shall kill myself afterward; I'm only living to kill you. Afterward what need'll I have of life? A pistol shot and I'm off to the Devil."

They were entering the village, the knell was still ringing, a great confused tumult was coming from the square with the plane tree; all the villagers were assembled in front of the Agha's door, howling.

"What is it they're shouting?" said Manolios, stopping to listen.

"You'll soon find out, curse you! Walk faster!"

The tumult grew louder, the words became more distinct; Manolios caught fragments; he guessed their meaning; he smiled bitterly and quickened his step. I'm coming . . . I'm coming . . . he murmured; don't shout so, I'm coming . . .

As soon as Manolios appeared in the square the crowd hurled itself upon him, in a frenzy; but Panayotaros advanced and stretched out his arms.

"No one's to touch him!" he bellowed; "he's mine!"

"Robber! Assassin! Bolshevik!" yelled the crowd, ready to tear him to pieces.

Priest Grigoris caught sight of him from a distance and rushed upon him, full of rage:

"Kill him, my children! Death to the excommunicated!"

But the Agha's door opened and Panayotaros with a kick had Manolios in the courtyard. The door closed again at once.

Cross-legged on a cushion of velvet, the Agha sat in his room; he was drinking in a stupor, his eyes fixed on the brazier's glowing coals; a mild warmth reigned in the room, the air smelled of raki and pork sausage, and the Agha blinked away, plunged in a profound beatitude. He listened to the villagers, who, gathered down below at his door, were shouting at the tops of their voices: "Manolios! Manolios! Give us Manolios!" He listened and smiled with satisfaction.

Devil's own race, these Greeks, he thought; the foxes, the ruffians, the demons! Wolves don't eat one another; Greeks do. Here they are now, wanting, for all they're worth, to eat Manolios! Why? what's he done to them? He's innocent, poor fellow; a bit crazy, but he never did anyone any harm. And yet: Give us Manolios; we want to eat him! You'd play the saint, would you, scoundrel? Then take what's coming to you! Well, let them eat him, if that's what they've set their hearts on; I don't care. Defend him? What's the good? it'd mean trouble; let them leave me in peace. There he is, take him, you blessed *romnoi,* and enjoy your meal! I wash my hands of it; I drink my raki, I savor these succulent camel sausages. Besides, I've also got my Brahimaki. And then there's my whip. I've everything I want, Allah be praised!

Steps sounded in the corridor, and the Agha raised his head.

The door opened, Panayotaros appeared. He closed the door, saluted the Agha and came forward, hobbling a little but with his face radiant.

"I've nabbed him, Agha. He was barricaded in the garden with his men, about twenty, armed to the teeth. The two who were with me got the wind up when they saw. 'Be off with you, cowards!' I told them, and I advanced by myself; 'Hands up, you swine! I'm Panayotaros!' Soon as they heard my name they ran in all directions. Manolios was left alone; to tell the truth, he never stirred. I caught him by the neck and I've brought him!"

"Bravo, my fire eater!" said the Agha, smiling into his mustache, which was freshly dyed black; "seems to me you've embellished the tale, but who cares? You're a Greek, and that means liar. Come, bring Manolios; we're going to have some fun!"

Panayotaros went out, seized Manolios by the arm, struck him with his fist and pushed him into the room. Manolios, with his arms folded, remained standing very calmly in front of the Agha, and waited.

"Shut the door, Panayotaros, and stay behind it!" the Agha ordered.

He filled his cup and emptied it at one gulp; he filled his mouth with sausage and began slowly munching and savoring it; half-shutting his eyes, he gazed at Manolios and smiled; he was happy.

"Poor Manolios," he said at length, "this is the second time you've got into my clutches; but this time I think you'll have trouble in getting out. Great crimes are weighing on your back, poor fellow; you've been robbing, they say, you've been killing, you've been setting fire to the village. Is it true?"

"It's true, Agha."

The Agha flushed, and lost his temper.

"Listen," he shouted, "try your nonsense on others; don't do what you did last time, don't ape the saints, d'you hear? Otherwise the Devil's going to get you. Understand? A poor innocent like you, rob, kill, set fire to things? Try it on others, I tell you; you won't fool me, my dear, see? Even if the Devil were in it, I wouldn't believe you!"

"It's me, Agha, it is me all right; I do ape the saints, I play the innocent, I keep my eyes downcast, I don't look men in the face; I pretend to be timid, but inside I'm a devil."

In the square the cries redoubled.

"Manolios! Manolios! Death to Manolios!"

"Do you hear? They want me to give you up to them; you won't come out of their claws alive. Make up your mind."

"I've made it up, Agha; give me up. I've only one thing to ask: let no one else be touched. The Sarakini had right on their side, but things couldn't be fixed up peaceably; so then I wanted to seize it by force, and I did what I have done. I am the cause of all these misfortunes, no one else! The Sarakini are fine people, Agha: honest, peaceable, hard working."

"Come now! I tell you they're bolsheviks; they want to bring down the Ottoman Empire."

"Don't you believe that, Agha; that's a lot of clever lies. Really they are poor people who want to live in peace and have roots in the earth; that's all."

The Agha clutched his head in his hands; the room had begun to go around.

"You *romnios* make me lose my bearings! I listen to this one and he's right; I listen to that one and he's right, too; I don't understand any more. By Allah, I'll hang the lot of you one day, to get a little peace and quiet."

At the door below more fullbodied yells rang out.

"Death to Manolios! Death to Manolios!"

"What the devil am I to do?" growled the Agha. "I'm sorry for you really, you poor innocent; I tell you once more, you're mad and a saint all in one; you want to cover all the villainies of the world with your wings, like a broody hen. I'm sorry for you, but what do you expect? If I don't do what they want I shall have trouble. After all, how do I know you're not a bolshevik? That devil of a priest, who excites the villagers to bawl themselves hoarse in front of my door, is quite capable of going and complaining before the pasha of Smyrna, and then—look out! Do you understand, my poor Manolios? Put yourself in my place; what would you do? Isn't it better I should give you up and let them do what they like with you, then that I should feel, day and night, the chill of the sword on the back of my neck?"

"You're right, Agha, give me up."

"But by all the devils, don't say it to me in that tone of voice; you're driving me mad! Come, admit that you're a bolshevik, so I can get in a rage and give you up without its breaking my heart. Otherwise I'm afraid of giving a lamb to the wolves. Will you ever understand what I want? I want my peace, that's all. For that, I've got to get rid of them and of you . . . Understand? If you confess you're a bolshevik, that's perfect."

"Well, I am a bolshevik, Agha," said Manolios; "now are you satisfied? I am dangerous to the Ottoman Empire; if I could, I would blow it sky high!"

"Go on, go on; confess, on your faith, that you have committed all the crimes; do all you can to set me in a rage!"

"This world is unjust and wicked, Agha; the best are hungry and suffer, the worst eat, drink and govern without faith, without shame, without love. Such a world must perish! I shall rush out into the street, I shall go up onto the house tops, I shall cry: 'Come, all who are starving and persecuted, let us unite, let us set fire to it, that the earth may purify itself and rid itself of bishops, notables and aghas!' "

"Go on, go on, Manolios, damn you; that's the way, I'm beginning to flare up!"

"I should like, Agha, to proclaim revolution over the whole earth. To rouse all men, white, black, yellow; to form an immense all-powerful army and enter into the great rotten towns, into the shameless palaces, into the mosques of Constantinople, and set fire to them!"

"Go on, go on, harder still! That's the way!"

"But I'm only a poor devil, a mere lackey, without power, lost in a village in the depths of Anatolia, and my voice can't make itself heard beyond Lycovrissi and the Sarakina. So I stand up between Lycovrissi and the Sarakina and I proclaim: 'Arise, starving brothers, my persecuted fellow beings; how long are we to remain slaves? How long are we to present our necks to the Agha's yataghan? Arise, the hour is come, liberty or death! They will not give us our rights peaceably, we will take them by war! Arm, downtrodden brothers, descend upon the replete village, kill those who resist you, set fire to the house of old Ladas, the dirty miser; Patriarcheas's house is yours, enter it and barricade yourselves in. When you have beaten the rich and the notables, arise again and strike the Agha: let him vanish from our lands, let him go to blazes! And then . . .' "

But Manolios had no time to finish; the Agha had leaped up, he was foaming at the mouth. He seized Manolios by the neck, shook him furiously, threw him to the ground, opened the door, and gave him a kick which sent him tumbling down the stairs, head first. He came down after him, caught hold of him again by the neck, dragged him into the courtyard and, with his foot, opened the entrance door wide.

The crowd recoiled, taken aback. The Agha, gasping and foaming at the mouth, was shaking Manolios by the scruff of the neck; behind him Panayotaros appeared and, with a grin on his blood-smeared face, signed to the villagers to draw near. Priest Grigoris was the first to rush forward, and advanced with his arms spread wide, ready to seize hold of Manolios.

The voice of the Agha rang out hoarsely, constricted by fury:

"Take him, kill him, tear him into a thousand pieces, the devil take you all!"

This said, he slammed the door.

The priest dashed forward; he was exultant. He clutched Manolios by one shoulder; Panayotaros took the other. The crowd threw itself upon him, howling, struck him, spat in his face. It bore him toward the church. Night had fallen; in the sky, not a star, nothing but great black clouds with, far-off toward the west, a noiseless flashing and extinguishing of lightning.

They passed the plane tree; the breathless crowd pawed Manolios; the shouting had ceased. The beadle ran up, pulled from his belt the enormous key of the church, and opened the door. The people surged in, behind the priest and Manolios. The three great silver lamps were lit, one before the icon of Christ, another before that of the Virgin Mary and the third before Saint John the Baptist. All the other martyrs and saints were drowned in darkness. Only, over the small doorway into the choir, there shone, phosphorescent, the two outspread wings of the Archangel Michael, the despoiler of souls. The church was fragrant with incense and wax.

The priest now held Manolios by the neck with both hands. He dragged him as far as the choir, threw him to the ground and set him on his knees before the archangel of death.

He was so delighted to have Manolios at his mercy, his vengeance was so certain, so sweet and so near, that he was unable to open his mouth and speak. The words tied themselves up in his throat, nothing came out but hoarse yells.

Panayotaros kicked Manolios who, with his head held erect, was gazing serenely at the feet of the archangel, shod in red lace-boots. Old Ladas pushed the crowd aside, approached breathlessly and spat on Manolios. Packed tight around the victim, the people waited in trembling eagerness for the moment when priest Grigoris would give the signal; they licked their lips in anticipation, seized suddenly by a burning thirst.

Priest Grigoris slipped his gold-embroidered stole round his neck and stood up before the icon of Christ; the three lamps above him threw their light upon his sweating face; the wound on his forehead had reopened and the priest's beard was red with blood.

He signed to Panayotaros, who caught Manolios under the arms and dragged him to the priest's feet; the crowd took another step forward, gasping.

"In the name of the Father, of the Son and of the Holy Ghost," boomed the voice of the priest, solemnly.

"Amen!" answered the crowd, making the sign of the cross.

"Brethren," cried priest Grigoris, "kneel down, and let us pray that God may descend upon our church and do justice. Lord, here he is at Thy feet, the excommunicated; he is trembling and waiting for Thy sword to fall on him! He has robbed, killed, burned, sown discord among the brethren, separated the affianced, stirred to a blaze the hatred between father and son; he has roused the ragged and the outlaws to rebellion; he has introduced them into our village, he has put our goods to the sack!

"As long as this man remains alive, O Lord, religion and honor will be in danger; as long as this man remains alive, Christendom and the Greek race, those two great hopes of the earth, will be in danger. He is paid by the Muscovite, that son of Satan, to make Thy name, Lord, vanish from the surface of the earth. We have assembled this evening in Thy church to judge this criminal, this blasphemer; descend, Almighty, from the vault of the church and judge him; and guide our hands to the execution of Thy judgment, Lord!"

He placed his foot on Manolios's back and began again to cry:

"I have lost my daughter and my brother. He has killed them. The Antichrist, the Muscovite, has entered into our village; he it is, on whom I have placed my foot, who opened the gates to him. The Sarakina is riddled with wasp nests, and he it is who has brought against us that poisonous swarm. Christian brethren, voice of the people, voice of God, judge him!"

At these words the crowd growled with rage; under the three silver lamps there gleamed bloodshot eyes, teeth, hands and twisted mouths. Panayotaros squatted and stared at Manolios in the eyes, as though afraid he would escape him; if Manolios moved slightly to the right, Panayotaros moved to the right; if Manolios moved to the left, he, too, moved to the left, ready at any moment to leap at his throat. Old Ladas, squatting on the stone flags of the church, remembered his burned-down house, his spilled oil and wine, and began to weep.

Priest Grigoris bent over Manolios.

"Accursed man," he shouted, "stand up! Have you heard the tale of the misfortunes which you have heaped upon our village?

Have you heard the tale of your crimes? Have you anything to say in your defence?"

"Nothing," replied Manolios tranquilly.

"You confess that you have robbed, burned, killed?"

"I confess that I am guilty of all the misfortunes."

"You confess that you are a bolshevik?"

"If bolshevik means what I have in my spirit, yes, I am a bolshevik, Father; Christ and I are bolsheviks."

The whole church rang with the howls of the crowd. Old Ladas stood up and began yelping:

"Let's kill him! Let's kill him! We have no need of other witnesses; he's confessed. Let's kill him!"

The crowd grew bold; all raised their fists. "Death! Death!" they howled.

Manolios freed himself from the grip of Panayotaros, and the people made way; he took a step forward and opened his arms: "Kill me," he said.

With his arms open, defenceless, unresisting: "Kill me," he repeated. He advanced in the lane opened for him by the surprised and silent crowd. The stupor of the crowd was such that if, at that moment, Manolios had opened the door and gone out, no one would have barred his way. But Manolios stopped in the middle of the church, just underneath the Pantocrator, the savage Almighty painted in the vault. He opened his arms again. "Kill me," he implored, the third time.

Priest Grigoris advanced and signed to Panayotaros to follow him.

"Bolt the door!" he ordered in a strangled voice; "bolt the door; he'll escape us!"

The beadle rushed to lock it and leaned his back against it.

The priest's voice had sent a shudder through the crowd; suddenly all were seized with fear at the idea that the quarry might escape them; in terror they crowded close around Manolios; their burning breath ringed his face.

For an instant Manolios's heart failed him: he turned to the door—it was closed; he looked at the three lit lamps and, under them, the icons loaded with *ex-votos*: Christ, red-cheeked, with carefully combed hair, was smiling; the Virgin Mary, bending over her child, was taking no interest in what was happening under her eyes; Saint John the Baptist was preaching in the desert. He raised his eyes toward the vault of the church and made out in the half-light the face of the Almighty, bending pitilessly over mankind. He looked at the crowd about him; it was as if in the darkness he saw the gleam of daggers.

The strident voice of old Ladas squeaked once more:

"Let's kill him!"

At the same moment, violent blows were struck upon the door; all fell silent and turned toward the entrance; furious voices could be heard distinctly:

"Open! Open!"

"That's the voice of priest Fotis!" cried someone.

"Yannakos's voice," said another; "the Sarakini have come to take him from us!"

The door was shaken violently, its hinges creaked; there could be heard a great tumult of men and women outside.

"Open, murderers! Have you no fear of God?" came the voice of priest Fotis, distinctly.

Priest Grigoris raised his hands.

"In the name of Christ," he cried, "I take the sin upon me! Do it, Panayotaros."

Panayotaros drew the dagger and turned to priest Grigoris.

"With your blessing, Father?" he asked.

"With my blessing, strike!"

Already the crowd had made a rush for Manolios; the blood spurted, sprinkled their faces; some drops fell, warm and salty, on the lips of priest Grigoris.

"Brothers . . ." rose the voice of Manolios, weak, mild, expiring; but he could not go on; he collapsed on the stone flags of the church and groaned softly.

The crowd, intoxicated, snuffed the blood and hurled itself upon the panting body; lips rose from it all blood; old Ladas bit the throat of Manolios with his broken-toothed mouth and tried to tear away a strip of flesh. Panayotaros wiped his dagger on his tawny hair; he anointed his ferocious jowl with blood and cried:

"You tore my heart, Manolios; I've killed you; we're quits!"

Priest Grigoris bent down, filled the hollow of his hand with blood and sprinkled the crowd with it:

"May his blood fall upon the heads of us all!"

The crowd received the drops of blood and shuddered.

"Open, murderers, open!" rumbled afresh the voices from outside.

Priest Grigoris made a sign to the beadle, who approached, staggering.

"Open the door," he ordered, "and come back and wash the stones quickly; don't forget that tonight, at midnight, we are celebrating the birth of Christ."

And, turning toward his flock:

"Let us go, Christians, my brothers," he said; "we have accomplished our duty, God is with us! Let priest Fotis come now and bury his friend!"

The beadle opened the door; threatening faces of men and women could be seen gleaming through the darkness.

"Where is Manolios?" shouted the breathless voice of Yannakos.

"Go and find him!" replied priest Grigoris; "draw aside, you others."

"If you have killed him," bellowed priest Fotis, "may his blood fall upon your heads and upon the heads of your children!"

"Go and find him!" repeated priest Grigoris.

"They've killed him!" roared Yannakos, and rushed into the church.

Toward midnight the bell began ringing, calling the Christians to the church to see Christ born. One by one the doors opened and the Christians hastened toward the church, shivering with cold. The night was calm, icy, starless. Only the house of Patriarcheas had its doors closed, and a great rumor of men's voices and of piercing lamentations of women could be heard coming from it.

Manolios was stretched out on Patriarcheas's great bed, swathed like a new-born child in a silk sheet which came from the trousseau of Michelis's mother. About him his companions watched, pale and silent; Yannakos had rested his head on Manolios's feet and was weeping like a child; he had tired himself out with crying out and beating his breast and now, with his head resting on the feet of his friend, he was weeping softly. Kostandis had gone to the Sarakina to look for Michelis; two or three women, squatting in a corner with their faces to the wall, were wailing and beating their breasts.

Leaning over his friend, priest Fotis gazed by the light of a lamp at Manolios's face, serene again and very pale; a knife blow had gashed it from the right temple to the chin. From time to time he stretched out his hand and arranged the hair of his dead companion; then he would withdraw again and plunge into his reflections: old Martha had just warned him that the Agha had already sent a messenger to the town with an urgent request for the aid of a regiment of infantry and horse; the bolsheviks have entered Lycovrissi, he had reported, and intend to kill him.

They will come with artillery, thought priest Fotis, clenching his fists; how can we resist them? They'll wipe us all out. Once more we must take to the road, and lose no time. How long, O Lord? Are You not good? Are You not just? I don't understand . . .

He extended his hand and tenderly caressed the face of Manolios.

Dear Manolios, you'll have given your life in vain, he murmured; they've killed you for having taken our sins upon you; you cried: "It was I who robbed, it was I who killed and set things on fire; I, nobody else!" So that they might let the rest of us take root peacefully in these lands . . . In vain, Manolios, in vain will you have sacrificed yourself . . .

Priest Fotis listened to the bell pealing gaily, announcing that Christ was coming down on earth to save the world. He shook his head and heaved a sigh: In vain, my Christ, in vain, he muttered; two thousand years have gone by and men crucify You still. When will You be born, my Christ, and not be crucified any more, but live among us for eternity.

At daybreak priest Fotis rested his head on the edge of the bed where Manolios lay stretched out, closed his eyes and fell, for a moment, into slumber. He had a dream: he had gone out in pursuit of a tiny yellow bird, a canary, at the foot of a bushy tree. He was still quite a small child, so it seemed to him, when this pursuit of the bird began. The years went by. He grew, became a young man, then a grown-up man with black hair and mustache; the years kept flying and his hair had become gray, then white; he was now an old man and still he was pursuing, vainly, the yellow bird. Defying capture, the little canary flitted from branch to branch, from flower to flower and sang as if possessed.

Priest Fotis had only slept for the space of a flash; but as he woke up it seemed to him that he had lived for thousands and thousands of years, that he had pursued a little canary for thousands and thousands of years without ever getting tired, with an ever-renewed vigor, indefatigable. Was it really a bird? In the depths of his being, priest Fotis felt that it was not really a canary, that yellow bird which sometimes whistled as if it were making fun of him and sometimes, with its head raised toward the sky, sang as if possessed.

"Whatever it may be, never mind, I shall pursue till my death," he murmured.

He stood up and gave a cry. He called his companions, men and women, assembled them in Patriarcheas's great courtyard; during the night those who had been dispersed over the gardens, vineyards and olive orchards had come in, and the courtyard was packed.

"My children," he cried, "take your heart in your two hands! Hard indeed is what I am going to announce to you, but we can bear anything and we shall bear this. Yesterday evening the news was brought to me that a Turkish army, horse and foot, with artillery, was marched out against us; arise, my children, quickly, let us not lose a minute, take away all you can on your backs, and let us be off! Let us leave Lycovrissi and Sarakina! We are no longer anything but a handful of Greeks on the earth; let us grit our teeth and go forward. No, they shall not get us; our race cannot die!"

"Don't worry, Father," cried Loukas, who had already seized up the banner of Saint George and was opening the door; "no, our race cannot die, Father!"

All rushed for the rich storerooms of Patriarcheas; Yannakos shared out the flour, oil and wine, priest Fotis the clothes, sheets and blankets; they took the door from its hinges and laid out on it the body of Manolios; four sturdy young lads loaded it onto their shoulders; the old men took the icons, priest Fotis placed himself at their head and all, with rapid steps, made for the Sarakina.

"We'll go first by the Sarakina," cried priest Fotis, "and there we'll bury our Manolios; then we'll dig up the earth and take out the bones of our ancestors and we'll march out once more. Courage, my children, fear nothing, grit your teeth, we are immortal!"

They reached Saint Basil's Well; priest Fotis leaned against it for a moment:

"My children," he cried, "today Christ has come down on earth;

let us carry Him with us: we have here mothers who will give Him suck. Happy Christmas, my sons and daughters!"

Yannakos came at the tail of the procession; he had laden his ass heavily and walked beside him in silence. From time to time the world seemed to him to grow dark; Yannakos wiped his eyes and again the world shone with the pale brightness of that winter morning. Lightly, tenderly, he touched his ass on the rump, and the beloved animal wagged his tail joyfully, turned his head and looked at his companion of the road; he could not understand. What was the matter with master? Why didn't he talk? Why hadn't he today stroked his belly, his neck and his long ears?

They took the sheer path up the Sarakina and the climb began. At the head went Manolios, laid out on the door; behind, his companions, men and women; no one spoke. The day was crystalline, the little church of the Prophet Elijah was sparkling at the first rays of the sun; over there, in the far distance, the mountains gleamed, some rosy, others pale blue.

Kostandis was waiting for them in front of the caves; he came up to priest Fotis.

"Father," he said, "Michelis won't come down from the Prophet Elijah's peak; he's taken with him a bundle, his silver Gospel book and Mariori's tresses, and he's settled in the old ascetic's cell. 'I'm all right here,' he told me, 'I don't want to see men any more, the good no more than the wicked; no one! I'll live and I'll die here!' "

Priest Fotis shook his head pensively.

"Perhaps, my dear Kostandis," he said, "perhaps he is right; let us not trouble his serenity. That is his way; let us take ours."

"And what's my way, Father?" Kostandis asked anxiously.

"As soon as we have buried Manolios, go back home, Kostandis," replied the priest, laying his hand on his companion's head; "go back to your wife and children; that is your way."

They lowered Manolios to the ground in front of the grotto which had served them as a church. The priest put on his stole and began to chant the burial service. From time to time sobs broke out among the companions, or else the voice of priest Fotis came to a standstill, cut off suddenly, unable to keep back its sobs . . .

All bent over the beloved dead and embraced him lingeringly and wept. The grave was dug and the priest advanced to its edge and tried to pronounce a few words of farewell to Manolios. But his throat was so tightened that the words could not come out, and suddenly priest Fotis burst out sobbing.

Then a little old woman grew bold, unknotted her white hair, gave a piercing cry and took farewell of Manolios:

> *The name of this fine young man was written on the*
> *snow;*
> *The sun has risen, the snow has melted and has borne*
> *away the name upon the waters.*

A few moments later, priest Fotis raised his hand and gave the signal for departure:

"In the name of Christ," he cried, "the march begins again; courage, my children!"

And again they resumed their interminable march toward the east.

A Note About the Author

NIKOS KAZANTZAKIS *was born in Crete in 1885. He studied at the University of Athens where he received his Doctor of Laws degree, later in Paris under the philosopher Henri Bergson, and completed his studies in literature and art during four other years spent in Germany and Italy.*

Before the last war, he spent a great deal of his time on the island of Aegina, where he devoted himself to his philosophical and literary work. In 1945 he was for a short while Minister of Education in Greece. He is President of the Greek Society of Men of Letters, but lives for the greater part of the year in Paris. His works are numerous and varied—in the fields of philosophy, travel, the drama and fiction. Perhaps the most outstanding, apart from his magnificently conceived novels, is his long epic poem on the fortunes of Odysseus, which begins where Homer's Odyssey ends. Mr. Kazantzakis' first book to be published in America, Zorba the Greek, received instantaneous acclaim last year and continues to enchant an ever-growing audience.